WIDER

Studies in Development Economics embody the output of the
research programmes of the World Institute for
Development Economics Research (WIDER), which was
established by the United Nations University as its first
research and training centre in 1984 and started work in
Helsinki in 1985. The principal purpose of the Institute is
to help identify and meet the need for policy-oriented
socio-economic research on pressing global and
development problems, as well as common domestic
problems and their inter-relationships.

Dominating Knowledge

Development, Culture, and Resistance

Edited by

Frédérique Apffel Marglin
and
Stephen A. Marglin

CLARENDON PRESS · OXFORD

This book has been printed digitally and produced in a standard design in order to ensure its continuing availability

OXFORD
UNIVERSITY PRESS

Great Clarendon Street, Oxford OX2 6DP
Oxford University Press is a department of the University of Oxford.
It furthers the University's objective of excellence in research, scholarship,
and education by publishing worldwide in

Oxford New York

Athens Auckland Bangkok Bogotá Buenos Aires Cape Town
Chennai Dar es Salaam Delhi Florence Hong Kong Istanbul Karachi
Kolkata Kuala Lumpur Madrid Melbourne Mexico City Mumbai
Nairobi Paris São Paulo Singapore Taipei Tokyo Toronto Warsaw

with associated companies in Berlin Ibadan

Oxford is a registered trade mark of Oxford University Press
in the UK and certain other countries

Published in the United States
by Oxford University Press Inc., New York

ISBN 0-19-828694-5

FOREWORD

An important task envisaged for WIDER when it was established in 1985 was to look at the processes and problems of development, particularly in Third World countries, from a broad perspective that would include the approaches and insights not only of economics but also of the other social sciences. This concern was so marked that the founding fathers of WIDER, in choosing a Director for this institute, weighed the merits of appointing an anthropologist with an opening to economics as against an economist open to the existence and value of other disciplines. They chose the latter and I have since then been concerned with bringing non-economic perspectives into the WIDER discourse. It was in this context that I encouraged Steve and Frédérique Marglin to develop a project on the effects of modernization or development on the cultures and values of traditional societies—in the hope that cultural anthropologists and economists working together could throw some fresh light on the cultural and social dimensions of development. This hope has, I believe, been vindicated.

The project has been built round a central issue: can rapid development in the conventional sense—industrialization based on the introduction of new technologies, increasing commercialization, new linkages with the world market—take place without disrupting traditional societies and without undermining the traditional value systems on which their social cohesion has so far depended?

Posed in this way, the project has been both controversial and highly topical. An emphasis on traditional value systems might be interpreted as 'backward-looking' and a denial of the very notion of development. Alternatively, it may be taken to imply that it is possible to distinguish between traditional values worth preserving and those other, equally traditional, values which should be discarded or at least questioned. As it happens, these are the very issues that many thoughtful people in the developing countries have been debating themselves—issues of growing political and economic importance, which not only deserve but demand systematic study.

The perspective taken by the contributors to this volume holds that indigenous systems have a coherence and logic of their own, that they constitute effective systems of production and consumption which maintain ecological harmony while ensuring the social and cultural cohesion of the group. Development strategies based on a sense of the superiority of the 'modern' and the 'scientific' and which fail to take seriously the cultural and social dimensions of societies not only destroy indigenous forms of culture and social life but also fail to cure the problems they set out to deal with. Indeed, they may create many new problems. These considerations give rise to the basic question with which this book deals: are the 'problems' of development—the persistence of poverty, ecological disasters, communal, ethnic, and religious confrontations—attributable merely to flawed *strategies*, or are they inherent in the 'project' of development itself, at least as it has been defined and conceived so far?

The challenge is to find ways of increasing well-being without indiscriminately destroying valued ways of living and 'knowing' and without placing unbearable strains on the environment. No one should question the importance of feeding the poor, clothing the naked, or healing the sick. Even Gandhi, arguably one of the most important political leaders of this century to question the goals of development, once said that if God expected a warm welcome from India's impoverished masses, He had better appear in the form of a loaf of bread. Two millenia earlier, Christ had said 'Not by bread alone . . .'.

This book is an attempt by contemporary social scientists to grapple with these age-old issues.

LAL JAYAWARDENA

ACKNOWLEDGMENTS

This is the first volume to appear under the rubric 'Development and Technological Transformation in Traditional Societies—Alternative Approaches', a project of the World Institute of Development Economics Research, United Nations University. This project began in July 1985, with a planning meeting attended by Arjun Appadurai, Tariq Banuri, James Boyce, Lal Jayawardena, Ashis Nandy, Ignacy Sachs, Amartya Sen, Stanley Tambiah, and the editors of this volume, who have doubled as project co-ordinators. Out of this meeting came an initial programme of research and a conference held in July 1986. (A list of the conference participants appears at the end of these acknowledgements.)

This book is by no means intended as conference proceedings or a conference summary. Many of the papers have been or will be published separately, or will appear in other WIDER volumes. And, in truth, the papers were so diverse that in our judgement no useful purpose would have been served by including them in a single book.

Notwithstanding, perhaps because of, the diversity of the participants and the range of opinions and viewpoints expressed at this meeting, the biggest debt of the authors of the present book is a collective one to the participants in the 1986 conference. Thanks are also due to the following for their comments on specific chapters: A. Tosun Aricanli and Ashraf Ghani for Chapter 1; J. F. Ade-Ajayi, Anjum Atlaf, Michael Best, Henry Bruton, Ali Ercelawn, Ramachandra Guha, Nancy Gutman, Arjo Klamer, Brian Levy, Siddiq Osmani, Robert Pringle, and Robert Walker for Chapters 2 and 3; Arthur Kleinman and Aditi Nath Sarkar for Chapter 4; Brian Spooner and Terence Turner for Chapter 6; and Abhijit Bannerjee, Jerome Bruner, David Corbett, Diana Eck, Arthur Kleinman, William Lazonick, Alain Lipietz, Sitakant Mahapatra, and David Washbrook for Chapter 7.

In addition to benefits received from discussion at the 1986 WIDER conference, the authors of this book received important feedback on other occasions. Chapters 2 and 3 were presented to the Conference for a Just World Peace (Paris, 1986); Chapter 6 was presented at the Symposium on Culture and Conservation (University of Pennsylvania, 1986).

Purna Chandra Mishra was an invaluable collaborator in the field research reported in Chapters 4 and 7. Art Stevens provided research assistance for Chapters 2 and 3, and Gillian Goslinga for Chapter 4. Elizabeth Tuchscherer's translation of Jacob Rösel, *Der Palast des Herrn der Welt*, into French was very helpful for Chapter 4.

Chapter 5 was written at the Committee for Cultural Choices and

Global Futures, Delhi. The field-work reported in Chapter 6 was supported by the National Science Foundation, the Joint Committee on South Asia of the American Council of Learned Societies and the Social Sciences Research Council, and the American Institute of Indian Studies.

The staff at WIDER contributed in a wide variety of ways: organizing travel, planning meetings, typing and retyping endless documents, and a million and one unseen (but not unnoticed) actions, without which this book would never have seen the light of day. If we single out one member of the staff, it is to personalize what must otherwise remain too impersonal a statement. Thank you, Anne Ruohonen.

F.A.M.
S.A.M.

May 1989

WIDER/UNU Conference
Development and Technological Transformation in Traditional Societies: Alternative Approaches

Helsinki, 4–7 August 1986

List of Participants

Charles Abeysekera
Social Scientists' Association
Colombo, Sri Lanka

Frédérique Apffel Marglin
Smith College
Northampton, Mass., USA
  and
WIDER
Helsinki, Finland

Arjun Appadurai
University of Pennsylvania
Philadelphia, Pa., USA

Tariq Banuri
WIDER
Helsinki, Finland

James Boyce
University of Massachusetts
Amherst, Mass., USA

Robert H. Cassen
Oxford University
Oxford, England

Newton Gunasinghe (deceased)
University of Colombo
Colombo, Sri Lanka

Gillian Hart
Boston University
Boston, Mass., USA

Trilokinath N. Madan
Institute for Economic Growth
Delhi, India

Stephen A. Marglin
Harvard University
Cambridge, Mass., USA
  and
WIDER
Helsinki, Finland

Bimal Matilal
Oxford University
Oxford, England

Chie Nakane
University of Tokyo
Tokyo, Japan

Ashis Nandy
Centre for the Study of Developing
  Societies
Delhi, India

Martha Nussbaum
Brown University
Providence, RI, USA

Jukka Oksa
University of Joensuu
Joensuu, Finland

Jussi Raumolin
Research Institute of the Finnish
  Economy
Helsinki, Finland

Savyasaachi
University of Delhi
Delhi, India

Amartya K. Sen
University of Oxford
Oxford, England
  and
WIDER
Helsinki, Finland

Stanley Tambiah
Harvard University
Cambridge, Mass., USA

Jit Singh Uberoi
University of Delhi
Delhi, India

David Vail
Bowdoin College
Brunswick, Me., USA

Shiv Visvanathan
Centre for the Study of Developing
  Societies
Delhi, India

Francis Zimmerman
École des Hautes Études en Sciences
  Sociales
Paris, France

Punam Zutshi
University of Delhi
Delhi, India

CONTENTS

LIST OF CONTRIBUTORS

Frédérique Apffel Marglin
Smith College, Northampton, Mass., USA, and WIDER, Helsinki, Finland

Arjun Appadurai
University of Pennsylvania, Philadelphia, Pa., USA

Tariq Banuri
WIDER, Helsinki, Finland

Stephen A. Marglin, Harvard University, Cambridge, Mass., USA, and WIDER, Helsinki, Finland

Ashis Nandy
Centre for the Study of Developing Societies, Delhi, India

Shiv Visvanathan
Centre for the Study of Developing Societies, Delhi, India

1

Towards the Decolonization of the Mind

STEPHEN A. MARGLIN

It became fashionable in the 1960s to decry growth without development and modernization. In this view, transformation of the economic, social, political, and cultural infrastructure is a necessary precondition for sustained growth, and growth which does not involve institutional transformation can provide but transitory gains.

This volume takes a different tack. Our criticism is directed against development and modernization, not growth. The chapters that follow have nothing to say against longer life-spans, healthier children, more and better-quality food and clothing, sturdier and more ample shelter, better amenities. Nor is any criticism levelled against the luxuries that people buy when their incomes grow enough to permit discretionary purchases, such as the radios and television sets that one sees even in very poor Third World villages.

To some extent these goods might be made available to the poor by redistributing existing supplies, but the politics of redistribution are not particularly encouraging, either within or across national boundaries. In the absence of redistribution, growth is at the very least a necessary chemotherapy for the cancer of poverty. (The metaphor can be extended: the necessity of *some* growth does not imply that more is better.)

1 Development, Modernization, and Westernization

Our criticisms are directed not at particular failures, which might be explained away as poor implementation of basically sound ideas, but at the theories which have undergirded and legitimized practice. But what is meant by development and modernization? Some might distinguish the two concepts, seeing development as a set of end states, and modernization as the means of reaching these end states. Development may then be defined in a variety of ways. At one extreme, development may be simply an extension of the idea of growth, taking into account growth in the capacity to generate consumption goods and progress towards a more equal distribution along with growth in consumption *per se* (Little 1982). Or development may be defined in terms of the fulfilment of basic needs like food, clothing, shelter, health care, and education (Streeten and associates 1981). Alternatively, development may be defined in terms of the levels of individual functionings and capabilities (Sen 1988a).

For our purposes, however, it is less the goals than the *processes* that matter, so we have little to gain from distinguishing between development and modernization. Of course, even with the focus on process, there still remains a diversity of views about what development and modernization mean. However we probably shall not go far wrong if we place the following at the core: on the economic side, industrialization and urbanization, as well as the technological transformation of agriculture; on the political side, rationalization of authority and the growth of a rationalizing bureaucracy; on the social side, the weakening of ascriptive ties and the rise of achievement as the basis for personal advancement; culturally, the 'disenchantment' of the world (to use Max Weber's terminology), the growth of science and secularization based on increasing literacy and numeracy.

These various aspects of modernity are not seen simply as complementary. As Daniel Lerner, a prominent student of development in the 1950s and 1960s, put it: economic, political, social, and cultural factors are 'so highly associated as to raise the question of whether they are genuinely independent factors at all—suggesting that [in the past] they went together so regularly because, in some historical sense, they *had* to go together' (1958: 438).

Lerner's view cannot be dismissed as an outmoded notion. Modernization theory is alive and well in our own time, like so many ideas that start out as the advanced scholarly thinking of one generation, only to reappear as the conventional wisdom of the next. In 1984 the US Bipartisan Commission on Central America (the so-called 'Kissinger' Commission) solemnly intoned its 'conviction that political, social, and economic development goals must be addressed simultaneously' (US National Bipartisan Commission, p. 60), having earlier observed that economic, political, social, and security (*sic!*) aspects of development 'are a seamless web' (p. 48).

This is for us the sticking point; to have economic growth, must we buy a whole package that changes the society, the polity, and the culture along with the economy? Another modernization theorist, S. N. Eisenstadt, put the point bluntly: 'Historically, modernization is the process of change toward those types of social, economic, and political systems that have developed in Western Europe and North America from the seventeenth century to the nineteenth . . .' (1966: 1). In a word, development means Westernization.

The very idea of development presupposes *some* model. 'Development' makes sense in analysing the transformation of a child into an adult precisely because adult behaviour is an agreed standard against which to measure the progress of the child—or was, until Carol Gilligan challenged the implicit masculine bias in the Western conception of the adult (1982). As in child development, so in the development of nations: since World War II, the West has provided the model by which to measure the progress of the rest of the world. Indeed, before the breakup of the European colonial empires in the aftermath of World War II, imperialism drew justification from the image of the colonized as 'children' (Nandy 1983).

The attractions of the Western model need no elaboration: the elevated levels of gross national product that have been achieved in the West permit broad masses of the population to enjoy levels of physical comfort to which only élites aspire in most of the world. But the Western model remains less than compelling. Environmental destruction, meaningless work, spiritual desolation, neglect of the aged—these are some of the characteristics of the Western model that make it a dubious example for the rest of the world to follow.

Indeed, in Chapter 2 Tariq Banuri suggests that the intellectual dominance of the Western model has derived not from its inherent and unequivocal superiority, but rather from the political dominance of those who believe in its superiority, and who have been able to devote attention and resources to legitimizing modernization-as-Westernization. This legitimization has succeeded so well that social progress has come to be defined in terms of the modernization project; the other side of the coin has been the foreclosure of alternative paths of development more congenial to indigenous cultural tradition.

In Banuri's interpretation, the evolution of theories of modernization is the outcome of a continuous process of challenge and response, an encounter between external critics of modernization—Third World intellectuals, Westerners who come from 'alternative' philosophical traditions, political activists, and the innumerable people who resist and rebel—and defenders who seek consistently to direct attention to the strengths of the modernization paradigm and to reject, contain, explain away, and (failing all else) assimilate challenges which focus on its weaknesses. Although the external critics have always existed, they have gained a broader hearing in recent years with the faltering of growth in the Third World, the emergence of social and economic problems within the West itself, and the global problems of the environment, ethnic violence, debt, and other growth-related concerns.

2 Development and Modernization as Expansion of Choice: A Critique

But perhaps we put the horse before the cart. Even if we define development and modernization as processes, should we accept without question the assumption that these processes—industrialization, technical transformation of agriculture, political rationalization, meritocracy, sec-ularization, and the spread of a scientific outlook—are simply means towards other ends? Would it not make as much or more sense to focus on the expansion of choice and to see these processes as among new possibilities opened up as choices expand? From this vantage point, we would judge modernization and development as outcomes of, rather than as preconditions for, growth. The case would be that development and modernization reflect an expansion of possibilities.

The desirability of expanding possibilities would hardly appear to be controversial. But, as Amartya Sen has pointed out, two separate reasons may be conflated into a single argument, since the expansion of choice may be considered desirable for both *intrinsic* and *instrumental* reasons (Sen 1987, 1988b). The expansion of choice is intrinsically desirable if valued for its own sake independently of the choices actually made, and it is instrumentally desirable if valued because it allows the attainment of preferred positions hitherto beyond the individual's reach. In the first case expansion of choice is an end, in the second a means.

The distinction between the two criteria lies in what we can infer from the choices people make. In particular, choosing new alternatives (the 'modern') in expanded arrays of choice is a necessary condition for the improvement of well-being under the instrumental criterion but not under the intrinsic criterion. In the instrumental view, people's choices 'reveal' their preferences for the new over the old. But in the intrinsic view it is the expansion of the array of possibilities rather than actual choices that is the critical point; even if people continue to choose along old patterns, welfare would be improved by the addition of new opportunities.

However, under both criteria well-being may be said to improve if people opt for the new alternative. Either way, a *sufficient* condition for welfare improvement is that people vote with their feet or their pocket-books or their ballots for the modern over the traditional. Under the intrinsic criterion, the choice of new alternatives is evidence that the array has indeed expanded, and, under the instrumental criterion, choice of the modern reveals that people rank the modern more highly than the traditional.

In both cases, however, it must be *assumed* that growth actually does expand choice in all relevant dimensions. For, on the one (intrinsic) hand, the possibility of the modern is not necessarily an enlargement of the domain of choice if the possibility of the traditional is removed at the same time. On the other (instrumental) hand, 'revealed preference' arguments fail if the new choice set does not include the old state. Now in the view that emerges from this book, a major problem is precisely that historically growth has expanded choice only in some dimensions while constricting choice in others. And if growth subtracts choices as well as adds them, we are in a position to argue that growth expands possibilities only if we are able to assume that an individual could reverse the process at will, and in effect could choose between two choice sets, the modern and the traditional. We could then defend growth-as-the-expansion-of-possibilities by arguing that the individual can choose between these two sets, which become the elements of a single meta choice set.

The problem with this characterization is that the development process is *irreversible*. Whether it proceeds in small steps or in one fell swoop, the result is generally the same: you can't go home again. Irreversibility is not *logically* fatal to the argument; it would not matter that the process is irreversible if individuals were endowed with perfect foresight. However, the inability to foresee all the consequences of the first steps down a path makes irreversibility crucial. Not only can't you go home again, but you can't figure out whether or not you want to until it's too late to change your mind.

An example may help. Development has generally meant an increasing focus on the commodities one consumes as the source of the meaning of one's life. Thus large numbers of people in the West are able to choose between Buicks and Hondas, but few can choose meaningful work. Lacking control over the work process and its product, most of us can endow our work with no more meaning than the pay-cheque at the end of the week. Even fewer of us would lay claim to transcendent social meaning in our work. By contrast, the humblest worker in Western society might once have found deep meaning as a participant, say, in the construction of a cathedral, as many people in non-Western societies regularly find transcendent meaning even in day-to-day activities. The contrast between craft weaving in an Indian village and work in contemporary Western society, explored in Chapter 7, expands on this theme.

Take another example, care of the aged. Our parents may have an expansive domain of choice when it comes to nursing homes, but how many can choose to spend their last days in their own homes? We middle-aged children, living in nuclear and even subnuclear families, are hardly freer to keep our ageing parents at home than members of traditional societies are free to put their parents in nursing homes. Even if we wanted to provide for our parents at home, we lack a family structure which would permit adequate home care.

It will be recognized that the emphasis on choice raises questions about the most basic social transformations that modernization has produced. Consider the political emancipation of peasants tied to the soil, whose labour was traditionally fixed by an ineffable mixture of power and custom and rewarded by a share of the harvest. Does transformation of peasants' status into free wage labourers expand their choice sets? Yes and no. The new status allows people to pursue non-traditional occupations, and to sell their labour power for whatever price the traffic will bear. But with freedom of contract comes a new vulnerability to market forces. Suppose drought, excessive rain, or some other calamity, natural or man-made, occurs, and the harvest fails. The free but landless peasant suffers not only from a diminished harvest, but also from diminished demand for his labour power, whereas the unfree peasant may have access to a more substantial portion of the harvest on the basis of traditional rights.

This is not to be read, I hasten to add, as a defence of slavery or serfdom, but as an illustration of the problematic nature of expansion of choice as a criterion for evaluating social change. The example also highlights the difference between the intrinsic and instrumental defences of freedom. An intrinsic defence of freedom might argue that emancipation constitutes an improvement whether or not the peasant is materially better off: freedom, it may be suggested, is more in keeping with the individual's human essence, even if it makes him or her more vulnerable. This is not an argument likely to appeal to the instrumentalist.

However, even when expansion of choice is interpreted as intrinsically desirable, it is not clear whether political emancipation enlarges freedom. In the absence of a 'social safety net', freedom of contract may be the freedom to starve in situations where the wage labourer is solely dependent on his earning power for access to goods; and if with Sen we give weight to the freedom to live a long and healthy life (1988: 280 ff.) as well as to freedom of contract, we may question whether the politically emancipated but economically dependent peasant is freer that his politically subservient but economically more secure brother.

As we have seen, the key problem, from both the instrumental and intrinsic viewpoints, is that choice sets shrink in some dimensions even while they expand in others. There are various reasons why this shrinkage takes place, and economics has given labels to some of them, no doubt in the view that to name a devil is to exorcise it. A major problem is what economists call *externalities*. The emission of sulphur compounds as by-products of electricity generation is in the process of destroying forests, lakes, and rivers in much of the temperate world. Acid rain diminishes the choice sets of all of us even as availability of electric energy expands them.

Another reason why choice sets contract is that many activities are *indivisible* and require a minimum scale to be feasible. The substitution of mass-produced articles for local craft products is conventionally seen as an enlargement of choice. And for many consumers this is exactly right: plastic buckets win out over clay pots in the market place because they are cheaper and more durable. But if the local market for pots shrinks to the point that it is no longer feasible for village artisans to carry on, not only are the potters adversely affected—their choice sets are almost certain to contract—but those villagers who might have continued to patronize the local producers also find their choice sets diminished.

In a longer view, the whole community may be the poorer once the potters' knowledge dies out. For this loss of knowledge is not likely to be reversible even if tastes, economics, or ecology reverses the ranking of clay and plastic. The force of this example, as the philosopher Bernard Williams has reminded us, is not limited to technical knowledge. Traditional ethical (and, one might add, aesthetic) knowledge may also be crowded out by the modern (1985: 167).

In short, the argument that growth expands choice fails to take adequate account of the many reasons why growth eliminates some choices at the same time it adds others. Hence one cannot interpret the rise of modern institutions in the Third World either as evidence for the expansion of choice sets or as the revelation of preferences for the modern over the traditional.

3   Development as Coercion

We have implicitly assumed up to now that the constraints which shape choices are the results of impersonal forces, like those that operate through markets. Externalities like acid rain are the by-products of production and consumption rather than the manifestation of a conspiracy bent on depriving us of an ecologically sound environment. Nobody deliberately tried to break down the family to the point that there is no room for the aged at home.

But the development process involves more coercion than meets the eye. Those who take an instrumental view of freedom might accept this coercion as leading sooner or later to higher satisfaction; one cannot, as they say, make an omelette without breaking some eggs. But for those who believe freedom is intrinsically desirable, the assaults on the autonomy of individuals and local groups in the name of development and modernization will be more disturbing. For example, drawing on an earlier work (Marglin 1974), Chapter 7 argues that the transformation of work into its modern Western form was the result of deliberate attempts to take control of process and product from the worker. If the factory does not impress contemporary Westerners as a curtailment of freedom, it is because we have grown used to this particular form of repression. But both in the West during the transition from household to factory production, and in parts of the Third World where the factory is still a novelty, it was, and is, abhorred for the very reason in which inheres the appeal of the factory system to bosses: the possibilities for supervision and control afforded by regimentation.

Chapter 4 explores the themes of freedom and force in the context of one of the great success stories of modernization—smallpox vaccination—and argues that coercion was used to impose vaccination in India *despite* (or perhaps because of) the availability of a good indigenous alternative, 'variolation'. Variolation, to be sure, involved a higher morbidity than vaccination, but it was superior in techno-economic dimensions like the cost of delivery and its availability in the countryside. Despite these advantages, the British felt it necessary to outlaw variolation, perhaps for political reasons and perhaps out of 'scientific' prejudice against indigenous techniques which were integrated into religious practice and worship. The British thus created the conditions for the realization of their prejudice. Deprived of variolation, Indians were left with the choice between traditional worship of the goddess of smallpox and Western medical practice. In such a choice, preferences *one way or the other* reveal little or nothing. Much more important than the choices people make in such circumstances are the constraints under which they choose. In this perspective, attention is focused on the process which eliminated the possibility of choosing a grass-roots technique of smallpox control that was integrated into the traditional belief system.

Post-Independence India has hardly improved on the low standard set by the British with regard to the use of force to implement its conception of development and modernization. Frédérique Apffel Marglin describes surprise attacks by paramilitary vaccinators, who would rout recalcitrant villagers out of bed in the middle of the night to accomplish the mission of vaccination.

In Apffel Marglin's view, the root cause of such a gross denial of freedom is the objectification of 'target' populations by the authorities. Whether it be in terms of the number of villagers vaccinated, or the number of acres brought under new 'high-yielding varieties' of crops, or the number of metres of cloth produced, once people are reduced to quantifiable targets, it is hard for the authorities (or anybody else) to take their freedom seriously.

The open question in all this is whether objectification is built into the very idea of development, or is rather a pathology of technological transformation. Apffel Marglin argues for the first position, at least in the conception of the vaccination programmes undertaken in post-Independence India. In her view, objectification of a target population is inherent in the binary opposition, illness versus health. The military language of the eradication programme is more than a set of unfortunate metaphors; it is inherent in the structure of thought itself. By defining health as the absence of illness, illness becomes an absolute negative and a target for eradication. Apffel Marglin contrasts this construction of illness with the indigenous Hindu one, in which health and illness are both represented by the same goddess. In the Hindu view, illness is an imbalance; no factor can be absolutely negativized and therefore put down for eradication. Furthermore, illness is the very source of regeneration, of new life. Illness is a necessary part of the cyclical process.

Apffel Marglin argues that along with the health–illness dichotomy goes the opposition of subject and object. Harbouring in its midst a deadly virus, the target population becomes a legitimate object of the activities of the state medical apparatus. The objectification of target populations is thus linked with specific Western conceptual structures, namely, those that rely upon exclusive, 'either–or', binary opposition. Coercion comes into play in even subtler ways. In Chapter 6, Arjun Appadurai examines the effects of commercialization of agriculture in a village in Western India. At first sight commercialization is one of those innovations which simply adds to the available possibilities: no cultivator is forced to produce for the market, adopt new methods of cultivation, change his mix of crops. However, the reality is more complex than this rosy view suggests. In much of India, timely irrigation is critical to agricultural success, and this is the case in the area Appadurai studied. But the change from a subsistence orientation to a commercial orientation dramatically changes the way irrigation is organized. Under subsistence agriculture, the typical arrangement was for several cultivators to share a well; sharing of risks associated with the water-supply was part and parcel of the social cohesion of the village. With commercialization comes a more individualistic attitude which undermines social cohesion in numerous ways, not least in promoting new attitudes towards water: sharing of wells comes to be perceived as a liability.

Cultivators may continue to co-operate for a time because the costs of sole proprietorship are beyond their means. But sharing is a strategy, *faute de mieux*, not a value. And if, as is likely, the village becomes more polarized with the passage of time, access to water will be limited to the large landholders with sufficient assets to obtain control of their own wells. The smaller cultivator will be excluded unless he participates fully in the new commercial opportunities—and maybe even then. He will find no more support for a claim on the well based on traditional right than did the small copyholder in opposition to the enclosers who transformed English agriculture between the fifteenth and nineteenth centuries.

In any case, the individualistic approach to freedom and force relies excessively on a legalistic interpretation of coercion. In any community of producers, be it a village or a factory, knowledge of the production process is essentially a social good—maintained, reproduced, and transformed by the community rather than by the individual. And with knowledge go values. As Appadurai shows, the shift to commercial agriculture kills the knowledge of subsistence agriculture along with the values. The individual cultivator is hardly freer psychologically or cognitively to practise subsistence agriculture once the community's orientation has shifted toward the market than he is free to practise commercial agriculture when subsistence is the rule.

Psychological and cognitive constraints on choice are explored in different ways throughout this volume. In Chapter 5, Ashis Nandy and

Shiv Visvanathan argue that the introduction of Western medicine marginalized traditional forms of medicine and effectively deprived Indians of the choices available within these more pluralistic systems of medical knowledge. And the loss of the knowledge of variolation, described in Chapter 4, would have rendered the traditional approach to smallpox control unavailable even if the mechanism for eliminating the indigenous technique had been a milder one than the outright prohibition to which the British authorities resorted. Chapter 7 is largely about how workers' resistance to modern work organization is constrained by the devaluation of their knowledge, both in their own eyes and in the eyes of others.

The psychological and cognitive constraints on choice are different from political and economic constraints but are, of course, heavily influenced by politics and economics. In this regard, colonial power relations have left an important legacy. In the colonial period, the political dominance of the West directly fostered Western values and attitudes. But the psychological constraints on choice continue despite the formal transfer of sovereignty in the post-war period. The adoption of Western values by Westernized indigenous élites stacks the cards against tradition. It hardly helps if Western values are expressed as universals which cut across cultural boundaries. On the contrary: the refusal to acknowledge the cultural source of the bias in favour of modernization makes it even more difficult to defend tradition.

4 Freedom as a Cultural Construction

These cultural biases are especially insidious when they are attached to ideas about freedom. Up to now we have provisionally accepted the idea that expansion of choice is desirable for both instrumental and intrinsic reasons and have criticized development on the grounds that choice is in fact curtailed in some dimensions as it is expanded in others. But the time has come to recognize the cultural biases that underlie both the instrumental and intrinsic rationales of freedom of choice and elevate expansion of choice to the status of a universal *summum bonum*.

On the one hand, the instrumental justification of inferring the superiority of the modern over the traditional from the choices people make is marred by the assumption that the values which guide choices are invariant with respect to the choice sets. Even if choice sets expand in all relevant dimensions, it must be recognized that 'preferences', as these values are misleadingly called, are *endogenous* and change dramatically during the process of growth. If a modernized person opts for a modern configuration of goods and social practices, this casts little light on the status of the traditional person's choices.

The intrinsic valuation of freedom of choice would appear to be more resilient to criticism, for a great deal of cross-cultural agreement surely exists on the undesirability of oppression. However, oppression is defined so variously that this agreement can hardly be equated to a common desire for freedom in the sense this term has in the West, where individual autonomy is privileged as the core meaning of freedom, and constraints on autonomy become the central meaning of oppression. This disposition to universalize a peculiarly Western interpretation does very little for cross-cultural dialogue and even less for mutual understanding. Indeed, in large parts of the world, the Western notion of freedom sounds suspiciously like licence, and the difficulties of distinguishing between the freedom to do one's own 'thing' and the freedom to become one's own person do not make it any easier to dispel these doubts.

In the West, the larger one's choice set, the freer one is. By contrast, the psychiatrist Takeo Doi (1971) has suggested that the distinctive nature of Japanese society can be understood by the high cultural value placed on *amae,* dependent love of the kind a child receives from his mother. The recipient—enveloped in indulgence, acceptance, and forgiveness—makes no choices. He does not have to since his needs are anticipated as part of the *amae* he receives. The important point is that *amae*—far from being outgrown, discarded by adults as a dependence fit for children and possibly for women—is highly valued by the Japanese male adult. The distinguishing characteristics of Japanese society, according to Doi, precisely reflect the value placed on being taken care of as against the value of autonomy. Reinterpreted through the prism of *amae*, autonomy is understood as the wilfulness of doing one's own thing.

Freedom-as-autonomy is closely related to freedom-as-control, and equally culturally bound. W. Arthur Lewis, awarded the Nobel Prize in economics for his studies of the growth process, once defended development in terms that suggested this identity not as a cultural construction, but as an obvious and self-evident truth. 'The case for economic growth', he wrote (1955: 421), 'is that it gives man more control over his environment, and thereby increases his freedom.' Outside the West, adaptation may commend itself as a better basis for freedom than control, a basis that might indeed spare the environment the despoliation that has been associated with development, arguably the consequence of the value attached to control in the Western model (Banuri and Apffel Marglin, forthcoming). Gandhian movements in particular have stressed control over self rather than control over the environment as the essential prerequisite of freedom.

5 Our Science, Their Superstition

By defending traditional cultural values against the onslaught of modernization, we run the risk of serious misunderstanding. If experience is any guide, the authors of the chapters that follow will, singly and collectively, be accused of promoting superstition, religious obscurantism, and even barbarity. As an Indian admirer of Western science put it early in this century, 'Benares and Puri [two pilgrimage centers for Hindus] have had their day. What is there in Benares but fat bulls and fat priests? What is there in Puri but cholera?' (Har Dayal 1912: 48). Do we really intend to defend the ritual immolation of widows on the funeral pyres of their husbands? Or foot-binding? Or female circumcision? Would we go so far as to defend the ritual sacrifice of virgins to forestall the anger of the gods?

There are many issues here, and it would be well to sort them out. First, there is the question of the particular and the general, the role of specific beliefs and practices within a cultural whole, rather than in isolation. It may be readily agreed that the sacrifice of a young woman on an altar in traditional society is barbaric, but in and of itself it is no more barbaric than the sacrifice of a young man on a battlefield in modern society. Such practices must be understood in context, as part of a cultural whole. But if it is the cultural whole that is at issue, we ought not let the particular be the excuse for an indiscriminate attack: female circumcision should not be a pretext for labelling African cultures as backward, or *suttee* a pretext for proclaiming the inferiority of traditional Hindu culture.

But can we not at least insist on the superiority of the modern over the traditional in terms of the epistemological basis of the two systems? Can we not distinguish practice based on true belief from practice based on superstition? And if we can call the belief false, can we not call the practice wrong, or at least unenlightened superstition? Observe, first of all, that this approach would require us to treat female circumcision more sympathetically if it is rooted in a consciously calculated system by which men control female sexuality, rather than in (say) the belief that uncircumcised women will bear inferior offspring. For in the first case although we might condemn both the premiss of the practice and the practice itself, we would not disagree with the logic that connects the practice to the premiss. In the second case, it is precisely the unscientific thought process which is at issue. We might condemn the practice in either case, but the specific conception of human dignity and equality that comes into play in the first instance would be recognized as culturally contingent in a way that the criticism of scientific truth appropriate to the second is not.

The implicit privileging of scientific objectivity is of course an old one. Bernard Williams has given it new force in suggesting that science, unlike ethics, will eventually converge to a unified understanding, expressible in a universal discourse, which reflects, in Williams's words, 'how things are' (1985: 136). This view is tempting, but it is hardly immune to criticism. One need accept neither a correspondence theory of truth, in which scientific statements reflect an objective reality independent of human consciousness and construction, nor a convergence theory of scientific 'progress', in which actual science proceeds, smoothly or fitfully, to a single system of scientific explanation. According to the philosopher Hilary Putnam, 'To say, as Williams sometimes does, that convergence to one big picture is required by the very concept of knowledge, is sheer dogmatism' (1988: 14). Many will find Putnam's critique persuasive, and will easily go the next step with him, which is to deny that we can take the convergence of scientific theory as the basis for an epistemological difference between scientific and ethical discourse.

But the absence of convergence in no way vitiates what Williams calls the 'absolute conception' of the world, the idea of a world independent of our conceptual structures. An absolute conception neither implies, nor is implied by, a convergence of theories about that world. Here however it is important to distinguish between the world of things and plants and the world of human beings. One who argues that the earth is flat is simply mistaken. Actions based on this belief may be noble or ignoble, but these actions are based on a false belief. There need not be a single theoretical structure to which natural science is converging, and the number of theories that encompasses the observed (or even the *observable*) regularities of the natural world may well be of a large order. But the absence of convergence does not rule out the possibility of eliminating egregiously false theories on the basis of greater knowledge of a world which is unaffected by our beliefs about it.

Contrast human sacrifice. Imagine the priestess called upon to explain the consequences of a failure to sacrifice the requisite virgins in the requisite manner. She might well say, 'Society will fall apart. Our women and our land will become barren because our men will become impotent as lovers and ineffective as cultivators.' *And she will be right.* Believing themselves to be impotent in the hammock and ineffective in the field, the men will be unable to perform in either context. The birth rate will decline, and the harvest will fail. Society *will* fall apart. Believing is seeing: beliefs bring about the very conditions that will make these beliefs come true.

Ah, but if you changed their beliefs? Ah, but if you change their beliefs, they won't be Aztecs any more. Precisely what is at stake is the power of belief to affect the world, so it will not do to modify the thought experiment to eliminate this factor. It is precisely belief which creates the *necessity* of sacrifice; sacrifice is efficacious within a particular cultural framework because people believe in it. By contrast, the natural world is not six thousand years old regardless of who may believe it. Thus propositions like 'the gods require human sacrifice' are culturally contingent in a way that propositions like 'the earth is flat' are not: there is no way of assessing their truth or falsity apart from peoples' beliefs; it is as if the earth cared whether you or I thought it was flat or six thousand years old.

Let us come back now to the case of female circumcision. Once the power of belief is recognized, the distinction we have drawn between 'scientific' and 'unscientific' defences of this practice dissolves. Quite apart from the very real possibility that female circumcision may simultaneously be defended ('scientifically') as a system of control of female sexuality and ('unscientifically') as a system of eugenics, the 'unscientific' defence may be as well-grounded empirically as any proposition of Western science: if parents, uncles, aunts, grandparents—not to mention the larger society—believe that the offspring of uncircumcised women are inferior, these unfortunate children may be reared in just the fashion that confirms their inferiority.

It would be a mistake to think that the power of belief is a characteristic of traditional society from which we are liberated by modernization. One cannot, I have argued (Marglin 1984, 1987, 1990, Marglin and Bhaduri 1990), understand the workings of modern capitalist society without understanding the power of belief. Indeed, the most enduring contribution of John Maynard Keynes to twentieth-century economics may turn out to be his insight into the social construction of reality, particularly as to the way in which belief mediates between profit and investment. In the Keynesian view, the key to prosperity is the 'animal spirits' (his phrase) of the capitalist class. If businessmen are optimistic and believe profits will be high, they will invest in new plant and equipment to take advantage of the high level of profits. In this case, production and employment will be high, and growth will be rapid. In a word: prosperity. Moreover, the level of profits will reflect the general prosperity, confirming capitalists' expectations and at the same time providing for the high level of investment which is the basis of successful economic performance. A virtuous circle is closed. By contrast, pessimistic animal spirits lead to low profit expectations, low investment, low production and employment, and slow growth. The low profits that result from general economic misery once again confirm capitalists' expectations and at the same time are in line with the needs of investment. The circle, now a vicious one, is once again closed.

The economic logic may be arcane but the central point ought not to be. In modern as in traditional society, there is a class of agents whose efficacy depends on belief. The capitalist society, no less than the Aztec society, is one in which reality is socially constructed, and belief creates its own truth. The sorcery of the Azande witch (Evans-Pritchard 1937, Tambiah 1985, ch. 2) is no less true or real than the profit expectations of the capitalist: both are endowed with a measure of self-fulfilling prophecy.

Evidently we need a terminology for distinguishing, not science from ethics, but the roles of *belief* in two classes of interaction of agents with the world, or more simply, between belief in two classes of propositions. Borrowing from Keynes (1921), I propose to use the label *organic* for propositions the truth of which depends on the beliefs of agents, and the label *atomic* for propositions the truth of which is independent of these beliefs. It is my assertion that propositions about the world of things and plants are atomic, while many if not all propositions about the world of human beings, the world of social relationships, are organic. (Note that the world of animals is an ambiguous one. The belief that my dog can point birds may be efficacious in training her; the belief that your elephant can fly is probably not similarly efficacious.) This being the case, there is no way of assessing the truth or falsity of organic discourse apart from peoples' beliefs. There is not only no objective truth in this realm, there is no objective falsehood either.

Observe that if the conventional opposition between scientific and ethical discourse has any epistemological validity, it is because normative statements are in some sense more likely to be organic, and descriptive statements more likely to be atomic. But any correspondence between normative and organic or between descriptive and atomic is *not* a logical one. Descriptive propositions as well as normative ones may involve agents organically: ethical propositions need not logically be organic, and organic propositions are certainly not all ethical. Williams is vulnerable for distinguishing science from ethics in terms of fit or lack of fit with an absolute conception of the world, but I share not only his view that there is a realm in which an absolute conception of the world applies, but also his suspicion that (unfortunately) this is not the realm in which most cross-cultural disagreement and misunderstanding takes place. The beginning of wisdom in cross-cultural dialogue may be an appreciation of the limits of atomic discourse.

6 Cultural Diversity as a Global Asset

So far the case for tradition has been largely a negative one: practices which appear to the outsider as backward, irrational, and even incoherent turn out to have a logic and efficacy of their own. The obscurantism lies not in seeking to understand this logic and efficacy but in denying the very possibility that it is the outsiders' prejudice which leads to labels such as 'backward'.

It still might be claimed that nothing really valuable is lost in the process of modernization, apart from what might capture the attention of the folklorist or anthropologist. But the issue is hardly folklore. It is rather the terms of change. Traditional does not mean fixed and unchanging. Tradition is actively constructed and dynamic—except when it is artificially frozen in an archaic pattern. The issue is the preservation of a *space* for a relatively autonomous transformation of indigenous cultures, not the preservation of cultures as static systems.

This alters but does not answer the basic question. It may still fairly be asked what the positive case is for maintaining a space in which traditional cultures can change on their own terms rather than in terms of the Western model. The answer must depend on whose viewpoint we adopt. From the vantage-point of those whose cultures are being undermined by modernization on the Western model, the question may appear the height of arrogance. From inside, the need to defend one's traditional culture may arouse anger and resentment when the same question is not put to Westerners. 'Because they are ours' may be all an insider feels required to say in defence of traditional ways.

From outside, the defence of traditional culture must be more self-conscious. A step in the right direction is the recognition that the present cultural dominance of the West is not the result of any intrinsic superiority in Western culture—unless one defines superior cultural fitness in terms of economic and political power, in which the West has surely excelled over the last five hundred years.

But even here the argument is hardly compelling. Are, say, rationalization and secularization necessary for material progress? If necessary under Western historical conditions, does a unique logic of growth compel Westernization as the price of growth? We know too little about the options that uncritical acceptance of the Western model has closed off to be able to answer these two questions with any degree of certainty.

The positive case for exploring these options is, or ought to be, obvious: the Western model of development, notwithstanding its considerable economic successes, has yet to produce an acceptable model for relationships between people or with nature. It is in our own self-interest as well as the global interest to promote cultural diversity, and a corresponding diversity of development models.

The argument is evidently one from uncertainty. Within the human species culture rather than instinct bears the primary load of the intergenerational transmission of knowledge. We cannot today know what crises we shall face in the twenty-first century—from nuclear holocaust to ecological despoliation to social disintegration, none can be ruled out. Nor do we know that the West will find the cultural resources within its own tradition to cope with these or other, less dramatic, contingencies. As in ages past, we may find that we have much to learn from outside the West. Should this come to pass, it would be a cruel irony to find the world remade in our own image.

Cultural diversity may be the key to the survival of the human species. Just as biologists defend exotic species like the snail darter in order to maintain the diversity of the genetic pool (see, for example, Myers 1983), so should we defend exotic cultures in order to maintain the diversity of forms of understanding, creating, and coping that the human species has managed to generate.

We will, in any case, defend cultural diversity if we are to be true to our own principles of self-determination. For, increasingly, traditional peoples are resisting modernization on the Western model. More, rather than less, coercion will be necessary if the development project based on this model is to be carried through, and it matters little that the principal agents of modernization are Westernized indigenous élites rather than Westerners.

The purpose of this volume is to explore the cultural dimension of the encounter between the modern, the Western, and the traditional. None of the authors of its several chapters would claim to be inside the traditional cultures we explore. Our claim is rather to a critical comparative perspective, which at the very least does not presuppose that Western theory and practice represent a standard to which others should aspire. From this perspective, indigenous practices which appear as backward, irrational, superstitious, obscurantist, or just plain absurd—when viewed against Western norms—turn out much more positively. This is so even in terms of economistic criteria which give no weight whatsoever to the role these practices play in the maintenance of the integrity of the indigenous cultural fabric. It is all the more the case when a 'holistic' attitude is adopted.

7 Dominating Knowledge: An Overview

Let us look at some of these traditional practices. In Chapter 3, Tariq Banuri develops an approach which can be used to contrast modern and traditional world-views from such a holistic perspective. Banuri describes two kinds of 'map', or guide to the universe we live in. He distinguishes between impersonal and personal maps and argues, first, that all cultures differ in terms of the balance between the two maps; second, that this balance keeps changing because of the tension between the two; and, most importantly, that the uniqueness of Western culture derives from the absolute priority which is accorded to the impersonal sphere. This asymmetry, which he terms the *impersonality postulate of modernity*, is, in the words Banuri borrows from Thomas Merton, 'at once its strength, its torture, and its ruin'. For Banuri, the emphasis on the personal in traditional cultures is evidence of the need for flexibility, spontaneity, sympathy, and openness to balance the rigidity, insensitivity, and closedness of impersonal relations. Banuri wants us to see balance and tension between the two maps not as the cultural immaturity of a 'pre-modern' society but rather as a *norm* against which to judge an extreme imbalance in the Western cultural model.

Chapter 3 frames the more specific contributions of the remaining chapters. These are in two sections, one on health-care delivery, the other on production. Together, Chapters 4 and 5 offer a powerful critique of the claims of Western medicine to a monopoly of medical truth. Apffel Marglin explores the genesis of vaccination as a prophylaxis for smallpox in the West and its extension to India. Far from being a contribution of Western science, vaccination appears to have been at the very most an adaptation of folk practice of inoculating with live smallpox matter and perhaps simply a direct imitation of a variant of traditional practice that employed cowpox matter as the inoculating agent. In this view, Jenner's contribution lay in his ability to listen to local people and take advantage of their knowledge rather than in independent invention. The traditional practice almost certainly came to Europe from outside; it was widespread, existing in the Middle East, India, and China. Although more risky than vaccination, variolation was an effective means of smallpox control, at least in rural areas where, during the ensuing period of contagion, inoculated individuals could be isolated from the population at risk. And unlike vaccination, which was associated with foreign rule under colonialism and with an urban élite that was almost as alien after Independence, variolation was integrated into the cultural fabric of the community. Inoculation was accompanied by worship of the goddess of smallpox, whose name was invoked by the inoculator as the smallpox matter was injected. The medical operation procedure was also a religious ceremony. According to Apffel Marglin, variolation was cheaper and more accessible in the rural areas, particularly to ordinary villagers, so that it might have been preferred to vaccination even without taking into account the cultural implications of the two alternatives.

Nandy and Visvanathan examine in the large the confrontation between Western and indigenous medicine which Apffel Marglin analyses in the particular case of smallpox control. Focusing on the criticisms of Western medicine in the context of the Indian national movement, Nandy and Visvanathan argue that voices as varied as those of feminists and theosophists of the ilk of Madame Blavatsky, opponents of industrialization such as Gandhi, and practitioners of indigenous medical science like G. Srinivasmurthi together anticipated the salient features of contemporary criticism of Western medicine, in the West as well as outside. These include, at one level, iatrogenic diseases (diseases caused by medical treatment), induced mutation (mutation caused by drugs, such as the emergence of chloroquine-resistant mosquitoes), inordinate cost, ecological dislocation (the destruction of the natural balance, as when DDT intended for house-fly eradication poisons the food chain and leads to bubonic plague), and drug dependence. At another level, the criticism focuses on the depersonalization of the patient, the reduction of the individual to a set of laboratory readings. This last, what Nandy and Visvanathan call the latent, as distinct from the manifest, critique, recalls a central theme of Banuri's discussion of modernization and development in Chapters 2 and 3. The latent and manifest critiques of medicine correspond roughly to the external and internal critiques of development, the manifest and internal critiques implicitly accepting the presupposition of Western culture that impersonal relations are inherently superior to personal ones, the latent and external critiques rejecting this presupposition. In a critical perspective, the 'impersonality postulate' is the root of many of the problems of modern medicine; moreover the rejection of this postulate was the basis, even if at times this was only dimly perceived by the critics themselves, of the criticism of Western medicine from the Indian perspective. It follows that the West itself might have been spared considerable grief if, less certain of its own scientific and cultural superiority, it had been open to the criticism that grew out of a different cultural perspective.

Chapters 6 and 7 focus on production. In Chapter 6, Appadurai investigates the transformation of techniques and relationships in Indian agriculture that have resulted from the reorientation of agriculture from subsistence to commercial production. Utilizing both the archive of indigenous-language exhortational   instructional manuals over the past century and his own observation of contemporary practices in a village in Western India, Appadurai finds that commercialization has had deleterious consequences, both economically and culturally. For one thing, it has made many peasants, particularly the poorer cultivators, run faster simply to stand still. For another, it has increased risks both for the individual and for the community as a whole. Third, and most important for Appadurai, commercialization has undermined the sociality of the village community. For instance, the agricultural and ritual cycles were once mutually embedded in each other. But now the agricultural cycle follows its own logic and rhythm, and the ritual calendar is subordinated to the exigencies of commercial agronomy. Also, as a result of commercialization, co-operation of the kind that joint operation and management of wells requires is now viewed as a cost and a risk, rather than as an affirmation and expression of deep ties which link villagers to one another.

Chapter 7 asks the question why workers in the West have accommodated themselves so much more readily than Indian workers to an instrumental role for work. Part of the answer, it is suggested, can be found in cultural differences. On the one hand, work in the West has a long history of negative moral connotation, starting from the conception of labour as punishment for the transgressions of Adam and Eve and the low status accorded manual work in certain Greek philosophical conceptions. By contrast, even relatively humble work such as weaving can be touched with divinity in the Hindu conception, as an analysis of the rituals, myths, and practices of a contemporary community of handloom weavers in Eastern India shows.

In addition, Western culture holds the knowledge of workers to be of an inferior sort; workers in the West are undermined by their own culture in their attempts to defend their work against the bosses' project of obtaining control over production. Once again, the Hindu conception differs: more pluralistic attitudes toward knowledge provide a cultural basis for defending the Indian worker's control.

Taken as a whole, this volume formulates a strong challenge to the claims made for the superiority of the Western model of development. Indeed, Western-style development and modernization have become synonymous with progress not because this path of social change is inherently superior, but because criticism has been marginalized and denigrated. That the intentions of the proponents of the Western model were in general benign speaks only of the paving material, not of the road travelled.

In particular, the Western technology for dealing with smallpox triumphed not because it was more efficacious in controlling smallpox, at least not until improved vaccines became available in the 1970s. Rather, it triumphed because of the power of the colonial government to outlaw variolation, as a practice tainted by its association with what in the West was perceived as superstition and idolatry. By the same token, Western medicine has achieved dominance outside the West not because it is proof to criticism, and not because the criticisms were not made, but because criticism was marginalized by the superior status of Western constructions of reality, buttressed by superior Western political power. Indeed, the very project of modernization has resisted indigenous criticism because of the marginalization of indigenous ideas of progress.

In agriculture, the transformation from subsistence to commercial agriculture appears to have transformed the indigenous Indian cultural model, but it is open to question whether, from the point of view of the marginal farmer, the economic gains have outweighed the costs in terms of the risks associated with heightened vulnerability to outside forces such as the course of distant markets. In the sphere of industrial production, the Western cultural model reinforces the economic model in robbing work of its meaning. While the economic model of small-scale Indian manufacture may be fairly similar to that which prevailed during the evolution of Western manufacturing, the Indian cultural model appears to open up possibilities for the Indian worker that were and are largely unavailable to his Western counterpart. (Unfortunately nothing guarantees that these opportunities will be seized.)

8   Some Lessons

Different authors draw different lessons from this research. Banuri uses the argument of Chapter 3 to point the way to a society that is decentralized economically, politically, and culturally, for it is only in relatively small-scale units that an appropriate balance can be struck between the personal and the impersonal.

Apffel Marglin finds differences in Western and Indian attitudes towards smallpox and technologies for dealing with the disease indicative of larger cultural differences. The Indian attitude presupposes an ecological balance among people and between people and nature; just as smallpox was accommodated by a combination of ritual and empirically based prophylaxis, so is nature to be accommodated; and along with nature, human society and the entire cosmos. By contrast, just as vaccination is the basis not of accommodation but of absolute control, so is nature and the 'other' to be conquered and dominated. Apffel Marglin sees in smallpox eradication a metaphor for the entire Western cultural project, going back to the Judaeo-Christian origin myth in which man (sic!) is given dominion over nature. In her view, this project is a model for repression rather than a model for Third World development.

Nandy and Visvanathan draw the lesson that strategies of dissent and confrontation are shaped by realities of political power rather than by the relationship of the intellectual content of the criticism to the content of what is being criticized. A challenge to the dominant medical system must also be a challenge to political and cultural dominance; both the dominant system and the alternatives are bound up in larger systems of power, values, and cultural perceptions.

Appadurai focuses on the issue of reproduction of the community, and suggests a line of argument that goes very much against the grain of current development policy. In Appadurai's view, the intrusion of the market into agriculture is dubious even on economistic grounds, once the economy is recognized to include not only the size of the pie but also how the pie is sliced and how vulnerable it is to shocks from outside; but, economics aside, this intrusion is dubious because it threatens the very foundation of the community—the web of social interaction and relationships which Appadurai calls sociality. In this view the market economy can be expected to overwhelm the traditional culture if the project of commercialization is left to the play of market forces. The difficulty of maintaining sociality is compounded by its status as an externality which nobody takes into account in determining his or her behaviour in an atomistic, individualistic context.

Finally, a major lesson of a comparison of work in India and the West is the light it sheds on *all* projects of social transformation which put the organization of work at their centre. For work to be an organizing principle of a decent society, it must be meaningful, and for it to be meaningful it must either be embedded in a system of values which give work a final, as distinct from an instrumental, purpose, or the worker's knowledge must be accorded sufficient respect to give the worker the cultural space to create his own meaning out of his labour. Both attributes are to be found in greater abundance among the poor handloom weavers of a village in Eastern India than among the affluent workers of a Western workplace.

Underneath these individual lessons lie collective lessons which weave in and out of the various essays. The issue of 'induced mutation', for example, is a concern not only of Nandy and Visvanathan but of Appadurai as well. Appadurai notes the long-standing view among Indian peasants (and shared by some researchers) that chemical fertilizers are 'addictive', that once a farmer embarks upon a regime of chemical fertilization the land will not produce at all unless the dose is maintained. The common thread to these arguments is that 'scientific engineering' is unworkable because it generates new problems more rapidly than solutions to old ones.

The problem has been well understood by scientists. Paul Mangelsdorf, a prominent corn and wheat breeder in the middle years of this century who also played a role in forming the institutions and shaping the strategy that produced the Green Revolution, put the problem succinctly in an essay on the evolution of wheat: '[T]he growing of new varieties over large acreages', he wrote in the *Scientific American* in 1953, 'increases the hazards from those diseases to which they are susceptible. The result is a never-ending battle between the wheat breeders and the fungi' (p. 59). But scientists, unlike their critics, remain confident that science can and will keep one step ahead.

This may be true, or it may not be; time will tell. For the present, confidence in scientific engineering must be recognized as an act of faith, a faith generated by the disposition of Western culture to regard nature as conquerable. Indeed, the Western confidence in the ability of science to stay one step ahead of the problems it generates is no less an assertion of faith than the criticism of the Western approach which comes out of the philosophical view that nature is to be accommodated rather than conquered.

There is another issue. Many of those who believe that Western science cannot in fact stay one step ahead of the problems it generates, that Three Mile Island, Chernobyl, Bhopal, acid rain, ozone depletion, and so on are only portents of catastrophes to come, would not accept the Western approach even if it were demonstrably workable. They find it objectionable on ethical, aesthetic and relational grounds that make feasibility a secondary issue. It is the very stance toward nature as an object that is found offensive.

Finally, I should reiterate the collective concern of the authors of this volume with the issue of force. We offer examples ranging from the heavy-handed coercion of paramilitary smallpox vaccinators to the subtle coercion of the commercialization of agriculture. Apffel Marglin has raised the question of whether the fundamental cause of the denial of freedom is a disposition to objectification rooted in binary oppositions of an 'either–or' kind. This volume makes no attempt to settle this question or even to make an agreed-upon statement, but it is worth noting the ubiquity of binary oppositions in the aspects of Western culture encountered elsewhere in this volume.

Banuri's impersonality postulate can be interpreted as the assertion that Western culture posits a binary opposition between the personal and the impersonal: the impersonal is privileged and defined as the absence of the personal. Banuri does not argue for a reversal of this opposition in favour of the personal but for a new mode of relationship between the two, one which is non-exclusive, non-hierarchical, and context-sensitive.

A binary opposition between health and illness is also central to the argument made by Nandy and Visvanathan. As in Apffel Marglin's analysis, the opposition between illness and health sets the stage for a subject–object dichotomy with dire consequences for the patient.

Appadurai briefly contrasts the Maharashtrian peasants' traditional, context-sensitive language of measurement to the new system's use of context-free units of measurement. He relates the context-sensitive, approximate language the peasants employ for measurement with the integral connection between sociality and economic activities, in contrast with the exclusion of sociality in the new system.

In the last chapter, it is argued that the absolute devaluation of workers' knowledge in Western cultures is central to workers' relative acquiescence in repressive modes of work organization. This absolute devaluation of workers' knowledge and the privileging of a universal, disembodied form of knowledge presupposes that these two forms of knowledge are related in a hierarchical, exclusive, either–or fashion.

The cultural specificity of exclusive binary oppositions is thus a running theme of this volume. Our views are in sharp contrast to a Lewis-type justification of development, namely, that 'economic growth . . . gives man control over his environment, and thereby increases his freedom'. The problem with this view begins with the binary opposition between man and the environment, which Lewis presupposes: man is the rational, active subject exercising control over a passive, objectified environment. Such an opposition may generate more repression than freedom.

At another level there is an even stronger unity in the collective message of the chapters that comprise this volume. Obviously, culture is seen by all of us as foundational. That is, we see culture as neither reflective nor instrumental. Culture is not a superstructure that emerges from and reflects a given material base. Nor is culture to be understood as the instrument which may facilitate or obstruct improvement in the material standard of living.

9 Cultures as Knowledge Systems

But what is culture? We are all accustomed to thinking of culture as a set of rules, largely tacit and unconscious, that structure our social interaction and at another level the values that underlie those rules and give them—and our actions—meaning. We have no reason to deny this conception of culture. But we have every reason to go beyond it.

In our view culture is not only rules and values, but ways of knowing. A culture is composed of many systems of knowledge. In Chapter 7, a knowledge *system* is defined in terms of four characteristics: epistemology, transmission, innovation, and power. Each system has its own theory of knowledge (or epistemology), its own rules for sharing knowledge, its own distinctive ways for changing the content of what counts as knowledge, and finally, its own political rules for governing relationships both among insiders to any particular knowledge system and between insiders and outsiders.

All the chapters in this volume utilize the notion of knowledge systems, although all do not use it the same way. Banuri conceptualizes different knowledge systems in terms of the axis of personal versus impersonal relationships. In this view the distinguishing and pathological feature of Western knowledge systems is the subordination of the personal to the impersonal. The characterization in Chapter 7 includes the personal-impersonal dimension but only as one of many oppositions that characterize distinctive knowledge systems. In the West, the knowledge system of management, particularly 'scientific management', is characterized not only by impersonality, by its insistence on logical deduction from self-evident axioms as the only basis for knowledge, but also by its emphasis on analysis, its claim that knowledge must be articulate in order to exist, its pretence to universality, its cerebral nature, its orientation to theory and empirical verification of theory, and its odd mixture of egalitarianism within the knowledge community and hierarchical superiority *vis-à-vis* outsiders. This system is called *episteme* in Chapter 7.

By contrast, labour's knowledge—called *techne*—is not only personal, it differs from *episteme* in other fundamental ways. The sources of knowledge of a *techne* range from intuition to authority; it defies the analytic decomposability of *episteme*; it is often implicit rather than articulate; recognizing the limits of context, it makes no claim to universality; it is tactile and emotional where *episteme* is cerebral; it is practical rather than theoretical, and geared to discovery rather than to verification; finally, *techne* reverses the power relations of *episteme*: it is hierarchical internally but pluralistic externally.

In my view, the accommodation of labour to capital owes much to the systematic subordination of *techne* to *episteme* in Western culture. The problem is that workers, sharing the dominant values of their culture, also share the devaluation of their own knowledge. More tentatively, Chapter 7 raises the question of whether Hindu culture is more open on this point. Non-Brahminical systems of knowledge (read *techne*) may or may not be hierarchically subordinate to Brahminical systems (read *episteme*). If they are, not even the Brahmins themselves attempt the equivalent of what is routine in the West; namely, the denial to *techne* of any place at all, the insistence on the reduction of *techne* to *episteme* as the condition of existence of knowledge.

The other chapters in this volume are principally concerned with the encounter between the dominant knowledge system of the West, *episteme*, with the traditional knowledge systems—the *technai*—of India. For Banuri, for Apffel Marglin, and for Nandy and Visvanathan, the central problem of the encounter is the imperialistic pretension to universality made on behalf of Western *episteme* and the total inability of its adherents to regard competing systems with anything but contempt, the inability indeed even to contemplate the existence of competing systems. Other systems of knowledge, particularly when they are embedded in myth and ritual, become superstition, the very antithesis of knowledge. The encounter is often fatal for indigenous systems because the supreme confidence of Westerners or Westernized élites in their knowledge is coupled to the superior means of political and economic force at their disposal.

According to Apffel Marglin, it is the union of this attitude towards knowledge and superior force which spelled the end of a cheap, effective means of smallpox control rooted in traditional knowledge and traditional religious worship. According to Nandy and Visvanathan, the same attitude closes the Western (and the Westernized) mind to 'unscientific' criticisms of 'scientific medicine'. Once labelled unscientific, criticism can be disregarded and the critics marginalized, irrespective of the merits of their arguments.

Appadurai emphasizes another aspect of the problem, namely the disembeddedness of Western knowledge systems from any social and religious grounding. For him, it is precisely the intrusion of disembedded knowledge in the form of an agronomic *episteme* that undermines the core value of sociality as commercial agriculture displaces subsistence.

All of this puts resistance to new technologies in a different light. What appears as obscurantism and superstition to the outsider can be at the same time resistance to alien cultural values, explicit or tacit, to the resisters. It is worth remembering that the followers of the original General Lud, whose name became synonymous with irrational resistance to progress, did not oppose the spinning-jenny but jennies in factories. Luddite resistance was not to technical progress but to the application of progress in ways which would destroy the birthright of ordinary folk to labour in their own cottages. In just the same way, the resistance to vaccination in the name of the goddess of smallpox can be seen as resistance to the cultural and political concomitants of vaccination, inseparably linked to vaccination in the minds of both the vaccinators and the vaccinated. To accept vaccination was to accept the culture of the vaccinator, hardly less alien when the culture of an urban Westernized élite had replaced the culture of the colonizers.

10   Decoupling Technologies from their Entailments

One final thought. These essays reflect a respect for the indigenous cultures of South Asia and the Third World generally. But this respect does not imply that we are disposed to preserve these cultures as artefacts are preserved in museums or animals in wildlife refuges. *None* of the authors is a preservationist. All of us recognize the need for growth and change as the first rule of cultural survival, certainly for the vast majority of cultures which exist in a world-wide web of economic and cultural exchange. Nor are we oblivious to oppression and abuse of power justified in the name of tradition.

It is precisely to preserve the option of organic growth for non-Western cultures that we are critical of the deference accorded to Western systems of knowledge, particularly to Western *episteme*, half a century after the process of dismantling the Western systems of empire got under way. We see this deference as an important obstacle to the empowerment of non-Western peoples, and, indeed, of Western peoples as well. The next round of decolonization, the decolonization of the mind, will require a critical re-evaluation of both Western and non-Western cultures, and the encounter between them. This re-evaluation is already taking place. We intend this volume as a contribution.

We have indicated that it is not our intention to call the growth of production and consumption of material goods into question; nor are we critical of the technologies that have brought material abundance to the West. Rather, our criticism is against the cultural and political *entailments* with which these technologies present themselves to the Third World. Once it is recognized that the threat to indigenous cultures and the real target of popular opposition mobilized in the light of this threat is the entailment rather than the technology itself, then a possibility opens up to separate, to *decouple* the technologies from the entailments.

We would hypothesize that such a decoupling may bring material benefits along with cultural benefits. If, for instance, variolators had been offered vaccination as an improved version of their traditional technology (which in historical fact it was, but that is not the central point for present purposes), satisfactory control of smallpox might have been brought about within the traditional cultural framework more quickly and at lower cost than was achieved by making vaccination part of a cultural confrontation between West and East, between modern and traditional.

Without this decoupling, it is difficult to see how growth in material standards of living can take place without modernization along the Western model. And we should be under no illusions about the inevitability of the quest for growth, whatever differences we may have about its prospects. Nobody, not even the most sceptical among us, will doubt the need to feed the hungry and clothe the naked, needs which were recognized long before growth came to dominate the Third World economic agenda. Whatever one's reservations may be about the necessity or utility of radios, televisions, motorcycles, and the like, the division between the necessary, the merely useful, and the wastefully luxurious is not ours to make; it is not our place to argue the virtues of simplicity and abstinence to those for whom material abundance is a distant dream. For their part, most Third World people, if given the opportunity, will not deny themselves a share in the riches that Western technologies have been able to produce.

The extent to which decoupling is feasible is an open question. But if the alternative is to make political disempowerment and cultural impoverishment the price of material abundance, surely it is worth making the effort to investigate the possibilities. Where there is a will, there *may* be a way. Where there is no will, there is certainly no way.

REFERENCES

Banuri, Tariq, and Apffel Marglin, Frédérique (forthcoming) *Who Will Save the Forests?*

Doi, Takeo (1971) *The Anatomy of Dependence*, Tokyo: Kodansho (English translation from the Japanese, 1973).

Eisenstadt, S. N. (1966) *Modernization, Protest, and Change*, Modernization of Traditional Societies series, Englewood Cliffs, NJ: Prentice Hall.

Evans-Pritchard, Edward (1937) *Witchcraft, Oracles and Magic among the Azande*, Oxford: Clarendon Press.

Gilligan, Carol (1982) *In a Different Voice: Psychological Theory and Women's Development*, Cambridge, Mass.: Harvard University Press.

Har Dayal (1912) 'The Wealth of the Nation', *Modern Review* (July), 12: 43–9.

Keynes, John Maynard (1921) *A Treatise on Probability*, London: Macmillan.

Lerner, Daniel (1958) *The Passing of Traditional Society*, Glencoe, Ill.: Free Press.

Lewis, W. Arthur (1955) *The Theory of Economic Growth*, London: George Allen and Unwin.

Little, Ian (1982) *Economic Development: Theory, Policy, and International Relations*, New York: Basic Books.

Mangelsdorf, Paul (1953) 'Wheat', *Scientific American* (July), 189: 50–9.

Marglin, Stephen A. (1974) 'What Do Bosses Do? The Origins and Functions of Hierarchy in Capitalist Production', Part 1, *Review of Radical Political Economics*, 6: 60–112.

—— (1984) *Growth, Distribution, and Prices*, Cambridge, Mass.: Harvard University Press.

—— (1987) 'Investment and Accumulation', in John Eatwell, Murray Milgate, and Peter Newman (eds.), *The New Palgrave*, London: Macmillan.

—— (1990) 'Lessons of the Golden Age', in S. Marglin and J. Schor (eds.), *The Golden Age of Capitalism*, Oxford: Clarendon Press.

—— and Bhaduri, Amit (1990) 'Profit Squeeze and Keynesian Theory', in S. Marglin and J. Schor (eds.), *The Golden Age of Capitalism*, Oxford: Clarendon Press.

Myers, Norman (1983) *A Wealth of Wild Species: Storehouse for Human Welfare*, Boulder, Colo.: Westview Press.

Nandy, Ashis (1983) *The Intimate Enemy*, New Delhi: Oxford University Press.

Putnam, Hilary (1988) 'Objectivity and the Science–Ethics Distinction', revised version of a paper presented to a conference on the quality of life, World Institute of Development Economics Research, Helsinki, 25–9 July 1988.

Sen, Amartya (1987) 'Food and Freedom', Sir John Crawford Memorial Lecture, Washington, DC, 29 October 1987.

—— (1988a) 'The Concept of Development', in H. Chenery and T. N. Srinivasan (eds.), *Handbook of Development Economics*, vol. i, Amsterdam: Elsevier Science Publishers.

—— (1988b) 'Freedom of Choice', *European Economic Review*, 32: 269—94.

Streeten, Paul, and associates (1981) *First Things First: Meeting Basic Human Needs in Developing Countries*, New York: Oxford University Press.

Tambiah, Stanley (1985) *Culture, Thought, and Social Action*, Cambridge, Mass.: Harvard University Press.

United States, National Bipartisan Commission on Central America (1984) *The Report of the President's National Bipartisan Commission on Central America*, New York: Macmillan.

Williams, Bernard (1985) *Ethics and the Limits of Philosophy*, Cambridge, Mass.: Harvard University Press.

2

Development and the Politics of Knowledge: A Critical Interpretation of the Social Role of Modernization Theories in the Development of the Third World

TARIQ BANURI

1 The Crisis in Development Theory

The period following World War II has witnessed the advent of a massive and unprecedented project of social engineering in Third World countries, variously termed industrialization, modernization, or development;[1] and justified on the basis of a supposed superiority of Western economic and political institutions and (initially at least) of Western values over non-Western ones. While the philosophical roots of the belief in the superiority of Western values can be traced back to the Enlightenment ethic of 'the rational pursuit of human freedoms', and the colonial ethic of 'the White Man's burden', contemporary writers generally legitimate their actions on relatively partial (and therefore more defensible) grounds, namely the need for and the desirability of transferring modern Western technology to Third World countries in order to bring about increases in per capita output (particularly in the high-productivity industrial sector), or the expanded provision of 'basic needs' (i.e. formal education, modern health facilities, piped water-supply, and so forth). Such a transfer is argued to be facilitated by other forms of institutional and structural change such as 'state-building' (i.e. the expansion of state power conjointly with the introduction of parliamentary and democratic institutions), and the inculcation of a particular set of development-enhancing 'modern' (i.e. 'Western') values and habits among the people of traditional societies.

The early days of this project were characterized by an unalloyed confidence in the ability of social scientists to help the people of Third World countries banish their inherited problems and construct a new

1. Terms such as Westernization or rationalization bring out other relevant aspects of this process. We use 'modernization' as an omnibus term to refer to the overall process of social change within which one or more specific streams may be present.

social reality from scratch.[2] Of course, even in that age of unbounded optimism there were several voices of doubt and dissent regarding the sagacity, desirability, or feasibility of such a gigantic endeavour; but the self-assurance of the theorists was so unequivocal and belief in their nostrums so widespread that doubters could readily be dismissed as irrational and misguided 'cranks' if not as malicious mischief-makers. Accusations of failures could similarly be disregarded as resulting from weaknesses not in the theory but in the application, because of the endurance of backward behaviour, values, and institutions in the countries concerned, or (at a later stage) from the inefficiency or venality of politicians and bureaucrats. Matters have changed, however. Although it may be too early to begin writing an epitaph for development theory, it is certainly not inopportune to record the passing of the era of blind faith.[3]

Today there is a crisis in modernization theory. Hardly a book or journal on development issues comes out which does not express disappointment, disillusion, or dissatisfaction with the ability of what Ashis Nandy has called a 'secular theory of salvation'[4] to live up to its promise to expand human freedoms.[5]

Many factors have contributed to this emerging crisis. The most obvious one is the extremely uneven record of development: of the persistence of poverty amid increasing affluence, of the increase in unemployment despite expanding production, and, in general, of the failure to ameliorate the condition of people in the poorest countries of Africa and Asia. A second reason is the increasing association of modernization and development with ecological disasters: the devastation of tropical rain forests and mountain watersheds, the deleterious (and unanticipated) ecological consequences of large dams and large irrigation systems, the loss of subsistence agricultural land to desertification in Africa and to water-logging and salinity in Asia, and the high energy-requirement and vulnerability of

2. The self-confidence of the scientists derived in great measure from the unqualified support they received from nationalizing élites (such as India's Prime Minister Nehru) in the receiving countries whose faith in the beneficence of Western rationality was, if anything, even more unequivocal.

3. While different writers suggest different dates for the onset of this period of disillusionment (in some cases as early as 1960), we see the mid- to late 1970s as the watershed. One reason is the series of events—Vietnam, OPEC, Watergate, prolonged recession—which helped to destroy the myth of permanent Western superiority.

4. Remark made in WIDER meeting on Technological Transformation of the Third World: Alternative Approaches, Helsinki, July 1985. See also Nandy, 1987: 20–1.

5. Prominent examples of such criticism from notable experts would include Henry Bruton 1985, Albert Hirschman 1981a, Amartya Sen 1983, and the various references cited therein. Equally important but less prominent are the expressions of disillusionment in influential textbooks on development: Meier's (4th edn., 1984) opening sentence talks about the 'dissatisfaction with the result of development efforts over the past three decades' (p. 5); in a similar vein, Ch. 1 of Yotopoulos and Nugent's (1976) textbook is entitled 'The Record of Economic Development and the Disillusionment With Development Economics'. Other examples could be given.

modern technologies. Another contributory factor is a similarly increasing association of development with higher levels of conflict and tension in much of the Third World, in almost all parts where the developmental project has been under way for a significant period of time, where such conflicts as wars, civil unrest, civic and ethnic violence, political repression, and urban crime appear to have increased tremendously.[6] Responsibility must also be placed at the door of a fourth consideration, namely the onset of a period of confusion, muddled groping, and search for new paradigms in economics as well as political science, the two mother disciplines of development theory.[7]

Notwithstanding the importance of each of the above, however, it seems that the single most important reason for the spreading disillusionment is a 'loss of hope', as Mary Kaldor once put it,[8] an erosion of the myth that development can create a just and humane society. This erosion has also permitted the increase in popularity and self-assurance of non-Western (and often anti-Western) social, cultural, and political movements in Third World countries. Some of the reasons for this can be summarized here.

1. There is a growing belief that it is not possible, given the earth's resources, for the entire planet to be able to emulate the consumption pattern of Western countries.

2. Tremendous unanticipated social and political problems accompanying development have raised the concern that, even if it were possible to 'become like the West', attempts to do so in the shortest possible time could be socially harmful.

3. Growing familiarity of Third World citizens with the mode of existence in the West has created serious reservations about the desirability of following this line of development. These reservations have surfaced in the West as well, and have no doubt helped to reinforce those in the Third World.

4. This process of doubt and discovery has been hastened by the events of the seventies (Watergate, Vietnam, OPEC, economic crises, the decay of cities, and the plight of the elderly or minorities in Western countries), which led to the gradual erosion of the myth that people in Western societies were in greater control of their destiny.

5. A similar disillusionment seems to have set in with regard to the Soviet model, with the publicization of the Stalinist purges, expansion of state control over peoples' lives, and a generalized denial of freedoms.

6. Escalation of the irrational arms race between the two superpowers and the accompanying intensification of belligerent rhetoric, despite widespread

---

6. And some of these, perhaps relatedly, in industrialized countries, most notably the United States, as well.
7. As Attewell 1984 argues, such redefinitions of the paradigms are also evident in recent Marxist thought.
8. Remark made in Conference on a Just World Peace, Paris, Dec. 1985.

popular resistance, have created doubts about the ability of the rational model even to ensure the survival of the species.

As a result of these and other factors, the two dominant Western models of progress have relinquished their hold over the imagination of Third World intellectuals, and a shift towards indigenous values has become more legitimate.

In this essay I take the resulting crisis in modernization theory as a point of departure to argue that it is essentially an affirmation of earlier doubts, and thus derives not from the discovery of some hitherto unobserved social costs, but rather from a newly articulated recognition of these costs. I shall argue that this recognition has helped, in turn, to reinforce deep-seated dissatisfaction with the modernizers' perspective on human society, and therefore, in order to understand the current crisis and to discover reasonable and coherent alternatives, it is necessary to examine in detail the intellectual and cultural roots of this perspective.

2   Towards a Sociology of Knowledge

There are several strands in contemporary modernization theory. Each strand, while reflecting an independent literature, and often an independent area of expertise, supports and is in turn supported by the assumptions and conclusions of the others. The motivating idea behind these different literatures is a search for explanations of the massive differences in income and productive capacity between Western countries (with Japan recently admitted as an honorary member) and countries of the so-called Third World; and the use of these explanations to discover methods by which the disparities can be overcome. Although some changes have occurred in recent years, the explicit objective of most such writings continues to remain one of teaching Third World countries how to 'become like the West', and how to do so in the shortest possible time; disagreements between various writings derive mainly from differences over the proper definition of the 'West', and over efficacious means of reaching this goal.

The list of subdisciplines in this literature would include: (1) *development economics*,[9] the cutting edge of the endeavour, with its competing paradigms[10] of *institutionalist mainstream*, *neo-classical*, and *structural*

---

9. Development economics focuses on economic factors, and seeks to bring about an increase in per capita output of Third World countries, the assumption being that other desirable attributes of Westernization will follow more or less automatically.

10. The various schools differ from each other in medium-term targets as well as in assumptions of exogeneity and endogeneity. The neo-classical approach considers the unfettering of the market as the key to economic development, the institutionalist and structuralist approaches, less sanguine, recommend direct action by the government.

approaches.[11] (2) The *political economy*[12] approach rooted in the Marxian tradition, including the *world systems* approach,[13] the *dependency* school,[14] and *non-dependency Marxists*.[15] (3) *Political development*, concerned with issues of state-building,[16] and finally (4) *social modernization* theory, which perceives 'correct' social values and behaviours as necessary prerequisites of development.[17]

While there are significant and profound differences between writings in the various subfields listed above, there are common grounds as well. These include:[18]

1. A linear view of history, in which Western countries are further along the path of progress than Third World countries, notwithstanding significant differences over the attractiveness of the contemporary social conditions in the former countries.

11. The tension between these schools is resolved in the form of substrategies which have themselves acquired the status of paradigms (e.g. basic needs, redistribution with growth, import substitution, export promotion, or rural development). The substrategies are both attempts to adapt development goals to popular needs, and (more cynically) efforts to make the development project more acceptable politically and hence more feasible.

12. While the political economy school has provided the major share of the criticism of mainstream theories (and hence should be placed in the category of 'alternative' views), its orthodox wing also shares with mainstream writers the linear view of progress according to which developing countries are on an evolutionary trail blazed by the industrialized countries. Recognizing this dualism, we have categorized such writings among the modernizing group as well as among the critical group.

13. The world systems approach was pioneered by the seminal work of Immanuel Wallerstein 1974 and built upon the ideas developed by dependency writers. Its distinguishing feature is an attempt to get away from the nation-state as a natural unit of analysis, and to see the emergence and development of capitalism as a global phenomenon.

14. The distinguishing feature of dependency theory is the analytical distinction between 'centre' and 'periphery' countries as a means for understanding the twin phenomena of 'development' in Northern countries and 'underdevelopment' in the South.

15. Unlike the other two Marxian paradigms, non-dependency writers give less importance to external factors and more to internal class conflict in explaining social evolution.

16. The prescriptive content of this discipline, derived from normative (Western) political philosophy, is the advocacy of 'superior' Western political institutions, including an efficient bureaucracy, some form of electoral democracy, political parties and pluralist associations, and the acceptance of abstract political rights. In theoretical terms, the issues boil down to a discussion of two dimensions of *power* in society, namely its expansion and legitimation. The former, brought about mainly by increasing the efficiency of the bureaucratic machinery, makes for more effective policy intervention; while the latter, whether through electoral means, media persuasion, or élite dominance, ensures that this effectiveness is not at the cost of future political stability (and, hence, future policy effectiveness), nor that of social and political rights. See e.g. Pye 1965.

17. These include the inculcation of Max Weber's Protestant ethic (later modernized in the form of Talcott Parson's pattern variables, McClelland's 'need for achievement' and Inkeles and Smith's overall modernity index), or Schumpeter's entrepreneurial values; or the overcoming of Banfield's 'amoral familism', or Hoselitz's ascriptive relations and diffuse functional identities. Once again, these writings assumed that the factors under consideration were exogenous, and that the overcoming of obstacles generated by their absence would lead to the breaking of other bottle-necks, and of an expansion in economic growth.

18. For another argument on the common grounds between mainstream and radical theories of development, see Wilber and Jameson 1984.

2. Again, notwithstanding significant differences over ultimate causes of the dramatic economic progress in the West, there is broad agreement that the proximate cause was the unfettering of rationality: the application of science to production, a mechanistic view of social relations, and an increased emphasis on efficiency.

3. Broad similarities in the analyses of core values, such as freedom, justice, equality, creativity, and even power as experienced and defined in the West.

4. Finally, although once again there are very significant differences over this issue, there is an implicit positivist assumption in a broad subset of these writings that the means for achieving social ends are separable from the ends themselves; and often also that moral considerations apply primarily to ends rather than to means.

The subject of this analysis then is precisely these common grounds: how, despite tremendous internal differences amongst the protagonists of modernization are these common grounds preserved in the face of substantial and often devastating critiques by outside theorists and activists?

In order to delineate this evolution, we have to begin with a sociology of knowledge of modernization theories, in other words, with a theory of why people write what they write. Here, I follow a common practice which sees the development of ideas in terms of challenge and response between theorists and their critics. To find our way through the complexity of this literature we shall use as our Ariadne's thread the notion of the 'external' critique, in other words, criticisms of modernization theory advanced by those who do not share the moral or intellectual perspective of its protagonists.

Theoretical progress and innovation, in this view, results from the creative effort of theorists to adapt their theories, assimilate new ideas into their paradigms, or successfully reject the claims contained in the challenge of the 'external' critique.[19] The set of feasible responses is, however, constrained by other goals of the theorists. Borrowing from the approach taken by the sociologist Paul Attewell (1984), I see these goals to be 'paradigm maintenance', 'prescriptive relevance', and the 'moral defence of modernization', the tension between which provides the principal endogenous mechanism of theoretical innovation.[20] The goal of prescriptive relevance demands a response to external critiques, but this

19. Thomas Kuhn's influence should be obvious in this discussion. Kuhn introduced notions like 'the priority of the paradigm' or 'normal science as puzzlesolving', as well as the role of anomalies and crises in theoretical evolution, which have been the major source of ideas in the sociology of knowledge literature. See Kuhn 1970, particularly Chs. 4–8.

20. The terms 'paradigm maintenance', 'prescriptive relevance', and 'moral defence of modernity' are meant to be self-explanatory. While they are somewhat different from Attewell's schema, a review of Attewell 1984: 17–36 can help clarify the concepts better.

response is often conditioned, constrained, or even inhibited by the need to maintain the paradigm and to defend modernization.

The most common response to an 'external' critique is the development of an 'internal' critique, i.e. one which shares the analytical and intellectual perspective of modernization theory, as well as the concern with a 'moral defence of modernization', yet criticizes some of the assumptions or implications of the accepted view.[21] In the short run this can introduce paradigmatic innovations over which a prolonged intellectual debate can ensue. Occasionally, a new paradigm might emerge from the discussion, effectively dividing the profession into two groups.[22] Often, however, paradigm maintenance is ensured by the 'policing' efforts of the orthodoxy, through which innovation can ultimately be incorporated into older paradigms. In some instances, of course, it is possible that the new ideas are rejected out of hand for being irrational or unfounded.

In any event, what this means is that while the 'external' critique presents a challenge to orthodox theory over its manifest failures, the 'internal' critique provides a means of addressing and assimilating this challenge.[23] Similarly, while the 'external' critique often seeks to *undermine* and thereby diminish the theory by attacking its moral base, the 'internal' critique seeks mainly to *complete* and thereby strengthen a theory by extending it to areas hitherto ignored. The discussion would be helped by a brief digression on the two types of critiques.

2.1 'Internal' and 'External' Critiques

'Internal' critiques of modernization, i.e. forms of criticism which accept the underlying moral argument for modernization and which are, therefore, assimilable into existing theories, include: (1) *intra-paradigmatic* criticism, i.e. the questioning of the assumptions and propositions of theories within the framework of a given paradigm;[24] and (2) *inter-paradigmatic* debate,

21. The various writings will generally be unified as a 'moral defence of modernization' only at a metaphorical or 'deep structural' level, to use a term popularized by Noam Chomsky, even though there might be substantial differences in their 'surface structure'.
22. The classic example of this is the 'Keynesian revolution', in which the innovative effort brought about a lasting schism in the economics profession.
23. It may be noted, however, that the distinction between the two types of critiques may be somewhat arbitrary in many instances, especially when it comes to the work of such 'iconoclasts' as Albert Hirschman, Paul Streeten, or Amartya Sen, who combine the critique with a way of assimilating it into the theory.
24. The term 'intra-paradigmatic' critique is perhaps self-explanatory. An example from the literature on development economics is the controversy over culturally specific institutions (e.g. the extended family) which influence behaviour in traditional societies. Some writers contend that the existence of such institutions should be taken as parametric and economic theory should be tailored to incorporate their effect on behaviour and welfare; others take a more functionalist approach to argue that these institutions serve a 'rational' purpose and therefore should be derivable from rational axioms of behaviour. Also, that their *raison d'être* will disappear with the advent of modernity.

i.e. the criticism of writers in different disciplines who may share the world-view of the impugned paradigm though not all of its maintained assumptions.[25]

'External' or 'alternative' critiques, on the other hand, are resistant to assimilation into modernization theories because they reject the basic notions of welfare and behaviour implicit in such theories, particularly those deriving from a presumed superiority of Western values and institutions. These can be either purely (3) *intellectual* challenges to modernization, or examples of (4) *socio-political resistance* and protest which undermine the certitudes of the regnant theories.

Intellectual challenges, i.e. 'alternative' intellectual or scholarly conceptions of social change and progress, include, in addition to writings with a specific Third World focus,[26] the literature which looks primarily at the problems emerging in Western countries after two or more centuries of capitalist development without any explicit reference to the concerns or predicament of Third World countries.[27]

Socio-political resistance includes, on the one hand, instances of political mobilization, resistance, and protest which challenge the attitudes and institutions supporting and enforcing modernity; and, on the other hand, examples of socio-psychological dysfunctioning or other non-intellectualized manifestations of popular disaffection with the results of development and modernization. Examples of such protest would include religious and ethnic revival movements, popular environmental movements, social welfare movements, women's movements, and movements of cultural interpretation and articulation.[28]

---

25. Examples include disagreements between political scientists and development economists over the role and function of the state, or between sociologists and economists over the proper analysis of institutions, or even the disputes between orthodox neo-classical development economists and those of a more eclectic persuasion.
26. These writings include the 'humanistic development' school, critics of the violent and disenfranchising nature of modern science and technology, and of their effects on social arrangements or the natural environment, writers who link the neo-colonialism of developmentalism with the psychological effects of political colonialism, advocates of a culture-based approach to welfare and progress as well as to notions of political conflict and to epistemological and methodological issues, and some writers in various religious traditions. See Section 3.8 for a more detailed discussion.
27. This literature would include the writings of the critical theory school of Marxism, social philosophers (Elster, Rorty) who focus on the uniqueness of unfettered rationality, Gramscians and other political theorists and political anthropologists who question the notion of the nation-state as a rationalization of social discipline; neo-structuralists and semioticians who highlight the hegemonic role of science and scientific methodologies, psychologists who raise the issue of alienation and socio-psychological anomie, and cultural anthropologists who point to the cultural specificity of modern Western values and institutions. See Section 3.8 for a more detailed discussion.
28. The concerns expressed by these movements have been echoed, and in some cases, anticipated by similar movements in Western countries. Particularly noteworthy are women's movements, the peace movement in Europe, and the Greens movement in West Germany.

2.2 Challenge and Response

What emerges from this discussion is the recognition that there exists a diversity of approaches to the development programme which, when viewed from the perspective of the predominant paradigm, appear as a hierarchy of critiques. At the farthest remove in this hierarchy is political resistance and protest as well as popular disaffection with the results of modernization, manifested in the form of socio-psychological dysfunctioning. The next level is that of intellectual and scholarly critiques of modernization, those which reject the notions of welfare and behaviour implicit in development theories and thus challenge the assumption of the superiority of Western values and institutions. Next come criticisms within the modernizing world-view, but from outside a specific paradigm. Lastly, there are the criticisms of policies or simplifying assumptions from within a paradigm.[29]

It can also be noted that each successive level of criticism brings the argument closer to a given paradigm; 'alternative' theorists interpret popular dissatisfaction and make it intelligible to Western intellectuals; sister paradigms make intelligible and manageable the criticism from extrinsic sources; and intra-paradigmatic critiques provide means by which such sisterly strictures can be assimilated and responded to.

It also follows from this discussion that the terms 'external' and 'internal' are relative to the subject of analysis. If we wish to examine a specific paradigm, only the intra-paradigmatic critique will be seen to be internal. On the contrary, if we look at the entire corpus of scholarly literature on social change in Third World countries, all critiques except for socio-political challenges by anti-Establishment forces will have to be treated as internal. I adopt a middle course here, in seeking to analyse the development of modernization theories alone, and see this development as a series of creative responses to the challenge posed by 'external' critics, whether intellectual or political.

To summarize, social theorists are challenged by many different critics as well as by some obvious failures in their predictions. They respond to these challenges creatively by adapting or modifying their assumptions, or by assimilating the criticism within their theories. This process, which gives theoretical systems their dynamism and strength, is in the case of modernization theories conditioned and constrained by the need of theorists to maintain their paradigms and to defend modernity.

The stability and resilience of the dominant world-view derived from its ability to assimilate or dismiss (as illogical, fanatical, or reactionary)

29. It may perhaps be apposite to note here that these distinctions between various criticisms are for purposes of clarification only, and need not have any direct congruence with particular writers or even particular articles, although in most cases this will indeed turn out to be the case. As mentioned earlier, 'iconoclastic' writers, such as Hirschman, Streeten, or Sen, may often fall into more than one category, even in the space of the same paper.

the external critiques, whether from intellectuals or popular movements. However, the increase in theoretical and analytical writings from contrasting perceptions, and the increase in self-assurance of the alternative popular movements, have strained the capacity of modernization theories to adapt or assimilate the criticisms, and have thus created a crisis in the dominant paradigms.

2.3 A Review of Modernization Theory

In the following sections, I use the notion of the 'external' critique to organize and guide us through the evolution of modernization theories in the post-World War II period. This exercise relies on a highly schematic construct of a series of intellectual challenges and responses in which the stages are: (1) dualism, (2) the role of values, (3) the 'meaning of development', (4) political development and political stability, (5) political participation versus organization, (6) appropriate technology and the social role of knowledge, (7) ecological, environmental, and natural resource questions, and (8) the cultural critique. Each of these represents a different challenge (or a modification of an earlier challenge) to modernization theorists from political and social developments and/or from 'alternative' intellectual criticism, and invites a different response. A simplified view of this evolution is presented in Table 1 below.

Although the following description will, at times, read like a chronological development, such is not the intent. First, many of the developments, particularly in stages 5–7, were more or less concurrent with each other and could have been presented in any order. Second, the notion of a 'stage' in the evolution of modernization theory represents the time when some ideas become popular or respectable, rather than when they first emerge. Intellectual roots of a controversy can often be traced back to many earlier writings, but the interesting question for sociologists of knowledge pertains not to these earlier (sporadic) works, but rather to the transformation of these ideas into a subject of concerted attention and debate in the profession.[30] This means that while a loose chronological ordering can be observed in the intellectual debates as asserted here, there is no necessary ordering in the emergence of ideas which are salient in these debates.

Table 1 presents the stages in schematic form. In the first stage, the recognition of significant socio-cultural differences within and across societies (dualism) caused some writers to construct alternative theories of economic behaviour, while others sought to demonstrate that existing paradigms of development could incorporate the observed differences. In

---

30. To give an analogy from another field of economics, the 'rational expectations' school of macroeconomics emerged in the late 1970s in response to the failure of existing theoretical approaches. It is this date which sociologists of knowledge will look at when trying to understand the evolution of modern macroeconomics, even though the idea of 'rational expectations' had emerged as early as 1959 in the writings of John Muth.

Table 1. Schematic Description of Modernization Theories

Stage	Title	External Critics	Political Event	Theorists' Response
1	Dualism	Boeke, Furnivall, cultural anthropologists	Political independence	Harmonious (economic) dualism
2	The role of values	Scott, Wolf, Hobsbawm Myrdal, Hirschman	Peasant wars Social unrest	Rational peasant Modernizing values
3	Meaning of development	Myrdal, Goulet, Schumacher, Berger	Political conflicts, civil wars	Redistributive policies, attack on poverty, basic needs
4	Political development	Dependentistas, political anthropologists	Political instability, civil wars	Political development, political stability
5	Alienation, disenfranchisement	Schumacher, Berger, Gran, Gramscians	Anti-systemic movements (NGOs)	Political development, rural development, political participation
6	Technology, social role of knowledge	Appropriate technology literature, Geertz	Ethnic violence, unemployment, formation of NGOs	Wrong prices, technologist approaches, state action
7	Environment and resources	Ecologists, Greens, Club of Rome	Ecological movements, anti-vivisectionists	Externalities, managerial approaches, neo-fascist approaches
8	Culture and resistance	Nandy, Geertz, Uberoi, Fanon, Freire, Dumont, neo-structuralism, Shariati	Indigenous revival movements	Neo-classical medicine, Gang of Four example, paradigm defence

the next stage the nature and timing of changes in these differences became a matter for discussion, calling for the involvement of sociologists and psychologists who hypothesized the existence of different values in traditional societies, and argued for the most part that such values needed to be eradicated and replaced by modern ones; while only a small minority asserted that alternative values may be important in their own right. The debate over values combined with some spectacular developmental failures to give rise to two related issues, the 'meaning of development', and the priority of political development. Next, these debates, together with expressions of political and intellectual dissatisfaction, led to an argument over popular participation in development and particularly over the role of development theory in denying such participation. Similar concerns surfaced over ecological and natural resource problems, over the absence of popular control of relevant decisions, and on the possibility that an erosion of social control was inherent in the nature of modern technology. These issues were subsequently brought together in what may be termed the cultural critique of development, to be taken up in the next section.

3 Dualism

The notion of 'dualism' was and continues to be a key organizing concept in attempts made in the various development theories to understand and remedy the massive differences in income, consumption, and productivity between Western and non-Western countries. Conventional explanations of this phenomenon note that while industrialized countries are sufficiently homogeneous, the so-called developing countries are generally characterized by 'dual' societies, in other words by the coexistence of a 'stagnant' traditional sector alongside a 'dynamic' modern sector, the latter reflecting conditions in Western countries. Development, in these explanations, is the gradual expansion of the modern sector until it completely displaces the traditional sector. As a result of this perspective, current development literature invariably uses the concept of 'dualism' to imply the inferiority of the traditional mode of existence.

While the concept of 'dualism' has been used from the very beginning to organize ideas about development, its normative and prescriptive content has gone through some very important changes, two of which are particularly noteworthy. First, there appears to have been a shift from a 'conflictual' to a 'harmonious' model of dualism, the latter being better suited to the imperatives and needs of development policy. Second, while it began as a description of the social and economic structure of non-industrialized countries, it has become increasingly relevant for the debates over the global economy (where the analogues of modern and traditional sectors would be the 'industrialized' and 'Third World' countries respectively).

3.1 Conflictual and Harmonious Dualism

The term 'dualism' was coined originally by the Dutch economist J. H. Boeke in his study of pre-Independence Indonesian development, to refer not to the coexistence, but rather to 'the *clashing* of an imported social system with an indigenous social system of another style' (Boeke 1953: 5; emphasis added). Though Boeke provided a name for this conflict, the idea itself was not new. Ian Little (1982) traces another version of this notion to colonial economists like J. S. Furnivall who, unlike modern development economists, considered 'development' (i.e. the opening up of an area for economic exploitation) to be antithetical to, and indeed inimical to, 'welfare' (i.e. the well-being of indigenous people).[31]

For modernization theorists the term dualism had a more harmonious connotation. They interpreted it to mean not a clashing of two different life-styles, but rather a 'displacement', as Henry Bruton was to put it later, of a backward and undesirable life-style by a dynamic and desirable one. Development economists refined the notion even further, from two different *life-styles* to two different modes of *economic behaviour*, coexisting because of differences in labour supplies in the two sectors (as in the W. A. Lewis 1954 and Ranis–Fei (Fei and Ranis 1964) models), or two different levels of technological or resource endowments (as in the Jorgenson 1967 model). Naturally, then, the transformation of the traditional into the modern sector began to be conceived not as a conflictual, but rather as an inevitable, desirable, and harmonious process in which people are pulled from the village to the city through the process of urbanization and industrialization, and economic rationality moves from the city to the village as rural life-styles change due to the import of capital and other resources and the consequent emerging shortages of labour.

Thus, while the notion of dualism emerged initially as an 'external' critique of the deleterious effects of development on local populations because of the underlying cultural conflict, modernization theorists transformed it into an 'internal' critique; a concept which had hitherto been a reflection of the conflict between development and welfare began to represent a congruence of the two concepts.

The timing of the shift from 'conflictual' to 'harmonious' dualism is particularly interesting. It coincides with the achievement of Independence of erstwhile colonies, whose new indigenous élites would need such justification in order to be able to defend the notion of development and its attendant policy aspects to their supposedly emancipated compatriots. Less cynically, it is related to the fact that after Independence the 'modern' sector was no longer purely expatriate but rather was increasingly

---

31. See Little 1982: 385 ff.: 'The liberal economists' assimilation of "development" to "welfare" constitutes a persuasive use of language, which is new as compared with the usage of colonial economists and writers before World War II.'

composed of indigenous elements who had evolved from their earlier 'backward' status. As such, the earlier conflict between foreign and local interests could now be argued to have metamorphosed into the problem of remaking the rest of the society in the image of the élite minority.

An innovation which is of particular importance in this context, and without which this transformation from 'conflictual' dualism to 'harmonious' dualism may not have been possible, is the 'linearization' of the concept of development. In the first place this occurred with the emergence of 'measures' of development, the most important of which, deriving from Simon Kuznets's earlier work, was the notion of national income or output.[32] This allowed the construction of a linear scale on which industrialized countries were unequivocally ahead of the Third World, and the 'modern' sector unequivocally ahead of the 'traditional' sector within the Third World. Another contribution to the 'linearization' of development, though not with the same mathematical precision, was Walt Rostow's influential theory of the stages of growth.

3.2 International Dualism

The diverse meanings of dualism continue to remain key organizing concepts, and can be argued to have given rise to competing schools of economic development. A 'conflictual' version of international dualism lies at the base of a very important paradigmatic innovation, this time in Marxist writings, namely dependency/world systems theory, in which the appropriate unit of analysis is considered to be the entire world rather than a nation-state, and 'Third World' and 'industrialized' countries are the analogues of 'traditional' and 'modern' sectors. Accordingly, dependency theorists argue that the development (or underdevelopment) of the Third World is the result of a dynamic interaction with the imperatives of the industrialized world, in the same manner as that of the 'traditional' sector within a country is of the imperatives of its 'modern' sector. The dependency approach raised many other important issues, most notably with regard to the relationship between local and foreign élites, and the role of the state in peripheral societies.

In contrast, a 'harmonious' version of international dualism can be seen to have fathered the emergence of 'institutional' development economics (an alternative to the orthodox neo-classical variety) which sought to incorporate cultural and behavioural differences into the formulation of economic theory and policy. This incorporation, however, was done at the expense of theoretical rigour, and led to an extended debate between proponents of the two schools over the appropriateness of theoretical innovations, a debate which continues to this day. Lastly, neo-classical development theory continued to insist that the only differences between

32. Kuznets 1941 first introduced National Income as a measure of social prosperity. This concept is applied to the Third World in Kuznets 1971.

the Third World and the industrialized West emanated from differences in resource endowments, rather than from differences in behaviour or rationality.

4 The Role of Values

The above controversies formed the basis of the next stage in the evolution of modernization theory, namely the question of social values of participants as well as theorists. First, there was a strong external critique of the desirability as well as the feasibility of the displacement of the traditional sector, by writers who asserted the existence of the 'rationality' and even the moral 'superiority' of traditional ways. These included Eric Wolf (1969), Eric Hobsbawm (1963),[33] and later James Scott (1976), and the 'Subaltern Studies' school in India (cf. Ranajit Guha 1982, 1983), and from a different perspective Albert Hirschman. The arguments of Wolf and Scott, derived from a Marxist perspective, are aimed at rediscovering the moral structure of the traditional (peasant) economy. They assert the existence and functional importance of such values as multi-stranded ties (particularly of the patron–client type) between individuals, of the corporate nature of the village, and of social guarantees of economic and social security through mechanisms of resource-sharing and reciprocal exchange. To get a little ahead of the story, these assertions about the peasant economy fall into the category of the 'personal' cultural map discussed in Chapter 3, and were intended as a critique of the unquestioning acceptance of the instrumental and 'impersonal' values of modernity.

These 'external' critiques of modernization derived their legitimacy from the strong resistance to the introduction of 'modern' institutions and practices into 'traditional' societies, particularly by peasants in the form of peasant rebellions, which seemed to belie the assertion of harmonious processes of change. This resistance, political as well as cultural, while particularly noticeable in South-East Asian countries (Vietnam, Cambodia, Laos, and later the Philippines and Indonesia), was also visible in South Asia and Africa. Looked at in another way, the intellectual critiques of dualism were attempts to make intelligible to modernization theorists, in scholarly terms, the values and aspirations which rural people in Third World countries seemed to be expressing in the form of political and social resistance.

In addition to overt political resistance, there were also examples of diffuse social and cultural resistance because of which the posited change

---

33. Hobsbawm does not exactly fit into this group. While he celebrates the heroism of the rebels, he regards them as 'primitive' (as evidenced from the title of his classic, *Primitive Rebels*, 1963), as archaic social movements which were 'against' history and hence doomed, but which were creating obstacles in the development of class consciousness.

was not proceeding apace. Examples of such resistance would include the reluctance of traditional people to send their children to school (occasionally going as far as burning schools), or to act upon various incentives (such as those for modern investment) provided by the government.

4.1 The Rational Peasant

In response to these criticisms, there have been three different developments in the modernization field. Writers of the so-called 'rational peasant' school (Samuel Popkin 1979, Theodore Schultz 1964, Sol Tax 1953, Raj Krishna) have tried to show that behaviour and values in peasant societies can be interpreted along the lines of conventional economic theory, and that therefore there is no difference in the morality to be ascribed to the peasant as opposed to his or her more modern counterpart. This literature is an attempt to interpret behaviour and institutions in non-Western societies along impersonal and functional lines, and thus to assimilate the concerns expressed by 'external' critics (Wolf, Scott). By contrast, whereas the latter also insisted that the peasants were 'rational', they claimed that there were 'different' forms of rationality, all of which were equally valid.

4.2 Social Modernization

A somewhat different response came from writers of the 'social modernization' school (Everett Hagen 1962, David McClelland 1961, Alex Inkeles and David Smith 1974, Bertholt Hoselitz 1960, Lucian Pye and Sidney Verba 1965), who sought to re-establish the moral superiority of 'modernity' by looking at the socio-psychological determinants of social values and value changes. Following the direction suggested by Max Weber's notion of the protestant ethic as a prerequisite for capitalism (Weber 1930) and later by Talcott Parson's pioneering work on pattern variables (Parsons 1951), these writers drew up lists of 'modern' values[34] and adduced socio-psychological explanations for their existence in particular cultures. The argument is that delay in adopting 'modern' values was due to the inherent conservatism of 'traditional' societies rather than to cultural resistance to domination. Furthermore, in the interest of the supposedly shared objective of modernization, this literature implicitly

---

34. These include McClelland's 'need for achievement' (i.e. things like punctuality, efficiency, long time horizon, pursuit of excellence, etc.), Hoselitz's formulation based on Talcott Parsons' famous pattern variables: ascription/achievement, universalism/particularism, specificity/diffuseness, and Pye and Verba's trust and loyalty to the nation state rather than to personal connections. Most writings are quite explicitly pejorative of traditional values, though this leads to ironic outcomes. For example, Inkeles and Smith 1974, after waxing eloquent about modernity, mention that they preferred the label 'modern' for this set of values instead of 'bureaucratic' or 'organizational', because the latter (although not inappropriate) had derogatory connotations.

legitimizes the forcible introduction of modernizing values into traditional societies.

While Hoselitz simply states that fundamental value orientations must change from particularistic to universalistic and from ascriptive to functional, McClelland and Hagen go into child-rearing mechanics to discuss how such changes are to be brought about. They argue, independently, that mid-childhood experience of safe behaviour in traditional societies induces a conforming attitude towards authority, while that in modern societies engenders a questioning attitude. Hagen goes on to explain that the emergence of a questioning attitude took place initially among the children of 'blocked minorities' who rejected their fathers' values. The overt prescriptive impact of these writings has been somewhat limited by the fact that it perceived the source of change to lie in mid-childhood experiences and the relatively resilient child-rearing practices.[35] Inkeles and Smith (1974), however, argue that the existence of modern institutions—such as schools, factories, political parties, cities— will, in itself, lead to the establishment of modern values in the populace, and that these changes can take place in adulthood as well.

In contrast to the above views, some writers, such as John Lewis and Morris Morris, have argued that the requisite cultural factors exist in all societies, and no change is necessary to induce development. Albert Hirschman (1965) goes one step further to assert that these so-called obstacles may actually be assets, or could be made into assets. In fact, he goes on to say that the attitudinal changes recommended by social theorists may be self-defeating because of the cognitive dissonance they introduce into the lives of constituent citizens.

4.3 Theorists' Values

Lastly, some writers (Gunnar Myrdal 1968, Albert Hirschman 1965) used this debate to assert the need for a sociology of knowledge of development theory, and particularly for the development theorist to become conscious of his or her own motivations in prescribing value changes or other policy prescriptions which derive from their own values, and will often reward those who share these values. This takes us directly into the next stage of evolution of modernization theories, where the issue was the meaning of development, and whether it was possible for social scientists to have an objective view of the aspirations of people in developing societies.

5   The Meaning of Development

The debate over cultural values raised many issues, among which an important one was the relativism of the values of the theorist himself or

35. However, they have probably had a fairly important effect on the thinking of theorists and policy-makers. To give but one example, Everett Hagen's theory of 'blocked

herself. Gunnar Myrdal, among others, pointed out that the cultural alienation of theorists could be due to the geopolitical situation of Western countries *vis-à-vis* the Third World, and that it was exacerbated by their haste in applying predetermined approaches to new-found problems. The mid-1960s, when these questions were being raised, was also a time of increased political conflict and tension in many rapidly growing economies (Pakistan, Ghana, Nigeria, Brazil).[36] The resultant instability revealed not only that there was latent dissatisfaction with the direction of social change in the countries concerned, but also that rapid growth could be self-defeating if it led to a subsequent slow-down. The first concern found expression in various writings on the 'meaning of development', which asked whether the assumed goals of development policy were indeed the ones sought by people who were supposed to benefit from this policy. The second concern led to questions on political evolution in Third World countries and to the emergence of the subdiscipline of 'political development', which is discussed in the next section.

The origins of the 'meaning of development' debate lie somewhat beyond Myrdal's criticism. In addition to the emerging political conflicts and tensions in Third World countries, particularly those enjoying respectable growth rates, there were also political and journalistic expressions of disaffection with the targets and goals of development policies. These were largely non-economistic and often expressed in popular rather than scholarly language.[37] In addition, many economists also challenged the unequal nature of development (e.g. Mahbub ul Haq's criticism of increasing economic concentration in Pakistan,[38] Albert Fishlow's 1972 work on inequality in Brazil, or Marxist critiques of asymmetric power relations under capitalism and the consequent effect on distribution of income and consumption).

Once again, we can observe an external political critique being translated first into anti-modernization and anti-development language and then into anti-growth language by intellectual intermediaries. At the scholarly level, the resulting debate on the 'meaning of development' has roots in social welfare theories, and heuristically, it asks whether growth in income increases happiness, and if not, whether the pursuit of this goal is a

minorities' may have no direct policy relevance, but the effect of the legitimation provided by modernizing theories as well as by supportive institutions (the school, the media, the state) can be seen to have created a 'blocked majority' in Third World countries, whose values and ideas are being rejected by its children as being irrelevant for the problems facing them.

36. Every country in Africa had a coup or some form of civil unrest during the 1960s. The situation in Latin America was not much different. See the various articles in Uphoff and Ilchman 1972, particularly Nulty and Nulty, and Zolberg.

37. These would include, for example, the political and spontaneous expressions of disaffection in East Pakistan (now Bangladesh).

38. Mahbub ul Haq first raised these issues in a public speech in Karachi in Apr. 1968, when he was the Chief Economist of the Government of Pakistan. See ul Haq 1976: 5.

reasonable human activity. Arthur Lewis (1955), who took this question to be central to development, suggested that happiness was not the issue, that what development did was to increase the range of choices available to a society. Other writers (Paolo Freire 1970, Denis Goulet 1971) were to ask whether development was the means to enhance peoples' core values, and if so, whether treating values as means of pursuing development was appropriate.

At this level, the question was one of larger values of freedom, liberation, or emancipation. However, by the time the debate arrived in the area of development economics, it had been translated almost completely into economistic terms. As such, instead of discussions of liberation or emancipation which are questions about the *process* of development, there were discussions only of desired *outcomes*, such as income distribution, poverty elimination, or basic human needs.[39]

Another aspect of the economists' response to this issue was perhaps unintended, namely that their contributions seemed designed to defuse the volatile political questions which had triggered the debate.[40] The concentration on an apolitical measure of inequality, namely the size distribution of income, rather than on more politically charged measures like functional, regional, or ethnic distribution of income is very instructive. So also is the almost immediate shift to other politically diffuse targets like basic needs or poverty eradication, and the direction of attention towards groups which had historically been politically passive or even resistant to social intervention, namely the rural masses in some countries. In other words, challenges to the theorists' right to intervene in the social and political life of the people of Third World societies were met by renaming goals, priorities, or even target groups in order to reassert the legitimacy of intervention. Stephen Marglin (1984) puts it very well when he accuses development theorists of seeking to exorcise the demons (released by external critiques) by naming them.

To recapitulate, I see the underlying motive for widespread political resistance to be the massive social intervention made in peoples' lives by the unfettering of organized and impersonal institutions including the market as well as the state, not to mention foreigners of various sorts. Critical theorists explained this resistance to be aimed against inappropriate government policies. Modernization theorists translated the issue into a need for discovering more popular (but equally objective) ends, which could then be pursued by benign governments and help restore their legitimacy. Development economists very carefully introduced alternative

39. This is not surprising, considering that economists often declare themselves incapable of dealing with non-economistic questions.
40. Similar 'depoliticizing' responses emerge in other areas as well, and result from a type of technological fix, which sees economic and political questions as being distinct. For a technological response to the environmental criticism of development, see Enzenberger 1974.

goals which might satisfy the theorists, but which would not become the subject of concerted political action or defence. Moreover, in so doing, they also managed to discover a moral basis for rejecting the demands of urban or other politically active pressure groups by invoking the poverty of the rural masses. It is not surprising, then, to note that despite vociferous discussion and controversy, alternative indices of development (equity, basic needs, quality of life) are not given much genuine attention by policy-makers, nor do they seem to excite much attention among people in general (Bruton 1985).

6   Political Development

A related consequence of the political unrest of the 1960s was the emergence, as an offshoot of what used to be called comparative political systems, of a new subdiscipline, political development, dealing with the nature of political evolution in Third World countries. As noted by pioneering writers in this subfield (Gabriel Almond 1956, Samuel Huntington 1968, Lucian Pye and Sidney Verba 1965), the optimistic ('benign line') view of political development—that economic development will automatically bring about beneficial changes in the political environment—was belied by the emerging conflicts and instability in growing Third World economies, and that therefore there was a need to analyse the determinants of stable political evolution.

'Beneficial political evolution' meant, in this literature, a progress towards the 'ideal type' contained in Western political philosophy dating back to Hobbes, Locke, and Hume, as characterized by electoral democracy, professional bureaucracies, and political stability. In many treatments, however, this ideal was assumed to coincide with existing political institutions in Western countries, most notably those of the 'nation-state'. This meant more than simply becoming independent from colonial rule. Additional qualifications were required, as expressed by Gunnar Myrdal's distinction between 'hard' and 'soft' states (Myrdal 1968: 895–900), the latter referring to the absence of the 'social discipline' necessary for modernization. Myrdal suggested that due to cultural or historical reasons—namely a 'legacy [of] a set of anarchic attitudes with an ideological and emotional force deriving from memories of resistance against the colonial power' (p. 897)—many Asian countries had 'soft' states, because of which 'rapid development will be exceedingly difficult to engender' (p. 899). The only exceptions in Asia, according to Myrdal, are China and Japan.[41] Other writers in the political development tradition were to see the difference in institutional rather than in cultural terms,

41. Myrdal's source is a 'traveller's report'. For a criticism of this notion in the case of India, see Bardhan 1984, particularly ch. 9.

implying that the necessary conditions for modernization could be created through institutional reform.

Accordingly, political development theories focused on the need for 'state-building', which includes the establishment of institutions that help 'expand' the level of 'power'[42] in a society, as well as those which increase the legitimacy of its exercise.[43] 'Expansion' of power required the strengthening of the bureaucratic machinery, particularly in its coercive activities, but also in technical efficiency, methods, processes, selection, training, and so forth. 'Legitimization' of power required a Hobbesian acceptance of the exercise of state power by the populace. Improved organization and acceptable mechanisms for recruitment to the bureaucracy would also help in this respect. At a macro-level, depending on the specific circumstances of each country, legitimacy could be increased either by expanded participation or by élite dominance.

An interesting deviation from this linear view of political development was provided by Myron Weiner (1965), who pointed out in his work on Indian political development that after Independence two distinct political cultures, the 'élite' and the 'mass', emerged in that country. The two operated at different levels of society,[44] and each had its strengths as well as weaknesses. In particular, this thesis of 'political dualism' pointed out very clearly the authoritarian bent of the rational and impersonal 'élite' culture, as well as the democratic possibilities of the relational and personal 'mass' culture. It is fair to say, however, that despite Weiner's personal eminence in the profession, the very provocative implications of his line of reasoning have not been followed up in the mainstream development literature.

Another impetus for the emergence of political development as an independent discipline was provided by Marxist and dependency theorists' writings (Paul Baran 1952, 1957, Fernando Henrique Cardoso 1972, Celso Furtado 1970, Andre Gunder Frank 1967) on the unequal distribution of power between the 'centre' countries of the world and those in the 'periphery', and the distorted nature of political change in the latter as a result. Contrary to the view of the liberal thinkers, these writers saw the

---

42. The term 'expansion' of power is used in Huntington's sense, namely to represent an increase in the ability of the 'rational' state to influence social decisions. A common remark in political development writings is that traditional societies have very little power but it is heavily concentrated in a few hands, whereas modern societies have a great deal of power which is distributed somewhat more widely.

43. For example, Huntington 1968 argues that political instability is the result of an explosion of mass political participation (due to urbanization, industrialization and educational expansion) relative to the institutional capacity which can absorb the new participants.

44. Weiner refrains from calling the two cultures 'modern' and 'traditional', since he believes that that would be an over-simplification and, given his unequivocal support of modernization, an unwarranted normative judgement that the former is good and the latter bad.

state itself as an arena of conflict as well as a reflection of the distribution of power in society,[45] rather than as a custodian of general welfare or popular needs and aspirations.

The prescriptive content of the political development literature was somewhat limited, partly on account of the cultural factors pointed out by Myrdal, but for other reasons as well. Included was the advice to strengthen the institutions of the state (to which reigning powers would presumably take kindly) and the establishment of stable mechanisms of transfer of power (which might be resisted), in addition to the inculcation of 'right' attitudes and behaviour among the populace (which might not be very feasible). As indicated, however, by the title of one of Huntington's later books, *No Easy Choice* (Huntington and Nelson 1976), the prognosis is not very optimistic.

The prescriptions which did have an impact were those aimed at increasing the legitimacy of policies or the stability of regimes in politically unstable societies, thereby increasing the 'hardness' of a state. Two examples should suffice. Some writers, concerned presumably with urban political instability, introduced the notion of countervailing rural groups which could be co-opted by modernizing élites to withstand the power of urban groups. This is reminiscent of Louis Napoleon's advice to the Prussian government to introduce universal suffrage because 'in this system the conservative rural population can vote down the liberals in the cities' (quoted in Bardhan 1984: 76). Similarly, the periodic invocation of the interests of 'the real poor concentrated in rural areas', while quite unsuccessful in persuading 'rural poverty' conveniently to disappear, did succeed in becoming a legitimization, perhaps unintentionally, of inegalitarian urban policies.

Other writers, such as Shahid Javed Burki (1976), argued in favour of efficient but superficially inequitable farm policies, because they supported the profit-maximizing 'middle farmers'—a concept with dubious empirical or theoretical backing—against the 'political maximizing' large farmers, even if the policies hurt the 'small farmer'. (For criticism of Burki's argument and methodology, see Alavi 1976.)

To summarize the last two subsections, two different inferences were drawn by social theorists from the political resistance and protest of disenfranchised groups in modernizing societies. First, that the goals of development chosen by government planners were unacceptable to many people; and second, that political unrest could effectively undo the gains made through the adoption of development policies. The first inference led to a debate on the meaning of development and to the search for objectively defensible goals. While this direction led into a series of interesting policy innovations (growth with equity, basic human needs,

45. Which meant, in the context of the Third World, groups connected with the 'centre' countries, in collusion with purely indigenous groups.

rural development) with which the profession seemed to be fairly satisfied, it did not really address the cause of the discontent, and so the popular critique as well as the resistance continued. This revealed, among other things, that the true source of popular dissatisfaction might have had more to do with the process, rather than with the objectives, of government decision-making.

The second inference indicated that economists had been mistaken in disregarding the political consequences of their prescriptions and in focusing only on the purely economic effects. The economists were, however, saved the extra effort because of the timely assistance of pioneering political scientists, who set up a new subfield of development theory, political development, to deal with this issue. But this, too, turned out to be an unsatisfactory resolution, since it was soon discovered that political development theorists did not have much in the way of prescription, and the little that they did have could be interpreted as attempts to legitimize the impugned actions of the ruling élites.

Furthermore, discussion of political stability and development brought to the fore another hitherto ignored issue, namely that of participation in civic or political affairs, which was not observed to increase necessarily with the establishment of the nation-state or even with the introduction of electoral democracy. These concerns were further reinforced by the legitimization provided by social scientists to emergent authoritarian and repressive governments because of the latters' association with growth-oriented policies. All these concerns were expressed by 'alternative' theorists, and used to challenge basic assumptions of mainstream theory.

7 Participation versus Organization

Political resistance to the state can be interpreted somewhat differently. Instead of seeing it as an opposition to particular policies of the state, or to a particular regime, or even to the system of functioning of a succession of regimes, we can see it as a questioning of the very concepts of the centralized, impersonal, and bureaucratically organized nation-state. Political development theory focused only on the pathologies of particular regimes, not on the idea of the nation-state as such. The emergence of conflict and instability in the Third World was also ascribed, in one way or another, to 'incomplete' modernization: absence of necessary political institutions, persistence of traditional behaviour patterns, or the like, rather than to a resistance to the rationalization and impersonalization of social existence entailed in the drive towards the formation of a Western-style nation-state.

Such an alternative interpretation, however, has indeed been the subject of a substantive literature in the West as well as in what is now the Third World, which questioned the disenfranchising potential of the modern nation-state. A classic example is the argument of writers on 'anarchism' (William Godwin, Pierre-Joseph Proudhon, Peter Kropotkin, Michael Bakunin),[46] even though their bias towards individualism created some paradoxes and conflicts.[47] Despite Marx's important differences with anarchist writers, most notably Proudhon, this line of thought also finds resonance in Marx's notion of self-alienation in capitalist social arrangements. Another writer who took up this argument was Max Weber, when he predicted the potential bureaucratization of capitalist society, mainly on account of the efficiency of the bureaucratic social organization.

In the twentieth century, significant contributions along these lines have been made in social philosophy by the Frankfurt School (Herbert Marcuse, Jürgen Habermas),[48] in political theory by Marxists like Antonio Gramsci and his followers (for example, Nicos Poulantzas 1978),[49] and in economics by radicals like Stephen Marglin (1974), and Samuel Bowles and Herbert Gintis (1986). In the context of the Third World countries, such ideas found their earliest expression in the works of writers like Peter Kropotkin,[50] M. K. Gandhi, and Lewis Mumford,[51] and later by Peter Berger (1976), Pierre Clastres (1977), Guy Gran (1983), Ivan Illich (1981), Ashis Nandy (1984, 1987), E. F. Schumacher (1973), and Elman Service (1975).

These writings sought to reopen some settled questions of Western political theory in the area of participation and responsibility. While there are several arguments here, a common theme is the rejection of the Hobbesian notion of the state of nature as the 'warre of every one against every one', and thus, equally, of the large and centralized organizations considered necessary today to maintain the public weal; and a criticism

46. For an excellent overview of the 19th-century literature on anarchism in Europe, see Woodcock 1986. As Woodcock notes, the association commonly made between anarchism and violence or terror may have contributed to the marginalization of this train of thought.

47. Such as Rousseau's familiar dictum on the difference between representation and participation in the context of the discussion on the general will. Anarchism's almost total acceptance of individualism and impersonality not only as values but also as essential human characteristics, distinguish it from much of the Third World literature on participation. One anarchist writer who takes an alternative position on this subject is Peter Kropotkin. See Woodcock 1986: 11–31.

48. See particularly Marcuse 1964; Habermas 1984. For a condensed description of the work and impact of the Frankfurt School, see Bottomore 1984.

49. For a recent discussion of Gramsci's work and its political and intellectual impact, see the various articles in Mouffe 1979.

50. Peter Kropotkin was, after Proudhon, the pre-eminent writer of the anarchist or anti-authoritarian tradition. In his classic (1902) study he presented detailed historical and anthropological evidence to argue, in opposition to the then popular Social Darwinist position, that mutuality and co-operation were significant forces in society, and that the coercive force of the state created obstacles in its exercise.

51. Mumford's (1961) classic study traces the evolution of the city from the dawn of civilization to the emergence of the megalopolises of the 20th century. It contains a devastating critique of the disenfranchising and oppressive consequences of political centralization associated with modernity. See particularly pp. 568–76.

of the disenfranchising effect of such organizations. Another theme is the distinction between the state and culture (or, in Gramsci's terms, civil society) as alternate means of social discipline, and the rejection of the former as the preferred alternative.

These critical writings drew their legitimacy from the continuing and heightened levels of political conflict and political resistance in Third World societies, notwithstanding the efforts made to strengthen state machineries. The continuing level of tension and conflict was later supported by the rise of what Immanuel Wallerstein (1974) has termed 'anti-systemic' movements in Third World countries.[52]

The response of modernization theorists to this criticism can be divided into three categories. First, there was the 'internal' criticism of neo-classical economists who claimed that government intervention in the *economic* sphere was undesirable on grounds of its manifest inefficiency as well as its authoritarian implications for society. This has led to a shifting of the debate from various specific issues of development theory, towards the single issue of freedom of exchange via liberalization of markets. Some relevant aspects of this shifting will be taken up in Section 10.5 below. It should suffice to note here that, paradoxically, the governments which chose to pursue a 'free market' path of development, were among the most authoritarian in the Third World. In fact, it has proven impossible to implement the free market path without the political foundation of an authoritarian state (see e.g. Sheahan 1980, Hirschman 1981b). Perhaps inadvertently, these examples were used to prescribe an authoritarian form of political development for the remaining developing countries.

Second, there was a set of critiques by mainstream development theorists (e.g. Tony Killick 1976),[53] who attacked the simplistic notions of the state and of government policies implicit in economic theory, and sought to replace them with more complete formulations. Partly as a result of this criticism, mechanistic planning exercises and social cost-benefit analyses, which were seen as the cutting edge of economics in the 1960s, have become *passé* in recent years. Plans are increasingly being seen as 'inputs into the process of economic decision-making', in terms of Killick's recommendations, 'rather than as outputs of this decision-making'. In contrast to the neo-classical critique, which appeared to favour 'hard' states, this criticism tended to undermine the 'hardness' by casting doubt on the certitudes of theorists.

52. These include such non-governmental organizations as women's movements in different parts of the world, movements such as Lokayan in India, 'base communities' formed under the auspices of liberation theology in Latin America, and the start of a return to rural areas in African countries.

53. Killick 1976 argues that economists should replace their monistic vision of the society and the state with one which recognizes the existence of tension and differentiation in them, and thus see policy as a balancing act, rather than the actions of a benevolent and omnipotent entity.

Finally, and perhaps somewhat paradoxically, some writers reasserted the superiority of the Western model of political development in general, and of the managerial approach to social issues in particular. This depended upon the possibility of increased social and political participation through concerted government effort (see Huntington 1968), through bureaucratic reorientation (BRO),[54] through increasing efficiency of government decisions,[55] or finally, by shifting the focus of development to areas hitherto neglected.[56] The main argument is that not only is it possible for a bureaucratic or impersonal machinery to be responsive to the needs of constituent citizens through the introduction of appropriate checks and balances, but that this is in fact the best means of ensuring the defence of freedom and sovereignty.

Once again, this literature can be interpreted as a synthesis of a tension between external critiques of modernization and the need for paradigm maintenance and moral defence of modernity in the face of such criticism. The primary challenge came from democratic or populist movements, particularly in Latin American countries, where the imposition of rational-bureaucratic governments was resisted, notwithstanding their supposed edge in bringing about rapid economic growth. 'Internal' critiques focused primarily on the freedom of the market, or else on the question of political stability, rather than on the broader issues of participation and freedom.

8 Technology and Knowledge

The existence of civic resistance and protest has been interpreted in other ways as well, particularly as being against the effects of the introduction of modern technology and its attendant institutions into society. Apart from the obvious actions of organized industrial labour, examples of such protest would include broad-based political action directed against the economically powerful groups in society, protest movements against specific projects or activities (e.g. against large dams, nuclear plants, and so forth), and a general unwillingness or inability to be subjected to industrial discipline. Actions like these and others have been interpreted by a large number of writers as being an indictment of the process of modernization.

This resistance can be interpreted either as a protest against the nature

54. See Rondinelli *et al.* 1983 for a review of the experience of decentralization in development.
55. This is exemplified by the introduction of more sophisticated models of economic and political functioning as a solution for the inadequacy of earlier models. For example, the simple macroeconomic models of yesterday have given way to mammoth Computable General Equilibrium models.
56. See ston 1977 for an ingenious explanation of the persistence of rural poverty as the result of an 'urban bias' among the national élites. Lipton indicates that the problem could, in principle, be cured.

and *process* of work in modern societies or, as a rejection of the *outcome* of these processes. It is fair to say that the 'alternative' critique has emphasized the former, while the 'internal' critique of modernization has focused on the latter.

One of the earliest of such critiques is Marx's argument detailing the alienation of the industrial worker both from the product and the process under capitalism.[57] A key point is the fact that technical division of labour under capitalism increasingly takes away from the worker the control of the nature, the pace, and the intensity of work, and that this loss of control is seen as the most compelling reason for social and political resistance (Marglin 1974, and Chapter 7 below). Just as the notion of a bureaucratic state can be argued to lead to disenfranchisement, so can centralized and hierarchical forms of economic organizations. In fact, this is the heart of the dispute over development and modernization, since it has often been asserted that modern culture is essentially a way of organizing people, resources, or ideas in a more efficient manner than traditional cultures do. As such, the suggestion that modern organization is a means of disenfranchisement hits at the very core of modernization.[58]

Writers of the Frankfurt School (Herbert Marcuse 1964, Erich Fromm 1942, Jürgen Habermas 1984) used Marx's argument to question the social basis of modernity, namely its technological and organizational imperative, not only in production, but also in consumption, distribution, and in the very processes of creation and dissemination of knowledge and information. This argument is taken further by Marglin in Chapter 7 below, where not only the institutional arrangements for work, but the very system of knowledge which gives rise to these institutional forms, are challenged.

In the Third World context, critics like J. S. Uberoi (1978), Ashis Nandy (1984, 1987), Reynaldo Ileto (n.d.), Frédérique Apffel Marglin (in Chapter 4 below), and Nandy and Shiv Visvanathan (in Chapter 5 below) argue that the 'scientific' approach to knowledge is not only far from perfect, but that it might lead to problems which were avoided by more 'humanistic' approaches. One of the main criticisms by partisans of this view pertains to the violent and undemocratic nature of modern scientific ways of understanding the world. This approach has often been used to criticize modern science and technology for not serving the needs of people. Since the modernizing approach is based on the assumption that the scientific method of understanding and manipulating the physical and

57. It has to be clarified here that in Marx's works, the existence of alienation is not restricted to capitalist society. However, alienation in production does increase under capitalism. For a review of the issues, see Josephson and Josephson 1962.

58. However, Marglin 1974 argues that the evolution of capitalist production led to a system which is not 'efficient' in the sense of producing more output with the same input. Rather, it produces more output by using more inputs. In other words, it is essentially a means of extracting more work (and more surplus) out of labour.

social environment is inherently superior, these alternative views present a challenge to their legitimacy.

The response of modernization theorists to these challenges has not been atypical. Rather than perceive the protest as being directed against the process of economic and social organization, or against the system of knowledge which gives rise to these processes, they have tended to focus attention on the outcomes of these processes. The internal critique which has been quite effective and forceful here is an 'economistic' version of Marxism, which sees the problems of capitalism to be essentially those of distribution (of consumption as well as leisure) and unemployment, and the solution to be a socialist state which will guarantee full employment and a more egalitarian distribution of income. The modern welfare state owes its existence, in part, to the appeal of such arguments.

One group which did recognize the social resistance to modern industrial organization was that of management experts. They saw it, predictably enough, as a managerial problem. The most celebrated of these views is the psychologist Abraham Maslow's notion of a 'hierarchy of needs', in which the need for physical survival ranks above other needs such as prestige or self-fulfilment. Social frustration, in this perspective, was seen to emerge from the rising expectations of a class which had managed to satisfy its lowest needs within this hierarchy and wished to achieve increased satisfaction by proceeding up the hierarchical ladder. Accordingly, they saw the solution in managerial terms, in providing job hierarchies, rewards and distinctions, leisure activities, and other means for workers to satisfy 'higher' needs in the work environment.

Another response, this time specifically in the Third World context, is that from the 'appropriate technology' school. By 'appropriate technology' is meant technology which is appropriate for the resource base of a country, and which will therefore not exacerbate unemployment in labour-surplus countries. The lack of appropriate technology is one of many reasons advanced for the existence of unemployment in Third World economies. Some writers argue that in this view, the problem lies not in science, technology, or knowledge, but rather in the absence of social and cultural factors which encourage enterprise. There is only 'one best way' of doing things, and the question of appropriate or inappropriate technology is therefore moot.

Those of a neo-classical persuasion argue that the problem is 'wrong' prices, set by government fiat or other political action, which interfere with market clearing. They argue that this problem can be corrected by getting the prices right, which often means lowering wages and raising interest and exchange rates. Appropriate technologies will appear in response to appropriate prices. It is on prices rather than on technologies that policy should concentrate. A third argument is advanced by 'technologists', who think that the wide diffusion of the benefits of appropriate technology inhibits research and development, and therefore that the solution is to subsidize research and development through government effort.

The contrast between these responses and the alternative view, identified with writers such as A. K. N. Reddy 1978 and Rudolf Bahro 1986, is based on differing notions of popular sovereignty. The alternative view would consider a technology to be appropriate only if it was under the direct control of the people who were affected by it or through people who were directly involved in the life of those so affected. The modernist response perceives market competition, governmental control, or legal remedies as suitable and sufficient substitutes for popular control. The connection between this controversy and that over popular participation should be self-evident at this point, as also would be the connection to environmental and ecological questions.

9 Natural Resources and Environment

The concern with the loss of sovereignty was also expressed in relation to a very important aspect of social life, namely the association of environmental deterioration with the replacement of community or social forms of control by bureaucratic arrangements. Similar concerns have also been expressed at the rapid depletion of non-renewable resources (Meadows *et al.* 1972). Following Ramachandra Guha 1985, we can identify the critics as falling into two groups, the 'idealists' (Lynn White 1972, Theodor Roszak 1969, Sunderlal Bahuguna 1983, and Rudolf Bahro 1986), and the 'ecological socialists' (Barry Commoner 1971, A. K. N. Reddy 1978, and C. P. Bhatt 1984). Both these groups place the blame for the observed problems on the instrumental, impersonal, and vivisectionist attitudes towards nature in the modern world-view. While the former group sees these attitudes as derived from the Judaeo-Christian ethic of the West, the latter writers perceive them to emanate from the nature of Western technology, and the asymmetrical social relations which determine this technology. Once again, we can categorize these critiques as being 'external' to the modernizers' perspective on social arrangements.

The alternative writings often connect the notion of environmental decay with ideas of violence. To see this point, one has only to notice the relationship of violence to the idea of excess, of going beyond certain limits. In the behaviouristic bent of the modern, impersonal world-view, the idea of internal constraints (relational or contextual limits) on people has been replaced by external constraints (market, state). However, these external constraints will work only if they are ubiquitous. If not, we will have the situation of 'market failure' or 'government failure'. While examples of these types of failure can be seen in various social interactions, the destruction of the natural environment is the most obvious example.

To follow this line of argument, the safeguarding of the environment cannot be done as long as the dominant value is one of external constraints.

These intellectual critiques of the impact of modernization have also been related to and supported by popular environmental movements in the West (various anti-nuclear movements, the Greens Party in Germany) as well as the Third World (Chipko Andolan movement in India, various popular movements in Asia and Latin America against large dams or nuclear energy).

The response of the defenders of modernization can be divided into three groups. Other than those who deny the criticism on the ground that technological change or price adjustments will take care of resource depletion, there are the 'managerialists' (Meadows *et al.* 1972, Paul Ehrlich *et al.* 1977, B. B. Vohra 1980), who argue for integrated environmental management and technocratic control—in other words, the expansion of external constraints; and the proto-fascists (Garrett Hardin 1968) who propose population control in addition to punitive sanctions, particularly against poor and Third World countries, to release the pressure on resources.

Once again, it can be argued that the criticism against the effect of modernization on the environment and resource availability had its roots in a world-view based on more personal connections to land and nature (the idealist view). The intellectual element of the critique brought the argument home to modernizers, who then proceeded to assimilate it into their world-view by translating these concerns into managerial and economistic issues, and presenting solutions which would meet some of the criticism, yet help retain the legitimacy of their own intervention into alien social and natural environments.

10   Cultural Critique: The Last Stage

Implicit in the discussion so far is the idea that the various challenges to modernization theory share a few common themes. However, since these different critiques were being made in different spheres of thought and action, they could either be partially assimilated or isolated and dismissed separately because of their lack of congruence with the dominant mode of analysis. The term 'cultural critique' implies a recognition and assertion of the underlying unity of the various strands in the argument, of the recognition of an 'Aquarian Conspiracy' in Marilyn Ferguson's terms (Ferguson 1980). In my view, this confluence is both the cause and consequence of a growing self-assurance generally of people of non-Western cultures, and particularly of the intellectuals who seek to articulate the world-views of these cultures for a scholarly audience.

The emergence of this unity should, however, be seen as the strengthening of a tradition of thought and action with a long and respected pedigree. An academic and intellectual critique of modernization on cultural grounds has long been expressed by a small but increasingly influential group of writers who identify the cause of many of the problems emerging in Third World countries as the very notion of a human being and human welfare implicit in modernization. They see the central problem as being the theories (and by implication modern Western culture) used by the modernizing élites of these societies to justify the imposition of unacceptable and undesirable policies and conditions upon an unwilling populace. These writers criticize the very basis of development, namely the supposed superiority of the values, institutions, and achievements of Western societies.

The fact that this literature has found new protagonists as well as a larger audience can be traced to three reasons. First, the increasing evidence of the dysfunctioning of societies, whether in the North or the South, which cannot be explained satisfactorily by available theories; second, because of the frustration with attempts to make piecemeal emendations in dominant modes of thinking; and lastly, because of the emergence of powerful anti-systemic and often anti-Western social and political movements of cultural revival in Third World countries as well as in some countries of the West.

10.1 Social Dysfunctioning

A key reason for the strengthening of the cultural critique is an exponential increase in the dysfunctioning of societies undergoing rapid modernization. Entire regions, previously peaceful and tranquil, are now almost un-inhabitable due to endemic civil war, ethnic conflict, political unrest, social and political oppression by militarized states, urban polarization and decay including a rise in violent crimes, environmental deterioration such as desertification, waterlogging, climate changes, or deforestation. There seem to be similar increases in socio-psychological problems assailing people in Westernized sections of the Third World, which are rapidly extending to other areas as well.

A related reason for the rejection of the modernizers' arguments is the emergence of somewhat similar problems in Western countries, phenomena to which one can collectively give the melodramatic title, 'the decline of the West'. Vietnam, Watergate, OPEC, macroeconomic problems (unemployment, inflation), micro-social problems (decay of cities, quality of life of old people, the position of women, and minorities) seem to have shattered the myth that people in Western societies are in greater control of their lives than are the people in 'backward' societies. Naturally, one of the reasons for the growing disaffection is the increasing familiarity of Third World citizens with the mode of existence of the West, an idea expressed charmingly by a character in *Mon Oncle d'Amerique*, a French film of the early 1980s. 'America does not exist,' he said, 'I've been there.'

A similar disillusionment seems to have set in with regard to the pre-Perestroika Soviet model. The publicization of the Stalinist purges, expansion of state control over peoples' lives, and a generalized denial of freedoms, have brought in their wake a growing disaffection with the other 'Western' vision of the good society.

As a result of these and other factors, the two dominant Western models of progress have relinquished their hold over the imagination of Third World intellectuals, and indigenous values have become more legitimate.

10.2 Frustration with Existing Theories

A related issue is the growing intellectual disaffection with the fact that piecemeal challenges to the orthodoxy do not seem to have any impact whatsoever. The criticisms and controversies in development literatures outlined in this chapter appear only to have helped to legitimize and reinforce existing prejudices, rather than to eradicate them. It is not surprising, then, that the focus of critical attention has shifted from particular controversies or problems towards a deeper issue, expressed with the appropriate degree of irony by the sociologist Gordon Allport. 'Social science', he is supposed to have said, 'never solves any problems. It just gets tired of them.' Opportunities for soul-searching by modernization theorists appear at regular intervals and disappear with equal regularity, leaving scarcely a trace on the focus and direction of the subsequent discourse.

10.3 Socio-Political Resistance

The single most important reason for the strengthening of the cultural critique is, of course, the influence exerted through direct political action undertaken by people as a form of resistance to modernization and as a simultaneous affirmation of traditional and religious world-views and ways of life. It is precisely these forms of resistance which are being interpreted and translated for a Western audience by the 'alternative' critics.

As an example of this form of resistance, take a phenomenon which has attracted a great deal of attention in recent years, in the United States and elsewhere in the West, namely the turn towards religious values in Islamic countries. In my view, to see this as an isolated occurrence in Islamic countries, and that too through the prism of dramatic[59] or tragic[60] events or of state activity,[61] is to ignore three important considerations. First, such indigenous revival movements are by no means restricted to Islamic countries, although for reasons of geopolitics and recent history

---

59. For example, the Iranian revolution, the Iran–Iraq war, the oil embargo, and other actions by OPEC countries.
60. Sadat's assassination, the Lebanese crisis.
61. Islamic laws in Pakistan, the *Panchsila* approach in Indonesia, the efforts to build an Islamic society in Libya.

the latter have attracted the greatest attention in the Western media; in fact, anti-systemic movements searching for a 'third way' out of the current impasse, often by invoking indigenous religious and traditional value-systems, are quite active in many parts of the globe, including Western countries.[62]

Second, while these movements often involve an explicit and emphatic rejection of Western capitalism, this has not, for the most part, led to a swing towards Marxism, since the conception of the West implicit in this rejection seems to encompass orthodox Marxism as well.

Third, whether in the context of Islamic societies or others, the use of the term 'revival' could be a little misleading, since a majority of the population had never entirely relinquished their traditional values or traditional modes of thinking in the first place. These movements are but contemporary articulations of beliefs and values which have long existed in these societies. In many cases, the change is only in the attitude of a Westernized minority which became alienated from or deliberately rejected traditional values.[63]

What this example illustrates is that it would be more appropriate to think of recent socio-political developments in many parts of the Third World as the result of a sense of discomfort with, or even an emphatic rejection of, the rational-technological model upon which people in the West as well as those in the developing world had pinned their hopes for the establishment of a humane and just society.

Among the Westernized élites in Islamic countries, this has taken the form of a rejuvenation of respect for Islamic values and ideals; in other societies, this has naturally taken other forms. Besides other religious and ethnic revival movements, mention can also be made of popular environmental movements, the most notable one being the Chipko movement in India; the rise of non-governmental organizations in various countries of the world, notable ones including various social welfare

62. ·Examples might include 'liberation theology' in Latin America (see Gutierrez 1973), various Gandhi-ist, environmentalist, and cultural revivalist movements in India (see Nandy 1984), as well as the Greens movement in West Germany (see Bahro 1986). Many other examples could be given. For instance, the journal *World Development* devoted an entire issue (July–Aug. 1980) to the subject of 'Religious Values and Development'. For an excellent review and discussion of the role of alternative movements, see Nerfin 1985.

63. There were many earlier Islamic revival movements, such as the ones inspired by Jamal-al-Din Afghani in Afghanistan, Syed Ahmed Shaheed in India, Sanusi and the Mahdi of the Sudan, among many others. For a brief description of these movements, see Mortimer 1982. As has been mentioned, these share certain similarities with other indigenous revival movements. The distinctly traditional flavour of various African nationalist movements has been noted by many writers; Hindu revival movements in India can be seen as intellectual precursors of the current rejection of Westernization. However, as Nandy 1983 explains in his penetrating analysis of the impact of colonialism, many of the visionaries in these movements tended to accept the norms of the colonizers while rejecting their domination––in contrast with Gandhi's approach.

movements, women's movements, or movements of cultural interpretation and articulation, such as the 'Lokayan' movement in India; and the formation of 'base communities' around the teachings of liberation theology in Latin America.

10.4 Intellectual Challenges

Very few social scientists, whether in Third World countries or in the West, have felt confident enough to jettison entirely the framework and assumptions of the disciplines in which they were formed and socialized. Nor have most of them been ready to take up alternative, 'backward', 'traditional', or religious discourses as a means of communicating their ideas. This situation is the one which seems to be undergoing the most rapid change in many Third World countries under the impact of the anti-systemic popular movements.[64]

As mentioned earlier, however, the intellectual roots of the current challenge to the intellectual orthodoxy go far back in history. In the twentieth century alone, a large literature critical of the multi-faceted modernization project has emerged in Western countries as well as in the Third World. While each of these sets of writings is very diverse in its approach, and many different issues have been raised which cannot be summarized here, a common theme can be identified. These writers tend to see the association between modernization and socio-economic deterioration[65] as endogenous rather than exogenous, and supported and strengthened in particular by the legitimization provided by 'neutral' social scientists. As a result of these considerations, this group of writers has chosen to focus their analysis on the discovery of causal connections between the project of modernization and the symptoms of social dysfunctioning. It is worth reiterating, however, that despite their many differences, these disparate critics of the functioning of modernity share, at a deep structural level, an alternative 'way of seeing', encompassing different notions of human behaviour, welfare, progress, and the role of knowledge.

In the Western literature can be included the works of the critical

---

64. To give but one example, up until the 1960s, radical intellectuals in Muslim countries like Pakistan used to perceive religion as completely antagonistic to their values and principles. Today, many radicals who are strongly opposed to orthodox religious parties or leaders as well as to the militaristic or pro-state views of these parties, will generally employ the Islamic idiom in their own political opinions, and even make explicit reference to the role of religion and tradition in determining their ideals. In other words, rather than accepting the overall dictates of the modernity project and opposing it at one or the other edge, these intellectuals are searching for an alternative framework to unify their different critiques.

65. E.g. political instability; ethnic and racial violence; political repression by the increasingly centralized states; the disenfranchisement of the population not only by the respective governments, but also by the introduction of new technology and institutions resistant to popular control; the alarming deterioration in the physical environment; rapid urbanization, with attendant costs in terms of social disintegration and decay.

theory school of Marxist analysis (Theodor Adorno, Erich Fromm, Jürgen Habermas, Max Horkheimer and Herbert Marcuse—for a summary, see Bottomore 1984), post-Wittgensteinian social philosophers (Jon Elster 1979, Maurice Godelier 1972, and Richard Rorty 1979); neo-structuralists and semioticians (Paul Feyerabend 1975, Michel Foucault 1980, Stephen Resnick and Richard Wolff 1982); psychologists who raise the issue of alienation and socio-psychological anomie in modern societies (Christopher Lasch 1979, Robert Bellah *et al.* 1985, James Hillman 1976, Phillip Slater 1970, and Jacques Ellul 1964); and cultural anthropologists (Louis Dumont 1977, Clifford Geertz 1973, Marshall Sahlins 1972, and Stanley Tambiah 1985) who point to the cultural specificity of modern Western values and institutions.

The comparative literature with an exclusive Third World focus is, if anything, even more disparate than the first one, but this work is similarly unified by a shared scepticism regarding the fruits of modernization and development. These writings would include the 'humanistic development' school (Richard Falk 1983, Denis Goulet 1971, Guy Gran 1983, Ivan Illich 1981, and E. F. Schumacher 1973), writers who link the neo-colonialism of developmentalist approaches with the psychological effects of political colonialism (Aimé Cesaire 1972, Franz Fanon 1968, and Ashis Nandy 1983), advocates of a culture-based approach to welfare and progress as well as to notions of political conflict and to epistemological and methodological issues (Arjun Appadurai in Chapter 6 below, Paolo Freire 1970, Reynaldo Ileto n.d., Ashis Nandy 1987 and J. S. Uberoi 1978), and writers in various religious traditions, particularly Islam (Fazlur Rahman 1979, 1982, and Ali Shariati 1979) and the liberation theology school in Catholicism (Denis Goulet 1971, 1980, and Gustavo Gutierrez 1973).

10.5 Neo-Classical Response: Trade Theory

In earlier cases of isolated critiques, some modernizing thinkers took up the challenge and tried to assimilate it into their own world-views while the rest of the profession continued on its predetermined path. Today, there are widespread expressions of confusion and disillusionment, as referred to in the opening section of this chapter, but very little constructive engagement. Paradoxically, the most common response of the development profession is a shift of the balance towards neo-classical rectitude, and a reassertion of the ideological purity which had been lost during piecemeal concessions to alternative views.

Such responses have generally come from neo-classical theorists, in the nature of a fresh declaration of faith in the market. A polemical expression of this view is put forward by Deepak Lal (1983), who claimed that development economics (meaning the mainstream, non-neo-classical, version) was dead, having been proved to be counter-productive for the purposes for which it was intended.[66] Similar arguments, albeit with less polemic and more reasoning, have been advanced by other neo-classical authors including Bela Balassa (1982), Peter Bauer (1981), Anne Krueger (1986), and Ian Little (1982), among many others.

The common element in all these writings is the interpretation of spectacular growth in the so-called 'Gang of Four' countries of East Asia (South Korea, Taiwan, Hong Kong, and Singapore) as a vindication of free-market policies, and therefore as an indictment of the *dirigiste* prescriptions of non-neo-classical approaches. The experience of these countries was retroactively labelled 'export-led growth', partly to acknowledge their superior export and growth performance, and partly to point to the trade and exchange rate policies which were claimed to have brought about this desirable outcome. The substantive aspects of this argument need not detain us. I have criticized these elsewhere[67] on account of their selective reading of the evidence, deliberate neglect of the *dirigiste* aspects of the South Korean and Taiwanese economies (see also Stewart 1985 and Toye 1985), and the inattention to the dramatic failures of attempts to replicate elsewhere the so-called free-market policies of these countries.[68]

For present purposes, it is more important to note the effect of the resurrected neo-classical argument on development literature as a whole. Since the 'free market' aspects of the 'Gang of Four' economies pertained to their macroeconomic trade and exchange rate policies, it began to appear as if the only relevant question for development economics was whether or not the liberalization of trade and exchange rate regimes was a panacea for all the ills of development, as claimed by neo-classical experts. It became commonplace to suggest that development economics had been taken over by trade theorists. As issues of trade theory assumed central importance in development literature, there was a concomitant decline in attention accorded to other problems, except to the extent that they had a bearing on the issue of openness.[69]

This development was further reinforced by the problems faced by many Third World countries (especially those in Latin America) of adjustment to the various external shocks of the late 1970s and early 1980s. Neo-classical writers, particularly those associated with the World Bank and the International Monetary Fund, claimed that difficulties in

66. For critical reviews of Lal's polemic against mainstream development economics, see Stewart 1985 and Toye 1985.
67. Amadeo and Banuri 1990. See also the various references cited in those papers, particularly Taylor 1987, Pack and Westphal 1986, Hughes and Singh 1987, Fishlow 1987, Aghazadeh and Evans 1985.
68. For the last strand in the argument with regard to the failure of the neo-classical experiment in Chile, see Foxley 1982.
69. This is not to suggest that there were no writings on these other issues. It simply means that issues of trade theory were the centre of everyone's attention, and the way to gaining prestige in the profession.

adjustment were caused by the inward orientation of the problem economies, and could be cured by the same liberalization policies which had earlier been recommended as solutions for growth problems. Both these institutions initiated programmes for financing structural adjustment, which provided additional incentives for the acceptance of these theories by resource-hungry governments.

10.6 Mainstream Response

This resurgence of neo-classical wisdom is surprising, coming at a time when even the more culturally sensitive writers of the institutionalist school were being assailed for their alienness by external critics. Non-neo-classical development economists, however, though on the defensive, were not entirely silent. As already mentioned, trade theorists in this group engaged the neo-classical school on the latter's assertion of the supposed beneficence of trade liberalization and other neo-classical measures. Others sought to identify the roots of the larger crisis, and to find ways of addressing them.

The most interesting of these responses are in the nature of 'internal' critiques of mainstream development theory by such writers as Henry Bruton (1985), Paul Streeten (1984), Albert Hirschman (1981, 1984), or Amartya Sen (1983). Each has argued, independently, that the paradigm of development economics is in need of a drastic overhaul, particularly with respect to the 'mono-economics' claim of some of its subfields. They have also identified quite clearly many of the concerns expressed in the popular critiques of modernization. In particular, they have questioned very effectively the theoretical certitude which often lies behind policies which are pushed to unwise extremes by their unsceptical advocates. Their recommendations are well-taken and thought-provoking for the development profession, especially those which acknowledge the necessity of a better understanding of the non-economic bases of economic behaviour and economic institutions. It is fair to say, however, that these ideas, however timely, are still at the fringes of the development profession.

11 Conclusions

George Bernard Shaw once said that 'all professions are a conspiracy against the laity'. While this accusation may not be true in a formal sense, at least in the case of the development profession it does contain more than a grain of truth—the profession has been continuously engaged in the task of forcing everything into its own way of thinking, of narrowing the options available for understanding, analysing, and resolving social problems, and of limiting the indigenously motivated potential for political, social, and economic change in the Third World. I have tried to show here that the current malaise in development theory is simply a continuation of earlier conflicts, which stemmed precisely from a resistance to such a narrowing of the options.

I argue that the project of modernization has been deleterious to the welfare of Third World populations not because of bad policy advice or malicious intent of the advisers, nor because of the disregard of neo-classical wisdom, but rather because the project has constantly forced indigenous people to divert their energies from the *positive* pursuit of indigenously defined social change, to the *negative* goal of resisting cultural, political, and economic domination by the West. In order for the improvement in welfare of Third World people to become possible, we have to stop believing that this is something only 'we' can do for 'them'; we have to stop trying to quantify and measure the 'quality of life' (or other indicators of 'development') because these measurements become a licence to intervene in 'their' lives on the grounds that 'we' know what is objectively and undoubtedly 'good for them'.

The problem with such definitions has always been their ability to disenfranchise people, to make it unnecessary for their opinions to be sought, and to make it impossible for them to change their preferences in the face of manifest problems. If the right to define welfare and progress were to be unconditionally restored to indigenous people, it is true that they would make mistakes, just as the development profession has made mistakes. But, unlike the latter, they will learn from their mistakes and they will adjust their behaviour, instead of continually trying to rationalize their errors, or to justify their actions, their privileges, and their right to intervene. As the hound said to the hare in the well-known fable, 'You have to be quicker than me. I am running only for my dinner; you are running for your life.'

Implicit throughout this critique has been the view that modernization is a particular 'way of seeing the world', and that it has continuously been confronted by 'alternative' ways of seeing, indigenous to native people. The task of the theorist has often been to speak on behalf of these people, to translate their views into the language of modernization, and to use this translation as a legitimization of further intervention. What we have learnt from the persistence of the unrest, of the unimaginable fury, against this endeavour is the indignity of speaking on someone else's behalf—to use Gilles Deleuze's description of Michel Foucault's contribution to our understanding of social processes (cited in Sheridan 1980: 114).

This is as far as the critique has gone. Within the assumptions of the dominant culture, this is as far as the critique *can* go. As long as these assumptions are accepted, the outside theorist or adviser (including the indigenous 'outsider') will continue to be empowered to 'speak on someone else's behalf', and to intervene, on the basis of superior knowledge, in the social milieu of Third World countries, without any safeguards against new manifestations of problems which have continually emerged from the use of knowledge considered superior. The pursuit of this important issue requires an analysis of the differences between 'modern' and 'alternative' perspectives, but that is rightly the subject of another paper. I take up this issue in Chapter 3, where I argue that the key distinction between these two perspectives is the cultural foundation which underlies their articulated forms. In Chapter 3, I use the notion of 'personal' and 'impersonal' maps (or ways of comprehending the world provided by all cultures), to argue that while indigenous approaches tend to maintain a balance between the two maps, modernity is premissed upon the superiority and universality of the 'impersonal' over the 'personal' map. I call this belief the impersonality postulate of modernity, and argue that the search for a better world, in the North as well as the South, must begin with attempts to restore the balance between what are in reality the two halves of our humanness.

REFERENCES

Alavi, H. (1976) 'The Rural Elite and Agricultural Development in Pakistan', in R. Stevens, H. Alavi, and P. Bertocci (eds.), *Rural Development in Pakistan and Bangladesh*, Honolulu, Hawaii: Hawaii University Press.

Almond, Gabriel (1956) 'Comparative Political Systems', in Heinz Eilau, S. J. Eldersvald, and M. Janowitz (eds.), *Political Behavior: A Reader in Theory and Research*, Glencoe, Ill.: The Free Press, pp. 34–42.

Attewell, Paul (1984) *Radical Political Economy Since The Sixties: A Sociology of Knowledge Analysis*, New Brunswick, NJ: Rutgers University Press.

Amadeo, Edward, and Banuri, Tariq (1990) 'Policy, Governance, and the Management of Conflict', in Tariq Banuri (ed.), *Economic Liberalization: No Panacea*, Oxford; Clarendon Press.

Bahuguna, Sunderlal (1983) *Walking with the Chipko Message*, Silyara (Tehri Garhwal, India): Chipko Information Centre.

Bahro, Rudolph (1986) *Building the Green Movement*, Philadelphia: New Society Publishers.

Balassa, Bela (1982) *Development Strategies in Semi-Industrial Economies*, Baltimore: Johns Hopkins University Press.

Banuri, Tariq, and Amadeo, Edward (1990) 'Worlds Within the Third World', in Tariq Banuri (ed.) (1990), *Economic Liberalization: No Panacea*, Oxford; Clarendon Press.

Baran, Paul (1952) 'On the Political Economy of Backwardness', *Manchester School* (Jan.), 20: 66–84.

—— (1957) *The Political Economy of Growth*, New York: Monthly Review Press.

Bardhan, Pranab (1984) *The Political Economy of Development in India*, Oxford: Basil Blackwell.

Bauer, P. T. (1981) *Equality, The Third World, and Economic Delusion*, London: Methuen.

Bellah, R. N., *et al.* (1985) *Habits of the Heart: Individualism and Commitment in American Life*, New York: Harper and Row.

Berger, Peter (1976) *Pyramids of Sacrifice*, New York: Doubleday.

Bhatt, C. P. (1984) *Himalaya Kshetra ka Niyojan Gopeshwar*, India, mimeographed (in Hindi).

Boeke, J. H. (1953) *Economics and Economic Policy of Dual Societies*, New York: Institute of Pacific Relations.

Bottomore, Tom (1984) *The Frankfurt School*, London: Tavistock.

Bowles, S., and Gintis, H. (1986) *Democracy and Capitalism: Property, Community, and the Contradictions of Modern Social Thought*, New York: Basic Books.

Bruton, Henry (1985) 'The Search For A Development Economics', *World Development*, 13: 1099–1124.

Burki, S. J. (1976) 'The Development of Pakistan's Agriculture: An Interdisciplinary Explanation', in R. Stevens, H. Alavi, and P. Bertocci (eds.), *Rural Development in Pakistan and Bangladesh*, Honolulu, Hawaii: Hawaii University Press.

Cardoso, Fernando Henrique (1972) 'Dependency and Development in Latin America', *New Left Review*, 74: 83–95.

Cesaire, Aimé (1972) *Discourse on Colonialism*, New York: Monthly Review Press.

Clastres, P. (1977) *Society Against The State: The Leader as Servant and the Human Uses of Power Among the Indians of The Americas*, trans. Robert Hurley, New York: Urizen Books.

Commoner, Barry (1971) *The Closing Circle*, New York: Alfred Knopf.

Dumont, Louis (1977) *From Mandeville to Marx*, Chicago: University of Chicago Press.

Ehrlich, Paul R., Ehrlich, A. H., and Holdren, J.P. (1977) *Ecoscience: Population, Resources, Environment*, San Francisco: W. H. Freeman.

Ellul, Jacques (1964) *The Technological Society*, New York: Alfred A. Knopf.

Elster, Jon (1979) *Ulysses and the Sirens: Studies in Rationality and Irrationality*, Cambridge: Cambridge University Press.

Enzenberger, H. M. (1974) 'A Critique of Political Ecology', *New Left Review*, 84: 3–31.

Falk, Richard (1983) 'Satisfying Human Needs in a World of Sovereign States: Rhetoric, Reality, and Vision', in Charles K. Wilber (ed.), *The Political Economy of Development and Underdevelopment*, Third Edition, New York: Random House.

Fanon, Franz (1968) *The Wretched of the Earth*, New York: Grove Press.

Fei, John C., and Ranis, Gustav (1964) *Development of The Labor Surplus Economy: Theory and Policy*, Homewood, Ill.: Irwin.

Ferguson, Marilyn (1980) *The Aquarian Conspiracy: Personal and Social Transformation in the 1980s*, Boston: Houghton Mifflin.

Feyerabend, Paul (1975) *Against Method*, London: Verso.

Fishlow, Albert (1972) 'Brazilian Size Distribution of Income', *AER* (May), 62: 391–402.

—— (1990) 'Some Reflections on Comparative Latin American Economic Performance', in Tariq Banuri (ed.) *Economic Liberalization: No Panacea*, Oxford: Clarendon Press.

Foucault, M. (1980) *Power/Knowledge: Selected Interviews and Other Writings, 1972–77*, trans. Colin Gordon *et al.*, Brighton, Sussex: Harvester Press.

Foxley, Alejandro (1982) 'Towards a Free Market Economy: Chile 1974–79', *Journal of Development Economics* (Feb.), 10: 3–29.

Frank, Andre Gunder (1967) *Development and Underdevelopment in Latin America*, New York: Monthly Review Press.

Freire, P. (1970) *Pedagogy of The Oppressed*, trans. Myra Bergman Ramos, New York: Herder and Herder.

Fromm, Erich (1942) *The Fear of Freedom*, London: Routledge and Kegan Paul.

Furtado, Celso (1970) *Economic Development in Latin America*, New York: Cambridge University Press.

Geertz, Clifford (1973) *The Interpretation of Cultures*, New York: Basic Books.

Godelier, Maurice (1972) *Rationality and Irrationality in Economics*, New York: Monthly Review Press.

Goulet, Denis (1971) ' "Development" ... or Liberation', *International Development Review* (Sept.), 13/3: 6–10.

——(1980) 'Development Experts: The One-Eyed Giants', *World Development*, 8/7–8: 481–90.

Gran, Guy (1983) *Development By People: Citizen Construction of a Just World*, New York: Praeger.

Guha, Ramachandra (1985) 'Eco-Development Debate: A Critical Review', *South Asian Anthropologist*, 6/1: 15–24.

Guha, Ranajit, ed. (1982) *Subaltern Studies: Writings on South Asian History and Society*, New Delhi: Oxford.

——(1983) *Elementary Aspects of Peasant Insurgency in Colonial India*, New Delhi: Oxford University Press.

Gutierrez, G. (1973) *A Theology of Liberation*, New York: Orbis Press.

Habermas, Jürgen (1984) *The Theory of Communicative Action*, Boston: Beacon Press.

Hagen, Everett (1962) *On the Theory of Social Change: How Economic Growth Begins*, Homewood, Ill.: Dorsey Press.

Hallowell, A. Irving (1955) 'The Self and Its Behavioral Environment', *Culture and Experience*, Philadelphia: University of Pennsylvania Press.

Haq, Mahbub ul (1976) *The Poverty Curtain: Choices for the Third World*, New York: Columbia University Press.

Hardin, Garrett (1968) 'The Tragedy of The Commons', *Science* (13 Dec.), 162: 1243–8.

Hillman, James (1976) *Re-Visioning Psychology*, New York: Harper & Row.

Hirschman, A. O. (1965) 'Obstacles to Development: A Classification and a Quasi-Vanishing Act', *Economic Development and Cultural Change*, 17/4: 385–9.

——(1981a) 'The Rise and Decline of Development Economics', *Essays in Trespassing*, Cambridge: Cambridge University Press, pp. 1–24.

——(1981b) 'The Turn to Authoritarianism in Latin America and the Search For Economic Determinants', *Essays in Trespassing*, Cambridge: Cambridge University Press, pp. 98–135.

——(1984) *Getting Ahead Collectively: Grassroots Experiments in Latin America*, New York: Pergamon.

Hobsbawm, Eric J. (1963) *Primitive Rebels*, New York: Praeger.

Hoselitz, Bertholt (1960) *Sociological Aspects of Economic Growth*, New York: The Free Press.

Huntington, Samuel P. (1968) *Political Order in Changing Societies*, New Haven: Yale University Press.

——, and Joan M. Nelson (1976) *No Easy Choice: Political Participation in*

Developing Countries, Cambridge, Mass.: Harvard University Press.

Ileto, Reynaldo C. (n.d.) 'An Alternative to Developmentalist Historiography in the Philippines', Manila: De La Salle University (mimeo).

Illich, Ivan (1981) *Shadow Work*, Boston: Marion Boyars.

Inkeles, Alex, and Smith, David (1974) *Becoming Modern*, Cambridge, Mass.: Harvard University Press.

Jorgenson, Dale W. (1967) 'Surplus Agricultural Labour and the Development of a Dual Economy', *Oxford Economic Papers*, 19: 288–312.

Josephson, Eric, and Josephson, Mary, eds. (1962) *Man Alone: Alienation in Modern Society*, New York: Doubleday.

Killick, T. (1976) 'The Possibilities of Development Planning', *Oxford Economic Papers*, 41/4: 161–84.

Kropotkin, Peter (1902) *Mutual Aid: A Factor in Evolution*, New York: McClure Phillips.

Krueger, Anne (1986) 'Problems of Liberalization', in Armeane Choksi and Demetris Papageorgiou (eds.), *Economic Liberalization in Developing Countries*, Oxford: Basil Blackwell.

Kuhn, Thomas S. (1970) *The Structure of Scientific Revolutions*, 2nd edition, Chicago, Ill.: University of Chicago Press.

Kuznets, Simon (1941) *National Income and its Composition, 1919–38*, New York: NBER.

—— (1971) *Economic Growth of Nations: Total Output and Production Structure*, Cambridge, Mass.: Harvard University Press.

Lal, Deepak (1983) *The Poverty of Development Economics*, London: Institute of Economic Affairs.

Lasch, Christopher (1979) *The Culture of Narcissism: American Life in an Age of Diminishing Expectations*, New York: W. W. Norton.

Lewis, W. Arthur (1954) 'Economic Development with Unlimited Supplies of Labour', *Manchester School* (May), 22/2: 131–91 (widely abridged and reprinted).

—— (1955) 'Is Economic Growth Desirable?', in *The Theory of Economic Growth*, Homewood, Ill.: Irwin.

Lewis, John (1962) *Quiet Crisis in India*, Washington, DC: Brookings.

Lipton, Michael (1977) *Why Poor People Stay Poor: A Study of Urban Bias in World Development*, London: Maurice Temple Smith.

Little, Ian M. D. (1982) *Economic Development: Theory, Policy, and International Relations*, New York: Basic Books.

McClelland, David (1961) *The Achieving Society*, Princeton: D. Van Nostrand.

Marcuse, Herbert (1964) *One Dimensional Man*, Boston: Beacon Press.

Marglin, Stephen A. (1974) 'What Do Bosses Do? The Origins and Functions of Hierarchy in Capitalist Production, Part I' *Review of Radical Political Economics*, 6/2: 60–112.

—— (1984) 'The Wealth of Nations', *The New York Review of Books* (19 July), 41–4.

Meadows, Donella H., Meadows, Dennis L., Randers, Jorgen, and Behrens, William W. III (1972) *Limits to Growth*, New York: Universe Books.

Meier, Gerald M. (1984) *Leading Issues in Economic Development*, 4th edn., New York: Oxford University Press.

Mortimer, Edward (1982) *Faith and Power: The Politics of Islam*, New York: Vintage Books.

Mouffe, Chantal, ed. (1979) *Gramsci and Marxist Theory*, London: Routledge & Kegan Paul.

Mumford, Lewis (1961) *The City in History: Its Origins, Its Transformations, and Its Prospects*, New York: Harcourt Brace Janovich.

Myrdal, G. (1968) 'The Beam in Our Eyes', in *Asian Drama: An Inquiry Into The Wealth of Nations*, Harmondsworth, England: Penguin Books, pp. 5–35.

Nandy, Ashis (1983) *The Intimate Enemy*, New Delhi: Oxford University Press.

—— (1984) 'Culture, State, and the Rediscovery of Indian Politics', *Economic and Political Weekly* (Dec.), 8: 2078–83.

—— (1987) 'Towards A Third World Utopia', in *Traditions, Tyrannies, and Utopias: Essays in the Politics of Awareness*, New Delhi: Oxford University Press.

Nerfin, Marc, ed. (1977) *Another Development: Approaches and Strategies*, Uppsala: Dag Hammarskjöld Foundation.

Parsons, Talcott (1951) *The Social System*, New York: The Free Press.

Popkin, Samuel (1979) *The Rational Peasant*, Berkeley, Calif.: University of California Press.

Poulantzas, Nicos (1978) *State, Power, Socialism*, trans. Patrick Camiller, London: NLB.

Pye, Lucian (1965) 'Introduction: Political Culture and Political Development', in L. Pye and S. Verba (eds.), op. cit., pp. 3–26.

—— and Verba, S. (1965) *Political Culture and Political Development*, Princeton, NJ: Princeton University Press.

Rahman, F. (1979) *Islam*, 2nd edn. Chicago, Ill.: University of Chicago Press.

—— (1982) *Islam and Modernity: Transformation of an Intellectual Tradition*, Chicago, Ill.: University of Chicago Press.

Reddy, A. K. N. (1978) 'The Transfer, Transformation and Generation of Technology for Rural Development' in K. D. Sharma and M. A. Qureshi (eds.), *Science, Technology and Development: Essays in Honour of A. Rahman*, New Delhi: Sterling Publishers.

Resnick, Stephen, and Wolff, Richard (1982) 'Marxist Epistemology: The Critique of Economic Determinism', *Social Text*, 6: 31–72.

Rondinelli, D. A., *et al.* (1983) *Decentralisation in Developing Countries: A Review of Recent Experience*, Washington, DC: World Bank Staff Working Paper No. 581.

Rorty, Richard (1979) *Philosophy and the Mirror of Nature*, Princeton, NJ: Princeton University Press.

Roszak, Theodor (1969) *The Making of a Counter Culture*, New York: Doubleday.

Sahlins, Marshall (1972) *Stone Age Economics*, New York: Aldine.

Schultz, Theodore (1964) *Transforming Traditional Agriculture*, New Haven: Yale University Press.

Schumacher, E. F. (1973) *Small is Beautiful: Economics As if People Mattered*, New York: Harper & Row.

Scott, James (1976) *The Moral Economy of the Peasant: Rebellion and Subsistence in South East Asia*, New Haven: Yale University Press.

Seers, D. (1969) 'The Meaning of Development', *International Development Review* (Dec.), 11: 1–16.

Sen, Amartya (1983) 'Development: Which Way Now?', *Economic Journal* (Dec.), 93: 745–62.

Service, Elman (1975) *Origins of The State and Civilization: The Process of Cultural Evolution*, New York: W. W. Norton.

Sheridan, A. (1980) *Michel Foucault: The Will to Truth*, London: Tavistock Publications Ltd.

Shariati, Ali (1979) *On The Sociology of Islam*, trans. Hamid Algar, Berkeley, Calif.: Mizan Press.

Sheahan, John (1980) 'Market-Oriented Economic Policies and Political Repression in Latin America', *Economic Development and Cultural Change* (Jan.), 28/2: 267–91.

Slater, Philip (1970) *The Pursuit of Loneliness: American Culture at the Breaking Point*, Boston: Beacon Press.

Stewart, Frances (1985) 'The Fragile Foundations of the Neoclassical Approach to Development', *The Journal of Development Studies* (Jan.), 21: 282–92.

Streeten, Paul (1982) 'A Cool Look at Outward-Looking Development Strategies', *World Economy* (Sept.), 5: 159–69.

—— (1984) 'Development Dichotomies', in Gerald M. Meier and Dudley Seers (eds.), *Pioneers in Development*, New York: Oxford University Press, pp. 337–61.

Tambiah, Stanley, J. (1985) 'An Anthropologist's Creed', Harvard University, Anthropology Department (mimeo).

Tax, Sol (1953) *Penny Capitalism: A Guatamalan Indian Economy*, Washington, DC: Smithsonian Institution.

Toye, John (1985) '*Dirigisme* and Development Economics', *Cambridge Journal of Economics* (Mar.), 9: 1–14.

Uberoi, J. S. (1978) *Science and Culture*, New Delhi: Oxford University Press.

Uphoff, N. T., and Ilchman, W. F. (1972) *The Political Economy of Development*, Berkeley, Calif.: University of California Press.

Vohra, B. B. (1980) *A Land and Water Policy for India*, New Delhi: Sardar Patel Memorial Lecture.

Wallerstein, Immanuel (1974) *The Modern World System: Capitalist Agriculture and the Origins of the European World Economy in the 16th Century*, New York: Academic Press.

Weber, Max (1930) *The Protestant Ethic and the Spirit of Capitalism*, trans. T. Parsons, London: George Allen and Unwin.

Weiner, Myron (1965) 'India: Two Political Cultures' in L. Pye and S. Verba (eds.), op. cit., pp. 199–244.

White, Lynn (1972) 'Technology and Social Change', in Robert Nisbet (ed.), *Social Change*, New York: Harper & Row, pp. 101–29.

Wilber, C. K., and Jameson, K. P. (1984) 'Paradigms of Economic Development and Beyond', in Charles K. Wilber (ed.), *The Political Economy of Development and Underdevelopment*, 3rd edn., New York: Random House, pp. 4–25.

Wolf, Eric (1969) *Peasant Wars of the Twentieth Century*, New York: Harper & Row.

Woodcock, George (1986) *Anarchism: A History of Libertarian Ideas and Movements*, Harmondsworth, England: Penguin.

Yotopoulos, Pan A., and Nugent, Jeffrey B. (1976) *Economics of Development*.

3

Modernization and its Discontents: A Cultural Perspective on the Theories of Development

TARIQ BANURI

1 Modernization and its Discontents

This chapter represents an intellectual journey of sorts. It is at once the product of, and an attempt to describe, the tension between the universe of those who study the Third World and the universe of those who inhabit this world. Like most other students of development, especially those from the so-called developing countries, I have long had serious doubts about the wisdom of many aspects of this body of knowledge, but was inclined to regard them as minor disagreements over a few policies or actions. Recently, however, I began to realize that these doubts derive from fundamental differences over 'ways of seeing' the world, rather than from a few specifics. It is this shift in comprehension that I shall attempt to develop here in the hope that it is relevant for current debates in the Third World.

While I believe, as I must, that the ideas presented here are important for a more complete understanding of the problems of development and progress, I am aware that they would not have been very relevant (and indeed, might not even have taken shape in my own thinking) were it not for the widespread feeling of a crisis in development theory. The current uncertainty in the profession has been a catalyst for many new attempts, particularly in Third World countries, to develop alternative approaches which can take into account more centrally the problems and failures of the process of modernization. This chapter is one more attempt in this direction.

Simply stated, I argue that in order to understand the current crisis we have to look at the impact of the entire corpus of modernization and development theories rather than focus on specific instances of their application. This is done by seeing modernization theories as artefacts of the culture which produced them and which contributed to their strengths as well as their weaknesses. Consequently, this essay also seeks to shift attention towards the intellectual, philosophical, and moral bases of the theory, and away from particular policies or actions which emerged from it under different circumstances.

To preface the succeeding remarks, I see a particular assumption—'that impersonal relations are inherently superior to personal relations'—to be the distinguishing element of the modernizers' world-view, and one which places them very firmly within 'Western' culture. This elegant and pedigreed assumption, which I shall label the *impersonality postulate*, introduces a powerful asymmetry in the analysis of social issues by concentrating intellectual energies only on those aspects of social behaviour which can be encompassed within an objectivist matrix. Alternative proposals, such as the one presented here, can then be interpreted as attempts to replace this asymmetry with a more balanced approach.

To avoid misunderstanding, I should clarify here that it is not my contention that the wise and able social scientists engaged in what appeared to many people to be a wholly admirable endeavour, namely the economic and social modernization of the Third World, were less than well-intentioned. Obviously they did not seek to bring about the pathologies and crises that have so stymied the profession today. However, just as one cannot look at an individual's action without taking account of the social, moral, and political contexts in which the action takes place, so also one cannot analyse out of context the intellectual contributions of development theorists who, notwithstanding their noble motives, may have contributed unwittingly to a host of problems. The problem is the context, not those who operated within that context.

A clarification is also in order with regard to my use of the term 'West', by which I mean the 'ideal type' of the 'West' presented as a model to Third World societies; I decidedly do not mean to refer to the observable culture lived and experienced by countless people in Europe and North America, except to the extent that their articulated form of self-definition is based on this 'ideal type'. Nor am I using 'West' as an antithesis of the socialist 'East'. These points will become clearer below.

Today, there is a crisis in development and modernization theories. Hardly a book or journal comes out without some expression of doubt, disappointment, and disillusionment with the record of almost half a century of planned development methods. It would be a mistake to think, however, that this crisis has emerged only because of some new-found problems. Indeed, Chapter 2 argues that the evolution of the various strands of modernization theory—development economics (institutional as well as neo-classical), political development, social modernization, dependancy and world systems, and non-dependancy Marxists—should be seen as a succession of responses by theorists to challenges from inside or outside their theoretical disciplines. Nevertheless, the current crisis is significant because it is helping to bring together a number of disparate criticisms of a process which had largely been accepted until recently.

Chapter 2 describes the evolution of contemporary theories of modernization and development in terms of a series of challenges and responses between 'external' critics—those who question the underlying intellectual, moral, and political basis of modernization—and the protagonists of modernization, whose responses to external critics have often taken the form of an 'internal' critique, which, while acknowledging weaknesses in the application of development theory, attempt to restore the credibility of the theory by finding ways of accommodating or assimilating the criticism into it. This conflict has generally revolved around differences in interpretation of the meaning and determinants of 'dualism', namely the significant socio-cultural differences, within as well as across nations, which accompany observable differences in economic productivity and wealth. External critics have often seen these differences in much the same way as J. H. Boeke, the originator of the concept, as 'the *clashing* of an imported social system with an indigenous system of another style' (Boeke 1953), in other words as 'conflictual dualism'. Champions of modernization, on the other hand, perceive dualism as the coexistence of an inferior life-style with a superior one; this leads to the notion of modernization as a harmonious process, as a displacement of the less desirable life-style by the more desirable one.

This debate between external and internal critics, or between 'conflictual' and 'harmonious' dualism, has continued, in varying forms, until this day, and can be used as a device for tackling the complexity of the modernization and development literature. For example, it can be used to analyse the formation of related subdisciplines, such as social modernization theory or political development. In the 1950s, social modernization theorists used psychological and sociological arguments to show why traditional systems of values and behaviour were objectively sub-optimal, and needed to be replaced;[1] while critics argued that traditional societies and alternative value systems had rationalities all of their own, which were meritorious not only in their own right, but also because of their relevance for understanding and combating some of the problems in modern societies (Scott 1976). Subsequently, the debate over values combined with some spectacular developmental failures to produce the new subfield of political development (e.g. Huntington 1968), in addition to a literature on the 'meaning of development' (Seers 1969).

More recently, the record of modernization and development has been criticized by some writers on account of its association with environmental deterioration (Guha 1985), socio-political violence (Nandy 1987*b*), erosion of political participation (Sheahan 1980, Hirschman 1981), and inappropriate and harmful technology (Chapter 7 below, Ellul 1964,

---

1. For a review of the literature, and a statement of this position, see Inkeles and Smith 1974.

Schumachar 1973). In all these debates, the external critics argued that the harmful consequences were inherent in the process of modernization itself, while the defenders of modernization either denied the existence or extent of the damage, or sought to expand the theory to accommodate the criticism into it.

These disparate criticisms have begun to come together in the form of a cultural critique, which replaces the modernizers' assumption of the superiority of the modern life-style with the earlier notion of the moral as well as socio-economic worth of different cultures and value systems. This essay is an attempt to provide a perspective which can integrate the various critiques and the responses they have elicited into an analysis of modernization and its discontents.

It is my argument that the many external critiques of modernization are unified at a deeper level by an alternative way of seeing the world. In this section, I shall elaborate on this argument in order to bring out more specifically the differences in 'ways of seeing' or 'cultural perspectives' between protagonists and antagonists of modernization. The object of the discussion is to present at the same time an alternative theory of behaviour, an alternative perspective on values, an alternative view on modernization theories, and an analysis of the legitimizing role of these theories in respect of certain values and actions.

2   Culture, Behaviour, and Values

In the following discussion, the terms 'culture', 'world-view', 'cognitive system', or 'way of seeing' are treated as synonyms. The use of these concepts is derived from an extensive literature in sociology, psychology, and anthropology which goes back at least to Max Weber's (1930, 1947) distinction between 'rational' and 'traditional' behaviour and their relationship with the 'problem of meaning', to Émile Durkheim's work[2] on the primacy of social structure in human behaviour and construction of meaning, Talcott Parsons's synthesis[3] of these two writers and his own views on the 'structuration' of human agency through meaning systems

---

2. Durkheim's view, presented in his two classic works, *The Division of Labor in Society* (1933, first published 1893) and *Suicide* (1951, first published 1897), is of society as interaction or relationship, rather than as a contract between individuals; the relationships define a moral order bound by shared sentiments. He rejected the then popular notion of the individual being prior to society, and argued that the understanding of society, including our approach to observed pathologies, had to take place at the social rather than the individual or psychological level.

3. Parsons's synthesis of the works of Weber and Durkheim (and Malinowski) derives from their shared interest in the 'problem of meaning'. Parsons noted that there was a complementarity between Weber's historical analysis of the variability of social structures in terms of their cumulative intellectual traditions, and Durkheim and Malinowski's work on contemporary societies which drew the distinction between intellectual processes for the construction of meaning on the one hand and those aimed at the solution of practical problems on the other. See Parsons 1954: 204–10.

and the legitimacy provided to existing social institutions by such construction, and George Mead's (1934) analysis[4] of behaviour as a tension between the 'I' and the social roles derived from the expectations of others (the 'me'). In anthropology, these ideas were taken up subsequently in the writings of Claude Lévi-Strauss, Louis Dumont, Clifford Geertz, and Stanley Tambiah, among others.

Much of what is said below is not new. The attempt is essentially to synthesize four well-known strands of thought in social science literature: the distinction between rational and traditional behaviour, the role of cognitive systems in determining behaviour, the 'structured' nature of cognitive systems, and the perception of behaviour as a tension between two aspects of this structured reality.

It is appropriate to begin with a definition of 'culture'. An elegant definition, provided by Geertz (1973: 50), is that of a super-structural system which fills the 'information gap' between 'what our bodies tell us and what we have to know in order to function'[5] or, to use a more recent metaphor, as the human 'software' which fills the gap between human needs and the available genetic 'hardware'.[6] This means, in Geertz's words (1973: 49), that there is

[No] such thing as human nature independent of culture. . . . [Our] central nervous system . . . is incapable of directing our behavior or organizing our experience without the guidance provided by systems of significant symbols. . . . Such symbols are thus not mere expressions, instrumentalities, or correlates of our biological, psychological, and social existence; they are prerequisites of it. Without men, no culture, certainly; but equally, and more significantly, without culture, no men.

Culture, this system of symbols, can thus be likened to a 'map' of the universe which we carry in our heads, and which enables us to integrate our values, choices, and actions. It is a 'design for living', a filter through which we assimilate all experience, physical as well as social, and which enables us to act in situations presented before us. 'All human action', said George Mead, 'is interaction—with others, ourselves, our natural and created physical world—within culturally defined contexts that determine not only action, but its meaning.' It is worth emphasizing that

4. George Mead 1934 stressed the role of communication in the development of the human agent. Communication allows individuals to assume the roles of others, and thus facilitates the simultaneous development of individualism as well as sociability. This led him to the observation that human behaviour will reflect the tension between the imperatives of these two roles, which he termed the 'I' and the 'me' respectively. Much of Mead's work complemented that of Freud.

5. The flexibility and learning capacity that this implies has often been remarked upon as the humans' source of advantage over other animals; equal, though less noted, is the disadvantage of our extreme dependence on such a system of learning.

6. This analogy was suggested by Oldrich Kyn in a seminar at the Applied Economics Research Centre at Karachi.

these 'culturally defined contexts', like languages, differ from society to society, indeed from 'culture' to 'culture'.

2.1 'Personal' and 'Impersonal' Maps

Theories of modernization are located in a particular ('modern' or 'Western') culture which is unique in a very important sense. In order to bring out this uniqueness, we will need the concepts of 'personal' and 'impersonal' maps. To get a little ahead of the story, these maps are integral elements of *every* cultural system, whether 'traditional' or 'modern'; the tension between the two provides the principal dynamic of cultural evolution and social change; and what distinguishes one culture from others is, in part, the uniqueness of the tension or balance between its component parts.

Now, what are these two 'maps'? It is easier to begin by describing them separately as two independent 'cultures' and then to talk about the blend or the balance between them in an observed cultural system. This is not to say, of course, that these maps exist in isolation anywhere; indeed, even the distinction between the two is unique to what we call 'modern' culture. To simplify matters, I shall concentrate on three key dimensions of the cultural maps: theories of the self (ontology), of knowledge (epistemology), and of the universe (cosmology).[7]

The 'impersonal' map can then be imagined as a culture in which everyone perceives herself or himself to have an impersonal relationship with other people, with the natural environment, and with knowledge. The distinguishing characteristic of this cultural perspective would be a perception of the individual as being separable or detached from the social, physical, or intellectual environment, as in the economists' Robinson Crusoe model of society; and the environment itself as being divisible into a finite number of partitions. A 'personal' map, in contrast, can be imagined as a culture in which every person sees himself or herself as having only personal relationships in each of the three dimensions. In this case, the sense of identity is created through identification rather than through separation. In fact, in this cultural system, the notion of an 'individual' (observer, agent, actor, what have you) is very hard to construct. Furthermore, the relational identity will not permit the conceptualization of the social or physical environment in terms of a finite number of attributes.[8]

7. See Uberoi 1978 for a discussion of modernity and its conceptions of ontology, epistemology, and cosmology.
8. This point is rather obvious, but worth emphasizing none the less. Think of the difference between a house and a home, between an animal and a pet, between the person in the street and a friend, etc. In each case, the former can be thought of in terms of a finite number of impersonal attributes (based on our needs?), while the complex nature of our relationship to the latter makes it impossible for us to perceive them only in terms of a few attributes.

The differences between the two maps are not merely cosmetic. They have implications for our values, orientations, and actions. Impersonal relations and attitudes are reflected in organization, rationality, linearity, and control; they need to be static and rigid, to constantly define terms and freeze them in place, to perceive time as discrete rather than continuous, and to place the world in a conceptual grid. Not surprisingly, therefore, 'hard' social sciences such as economics and political science focus on relationships of exchange and power respectively, both of which belong in the impersonal sphere.

Personal relations and attitudes are manifested in spontaneity, fluidity, and bilateral vulnerability; they must evolve dynamically and they have to be flexible, concepts and definitions keep changing and evolving, time is seen as continuous, and attention is directed mainly towards those aspects of social reality which elude the conceptual grid of impersonality.

Modern culture is unique in a very special sense. It is the only one which wishes consciously to separate these two dimensions of culture from each other, and to place them in a hierarchy in which the 'impersonal' is superior to the 'personal'.[9] This what I have called the *impersonality postulate of modernity*: 'That impersonal relations are inherently superior to personal relations.' Before arguing this point, it would be helpful to have a more detailed description of the three dimensions of culture.

With regard to self-definition or *ontology*, the 'impersonal' view can be described by what the anthropologist Louis Dumont calls 'individualism', a characteristic of those (Western) societies, which value, 'in the first place, the individual human being: every man is, in principle, an embodiment of humanity at large, and as such he is equal to every other man, and free' (Dumont 1977: 4). This means, among many other things, that individualism provides a sense of personal identity independent of relationships, and based on such 'impersonal' elements as abstract rights, attributes, desires, preferences, or even professional occupation.[10]

Dumont contrasts individualism with 'holism', a characteristic of those contemporary or ancient societies in which value is placed 'in the first place, on order: the conformity of every element to its role in society—in a word, the society as a whole' (Dumont 1977: 4).[11] Since my emphasis

9. This impersonal/personal contrast has close analogies with Dumont's individualism and holism, Tonnies's *Gesellschaft* and *Gemeinschaft*, Maine's contract and status, Durkheim's contractual solidarity and organic solidarity, Sen's self-interest and commitment, and Habermas's rational-purposive action and communicative action.

10. That 'modern' societies are 'individualistic', where the goals and preferences of individuals are taken to be metaphysical entities, has also been noted by various other authors. For example, see Polanyi 1944: 163–91, Durkheim 1933: 200–32, Slater 1970, Lasch 1979. A similar distinction is made by Sen 1977. My differences with Sen are along the lines taken by Das and Nicholas 1982.

11. This broad distinction has a wealth of implications. For example, in individualistic societies, but not in holistic ones, relations between people are subordinated to the relations between people and things; and economic aspects of society are segregated

is on the nature of personal identity in different cultures, a better name for this view is 'relationalism', in which the individual sees herself or himself simply as the nexus of a web of relationships.[12] These relationships and roles acquire a metaphysical and symbolic (as opposed to a literal) quality, just as rights, desires, and preferences acquire a metaphysical quality in individualistic cultures. The relational culture tells us what, for example, it means to be a spouse, a neighbour, a friend, a patron, or a client, but is silent on what it means to have preferences, attributes, or rights independent of their cultural nexus.[13]

Similarly, in our theories of the universe or *cosmology*, the impersonal view is represented by what can be called 'instrumentalism', i.e. perceptions of such things as land, the village, the home, trees, forests, animals, stars, goods, and even people, primarily as sources of gratification. Alternatively, the 'personal' view would see all these entities in a relational context: a home is not just the place where you are living at the moment, but also an integral part of your history as well as of your future.

The 'instrumental' view sees everything as being replaceable or substitutible, whereas the 'relational' perspective finds everything unique and irreplaceable. It follows that 'impersonality' implies the attribution of only a finite set of qualities or characteristics to each object, while 'relationality' sees infinite dimensions in each in terms of its attributes.

Lastly, it is also possible to identify two broad alternatives in the theory of knowledge or *epistemology* provided by a cultural map. The impersonal view is represented by the Cartesian 'positivism/literalism' which found its most forceful exposition in the works of the logical positivists of the Vienna Circle.[14] In this view, valid knowledge derives only from the separation of the observer from the object of knowledge, and the expansion of knowledge takes place through its division into separate self-contained divisions with cause and effect relations restricted to each subdivision.[15]

Alternatively, in the 'personal' view encompassed in the practice of 'communication',[16] 'hermeneutics' (Rorty 1979, especially ch. 7), or

from the remaining part of social arrangements.

12. A somewhat similar distinction is made by Gilligan 1982 between 'masculine' and 'feminine' forms of self-definition in Western countries. Gilligan sees men as defining the world in terms of moral absolutes, while women define it in terms of relationships.

13. The last sentence should indicate quite clearly that the 'personal' and 'impersonal' maps are not intended to represent any real society or culture, since it is difficult to imagine any culture which would be silent on the role of personal attributes or preferences in forming one's identity.

14. For a discussion of the effect of positivism on economic thinking, see Caldwell 1982.

15. For a critique of the authoritarian implications of this approach to knowledge, see Nandy 1987a. Habermas's distinction between rational-purposive action and communicative action is also relevant here. See Habermas 1984, particularly pp. 157–85, 186–215.

16. This sense is related to Habermas's distinction between rational-purposive action and communicative action, the latter aiming at legitimacy, sincerity, and comprehensibility, rather than at 'truth' defined in an abstract and universal sense (see Habermas 1984).

'semiotics' (as espoused by Foucault, Habermas, or others), valid knowledge derives from identification with the object of knowledge, in other words through a personal relation between the observer and the observed, which precludes the attribution of finite dimensions or of independent cause and effect relationships in each of these dimensions of analysis.

2.2 Culture and Behaviour

To paraphrase Anthony Giddens, these cultural 'maps' are both constituted by human agency and yet at the same time they are the medium of such constitution: they exist prior to each individual, and yet at the same time individuals determine, through personal experiences and actions, not only the precise configurations of their own 'maps' but also the maps of people connected to them.

A little reflection will reveal that the two 'maps' are in no sense alternatives. Both of them exist in *every* culture. Indeed, in our everyday lives we commonly rely on both ways of seeing without consciously distinguishing between them. Every culture provides people with 'impersonal' as well as 'relational' identities, with symbolic as well as instrumental connections to nature, and with semiotic or hermeneutic as well as 'rational' explanations of natural or social phenomena.

Approached in this manner, social values as well as individual and social behaviour can be seen to be derived from the specification of cultural maps. The issue of values is discussed in more detail below. Here it suffices to mention that it can be approached either directly as a question of the good life, or indirectly, as differences in perception of moral conflicts. The direct approach would take up some broad and presumably shared value, such as freedom from domination, and ask how this value might be expressed differently in different cultures, and how these differences in perception might lend support to very different social, economic, and political structures in different societies. This line of argument is followed in Section 2.6 below.

The indirect approach would focus instead on differences in individuals' perception of moral values, and therefore of moral dilemmas. One version of this approach is adopted by psychologists like Carol Gilligan (1982) in her discussion of the difference between masculine and feminine ways of perceiving the world. Gilligan argues, in effect, that moral values can emerge from each of the two dimensions of culture, and therefore that moral dilemmas are interpretable either as conflicts between abstract principles in an impersonal (and in her terms, masculine) world-view, or as conflicts between obligations in a relational (or feminine) view.

Another version of the psychological approach, perhaps more important

A related notion emerges from Mead's view of the development of thinking as the result of communication (see Mead 1934).

for our purposes here, is the one adopted by George Mead (1934), who interprets moral conflict as a tension between the (impersonal) 'I' and the (relational) 'me'. This approach is pertinent here because it leads us directly from the discussion of values into the analysis of social behaviour.

To follow this line of argument, in every culture a decision, whether individual or collective, represents the resolution of a tension between the conflicting demands of the two maps. This suggests that while all humans are alike in the sense that their actions represent a playing out of the tension between the 'personal' and the 'impersonal', they are all none the less different, because each individual (and indeed, each action) represents a different resolution of the tension.

In the same sense, all cultures are similar yet different. All cultures manifest themselves in the form of a tension between the two cultural maps, but each represents a unique balance and a unique tension. This point is worth elaborating.

Cultures differ from one another because of three different factors. First, it is only a slight exaggeration to say that the 'personal' map is context-specific while the 'impersonal' map is universal; in other words, cultural specificity derives in the first instance from the 'personal' map. Second, they will differ also in the relative weight they give to the two maps in different spheres of human activity, in other words in how they blend and balance the two maps in the consciousness of their constituent individuals. Lastly, as has already been noted, the nature and intensity of the tension between the 'personal' and 'impersonal' maps will be different in different cultures.

Indeed, the tension between the two maps can be seen as the primary source of cultural and social change. In other words, 'culture' is not a static phenomenon, but rather is something which changes endogenously through the resolution of the tension between its component elements. All cultures can be seen as unique and evolving resolutions of the dialectic between the 'impersonal' and the 'personal'.

In fact, it is possible to go even further and to argue that the coexistence of the 'personal' and the 'impersonal' is not accidental. In fact, the two ways of seeing are necessary as complements to each other: each helps to limit the excesses which can result from an unfettering of the other.[17] No human society can exist without both of these maps as components of its culture.

2.3 The Impersonality Postulate

The project of modernity has, however, taken upon itself precisely the task of distinguishing between the two maps by asserting a hierarchical

---

17. Here it may be useful to suggest an analogy. Just as we argue that the impersonal and personal maps are necessary for each other because they help limit each other's excesses, it can be argued that the notions of 'cultural relativisim' and 'cultural absolutism' are

relationship between them. It has the confessed task of 'rationalizing' the whole world, of placing the world in a conceptual grid, and therefore of separating the two halves of human consciousness and strengthening one at the expense of the other.

As Polanyi 1944, Dumont 1977, 1980, and others have pointed out, 'modern' culture is unique in a very important respect. It is the only one which creates an explicit dichotomy between the two forms of self-definition, and, at least in its articulated and self-conscious form, concentrates only on the imperatives of the impersonal aspect, relegating the notion of personal connections to a supervenient 'private' sphere. In other words, the 'way of seeing' in modern cultures is motivated by a powerful asymmetry, which I call here the *impersonality postulate*: 'Impersonal relations are inherently superior to personal relations.' Despite its apparent 'arbitrariness', this postulate is pervasive as the foundational element of various Western theories, in fact, of the entire sensibility which, without seeking to be polemical, I would describe as 'Western'.

This asymmetry in the modern culture, to borrow Thomas Merton's eloquent words, is at once its strength, its torment, and its ruin. While it provides for a tremendous (perhaps temporary?) increase in the ability to control nature, it is also the cause of a myriad of problems including a loss of meaning in peoples' lives, increase in alienation and anxiety, creeping disenfranchisement, an unprecedented rationalization of violence, and destruction of the environment.

Yet this attitude has not been completely internalized by people in any society, West, East, North, or South: witness the resistance implicit in the refusal, at great personal cost, of people in the Third World as well as in the West to give up traditional approaches to knowledge; or in the rejection of such impersonal institutions as the state, the market, the school, the media, or social experts; or even the social and psychological dysfunctioning observed in places where there is a protracted history of the forcible intrusion of impersonal institutions.

Yet it is evident that Western culture in general and its articulated intellectual form in particular reflect precisely an acceptance of this postulate. To elaborate on this argument, it would be helpful to discuss the nature of assumptions in the dominant analytical schools of social science.

2.3.1 Impersonality and Modernization   The literature on modernization is replete with adverse references to the existence of personal relations in traditional societies which are said to impede the smooth functioning of the economy. Examples would include: multi-stranded

also necessary for each other, since they similarly limit the excesses which might result from an asymmetric reliance on one or the other viewpoint as a guide to behaviour.

instead of single-stranded relationships (Scott 1976, Popkin 1979), kinship ties, labour immobility, restrictions on the sale of land, subsistence rather than market production, mystical or religious instead of scientific ways of approaching production, and gift or reciprocity instead of commodity exchange, among many other examples. Similar observations are found in anthropological analyses, most often without the derogatory connotations; e.g. gift or reciprocity instead of commodity exchange, the existence of particularism and personal relations in the organization of social life in traditional environments.[18]

The attitude that behaviour based on impersonal considerations is the only legitimate form of behaviour is even more pronounced in the 'objective' or 'hard' social sciences, such as economics, political science, political economy, and their offshoots in the area of development theory.

It is most in evidence in neo-classical economic theory, which clearly defines the self as separate from the environment by treating preferences and attributes as metaphysical entities and the environment as an external datum. In other words, instead of seeing behaviour as the result of a tension between the demands of the 'personal' and 'impersonal' maps, with this assumption neo-classical theory allows itself to focus only on conflicts between different objectives within the impersonal sphere alone.

This would not be an invalid approach if in a particular instance it was conceded that the impersonal sphere is clearly dominant or that the personal side is completely irrelevant. In such an instance, if the various desires of the impersonal self are stable over time then empirical observation would also lead to predictive ability, which is the claim made by neo-classical economics.[19]

In a like manner, political science perceives individuals to be in pursuit of power, and political institutions to be the means for efficiently exercising and legitimizing power in society. Economic determinists see this simply as an alternative way of saying that individuals pursue higher utility, since power may be a means to the achievement of goods which provide such utility. Nevertheless, the legacy of liberal political philosophy and economics has helped legitimize the existence of the modern 'nation-state', with its impersonal and bureaucratic authority for the regulation of the behaviour of its citizens on the basis of reason and consent, as the 'rationalization' of civil society, and hence as a modernizing ideal for the Third World.

18. See e.g. Donham 1981 on labour exchange among the Malle, or Weiner's 1978 account of the role played by yams in Trobriand social life.
19. It should be noted here, though, that if the personal aspect was dominant instead of the impersonal one, even then the primary tension would be readily resolved, and would similarly give rise to another secondary conflict—that between different relationships, or different obligations. This has obvious parallels to Gilligan's 1982 argument, regarding different ways of perceiving moral dilemmas, either as conflicts between principles, or as conflicts between obligations. Here also, if a model could be specified with as much

What unites both of these disciplines is a judgement concerning the superiority of impersonal over personal relationships within society, whether within the sphere of exchange or power, and a methodology which uses these alleged sources of human motivation to discover empirical regularities in society. Finally, they both share a refusal to look at sources of motivation other than the pursuit and maximization of self-interest, even if they are more relevant and of greater predictive value in particular instances.

This approach could be justified on any one of three grounds:

1. That the theory is meant to apply only in the limited number of situations where impersonality is dominant. This could mean a demarcation of the area within the purview of theory, as that where relationships are clearly perceived as impersonal. (See Godelier 1972: 251–79.)

2. In addition to (1), that the domain of impersonal relations is the only important area of social interaction, either because (a) other aspects are intrinsically less important, since they do not determine issues like production, distribution, or consumption, nor those relating to power; or (b) that the arena of personal connections is not similarly subject to change, and hence can be assumed to be 'given'; or, finally (c) that the area of impersonal relations is the most predictable, and hence the most susceptible to control.

3. Finally, that everything is reducible 'in the last instance', to impersonal desires. In other words, it is possible to interpret even personal commitments as forms of impersonal desires; or, more strongly, that all relations *are* impersonal. (See Sen 1977.)

Even though one occasionally finds disclaimers in economic and political science texts to the effect that the theory is not universally applicable, such humility is rare. Neo-classical economists, in particular, believe that the same theory applies to all possible times or places,[20] and that choice is ultimately reducible to a conflict between different impersonal preferences.[21] In fact, a great deal of effort is expended in proving this type of reducibility.

Institutional economists acknowledge the weakness of this assumption, and modify the analysis to allow behaviour to be constrained by existing social or political institutions, or to be motivated by considerations other than the pursuit of profit. Yet, in many cases there are problems because

precision as the neo-classical model, a similar predictive ability could well be obtained.

20. An extreme, but by no means isolated, example of this attempt at universalization is Gary Becker's 1974 application of the neo-classical method even to the analysis of personal and intimate relationships.

21. It should perhaps be pointed out here that it is equally possible to reduce the analysis in the other direction, and to perceive even the impersonal form of self-definition as another socially determined 'role', which can come into conflict with personal 're-lationships', i.e. other 'roles'. So, for instance, it is just as possible to say, 'I may be a businessman, but I am also your friend,' as it is to say, 'I may be your friend, but I am also a person.'

of the mechanical way in which institutions are introduced into the analysis.

Rather than focus on the conflict between the demands of the 'personal' and 'impersonal' maps, the institutional analyses often refer to the former only as the generator of a set of boundary conditions which frame the conflict within the impersonal sphere. While such a concession may increase the predictability of some models, it is likely to be problematic, since it requires the institution to act as a rigid constraint rather than as the basis of a continuous tension with impersonal desires.[22] Furthermore, this concession also aims to preserve what may be the implicit target of the alternative critique, namely the right of the outside bureaucrat, policy-maker, adviser, or theorist to intervene in the social milieu. Related to this is the fact that institutionalist approaches often sought to introduce the impersonal institution of the state to supplement or balance the other impersonal institution of the market, which led to debates over 'government failure' versus 'market failure', discussed earlier.

Marxian political economy presents an interesting ambivalence over the impersonal/personal divide. While many of the ideas on the alienating influence of modern social and economic arrangements had been developed by the 'early' Marx, they have not been pursued too vigorously by orthodox Marxist-Leninists. In Marx himself, we can see the transition from a perspective which saw the conflict as being within individual consciousness, to one in which it was transferred to social classes; and it was this later 'economistic' phase of Marx which has been incorporated more extensively into his own subsequent theoretical writings, as well as into mainstream Marxist literature.[23]

In this economistic phase, one can discern a bias in favour of impersonal forms of self-definition, albeit from a very different perspective and with very different objectives. Karl Marx saw the history of all hitherto existing societies to be a history of conflict between classes. In pre-capitalist societies, this conflict was mediated by the presence of all types of personal connections between the élite and the subordinate classes. The uniqueness of capitalist society lay in the fact that the dominant class, the bourgeoisie, did not claim any but the cash nexus with the subordinate class of the proletariat; and this, in a nutshell, is why the proletariat will become conscious of the nature of its exploitation, and will act to overthrow it.

---

22. The argument here borrows from Leibenstein 1976 and the surrounding debate over X-efficiency.
23. The protean nature of Marxist theory makes this a somewhat unfair comment. As Attewell 1984 among others has pointed out, recent radical writings can be seen as a response to new problems and challenges, often with a significant adaptation of the basic paradigm. There is also the existence of such schools as the structuralists, or the critical theorists, who see the central contribution of Marx to lie in his epistemological breakthrough. See Resnick and Wolff 1982. It is fair to say, however, that the *mainstream* of Marxist theory is liable to the accusations levelled at it in the text.

The bourgeoisie emancipated itself from the myriad personal connections and restraints which had (ineffectually) held earlier dominant classes in check, and this emancipation created conditions whereby the proletariat would also emancipate itself, first by becoming like the bourgeoisie, and then by overthrowing it.

2.4 Legitimization of Modern Values

Not only is the asymmetry between the impersonal and personal forms of understanding implicit in Western social theories, these theories have actually helped to legitimate this asymmetry as intrinsically desirable, and to make it an important and valued aspect of Western culture. To see this, it is only necessary to remark upon the way these theories have conditioned the discussion of valued goals in society. To give but a few examples:

1. *Exchange Theory*: impersonal relations between buyer and seller ensure freedom of exchange. In many writings, this is seen as a primary form of freedom.
2. *Production Theory*: impersonal relations between employers and employees ensure that resources will flow to their most efficient uses.
3. *Jurisprudence*: 'blindness' of justice, and the principle of natural law, 'that no man shall be a judge in his own cause', suggest that impersonal relations between the judge and the litigants are necessary to ensure justice.
4. *Education Theory*: the separation of the content of education from the personality of the participants may be necessary not only for the pursuit of efficiency, but also to maintain the myth of the equality of opportunity.
5. *Political Science*: a bureaucratized, efficient state is seen as one which will be able to implement most effectively the will of the citizens, leading not only to effective decision-making, but also to the protection of freedoms.
6. *Technology*: the notion of experts, and the partitioning of knowledge that it entails, is legitimized on grounds of efficiency, as well as of innovation and growth.
7. *Moral Philosophy*: based on abstract rather than relational principles, it is legitimized on the grounds of it being universal and objective—and thus fair.
8. *Communication*: that a free, impersonal, and impartial press will provide true information, in contrast to the tainted news supplied by politically motivated sources.

The upshot of the argument is that core values like freedom, justice, equality, fairness, universality, efficiency, and growth, are all being seen through the prism of impersonality. As such, it is not only social theory which perceives a focus on impersonal relations to be useful for pedagogical or substantive purposes; rather, the view that core values of society can be safeguarded only by understanding everything through the lens of impersonality, has gradually become the dominant form of conscious belief in Western societies. This is not the place to go into a discussion of why such an evolution took place; suffice it to say that the legitimizing endeavours of social theorists played no small role in it, as also did the unprecedented economic growth which accompanied this process, and the tremendous social costs which were (and are still being) imposed on those who resisted its advance.

2.5 Alternative Approaches

The 'alternative' approaches discussed in the previous sections can be interpreted as being critical of the assumed superiority of the impersonal over the personal as a way of thinking about the world; and indeed one may go so far as to suggest that the primary objective of the modernist hierarchy is not pedagogy but control; not helping to understand the world, but rather helping to maintain existing (often oppressive) structures of power; not expanding human freedoms, but legitimizing the denial of sovereignty to the populations of the Third World, as also to the common men and women in Western countries.

Another basis for the alternative critique is the fear that since self-definitions are culturally determined, the acceptance of impersonality as socially desirable at an intellectual level can actually result in it becoming a dominant value at a popular level,[24] and that this may not in the long run be in the interest of human society.

The above arguments have their roots in the familiar criticism of the hegemonic panopticism[25] inherent in Western liberalism's method of binary opposition; in the supposed hierarchical rather than dialectical relation between health/sickness, truth/error, objectivity/subjectivity, universality/contexuality, purpose/drift (spontaneity), light/dark, Apollo/Dionysus, or stability/volatility (Spanos 1985; Chapter 4 below). Following these critiques, I would argue that many of the seemingly insoluble problems of today's world stem precisely from the implicit assumption of a dichotomy and a hierarchy between the impersonal and the personal spheres of culture, and that in our search for solutions we need to replace this hierarchy with the notion of a tension or a dialectic between the two.

So what does this alternative perspective propose about possible ways

24. Modernity is often said to have universalized the market as a social mechanism, but the reverse effect has not been given equal attention, namely that the impersonal relations expressed through a market exchange are also important for modernity to have continued to maintain its hold on peoples' consciousness.

25. The term 'panopticism' suggests centralized surveillance and control. It comes from the 'panopticon', an ingenious building design suggested by Jeremy Bentham, the father of utilitarian liberalism, in 1787, as a model for the construction of prisons, factories, schools, houses for correction, homes for deserted young women, nurseries, lunatic asylums, and even chicken coops. It was a circular building with a central surveillance kiosk and listening tubes, constructed in such a way that a single warden could see and hear all the inmates without being seen by them. See Foucault 1978, part 3, ch. 3; 1980, ch. 8.

out? At this stage, it can be suggested that the assumption that the impersonal world-view is the only important and relevant one for understanding human behaviour is seriously flawed; the inadequacy of the incomplete theory manifests itself in the form of poor predictive power,[26] as well as in the breaking down of the economic system wherever such predictive ability is used for prescriptive purposes.[27] This approach needs to be replaced by a more complete analytical framework, one which will take into account the underlying tension between the two modes of self-definition. In particular, it is possible to reverse the fundamental assumption of economic theory—that all actions are reducible to the impersonal aspect of behaviour—and to see human actions as deriving from a tension between conflicting obligations and commitments.

Some specific ideas, listed below, are intended to indicate two things. First, that in practice social systems are based on an admixture of the personal and impersonal perspectives, notwithstanding the overemphasis of the modernization approach on the latter. Second, that a perfectly coherent and logical argument could be based on the 'personal' map just as easily as on the modernizers' exclusive reliance on impersonal arguments. It is not to be inferred from these descriptions that a well-ordered and humane society could exist and endure based only on one of these two supports.

1. *Exchange Theory*: economics assumes that 'no one enters into an exchange unless she or he is thereby made better off'. In contrast, one can suggest that people might enter into exchanges to sustain durable human relationships; an 'economic' exchange is only the limiting form of such a relationship, where the expected duration of time is zero. The entire discussion on gift and reciprocity becomes relevant in this issue (Sahlins 1972: chs. 4–5).

2. *Production Theory*: in production, the same type of arguments would apply, since the 'exchange' of labour for wages may be determined as much by social and relational factors as by abstract needs and attributes. (See the excellent discussion by Donham 1981.)

3. *Jurisprudence*: Legal arrangements based on the institution of village elders employ the maxim that no one shall judge a cause unless they are interested in the welfare of the participants. This corresponds to the notion of 'punishment as atonement', and not 'punishment as retribution'. Legal systems always combine the two principles, for example into 'courts of law *and equity*', as the British institutions are called.

4. *Education*: elaborate systems of education have been based on a direct personal relation between the teacher and the student, and the interest of

26. Such ineffectiveness in prediction is often remarked upon in the case of Third World countries, but it could apply equally well to the areas of economic theory in the West, where personal factors are important, but not given adequate recognition. The most obvious example would be wage behaviour.

27. This might include alienation and its attendant psychological problems, the increase in violence, declines in productivity, etc.

the teacher not only in the subject-matter, but also in the welfare of the student as a complete person. These include informal education (in the family, the neighbourhood), master–apprentice relationships, and even the structure of post-graduate education in Western countries.

5. *Political Science*: alternative approaches emphasize 'face-to-faceness', in other words, a political system built around personal relationships as a guarantee against oppression, a protection of rights, and the allocation of civic responsibilities (Service 1975).

6. *Technology*: to follow Stephen Marglin's distinction (Chapter 7 below), the 'impersonal' approach assumes that all knowledge is ultimately 'epistemic', and that the persistence of *techne* is a residual from the past. It could be argued that ultimately all real knowledge is based in the context, that *episteme* is really another form of *techne*. Lastly, that while knowledge has to be organized somehow, in order to be rendered comprehensible, it could be done along a dimension which would make it accessible to participants in an immediate and socially relevant fashion, around a (social or natural) community, rather than around an impersonal discipline.

7. *Moral Philosophy*: relational values can be the basis of a moral philosophy, which emphasizes claims and obligations—to people, to animals, to nature in general, to the community—rather than abstract and universal principles. (A variation of this argument has been made by Gilligan 1982.)

8. *Communication*: that one trusts information only from a trusted source, notably from a person who is interested in the welfare of the recipient of the information. The success and popularity of television newscasters who 'appear sincere' is a testimony to the fact that people, even in Western countries, use personal judgements in evaluating the soundness of the information.

It will be noted immediately that notwithstanding the overt belief in the superiority of the impersonal, these alternative perceptions continue to exist even in modern societies; indeed, it is possible that their existence is what makes these societies human and liveable. In other words, this implies that the current crisis in development theory has the potential of suggesting alternative ways of thinking about such basic values as progress, freedom, and social change, not only for the Third World, but also and perhaps more importantly for the Other Worlds of this planet. These alternative ways of thinking have embedded in them alternative prescriptions for action, whether individual or collective, and alternative suggestions for institutional and social reform. Rather than look very generally at some social values and preferences, I shall focus on the issue of freedom and oppression to guide the discussion on the issue of the long-term impact of the impersonality postulate.

2.6 Culture and Values

To go from behaviour to values, we need to reopen some settled questions. Development theory had accepted uncritically the notion that progress in

Table 2. A Taxonomy of Cultural Constraints

	Impersonal	Personal
External	property rights	status, prestige
Internal	universal morality	contextual morality

the Third World is identical to a progressive emulation of the social, political, and economic institutions in Western countries. Once this certainty is questioned, there arises the need for a new definition of progress to begin the discussion.

Ashis Nandy (1987a) has provided a definition, to which, I believe, there should be little opposition. He defines progress as 'an expansion in the awareness of oppression'. The assumption is that it is the awareness of oppression which creates resistance, and hence leads to its melioration. Since oppression is directly related to the notions of freedom and domination, this definition can be used as a starting-point to discuss the specific role played by modernizing theories in human emancipation.

All cultural systems recognize the need for interdependence of people in a society, and hence of the existence of constraints upon their behaviour. To analyse these issues, we can distinguish between 'internal' (i.e., those stemming from the individual's self-definition) and 'external' constraints (i.e. those stemming from the individual's recognition of certain or probable loss of personal utility if the constraints are violated).

In each category, we can further distinguish between 'personal' or 'impersonal' constraints, depending respectively on whether they are imposed in the context of a personal relationship, or by an impersonal agency.

Finally, in every particular situation, a constraint could either be 'acceptable' or 'unacceptable', and, if the latter, would give rise to a situation of un-freedom and resistance. 'Acceptability' means, in the case of internal constraints, that they are consistent with one's self-definition; and in the case of external constraints, that they are considered to be legitimate. Before I discuss this, however, it would be useful to give names to these constraints. This is done in a diagrammatic summary (see Table 2).

The acceptability or unacceptability of constraints derives from the socialized notions of freedom and fairness. In the approach taken and legitimized by modern social theory, it is only the impersonal constraints which are considered to be 'fair' or acceptable, and only the external constraints which are considered necessary or reliable.[28] As such, it is

28. In the case of internal constraints, this is self-evident in the superiority accorded to universal over contextual or relational morality (see Gilligan 1982). Similarly, for external constraints, it is equally obvious in the notion of 'rule of law', or a criticism of 'paternalism'; in the delegitimation of the authority of those who have a direct

also possible to understand the introduction of modernity as an attempt
to replace personal and internal forms of constraints with impersonal and
external ones. The shift in our perception of the natural environment,
from one which saw it as a personal constraint to the modern view of it
as an impersonal constraint, has been noted and criticized by a number
of psychologists.[29] A devastating critique of this trend is offered in a
proposal for a new 'dialogue with nature', made by the Nobel Laureate
physicist Ilya Prigogine (with Isabelle Stengers, 1984) to avoid the
destructive social and environmental implications of the profound and
implacable silence which (paradoxically, since the self-awareness of the
'rational' man was necessary for the dialogue) greeted the post-Newtonian
attempt at such a dialogue.

2.6.1 Constraints and Property Rights   In social theory, external
constraints are often referred to as 'property rights', which are supported
by two institutions: the market and the state. The former facilitates social
interaction once property rights are generally accepted, while the latter
ensures that they will be so accepted. Economic theory considers the
creation and expansion of property rights to lead to freedom, and the
absence of such rights, referred to as 'externalities', to lead not only to
inefficiency and sub-optimal performance, but often also to social conflict
and un-freedom.

However, the creation of rights alone is not enough; they also need to
be enforced. *Ubi jus, ibi remedium*, says the legal maxim, 'where there is
a right, there is a remedy'. In other words, 'if there is no remedy, there
is no right': in order to obtain the desired solution, it is also required
that a legitimate enforcement mechanism be created, hence the state.

This position has several problems, not the least of which is the fact
that property rights can suffice for the creation of a free and harmonious
society only if they can cover all possible transactions. Given the necessity
of enforcement mechanisms, however, one can expect either an increase
in surveillance and monitoring of individuals, or an increase in punitive
costs, such as a threat of starvation or a direct expansion of terror in
society.[30] These two tendencies are increasingly apparent throughout the
world today as the modernization project makes headway.

personal interest in the welfare of whoever is subject to such constraints; as also in the
increased legitimacy of the authority of impersonal agents, be they law-enforcers,
managers of organizations, sellers of products or of expertise, or those fulfilling a
contract.

29. See, for example, Hillman 1976. He argues that many problems in psychoanalysis as
well as in social functioning can be traced back to the depersonification of nature. He
is loosely in the Jungian tradition of archetypal psychology, although he is criticized by
many Jungian psychologists for being a deviant.

30. For an analysis of these consequences, see Bowles and Gintis 1986: ch. 5. Also see
Berger 1976 and the various works by Foucault on panopticism, particularly 1978, 1980.

Another problem pointed out by several writers, beginning with Adam Smith in the *Theory of Moral Sentiments* (1976), is the idea that the pursuit of self-interest in economic matters is socially desirable only if everyone (or almost everyone) follows a generally recognized moral code and has a shared sense of justice; in other words, if there are sufficient internal constraints. Durkheim 1933 goes one step further to argue that impersonal constraints need to be complemented by personal ones; in his terms, given the uncertainty surrounding our actions, it is not possible for a social system to be based purely on 'contractual solidarity', and that 'organic solidarity' is necessary for the smooth functioning of the economy. For the fact of the matter is that the inculcation of internal restraints also requires the acceptance of personal constraints. Notwithstanding the behaviourist school of psychology, it is difficult to imagine that rewards and punishment by an impersonal authority will suffice to teach moral values; this approach is more likely to induce behaviour aiming to beat the system.

The shift from personal to impersonal constraints, and from internal to external ones, has three important consequences. First, it creates a strong advantage for centralized organizations, since such organizations are consistent only with strongly centralized forms of control and acceptance of impersonal authority; as such, this induces people to form organizations simply in order to defend themselves against organized or collective forces. Also, as noted, they are accompanied by the establishment of powerful and impersonal structures of surveillance and control at the level of knowledge (technology), politics (organization), and architecture, which are to a certain degree irreversible.

Second, the imposition of such structures is resisted by people as a loss of their sovereignty, and has to be introduced by force. Such resistance is strongest where the penetration of impersonality is the most widespread, and where the cultural community is the most self-assured.

Third, it is generally possible to wean away only the younger people to this new form of thinking, and as such it requires the undermining of the authority of their elders. All of these developments can be recognized as part of the process of the introduction of modern values and institutions. As such, I would see the rise of various forms of resistance to modernization as a rejection of the above changes in society.

2.6.2 Culture as Resistance   While each of the above changes reinforces the others, and so cannot really be addressed in isolation, the discussion can be started from the one which is most directly connected to the issue of freedom and resistance, i.e. the shift from personal to impersonal constraints. Note that resistance of whatever form is associated with the existence of unacceptable constraints upon one's behaviour, and of a general absence of freedoms. Hence, if impersonal constraints are not recognized to be fair and just in a society, their imposition is likely to be resisted; thus differences between various theorists over the interpretation of cultural resistance stem from underlying differences over definitions of freedom and of acceptable constraints.

Now, the acceptability or otherwise of these constraints arises from the nature of the world-view and self-definition imparted by a cultural system. Internal constraints emerging from one social role may be unacceptable if they come into conflict with the needs of another role; likewise, if they come into conflict with the notion of the rights and needs of the abstract individual. Conversely, external constraints imposed by legal or contractual obligations, or by paternalistic intervention, may be unacceptable if they come into conflict with implicit notions of social relationships or of abstract rights.[31] As discussed earlier, this conflict plays itself out in every decision, and alters the nature of the underlying roles and relationships.[32]

Be the above as it may, it is useful to ask how people respond to the introduction of impersonal constraints. In a completely impersonal environment, such constraints can and often do create incentives for evasion. In a personal environment, on the other hand, they create incentives for the 'humanization' of the constraints—by changing the nature of relationship through loyalty, submission, and even resistance, but above all by the establishment of personal connections.[33] In both cases, there will be a decline in the short-term efficiency of the operation, either through non-co-operation or through the introduction of un-predictable personal factors into the equation. In many instances, however, the long-term efficiency will actually increase through greater motivation as well as through a better recognition of implicit costs and benefits.

To summarize, the above argument raises three issues: first, that external constraints are not sufficient by themselves to establish a harmonious

31. As Gilligan 1982 has shown, it is possible to argue from both perspectives. We can say that there is a conflict between two abstract attributes, loyalty and truthfulness; or that there is a conflict between two social roles/relationships.

32. This point arises in the elegant critique levelled at Western liberal theory by Bowles and Gintis 1986. They argue that the notions of freedom and democracy in liberal political thought were strongly grounded in a separation between 'learners' and 'choosers'. While the latter were thought to be fully formed individuals, who had the right to make choices without any unnecessary constraints, the former (i.e. children, workers, people from non-European cultures or races) were implicitly regarded as unready for such a responsibility, and therefore to be denied this freedom while they were in the learning stage. We can take their argument one step further, and raise the issue that, after all is said and done, 'learning' does require a submission of the ego, and hence the acceptance of external constraints, and the problem is not so much in the fact that 'learners' do not have freedom of choice, but rather that people are placed in this category only to sustain and legitimize the existing distribution of power; and, more importantly, that these constraints over the 'learners' are intended to be impersonal in character.

33. See Scott 1976 for an analysis of peasant resistance and protest in an alternative cultural setting. Also see Janeway 1981 for an argument on the ability of the 'weak' to create autonomy and challenge oppression.

society; second, that the inculcation of internal constraints requires the strengthening of personal connections; and finally, that the imposition of impersonal constraints is resisted by various methods. The last point carries us back to the observed sources of dissatisfaction in Third World countries today, since, as I have argued, this dissatisfaction is related not to any new costs of modernization, but to the establishment and multiplication of impersonal constraints.

Accordingly, I interpret the resistance of 'traditional' cultures to 'modern' values and practices as an attempt to avert problems which arise on account of this asymmetry, and to retain control over their own actions and their own environments. Development theory had set for itself the task of breaking down this resistance and thereby facilitating the introduction of modernity into the midst of traditional cultures. The abandonment of this project would require a re-evaluation of the built-in cultural biases of the theory, and cannot be restricted to a marginal change here or there.

3 Progress, Welfare, and Development

Modernization theories present us with a vision of the future, a 'theory of salvation' in Ashis Nandy's words (1987a: 22), based on the presumed superiority of the impersonal world-view and the alleged untenability and undesirability of personal constraints upon action. They promised an end to the oppression created by poverty, under the assumption that whatever actions were adopted in pursuit of this goal would have no deleterious effect on other aspects of human freedoms, and could in fact provide a positive stimulus to those as well. The history of the last four decades tells another story, as the levels of state-sponsored oppression as well as civic violence in most countries have increased exponentially. It is possible to argue that notwithstanding the justification of modernity as a means of enhancing human freedoms in the Third World, it has served invariably to reduce freedom and to deny sovereignty to people wherever it has been introduced, and that the target of popular protest and resistance is precisely this disenfranchisement.

In the search for an alternative vision, I started with the notion of progress as being 'the expansion of the awareness of oppression in society', and argued that contrary to the claims of modernization theorists there is no positive relationship between impersonality and progress; indeed, in the modern world it is possible to infer the existence of an inverse relationship between the two. This, however, is only a negative comment. To go from this to a positive vision of the future as contained in the 'alternative' writings, the following points can be made.

First of all, this definition of progress is rather vague and general, but that is deliberate. It is an attempt precisely to deny the validity and legitimacy of universal and objective definitions, and thus to transfer the power of defining the problems and goals of a society from the hands of outside experts into those of the members of the society itself. In our view, the main problem with the debate on the 'meaning of development' was its aim of 'technocratizing' the notion of progress, of simplifying and quantifying it in such a fashion that anyone equipped with a handy and simple tool-kit could pronounce judgement on the desirability of a course of action or a set of policies for any group of people, whether or not the evaluator had any direct interest in their welfare.

Gilles Deleuze recently characterized Michel Foucault's contribution to social theory in the following words, 'You have taught us something absolutely fundamental: The indignity of speaking on someone else's behalf' (quoted in Sheridan 1980: 114). The criticism of the debate on the 'meaning of development' and the replacement of economistic measures with a broader social definition is motivated by this very concern, the indignity of speaking on someone else's behalf. In other words, the idea is that as communities became aware of oppression, whether it stems from ignorance, poverty, or other natural causes, or from injustice and inequity, they will define their own priorities and undertake social and political action to articulate and pursue them. On occasion, this may entail a prior emphasis on such conventional objectives as economic growth, consumption, industrialization, equity, or basic needs. On other occasions, other goals may assume greater importance, such as political participation, social harmony, ecological conservation, or the maintenance of social and cultural values. It is not for the outside expert to insist that the goals which she or he thinks worth pursuing are the ones which should be pursued by all societies.

However, the alternative vision of progress is not confined to de-legitimizing the role of the expert, even though that is important. Once the role of the expert is called into question, other issues also emerge. The first is that of the theory of change which forms the basis of the theory of progress. The legitimization of the experts' definition of progress stems from the assertion of a crisis in the region of interest, which is used to justify immediate action for the amelioration of the problem, and thus the legitimacy of large-scale and centralized intervention and the concomitant loss of sovereignty of the people. Note however, that 'immediate action' means simply that the government or other centralized bodies will feel justified in their actions, not that the problems which require such attention will be resolved: witness the snail's progress on such 'crisis' issues as poverty, hunger, malnutrition, and environmental damage, among many others.

This does not mean that there are no crises in the Third World which require immediate action. A shared sense of a crisis may exist over some extreme situations (e.g. a famine or an epidemic) in some parts of the

Third World, and in these cases immediate action would be fruitful, in part because the urgency of the situation would help in mobilizing the populace for necessary action. But such extreme situations are rare. In other places, while there may be many problems, the absence of a shared sense of crisis means that centralized interventions will not only be ineffective, but may actually create more problems than they can or do solve. Indeed, in most places, it will be discovered that the crisis, if any, stems precisely from the centralized intervention itself.

The alternative vision starts with a denial of the legitimacy or even the desirability of these 'quick fixes'. Hence it must deny also the theory of discontinuous change which follows from the invocation of a crisis. This is replaced by a theory of continuous change, a change which takes place as the result of resistance, protest, and challenges from below, rather than from an imposition from above. In fact, the main task of the theorist, in this sense, is to help strengthen resistance against oppressive institutions.

A corollary of this approach is to cast doubt upon the legitimacy of the expert, who relies upon impersonal, universal, and 'objective' knowledge. Clearly, the legitimacy of experts is derived from the belief that they have a claim to truth by virtue of a superior understanding of social phenomena. The manifest failures of the developmental project, however, cast doubt on such an unequivocal claim, not because economists, for example, do not understand economics, but because they do not understand politics, sociology, psychology, and other areas in which the policies of economists have induced pathologies and problems.

This means that the traditional division of social science into separate disciplines is not a useful way of approaching issues. It would be more productive to divide up the area of knowledge into geographical or cultural subdivisions. But if we do this, then the contextuality of knowledge will increase, making the expert, trained in universal sciences, an anachronism. Furthermore, as Jürgen Habermas has indicated, the claim to validity of someone speaking in a geographically isolated context would be based on 'truthfulness' (or 'sincerity') and not 'truth', and therefore be subject to various other stresses and strains (Habermas 1984: 75–101).

Second, the demand that this imposes on the social theorist is, in Tambiah's (1985) words, to take responsibility for the longer-run consequences of their prescriptions, including those which are normally the subject-matter of other disciplines.

Third, this approach will seek to legitimize and strengthen indigenous ways of knowing, particularly those based on a direct personal relationship with the limits of the social and physical environment; and will desist from creating élite ways of knowing which cannot be used by the subjects themselves. Given the prescription for resistance to impersonal intervention, it is obvious that the alternative approach will take place over a long time-span, and will not seek to create a new world overnight.

What will be the features of the longer-term objective?

The popular and intellectual resistance to processes favouring cent-ralization of authority, power, and knowledge indicate that a vision of the future in the Third World must explicitly be one of a decentralized polity, economy, and society. In addition to the obvious forms of political and economic decentralization, there is also a need for what may be termed epistemological decentralization.

At the political level, the role and function of the nation-state has come under a great degree of stress. Given the centralization of power and authority in the institutions of the modern state, it has been practically impossible for most Third World countries to maintain even a semblance of democracy for any significant length of time. Ethnic and linguistic differences in most of these countries have exacerbated the pressures on the state, as also have the dramatic increases in urban population, far faster than the increase in the governments' ability to manage the cities. It seems to us that a shift towards a decentralized polity is the only solution for most Third World societies.

Such decentralization would mean an increase in the powers and functions of 'local' governments, whether at the level of a village, a group of villages, small towns, or possible subdivisions of large cities. 'Increase in powers' refers to the ability to raise revenues, to spend them on development, redistribution, or on the maintenance of social peace. Such a system would also necessitate the establishment of institutions which can co-ordinate the actions of decentralized units. Decentralization also implies bringing the political unit to the level where the shared values and cognitive systems can facilitate the development and maintenance of 'organic solidarity', in Durkheim's words.

Legal decentralization would imply the transfer of legislative and executive powers to the decentralized units. Economic decentralization refers to the development of production systems which can facilitate direct participation in economic decision-making by people involved in the production process. This is related to the notion that the knowledge as well as action should be responsive to the environmental (social as well as physical) boundaries of the participants' world.

This notion of limits has a relationship with the notion of non-violence—with respect both to other human beings and to nature. Impersonal and instrumental forms of knowledge permit violence, un-derstood as actions which go beyond acceptable limits and are therefore irreversible in a larger social sense. This is exhibited in the wanton destruction of the environment which has become a fact of life in many parts of the Third World—deforestation, pollution, wasteful use of non-renewable energy and other materials—as well as in the organized forms of violence against human beings. The shift in perception away from this universal and impersonal perspective towards one based on direct human connections can help create the notion of sustainable development as a fundamental human value, and therefore also the basis for popular resistance against violence.

In my view, however, the most important issue is that of epistemological decentralization. This means the approach to knowledge which emphasizes its shared nature. Repeated experiences in the Third World (as well as recently in the West), have shown that alien forms of knowledge can be accepted by people in a situation of crisis, or as a temporary measure, but not in 'normal' times as a permanent feature of social existence. For example, there is the common observation that it is easy to build systems (e.g. factories, transport systems, other urban services) in the Third World but very difficult to maintain them. The first can be accepted as a temporary feature, but the second requires a radical shift in orientation which is difficult to bring about. The only solution is to cast the problem in the indigenous metaphor, whether of ritual or science. The idea behind this line of argument is that systems should be looked at in terms of their susceptibility to popular control, rather than to technical efficiency or the like.

Finally, it should be clear that a vision of this type is simply a means of organizing ideas, of indicating the possibility of alternatives. The details must differ from place to place in accordance with the specific cultural characteristics peculiar to each place.

REFERENCES

Attewell, Paul (1984) *Radical Political Economy Since The Sixties: A Sociology of Knowledge Analysis*, New Brunswick, NJ: Rutgers University Press.

Becker, Gary (1974) 'A Theory of Marriage', *Journal of Political Economy* (July–Aug., 1973), 813–46 (Mar.–Apr., 1974), 11–26.

Berger, Peter (1976) *Pyramids of Sacrifice*, New York: Doubleday.

Boeke, J. H. (1953) *Economics and Economic Policy of Dual Societies*, New York: Institute of Pacific Relations.

Bowles, S., and Gintis, H. (1986) *Democracy and Capitalism: Property, Community, and the Contradictions of Modern Social Thought*, New York: Basic Books.

Caldwell, Bruce (1982) *Beyond Positivism: Economic Methodology in The Twentieth Century*, London: George, Allen and Unwin.

Das, Veena, and Nicholas, Ralph (1982) *'Welfare' and 'Well-being' in South Asian Societies*, ACLS-SSRC Joint Committee on South Asia, Subcommittee on South Asian Political Economy—Project II.

Donham, Donald L. (1981) 'Beyond the Domestic Mode of Production', *Man*, 16/4: 515–41.

Dumont, Louis (1977) *From Mandeville to Marx*, Chicago: University of Chicago Press.

—— (1980) *Homo Hierarchicus: The Caste System and its Implications*, trans. Mark Sainsbury, Louis Dumont, and Basia Gulati, revised English edn., Chicago: University of Chicago Press.

Durkheim, E. (1933) *The Division of Labor in Society*, New York: The Free Press.

Durkheim, E. (1951) *Suicide*, trans. J. A. Spaulding and G. Simpson, edited and introduced by G. Simpson, Glencoe, Ill.: The Free Press.

Ellul, J. (1964) *The Technological Society*, New York: Alfred A. Knopf.

Foucault, Michel (1978) *Discipline and Punish: The Birth of the Prison*, trans. Alan Sheridan, New York: Pantheon.

—— (1980) *Power/Knowledge: Selected Interviews and Other Writings 1972–77*, trans. Colin Gordon, Brighton, Sussex: Harvester Press.

Geertz, C. (1973) *The Interpretation of Cultures*, New York: Basic Books.

Gilligan, Carol (1982) *In a Different Voice: Psychological Theory and Women's Development*, Cambridge, Mass.: Harvard University Press.

Godelier, Maurice (1972), *Rationality and Irrationality in Economics*, New York: Monthly Review Press.

Guha, Ramachandra (1985) 'Eco-Development Debate: A Critical Review', *South Asian Anthropologist*, 6/1: 15–24.

Habermas, Jürgen (1984) *The Theory of Communicative Action*, Boston: Beacon Press.

Hillman, James (1976) *Re-Visioning Psychology*, New York: Harper & Row.

Hirschman, Albert O. (1981) 'The Turn to Authoritarianism in Latin America and the Search For Economic Determinants', in *Essays in Tresspassing*, Cambridge: Cambridge University Press.

Huntington, Samuel P. (1968) *Political Order in Changing Societies*, New Haven: Yale University Press.

Inkeles, Alex, and Smith David, (1974) *Becoming Modern*, Cambridge, Mass.: Harvard University Press.

Janeway, E. (1981) *Powers of The Weak*, New York: Alfred A. Knopf.

Lasch, Christopher (1979) *The Culture of Narcissism: American Life in an Age of Diminishing Expectations*, New York: W. W. Norton.

Leibenstein, Harvey (1976), *Beyond Economic Man*, Cambridge, Mass.: Harvard University Press.

McPherson, C. B. (1962) *The Political Theory of Possessive Individualism*, New York: Oxford University Press.

Mead, George H. (1934) *Mind, Self and Society*, ed. C. W. Morris, Chicago, Ill.: University of Chicago Press.

Nandy, Ashis (1987a) 'Towards A Third World Utopia', in *Traditions, Tyrannies, and Utopias: Essays in the Politics of Awareness*, New Delhi: Oxford University Press.

—— (1987b) 'The Politics of Secularism and the Recovery of Religious Tolerance', Delhi: Center for the Study of Developing Societies (mimeo).

Parsons, Talcott (1954) *Essays in Sociological Theory*, Glencoe, Ill.: The Free Press.

Polanyi, Karl (1944) *The Great Transformation: The Political and Economic Origins of Our Times*, Boston: Beacon Press.

Popkin, Sam (1979) *The Rational Peasant*, Berkeley, Calif.: University of California Press.

Prigogine, Ilya, and Stengers, Isabelle (1984) *Order Out of Chaos: Man's New Dialogue With Nature*, New York: Bantam Books.

Resnick, Stephen A., and Wolff, Richard D. (1982) 'Marxist Epistemology: The Critique of Economic Determinism', *Social Text*, 6: 31–72.

Rorty, Richard (1979) *Philosophy and the Mirror of Nature*, Princeton, NJ: Princeton University Press.

Sahlins, Marshall (1972) *Stone Age Economics*, New York: Aldine.

Schumacher, E. F. (1973) *Small is Beautiful: Economics As if People Mattered*, New York: Harper & Row.

Scott, James C. (1976) *The Moral Economy of The Peasant: Rebellion and Subsistence in South East Asia*, New Haven: Yale University Press.

Seers, D. (1969) 'The Meaning of Development', *International Development Review* (Dec.), 11: 2–6.

Sen, Amartya (1977) 'Rational Fools: A Critique of the Behavioural Foundations of Economic Theory', *Philosophy and Public Affairs*, 6: 317–44.

Service, Elman (1975) *Origins of The State and Civilization: The Process of Cultural Evolution*, New York: W. W. Norton.

Sheahan, John (1980) 'Market-Oriented Economic Policies and Political Repression in Latin America', *Economic Development and Cultural Change* (Jan.), 28/2: 267–91.

Sheridan, A. (1980) *Michel Foucault: The Will to Truth*, London: Tavistock Publications Ltd.

Slater, Philip (1970) *The Pursuit of Loneliness: American Culture at the Breaking Point*, Boston: Beacon Press.

Smith, Adam (1976) *The Theory of Moral Sentiments*, Oxford: Clarendon Press. Originally published in 1759.

Spanos, W. A. (1985) 'The Apollonian Investment of Modern Humanist Education: The Examples of Matthew Arnold, Irving Babitt, and I. A. Richard', *Cultural Critique*, 1/1: 7–72.

Tambiah, Stanley J. (1985) 'An Anthropologist's Creed', Harvard University, Anthropology Department (mimeo).

Uberoi, J. S. (1978) *Science and Culture*, New Delhi: Oxford University Press.

Weber, Max (1930) *The Protestant Ethic and the Spirit of Capitalism*, trans. T. Parsons, London: George Allen and Unwin.

——(1947) *The Theory of Social and Economic Organization*, trans. A. M. Henderson and T. Parsons, New York: Oxford University Press.

Weiner, Annette B. (1978) 'The Reproductive Model in Trobriand Society', in J. Specht and J. Peter White (eds.), *Trade and Exchange in Oceania and Australia*, special issue of *Mankind*, 11/3: 175–86.

4

Smallpox in Two Systems of Knowledge

FRÉDÉRIQUE APFFEL MARGLIN

1 Introduction

This chapter challenges the claim of Western science to be a superior form of knowledge which renders obsolete more traditional systems of knowledge. Today the adjective 'non-scientific' is often used synonymously with 'irrational'. A system of knowledge which makes no distinction between naturalistic forms of explanation and religious forms of explanation is deemed irrational and inferior. Although the knowledge system of Western scientific medicine has come under critical scrutiny by several scholars (Canguilhem 1978; Foucault 1975; Illich 1976; Turner 1984), it has rarely been the focus of challenge in the context of development studies. In this realm, the Western scientific medical system is spared scrutiny because of the widely shared belief that it is superior to other methods.

For my critical appraisal I have deliberately chosen a case which has been seen as an unqualified success: the eradication of smallpox. Through this case I intend to challenge the entire project of modernization. In order to do so I will draw upon Derrida's[1] deconstructive method and focus on the type of binary oppositions which underlie the dominant strands in Western systems of knowledge. Oppositions such as rationality/irrationality, subject/object, health/illness, mind/body, life/death, nature/culture, and many more, form the structure which upholds systems of thought particular to much of the Western tradition. This system of thought has been labelled 'logocentrism' by Derrida and renamed 'phallogocentrism' by feminists. It is a system of thought which posits first principles and ultimately *a* first principle, an ultimate ground or *logos* which lies outside the system of differences which constitutes meaning in language. According to Derrida,[2] all acts of signification depend on difference. For example, the sound *bat* is a signifier because it contrasts with *pat, mat, bad, bed*, etc. The noise that is present when one says *bat* is inhabited by the traces of forms one is not uttering. The sound *bat* can

1. For a succinct and readable discussion of Derrida see Culler 1982; see also Eagleton 1984 and Derrida 1976, 1979.
2. For the Anglo-Saxon tradition arguing for the ultimate relativity of meaning in all acts of signification, see Mertz and Parmentier 1985; see also Lakoff 1987.

function as a signifier only in so far as it consists of such traces. What is voiced is marked by all the sounds that are not voiced; the presence of the sound is a product of unvoiced contrasting sounds, a product of differences.[3] Each element in a system of signification is constituted by reference to the trace in it of the other elements in the system. Binary oppositions of the exclusive type function precisely by negating this fact. One element of the opposition is defined as the absolute absence of the other element. Binary oppositions are of the logical form A/not A. Irrationality is what is *not* rational. Nature is what is *not* culture. Health is the absence of illness; and so forth. Oppositions such as subject/object, nature/culture, and mind/body are fundamental in the dominant currents in Western thought. They underlie and frame the very possibility of discourse; they ground thinking in the very reality of things.

Smallpox in modern medical discourse is a disease, and health is the absence of disease. There is an absolute boundary between the two terms which mutually define each other as presence and absence. Smallpox in non-modern India is a goddess who is *both* the presence and the absence of the disease. Goddess Śītalā is both the disease and its cure or its absence, health. The former view of smallpox is part of a logocentric mode of thought and the latter view part of a non-logocentric mode of thought. In this chapter I am particularly interested in the political implications of these two contrasting modes of thought.

The logocentric view of smallpox rests on a particular strand in biomedicine which is based on the assumption of a single necessary and sufficient cause for each disease. It is a strand which was much reinforced by the discovery of the germ theory of disease and which leads to the logic of eradication, as well as to the universalizing of medical knowledge and the transfer of technology world-wide.[4] This strand competes with another one in epidemiology, medical ecology. Medical ecology is in fact much closer to the indigenous non-logocentric mode of thought discussed in this chapter. In this area of biomedicine there is no clear boundary between health and disease, no exclusive dichotomy. In such a view disease is a process of interaction and adaptation between a host and its environment. Such a view is critical of eradication and instead proposes prevention and control as public health measures.[5]

The worship of Goddess Śītalā and the traditional practice of prophylaxis called 'variolation' were not part of any of the realms of 'high' medical

3. For an extended discussion of this issue see Culler 1982: 96–8.
4. Major spokesmen for this tradition in public health medicine are Charles Chapin in the early 20th century in the US and Fred Soper more recently. See Kunitz 1987: 381–3. I am particularly grateful to Arthur Kleinman for this reference.
5. Two of the most eloquent proponents of this view are John Gordon (see Kunitz 1987: 39) and René Dubos. Dubos 1972 argues for the impossibility of eradication of infectious diseases and warns that unless life is lived in closer accordance with the requirements of the ecosystem, the death of the human race will occur.

culture in the subcontinent such as Ayurveda, Unani, or Siddha. According to the historian Paul Greenough, the variolators were not physicians. Variolation was

imbedded in a series of ritual acts principally intended to ward off the anger of the smallpox goddess and was therefore unlikely to have been conceived of as a medical procedure at all. Like snake-charming and spirit-expelling, it seems to have been regarded as a useful, specialized religio-somatic practice that by Indian norms did not intersect with the cultural realm of medicine (Greenough 1987: 19).

However, I argue in Sections 3.1 and 3.2 that there are continuities between basic Ayurvedic practices and practices surrounding the cult of Śītalā.

The resounding success of the World Health Organization's programme to eradicate smallpox world-wide—achieved officially in 1977—has produced several scholarly studies on the history of smallpox. Before Jenner's discovery of vaccination with cowpox at the end of the eighteenth century there existed several traditional methods of coping with and containing the disease. The method which will be examined in this paper is the one employed in India, called 'variolation' or 'inoculation'. This consisted in inoculating healthy persons by pricking the skin with a needle impregnated with human smallpox matter. (By contrast, vaccination uses cowpox matter.) The technical operation was accompanied by worship of the goddess of smallpox. The two aspects of the treatment were not experienced or thought of as being separate or as belonging to two different modes of thought and action.

Vaccination was brought to India shortly after it was discovered in England, in the very first years of the nineteenth century. There, unlike in Europe and the Americas, it did not displace variolation, which continued to be preferred by the bulk of the Indian population. In spite of several reports by British physicians on the efficacy of variolation for controlling smallpox epidemics, the British government in India outlawed variolation in 1865. This action by the colonial government dealt a death blow to the practice and knowledge of the variolators, which has irretrievably disappeared, although the worship of Śītalā continues. The present study questions the validity of the view that considers the loss of such knowledge no real loss since it has been supplanted by a superior form of knowledge, that of vaccination and the monocausal view of disease.

After outlawing variolation, the colonial government proceeded to make vaccination compulsory in several provinces. Resistance to vaccination became a political phenomenon protesting against an alien rule and the imposition of an alien practice. After Independence in 1947 the Government of India made smallpox vaccination the top priority of its public health programme. The popular resistance to vaccination continued. It was seen by both foreign experts and governmental experts and administrators as evidence of the obscurantist and superstitious nature of India's masses.

During the colonial era vaccination and the system of knowledge that came with it was imposed by fiat. After Independence the domination of this system continued by default since indigenous knowledge was lost. However, it is doubtful that even if variolation had not disappeared, the modern experts and administrators of India's independent government would have considered it a real alternative. The scientific system of knowledge is dominant in the world of development experts and the élites of the new nation-states of the Third World. It is a system which takes as axiomatic the separation between rational thought and beliefs in 'supernatural beings'.[6] By contrast variolation was embedded in religious belief and practice, and the resistance to vaccination in India was in the name of the goddess of smallpox. Therefore resistance was seen not as a political act but as obscurantism and superstition. Such a position needs to be challenged not only because it is fallacious but also because it is dangerous, as well as morally arrogant.

The danger of labelling resistance to vaccination in the name of Śītalā as obscurantism and superstition is that it forecloses the need to examine the political entailments of the state's vaccination programme. By being identified as superstitious, overcoming resistance by any means is justified.

Rituals and festivals in honour of Śītalā are perceived as inefficacious methods of dealing with smallpox. Such a view tends to obscure a different efficacy of such rituals which—after the loss of the knowledge of variolation—lies outside the field of epidemic control. Their present efficacy lies in their ability to regenerate the community, to create or re-create social congruence. In a word, they have political efficacy. Such regeneration—as will be seen in a later part of this chapter where such a ritual is discussed in detail (Section 3.3)—arises out of a communal immersion in the symbolic illness of the deities. Health, renewed life, can only be achieved through an immersion in illness and death. Every twelve years the deities actually die. In this system, health is not the absence of illness, nor life the absence of death. For health and life to reassert themselves, illness and death have to be experienced. The presence of health and of life depend on the presence of illness and of death, not on their absence. We are here faced with a non-logocentric mode of thought. This chapter examines the political implications of both logocentric and non-logocentric systems of knowledge.

2 Variolation and Vaccination

2.1 Variolation: Indigenous Disease Control

Long before Jenner's discovery of vaccination using cowpox matter in 1798, there is evidence for the widespread use in several parts of the

6. I put these terms in quotation marks because in a Hindu context the word 'supernatural' is a misnomer, as I will argue further on in this chapter.

world of variation (also called 'inoculation'). This method utilizes human smallpox matter to inoculate susceptible persons previously unexposed to the deadly form of smallpox; 'the inoculee gets an attenuated case of smallpox—lower fever and less exanthema which is very rarely fatal and confers immunity from further infection' (Greenough 1980: 345). It differs chiefly from vaccination in that an inoculated person is fully contagious whereas a vaccinated person is not.

Variolation appears to have been brought into Europe during the seventeenth·century and is recorded to have been a folk practice among Polish, Greek, French, and Welsh peasants (Hopkins 1983: 46; *History of Inoculation and Vaccination* 1913). The folk practice, called 'buying the smallpox', was not utilized in urban centres, where the only method relied upon to control epidemics of smallpox was isolation and quarantine. At the turn of the century several reports of vastly more effective methods of disease control reached British physicians. In 1700 two reports reached the Royal Society describing the Chinese method of inoculation. This consisted of blowing the dust of powdered scabs from persons previously infected with a mild case of the disease into the nostrils of the susceptible person. In 1714 a Fellow of the Royal Society read a report of inoculation practices in Constantinople communicated to him by an Italian physician residing in that city. This consisted of scarification of the skin in 2 to 5 places with a needle until some blood appeared and dropping in those places from a bottle variolous matter freshly taken from the pustules of a naturally infected person (Hopkins 1983: 46).

This method was said by the Turks to have been introduced from Circassia (the region to the north-east of the Black Sea) some forty years earlier. It is identical to the one employed in the Arab world from the westernmost part of Africa to the Middle East. In 1726 Dr Russell, a British physician residing in Aleppo, reported this same method from a female bedouin informant who called it 'buying the smallpox'. He found that the practice was known to older people who remembered having heard of the custom from their elders (*History of Inoculation and Vaccination* 1913: 30–1).

The similarity in inoculation technique and in the name for the practice—'buying the smallpox'—points to the Arab origin of this European folk practice, reported as early as the second half of the seventeenth century from the northern shore of the Black Sea to the western part of North Africa.

The earliest report of variolation from India dates from 1731 (Dharampal 1971: 141–2 cited in Nicholas 1981: 28). It is described by one Robert Coult in a letter to a relative in England:

Their method of performing this operation is by taking a little of the pus (when the smallpox are come to maturity and are of a good kind) and dipping these in the point of a pretty large sharp needle. Therewith make several punctures in the hollow under the deltoid muscle or sometimes in the forehead, after which they cover the part with a little paste made of boiled rice.

The fever ensues later or sooner, according to the age and strength of the person inoculated, but commonly the third or fourth days. They keep the patient under the coolest regimen they can think of before the fever comes on and frequently use cold bathing.

From the description the technique seems to be identical to the Arab one. A later report (1767) by the British physician Holwell, also describing variolation practices in Bengal, reports what seems to be an improved version of the practice: scratching the skin with a needle, the variolator uses a piece of 'cotton, which he preserves in a double callico rag . . . saturated with matter from the inoculated pustules of the preceding year, for they never inoculate with fresh matter, nor with matter from the disease caught in the natural way, however distinct and mild the species' (Dharampal 1971: 150–3). 'Throughout the operation, the inoculator continuously recited the worship of the Smallpox Goddess, Gūṭikā Ṭhākurāṇī' (Nicholas 1981: 29). This represents a new and third method which seems greatly to lower the chances for the spread and eruption of the more severe form of the disease. This safer method never seems to have been introduced in Europe.

No student of the history of smallpox has been able to identify definitively where and when variolation was invented. The existence of three separate techniques would point towards multiple discovery. But given the trade links between the Arab world and India (Obeyesekere 1984: 530–5) and the similarity of the Arab and Indian techniques, diffusion from one to another is possible.

Dr Donald Hopkins of the Center for Disease Control in Atlanta, who himself participated in the World Health Organization campaign to eradicate smallpox, leans towards India as the originator of the scarification method of variolation: 'It is almost certain, however, that inoculation with smallpox virus was practiced in India in ancient times' (p. 17). He bases this opinion on the authority of a British army officer, one Colonel King (Colonel W. G. King of the Madras Medical Service, but not identified as such by Hopkins). King in turn relies on a text on variolation with both cow and human pox attributed to Dhanwantari, some two thousand years before Jenner: 'take the fluid of the pock on the udder of the cow and on the area between the shoulder and elbow of a human subject on the point of a lancet, and lance with it the arms between the shoulders and elbows until the blood appears. There, mixing this fluid with the blood, the fever of the smallpox will be produced' (*History of Inoculation and Vaccination*, 13–14).

A recent article by Dominik Wujastyk considers the origin and veracity of this quote. Wujastyk traces the Sanskrit quote to a fraud originally perpetrated to overcome native resistance to vaccination in India at the beginning of the nineteenth century. He quotes Baron, the biographer of Jenner, who enquired from an eminent Sanskritist, Sir John Malcolm, concerning this report (Baron 1827: 557 in Wujastyk 1988: 145):

On the introduction of vaccine inoculation into India it was found that the practice was much opposed by the natives. In order to overcome their prejudice the late Mr. Ellis, of Madras, who was well versed in Sanskrit literature, actually composed a short poem in that language on the subject of vaccination. This poem was inscribed on old paper, and said to have been found, that the impression of its antiquity might assist the effect intended to be produced in the minds of the Brahmins while tracing the preventive to their sacred cow. The late Dr. Anderson, of Madras, adopted the very same expedient in order to deceive the Hindus into a belief that vaccination was an ancient practice of their own.

The authenticity of the quote had been vigorously defended by Colonel King in the pages of the *Madras Mail* (11 May 1905, cited in Wujastyk 1988: 162). Wujastyk follows closely a lengthy debate spurred by King in the *Madras Mail*; his researches also fail to turn up the Sanskrit text to which the quote is attributed. The most powerful reason, however, to doubt the authenticity of the quote is the fact that the cowpox virus has never existed naturally in India:

When vaccination first became known, it was natural that physicians in India should try to find the life-saving virus in the local cattle. This would have obviated the great labour involved in bringing the virus all the way from England. Several attempts were indeed made to find cowpox, and two distinguished doctors have left written reports that no such virus was found in India (Wujastyk 1988: 165).

Wujastyk concludes that 'On balance, it does seem likely that a "pious fraud" was perpetrated at the beginning of the nineteenth century in Madras, Bengal, or both, and perhaps more than once, in order to popularize vaccination' (p. 167).

In his careful historical study of Indian medical texts bearing on smallpox Nicholas concludes that by the sixteenth century in India there was only a humoral and a theurgic (i.e. divine causation) explanation of the disease. Variolation is not mentioned, let alone vaccination.

There is a further question—namely, the possibility that a non-textual popular tradition concerning variolation may have overlapped with a more élite textual tradition. Smallpox inoculators have been recorded as belonging to a non-élite, popular social milieu; Hindu and Muslim cultivators in Dinajpur District, garland-makers and barbers in Dacca, and lower-caste Vaidyas (Vaidyas are Ayurvedic doctors), low-ranking astrologer Brahmins in Serampore, and barbers. Risley (1891) reports that the latter 'possess a textbook, Vasanta-tika (smallpox inoculation), but few study it' (cited in Nicholas 1981: 28–9). Holwell reports that 'a particular tribe of Brahmins' were inoculators in eighteenth-century

Bengal but Nicholas points out that a job requiring bodily contact with people from all walks of life is not an estimable occupation for a Brahmin. Since the procedure requires drawing blood this would further lower the status of Brahmins practising inoculation. Even those groups, such as the barbers, who have a textual tradition, do not seem to rely primarily on it. (This is similar—in my experience—to dance teachers in Orissa whose tradition is recorded in vernacular, as well as Sanskrit, texts, but who seem to rely exclusively on oral transmission.)

As Zimmermann has shown, the low-status oral medical traditions which involve the drawing of blood, operations, and generally non-humoral, i.e. non-'expectant' practices are part of an ancient orthodox medical discourse which he terms the 'operative' discourse. He sees within the Indian medical tradition from the earliest textual evidence a double, seemingly contradictory discourse. The expectant model is today associated with such Brahminical practices as vegetarianism and non-violence. The operative model, characterized by empirical observations of anatomical facts and the fulfilment of practical tasks, is today associated with low-ranking castes but is heir to an older tradition connecting the physician with the king, war, and the shedding of blood (Zimmermann 1978: 100).

The practice of inoculation seems to fit in well with Zimmermann's 'operative' model: it involves empirical observation, the fulfilment of a practical task, and the drawing of blood, and is carried out by low-status persons who depend primarily on oral transmission of their knowledge. Zimmermann's work sounds a note of caution for those who would too hastily dismiss the possibility that the practice of variolation in India is much older than its reported existence at the turn of the seventeenth and eighteenth century and may have existed much earlier even though it is not mentioned in any Sanskrit or Bengali medical texts up to the sixteenth century.

How effective was variolation as a method of disease control? According to the method employed, the risk of death from variolation varied between 1 to 3 per 100 (Buchanan-Hamilton MSS D-71/81, F; quoted in Greenough 1987: 17); this contrasts with a death rate in naturally acquired *variola major* during epidemic phases ranging between 1 in 2 to 1 in 6 persons. In a paper on variolation Paul Greenough (1987) cites various eighteenth- and nineteenth-century sources on the efficacy of variolation. In the late eighteenth century Holwell noted that 'it is no uncommon thing for [the *tikadārs*] to ask parents how many pocks they choose their children should have . . . [and] they hardly ever exceed, or are deficient, in the number required' (Dharampal 1971: 150). In 1867 Thomas Wise reported that

a timorous mother will be satisfied with few [pustules], while a robust father will require more, and the interesting fact is that the inoculator can regulate the profuseness of the eruption by the kind and in particular by the quantity or state of dilution in which the smallpox matter is introduced (Wise 1867: ii. 545).

Another physician, T. E. Charles, estimated the fatality rate as 1 in 200 (Charles 1870). There is no question that variolation was a most impressive discovery. '

In 1723 Dr James Jurin presented to the Royal Society of London a statistical study of the impact of variolation in England. Jurin concluded that 'the risk of dying from smallpox was about two out of seventeen, and that in recent epidemics of smallpox, about one out of every five or six victims died. In comparison, he showed that only one out of every 91 persons inoculated in England died of smallpox inoculation' (Hopkins 1983: 50). In terms of epidemic control, Razzell's social historical research attributes the increase in life expectancy at birth in eighteenth-century England to the introduction of inoculation. However, he shows that epidemic control due to inoculation was substantial in rural areas but sporadic in urban areas (Razzell 1977, cited in Hopkins 1983: 76).

Razzell's work on variolation in eighteenth-century England converges with the reports by Dr Buchanan-Hamilton at the beginning of the nineteenth century from Eastern India, where, since variolation was widely diffused, only about 1 in 100 persons died even during epidemic phases of the disease (Greenough 1980: 346). Razzell's evidence for eighteenth-century England and the evidence for eighteenth- and early nineteenth-century India shows that variolation, when practised fairly extensively in the population, was an impressively effective method of controlling the disease. A survey of Bengali villagers in 1850 reveals that 81 per cent of the population had been variolated (Greenough 1980: 347). This can be compared with the figures of the early 1960s Government of India smallpox eradication programme, where the target was to vaccinate 80 per cent of the population of the country.

One of the criticisms made after Jenner's discovery was that variolation would spread the acute forms of smallpox to susceptible persons by natural contagion. Greenough states that: 'This question is answered in the negative by Razzell. He argues, with considerable evidence, that when large numbers were regularly inoculated in rural areas—areas where the bulk of the population had been previously exposed to smallpox or variolated—there was little chance for variolation to increase the rate of natural infection' (Greenough 1980: 345 referring to Razzell 1977: 26–33).

Razzell's study of eighteenth-century England corroborates Holwell's view regarding variolation in eighteenth-century Bengal; the latter states that 'notwithstanding the multitudes that are every year inoculated in the usual season it adds no malignity to the disease taken in the natural way, nor spreads the infection, as is commonly imagined in Europe' (Holwell

1767 in Dharampal 1971: 144, cited in Greenough 1980: 346). It must be kept in mind that the technique of inoculation reported by Holwell to be in use in Bengal was, of the three techniques so far reviewed, the safest, since it used variolated matter only from the pustule of previously inoculated persons, thus greatly increasing the chance for a mild case to occur in the inoculee. This method seems to have been current only in India since the European, Turkish, Arab, and Chinese methods all used variolated matter taken from a person having caught the disease by natural means.[7]

Besides being efficient, variolation in Bengal was also cheap and popular:

'The tikadār' [variolator], we are told, goes 'down one side of the street and up the other, and is thus employed from morning until night, inoculating sometimes 8 or 10 in a house' (Holwell 1767 in Dharampal 1971). This intense intra-village coverage, combined with the movement of tikadārs throughout Bengal, Bihar and eastern Uttar Pradesh as described, leads one to think inoculation was perceived to be effective (Greenough 1980: 346).

Jenner's vaccine was introduced in India early in 1802 but as the 1850 survey of Bengali villagers revealed, the overwhelming majority of the population continued with the traditional variolation rather than with vaccination; the traditional method flourished until the colonial government outlawed it in 1865 (Greenough 1980: 347).

One historian of vaccination has characterized this practice as the 'chief medical contribution of the Enlightenment' (G. Miller 1957, cited in Hopkins 1983: 77). But in actual fact, Jenner's discovery grew out of the practice and knowledge gained from inoculation in eighteenth-century England. The medical establishment in Europe lagged behind folk practice by over half a century and behind the adventurous spirit of Lady Montague, who was the first member of the European élite to use inoculation in her family. She was the wife of the British ambassador in Constantinople and had witnessed the practice there, where inoculation was carried out by old women. She had her son inoculated in Constantinople—albeit by the embassy surgeon—in 1718 and her daughter in 1721. Her attitude contrasts sharply with that of one contemporary British doctor, Dr William Wagstaffe, who around that time composed the following gem of European ethnocentricity and sexism:

Posterity will scarcely be brought to believe that a method practiced only by a few Ignorant Women, amongst an illiterate and unthinking People should on a sudden, and upon a slender Experience, so far obtain in one of the most Learned and Polite Nations in the World as to be received into the Royal Palace (Stearn 1950: 115 cited in Hopkins 1983: 47).

7. However, the Chinese did take care to choose only mild cases for their variolation matter (cf. Needham 1980: 15–17).

This was written at a time when independent reports of the Chinese, Turkish, and Arab method of variolation were being received by European physicians. The turn of the seventeenth and eighteenth century was, according to historians, a period of terrible smallpox epidemics. In the face of these two factors Hopkins is moved to remark that '[t]he failure of European physicians to respond immediately to these efforts . . . is curious' (p. 46).

By the end of the eighteenth century, inoculation had been accepted by British physicians and Jenner was an inoculator who had himself been inoculated as a child of eight. While he was studying surgery and pharmacy as an apprentice in 1762 in Sodbury he learned from a country girl that she could not be infected with smallpox because she had already had the cowpox. Such knowledge had apparently been common among peasants in England for over a century. He experimented on his own children by inoculating them with cowpox matter and then noticing that a subsequent smallpox inoculation produced no result (Hopkins 1983: 77–8). Clearly the technique used by Jenner was that of variolation. Combining this with folk knowledge concerning the relationship between cowpox and smallpox enabled him to achieve his famous discovery. This continuity between variolation and vaccination is not only manifested in the realm of biological knowledge but sociologically as well. As Hopkins notes,

the experience with inoculation as an effective specific tool against smallpox, in Europe and North America especially, enabled inhabitants of those two continents to exploit Jenner's vaccine almost as soon as it was discovered. In that sociological, nonbiological sense, Jennerian vaccination was not an abrupt break with the past, but the direct descendant and heir of inoculation (Hopkins 1983: 77).

Given the similarity in technique and type of knowledge involved in variolation and vaccination, the Indians' strong preference for the former during the nineteenth century cannot easily be attributed to blind adherence to superstitious tradition or obscurantism as has often been done (see Mather and John's view about the need to remove the superstitious belief in a smallpox goddess for effective treatment of the disease, 1973: 195).

2.2 Resistance to Vaccination in India

In order to approach the topic of the resistance to vaccination in India, we need to summarize our understanding of the history of indigenous knowledge and practice concerning smallpox in India. Smallpox as a disease is named and described in the earliest Sanskrit medical treatises, those of Caraka and Suśruta which scholars date to the fourth century AD. The disease is called *masūrikā* from a word meaning 'lentil' or 'pulse' since the boils resembled in colour and shape a local variety of that legume (Suśruta, Ni. 6, 18; Caraka, Ci 12, 93. Quoted in Nicholas 1981). In those earliest texts and in later commentaries to those texts such as the eighth-century Nidāna of Mādhava-Kāra and the text by Ḍalhaṇa of the eleventh to twelfth centuries, the treatment of smallpox belongs to the ancient Ayurvedic system of humoral explanation and consists of diet and external efforts at restoring imbalances between, for example, hot and cold. There is no mention of variolation or of the goddess. By the twelfth century, Sanskrit texts such as that of Ḍalhaṇa give other names for the disease which are all variants on the word *śītala* (meaning 'cold' or 'cool'), such as *śītalā*, *śītalikā*, and *śītalī* (Meulenbeld 1984: 91).[8] By the end of the fifteenth century or beginning of the sixteenth, another Sanskrit text, an appendix to the eighth-century Nidāna of Mādhava-Kāra, mentions for the first time that the disease is caused by the goddess Śītalā (Nicholas 1981: 26). Can we conclude from this textual evidence that smallpox was not connected to the goddess of smallpox Śītalā until the end of the fifteenth century? Probably not. There is iconographical evidence from the ninth century in Rajasthan for the existence of such a goddess (see Plate 23 in Hopkins 1983). By the twelfth century there are several instances of iconographical representations of the goddess Śītalā (Nicholas 1981). Since in Ḍalhaṇa's twelfth-century text the disease's name is changed to *śītala* or variants of that word, I think it is safe to assume that in practice smallpox has been connected to the goddess Śītalā at least since the twelfth century.

The earliest mentions of variolation come from Europeans in India and date from the early eighteenth century. Variolation as a method of controlling epidemics was associated with the worship of the goddess of smallpox who was believed to cause the disease. The tradition of the variolators is a vernacular, predominantly oral, and low-status one, contrasting with the earlier Sanskrit textual tradition. What needs to be emphasized is that since at least the twelfth century, a dietetic-*cum*-humoral understanding of the disease was associated with the worship of a goddess of smallpox and that at least since the eighteenth century another understanding of smallpox had created the practice of variolation which was also associated with the worship of the same goddess.

It is well to point out once more that the religious language concerning smallpox, the humoral theory, and the technique of variolation with its implicit knowledge of infection and contagion, were thought of and experienced as a unified field. Although Foster and Anderson's distinction between personalistic (including supernatural) and naturalistic medical systems is useful, since it avoids certain terminological difficulties, I find it problematic since it presupposes a nature–culture and/or a nature–supernature dichotomy (Foster and Anderson 1978: 53). There is no good

---

8. I wish to express my gratitude to Francis Zimmermann for having helped me with the Sanskrit references and having sent me the relevant parts of Meulenbeld's article.

basis for setting up a binary opposition between a naturalistic discourse and a religious discourse.

As Nicholas puts it, this evidence makes it clear that the cult of a goddess of smallpox did not prevent or displace the two 'naturalistic' understandings of the disease. Quite the contrary; indigenous medical treatment of smallpox in India was associated, as we have seen, as far back as the twelfth century with the worship of Śītalā. In the eighteenth and nineteenth centuries impressively effective practices of inoculation and epidemic control are similarly associated with the worship of the same goddess. Since more often than not the reported resistance to vaccination in the twentieth century has been in the name of Śītalā, it is necessary, before going any further into the nature of this resistance, to investigate more precisely the nature of the relationship between a so-called religious discourse and a so-called naturalistic discourse on smallpox.

Even though the link between Śītalā and a humoral explanation of smallpox is not seen in the classical (and earliest) Ayurvedic treatises, these texts exhibit a 'constant desire to justify material activities and physical processes by considerations borrowed from the surrounding tradition, and which in the final analysis belong to the religious domain' (Zimmermann 1982: 224; my translation). But as the whole of Zimmermann's book on Ayurveda abundantly attests, the human and what Westerners would call the 'supernatural' are merely continuations and refinements of the natural. Our familiar Western oppositions between the natural and the supernatural or between nature and culture are dissolved. In the Ayurvedic discourse it would be doing violence to its vision of reality to speak of naturalistic versus religious explanations of disease. The human body and the earth are both irrigated by fluids. The drainage of the human body (i.e. medicine) and the cultivation of drained land are a single theme. Vegetal growth, i.e. agriculture, human growth or maintenance of health, and the worship of deities are all part of a single chain of being where the continuities are assumed by processes of cooking and mixing of essences (rasa). Sun, water, and wind (i.e. fire, water, and air) in the right combination assure growth of vegetation, cooking, digestion, and the transmission of the oblations to the deities. Fertility of the land, life, and the blessings of the gods all depend on the same principles of proper congruence between these three elements in each of the three realms. Furthermore, the human body is sustained by the land, its fauna and flora, and the gods are sustained by the food offerings from humans. Through the kitchen fire and the digestive fire (bile, one of the three humours), the cooking water and the water in the body (phlegm, another humour), the air which keeps the fire burning and the air in the body (wind or breath, a third humour), humans appropriate their environment into themselves. The right kind of appropriation, or one could say the right way of absorbing one's environment, depends on a congruence between corresponding elements, vital fluids (saps, essences, and so on) and substances, between the land and the body. The link between the three major realms of environment, humans, and deities are the transformations such as cooking (*saṃskāra*) and combining (*saṃyoga*) which enable humans as well as deities to be sustained. There is a continuous 'chain of beings which rises from the sap which plants extract from the soil up to the gods who nourish themselves from the fragrance emanating from the sacrificial fires' (Zimmermann 1982: 198).

This simplified summary of Zimmermann's study is intended to alert the reader to the absence of a nature–supernature or nature–culture dualism in non-modern India (see also Egnor 1978; Daniel 1984). When we narrow our focus on the worship of Śītalā as a healing cult we must shift our attention from the level of general conceptual structures to the level of language. In later Sanskrit medical texts the disease itself is called Śītalā and in everyday discourse the person suffering from smallpox is spoken of and to as if she or he were the goddess herself. Treating the patient and worshipping the goddess are one and the same set of actions and words.[9] The diseased person, male or female, is addressed as 'mother' (*mā*); he or she is offered cooling drinks and food, the leaves of the neem tree which are said to be cooling as well as being a disinfecting agent.[10] In other words, the patient is offered the same substances which the goddess might simultaneously be offered in her temple, as well as being spoken of and to as if he or she were the goddess herself.

The disease is discussed in terms of an excess of heat, the pustules being the visible signs of an overboiling blood erupting through the skin and the fever being the immediate indication of an excess of heat escaping from the body. It can also and simultaneously be spoken of as the anger of the goddess. In the continuous chain of beings material substances transform and refine themselves (*saṃskāra*) into feelings, thoughts, and consciousness (Egnor 1978: 131). Anger is an excess of heat; heat is fire; heat is bile; heat is the sun. Heat out of congruence is disease, which is the anger of the goddess. The distinction between the literal and the metaphorical is blurred to the point of being dissolved; it is replaced by what Daniel has called 'figurative reality'. One should not assume from this that Indians are incapable of distinguishing between the literal and the metaphorical, but rather that they have an awareness of what the English linguistic philosopher J. L. Austin has called the illocutionary and perlocutionary power of words. Words can do things, can change the world, can create new realities (Daniel 1984: 106–8).

It is thus distorting to speak as Nicholas does of two indigenous

9. For ethnographic descriptions see Babb 1975; Bang 1973; Bhattacharyya 1952; Beck 1969; Egnor 1984; Junghare 1975; Kolenda 1982; Mather and John 1973; Morinis and Brilliant 1981; Nicholas 1981; Roy 1927; Wadley 1980.
10. On the antiseptic properties of neem (*Azadirachta indica juss*) see Radwanski 1977.

explanations of the disease, one humoral (naturalistic) and one theurgic (religious); we are in the presence of a unified discourse perceived as two through the distorting lenses of Western dualistic conceptual structures. Furthermore, it is clear that the knowledge of some sort of viral infection and of contagion necessary to produce the knowledge of variolation was not experienced as contrasting or conflicting with the other two manners of speaking of smallpox. Not only did the variolators recite hymns to the goddess while inoculating and have the inoculees recite along with them, but the inoculees had to prepare themselves before the visit of the variolator by following a cooling diet which they continued for a prescribed period after the inoculation (Coult in Dharampal 1971: 141–2, cited in Nicholas 1981: 28).

With this background, resistance to vaccination on the grounds that it would offend the goddess can be interpreted 'from below' in a very different way from the interpretation 'from above'. It is not a simple matter of religion and/or blind faith in tradition on the one hand and a rational, naturalistic, progressive scientific world-view on the other. The language of Śītalā is a non-logocentric language, dissolving all binary oppositions. As for efficacy, the touchstone of Western science, it is worth repeating that when the British outlawed variolation in India in 1865, it was an effective, cheap, popular, and grass-roots method of disease control. On the basis of the evidence from the early 1960s vaccination campaigns, India did not approach this effectiveness until the 1970s.

The Government of India's smallpox eradication programme of the early 1960s had the target of vaccinating 80 per cent of the population because it was assumed that this immunity level would stop the disease. The vaccination target was not reached; an assessment of the programme by the National Institute of Communicable Diseases in Delhi in 1963 found that recorded figures for both vaccination and re-vaccination were much higher than those found in the surveyed population (Basu, Jezek, and Ward 1979: 23). Since the recorded figures show that 68 per cent of the population was vaccinated between 1962 and 1965, many of these were re-vaccinations and the percentage of newly vaccinated persons must have been a great deal lower (Gelfand 1966: 1640). It was only in 1977 that the World Health Organization (WHO), in collaboration with the Indian government, successfully eradicated smallpox.

It is my contention that the resistance to vaccination was essentially of a political nature. Let me begin with some history. Nicholas's research has shown that beginning in 1750 in Bengal there took place a sudden outpouring of vernacular hymns and ritual texts pertaining to Śītalā, most of which were written in Western Bengal. The marked increase in literary works elaborating on the mythology of Śītalā was of such a magnitude that according to Nicholas the status of Śītalā shifted from that of a minor deity to that of a major one. He is able to show that this phenomenon

correlated with major smallpox epidemics which ravaged this area of
Bengal between the 1740s and 1770s. Politically this was a period of major
upheavals which saw the collapse of the Mogul empire and a countryside
ravaged and profoundly disrupted by Maratha and English armies. After
their victory at Plassey in 1757, the British took control of the two western
districts of Bengal, Burdwan and Midnapur. Pillaging by Maratha cavalry,
increasing pressure on the cultivators from British revenue-collecting, and
a severe drought in 1769 all built up to a major famine and smallpox
epidemic in 1770 in which 10 million people are said to have died (Sinha
1967: 88, cited in Nicholas 1981: 33). A contemporary Dutch naval
commander wrote the following of this tragedy, which he witnessed:

This famine arose in part from the bad rice harvest of the preceding year; but it
must be attributed principally to the monopoly the English had over the last
harvest of this commodity, which they kept at such a high price that most of the
unfortunate inhabitants—who earned only a sou or a sou-and-a-half a day to
sustain their family—found themselves powerless to buy the tenth part of what
they needed to live.
   To this scourge was added smallpox, which spread among persons of all ages
and of which they died in great numbers (Stavorinus 1798: 125–8, in Nicholas
1981: 33).

The increased movement of displaced persons due to invasions and the
movement of armies themselves both contributed to the spread of infection.
The relationship between tax-collecting, famine, and smallpox could not
but have been deeply etched in the consciousness of the villagers of
Western Bengal.
   Political turmoil also disrupted the annual work of the variolators as
well as quarantine arrangements for variolated persons. As Nicholas
remarks, all these factors transformed a disease into a calamity (1981:
34). When revenue extraction pushes the villagers to extreme poverty,
malnutrition lowers the population's resistance to infectious disease. Wars
disrupt the villagers' indigenous mode of disease control through the
regular annual visits of the *tikadārs*; diet and inoculation fail; all they
have left is their capacity to write and sing hymns to the goddess, which
the government's destructive activities cannot rob them of.
   Even though vaccination was introduced by the British in India at the
very beginning of the nineteenth century, vaccination did not naturally
displace variolation in India as had been the case in Europe, since
variolation largely answered the Indian conception of effective protection.
The British physician Buchanan-Hamilton corroborated this 'when he
found in 1812 in Bhagalpur district that the general adoption of the
practice (of variolation) render[s] the introduction of the vaccine of very
little importance' (Greenough 1980: 347).
   It is my contention that vaccination was resisted because of its

entailments, political and cultural. For example, it was not the traditional custom to cremate the body of a person who died of smallpox since it was considered that this would enrage and further exacerbate the heat of the goddess (Hopkins 1983: 163). But, in Bangladesh as late as 1977 rumours circulated of the house and body burnings of victims of smallpox which were practised by the colonial government (Foster 1978: 448). Other rumours recorded in the nineteenth century reveal that vaccination was associated in people's minds with the government and acceptance of it as tantamount to acceptance of foreign rule. Indian priests at Benares were reported at the end of the century to tell of a prophecy 'that India would expel the British through the leadership of a black child with white blood. Vaccination, the priests charged, was how the English intended to find that child to kill him' (Hopkins 1983: 147). Another rumour was that the purpose of vaccination was to put a ' "Government mark" on the arms of every child. When older, the male children with this mark would be sent as coolies to other British colonies, or forcibly drafted into the army. Girls with the mark would be forced into harems. Another version of the rumour was that the mark was part of a census of the people with the view to imposing a new tax' (Wujastyk 1988: 153–4).

In Sri Lanka the rumour was that vaccination meant taking an oath in favour of British rule. Such rumours were no doubt fanned by the autocratic behaviour of the colonial government in outlawing variolation and then proceeding to make vaccination compulsory in many parts of the country. After Independence the Government of India made preventive vaccination the single most important activity of its public health agencies. But due to 'incomplete coverage of the population and the relative ineffectiveness of liquid lymph vaccine in a warm climate, the disease retained its high endemicity and its tendency to recur periodically in epidemic fashion' (Gelfand 1966: 1635).

The history of the eradication programme is instructive on the nature of resistance. In 1959 pilot projects were set up to initiate a programme of total eradication; by March 1961 they came to an end due to poor results. In 1962 the National Smallpox Eradication Program (NSEP) was created in Delhi. Dr Gelfand reviewed the operations of this vast bureaucratic endeavour between 1963 and 1965. The target of immunizing 80 per cent of the population was not even approached. Massive bureaucratic failures were basically the cause for the disappointing results; these failures ranged from poorly motivated health workers, to reporting vaccinations that had not been performed so as to fulfil an expected quota and avoid retribution (Foster 1978: 148). The recording task seems to have broken down almost totally; in some cases the registers of recorded vaccination were prepared by copying information from the 1956 electoral rolls (Gelfand 1966: 1644), whereas in other districts 'persons deceased for several years before NSEP began were not only registered but were also recorded as being successfully vaccinated!' (p. 1646). Vaccinators were noted on occasion to be not only technically inefficient but abrupt and callous in their approach to people (p. 1642). As a result of the failure of the programme several changes were made. The target was changed to 100 per cent of the population and the target date to March 1966. 'Attack phase teams are now instructed to move as rapidly as possible through individual communities, vaccinating as many as possible . . .' (p. 1639). In other words, response to failure was a more comprehensive and aggressive programme, ideal circumstances for multiplication of abuses. One of the most vivid reports of forced immunization by government vaccinators backed by police is given by Brilliant and Brilliant (1978: 359):

In the middle of the gentle Indian night, an intruder burst through the bamboo door of the simple adobe hut. He was a government vaccinator, under orders to break resistance against smallpox vaccination. Lakshmi Singh awoke screaming and scrambled to hide herself. Her husband leaped out of bed, grabbed an ax, and chased the intruder into the courtyard. Outside, a squad of doctors and policemen quickly overpowered Mohan Singh. The instant he was pinned to the ground, a second vaccinator jabbed smallpox vaccine into his arm.

Mohan Singh, a wiry 40-year-old leader of the Ho tribe, squirmed away from the needle, causing the vaccination site to bleed. The government team held him until they had injected enough vaccine; then they seized his wife. Pausing only to suck out some vaccine, Mohan Singh pulled a bamboo pole from the roof and attacked the strangers holding his wife.

While two policemen rebuffed him, the rest of the team overpowered the entire family and vaccinated each in turn. Lakshmi Singh bit deep into one doctor's hand, but to no avail.

One of the authors of the piece, a former board member of the American Civil Liberties Union, muses about 'what would happen . . . if society used force on every dissenter in the name of public health?' (p. 6). Another observer reports witnessing a sixty-year-old vaccinator pursuing an even more elderly woman up a tree to immunize her (Morinis 1977: 359). Uniformly, the literature on the government's smallpox eradication programmes opposes the people's knowledge and beliefs concerning smallpox against science; those who carried out vaccination were on the whole not part of the communities in which they worked and they believed themselves to be representing a vastly superior form of knowledge completely divorced from the conceptual universe of the people they were attempting to immunize. This is in sharp contrast with the practices, social status, and attitudes of the indigenous tikadārs of the eighteenth and nineteenth centuries. Such a situation is almost certain to create animosity rather than co-operation; as the WHO report on the eradication of smallpox in India puts it: '[n]ot infrequently a young, aggressive vaccinator would fail to observe the courtesies and respect due these older people, an action which provoked resentment and animosity, rather than cooperation' (Basu, Jezek, and Ward 1979: 113).

Resistance voiced in the language of 'the anger of the goddess' should be read as a sign of political resistance to the logocentric, authoritarian, top-down disciplinarian activities of the government. To see it as superstitious, anti-progressive, and ignorant is simply to protect logocentric structures of power.[11] The many reports in the literature of the resignation of the Indian peasant in the face of smallpox, explained by the fact that it is the grace of the goddess, and the attitude of passivity in the face of this calamity in the name of not angering the goddess, are singularly reminiscent of the stereotype of the passive Native American. Worsley invites us to unmask the stereotype in the following manner:

Such is the stereotype of Indian [that is, Native American] passivity and resignation, which are, in reality, neither conservative commitment to entrepreneurial tradition nor a lack of the entrepreneurial spirit, but refusal . . . [W]hen hope—and organization—become possible, refusal becomes resistance, resistance protest, and protest eventually turns into positive demands for alternatives . . . It is not a search for purely economic opportunity, but far wider: a struggle for the reassertion of the wholeness of the human personality . . . and a cultural reassertion, too, of the value of long-despised forms of knowledge, from traditional medicine (actually always innovative) to modes of experiencing the world and conceptions of the relationship of humankind to Nature which are often far richer than those either of the West or of a Second World hell-bent on socialist accumulation, meritocratic mobility, and cultural modernization (Worsley 1984: 291–2).

With the advent of the collaboration between the Government of India and WHO in 1970, a markedly different strategy was employed to eradicate the disease. One of the most fundamental among the various changes— both technical and organizational—which took place in the early 1970s was the shift from mass vaccination to the policy of 'surveillance and containment'. Based on field experience in Nigeria, this new strategy consisted in locating every outbreak of the disease, and then sending vaccinators in to contain the outbreak by vaccinating everyone not yet immunized in the vicinity of the outbreak. The necessity for the co-operation of the public became essential. Re-education of public health staff, monetary rewards for reporting cases of smallpox, and the hiring of local villagers to aid health workers in containment were the most important measures taken to achieve co-operation. In an interview with Dr Foster of the Bureau of Smallpox Eradication, Center for Disease Control in Atlanta, Georgia, I was struck by two things; one was his statement that 'resistance totally disappeared when we hired local inoculators' and the other was the absence of derogatory remarks concerning beliefs and practices surrounding Śītalā. He and one of his

11. For a similar argument in the case of cholera epidemics in the Philippines see Ileto (n.d.).

colleagues who had also participated in the eradication programme in India maintained a studiously neutral and non-committal position with regard to the worship of Śītalā. This was all the more evident since I asked questions concerning resistance to vaccination due to beliefs in the goddess. He handled my questions by emphasizing the success the government–WHO programme had in winning popular support. In fact, he reported to me having seen a smallpox vaccine needle and vial on an altar of the goddess in Bangladesh in 1974. From his published statements it is clear that the recognition of the 'absolute priority need for the public's participation' (Foster 1977: 247) prompted an attitude of actively avoiding expressing arrogant or deprecatory attitudes towards the people's practices. Aided by the expert knowledge of anthropologists on information flows in rural India (see Morinis 1980), and by sophisticated marketing-type promotional tactics including dropping leaflets from aeroplanes, the new surveillance and containment strategy proved successful. But, according to Dr Foster, the key ingredient was the ability of the staff of the eradication campaign to create—artificially and at great cost—grass-roots involvement and support for the campaign. It is well to recognize that this reorientation does not express a newly found respect for the people's own systems of knowledge or even a new political endorsement of grass-roots participation, but rather represents an imaginative and effective response to the necessity of involving the public at large which the new surveillance–containment strategy required. The fact that resistance was overcome when local people were involved also seems to confirm my own interpretation, namely that resistance was basically a political phenomenon in a religious garb.

India was officially declared free of smallpox in April 1977, two years after the last case of smallpox was reported in May 1975 (Basu, Jezek, and Ward 1979: 26–7).

2.3 Socio-political Implications

Perusing the literature documenting the smallpox eradication campaign, one cannot but be struck by its use of military language to communicate its key concepts. A few examples will illustrate the point: 'Intensive Search and Containment'; 'a strategy based on the national mobilization of health resources for the main battle against smallpox . . . the Government of India, the state Governments and WHO . . . decided to launch an intensified campaign . . .'; 'Operation Smallpox Zero'; 'Periodic active search operations'; 'villages, localities, mohallas, corporations were routinely searched'; 'children in school were one of the main targets', etc. (Basu, Jezek, and Ward 1979: 29, 32, 158). The 'campaign' was carried out with support from the police, as was discussed in Section 2.2. The eradicators not only made use of military language but also of military equipment such as helicopters, walkie-talkies, motor-launches, etc. (personal communication from James Boyce, who witnessed these activities in the early 1970s in Bangladesh).

The non-ecological, monocausal approach to disease leads to a policy of eradication; such a policy in turn lends itself to a military approach since the cause of the disease can be isolated and therefore targeted for destruction. As René Dubos clearly saw, such an approach to disease is anti-ecological and courts disaster (1972). The politically repressive potential in such an approach is captured in the military language used by eradicators. According to Kunitz, smallpox is the only disease to have been totally eradicated. It has not worked with other diseases such as tuberculosis and malaria. The monocausal, what I have termed logocentric, approach to epidemiology is no longer the dominant model in biomedicine today (Kunitz 1987: 401). My contention is that the success of the smallpox campaign has been achieved at a high political and cultural cost and that smallpox could have been successfully controlled rather than eradicated had other approaches been followed. The campaign to eradicate smallpox was carried out from the top down, and local knowledge was ignored and deprecated. What is surprising to me is that the existence in biomedicine of an ecological model—which according to Kunitz was the only model available to the mid-nineteenth-century physician in America (1987: 38)—did not generate a more respectful attitude towards variolation. The following characterization by Charles Rosenberg of nineteenth-century medicine in America is remarkably reminiscent of the Indian system of knowledge concerning variolation and Śītalā:

The model of the body, and of health and disease . . . was all-inclusive . . . capable of incorporating every aspect of man's life in explaining his physical condition. Just as man's body interacted continuously with his environment, so did his mind with his body, his morals with his health. The realm of causation in medicine was not distinguishable from the realm of meaning in society generally (1979: 10, cited in Kunitz 1987: 380).

What probably prevented the recognition of variolation and the worship of Śītalā as being similar to this model is the natural–supernatural exclusive dichotomy. Variolators, as low-caste 'priests' of Śītalā, were probably associated with a supernatural model of disease causation and thereby easily dismissed as superstitious.

Although I have no information on the motivating factors behind the colonial government's decision to outlaw variolation, the logocentric approach to disease gave it an opportunity to take control of and institutionalize an activity heretofore outside its purview. Non-logocentric approaches to disease, be they Western or Indian, lend themselves with much greater difficulty to control by a centralized state.

Even though a multicausal, ecological approach in biomedicine seems to have existed side by side with a monocausal medical model, logocentric modes of thought seem to have predominated when it came to the perception of deities such as Śītalā. Earlier, foreign commentators naively dismissed these deities as demons. In the more recent scholarly literature this phenomenon has been dealt with by labelling the name of the goddess a 'euphemism'. By calling the dreaded goddess of smallpox, who sends deadly fevers and pustules, by a name which conjures the opposite, 'the cool one', her worshippers, it is argued, attempt to cajole and flatter her into becoming cool.

Such an interpretation is prisoner of a logocentric, either–or mode of thought. Śītalā angry and heated up *is* the diseased person, quite literally. Pacified and cooled, she is the cured patient and the beatific and beautiful woman represented in her iconography. In both her manifestations she is worshipped. A patient suffering from smallpox is addressed as if he or she were the goddess and is worshipped. Treatments in the form of administration of special cooling foods and drinks, of neem leaves, of cooling sandal paste, of reciting and chanting hymns to the goddess and of prostrating oneself in front of the patient are the same actions that constitute the goddess's worship in her temple. Such an understanding of disease prevents a search and destroy response. There is no enemy to be eradicated. Both Greenough and Nicholas in their historical studies of smallpox in India point out that the variolators did not pressure those people who refused to be variolated, as certain castes and sects did. Furthermore, the work of the indigenous variolators was totally independent of state authority; no police or other state agents were involved. The work of the variolators and the co-operation of the people were spontaneous expressions of grass-roots action. The disease calls for efforts to re-establish a lost congruence between various elements. In such a view the disease cannot be objectified as existing separately from a healthy subject. This is why Śītalā is both the disease and the absence of the disease, or the illness and its cure.

Michel Foucault's historical study, *The Birth of the Clinic* (1975), has perceptively shown the similarities between the hospital and the prison. In the prison the enemies of society are placed under police surveillance. In the hospital the enemy of health is placed under surveillance. In the eradication approach to epidemiology, where the enemy is spread out among the population, the police are called upon to second the medical experts in destroying the enemy. The possibilities for abuses of power are great. Nor are they theoretical: the Brilliants' eyewitness account (quoted above) of a surprise attack on a terrified and unwilling peasant family testifies that such abuses have indeed occurred. In India the strategy to eradicate smallpox shifted from a more directly authoritarian one in the 1950s and 60s to one employing the subtler methods of marketing techniques when WHO joined the venture in the 1970s. But the strategic change did not reflect a conceptual change.

To the dichotomization between health and disease corresponds a socio-political dichotomization between the target population which is objectified and the agents of the state: medical experts, medical technicians, police (and other state-hired experts) who are the subjects in charge of searching and destroying the enemy. That is, a subject–object dichotomy corresponds to the health–disease dichotomy. One side of the equation is passive and acted upon and the other is active. This contrasts with the view of the smallpox patient as the goddess incarnate to be worshipped by all including the variolators and other health specialists. Resistance to vaccination both during the colonial era and after Independence is a political act of refusal to be disenfranchised by such a division between legitimately acting subjects and a disempowered population objectified as the target. Resistance to vaccination in the name of Śītalā is a rejection of politically repressive dualistic conceptual structures—Śītalā defies dualism in her very being; she is both illness and health.

The health–illness binary opposition parallels a life–death opposition. Death is the outcome of an unsuccessfully treated disease. It is absolutely opposed to life. The logic of the logocentric approach to disease makes death the enemy to be conquered as it makes disease the enemy to be destroyed. This gets translated into such practices as keeping terminally ill patients alive beyond their own wishes, the cryonics movement in the United States which freezes bodies after death to preserve them until the time when their diseases will have been conquered and they can be thawed back to life, and many other similar practices. As one participant at a recent meeting of development experts succinctly put it: 'death always represents a failure'. Death becomes absolutely negativized, the ultimate enemy.

I can do here little more than summarize Robert Jay Lifton's (1983) arguments concerning the grave dangers both to the individual and to society of such an attitude towards death. The logocentric medical (and developmental) discourse constructs death as the absolutely negative. Such a view corresponds to social conditions in the advanced industrial countries in which the old are no more than unproductive members of society, kept out of sight in old folks' homes. The old uncomfortably remind the productive members of approaching death, hence the efforts to keep them invisible. The visible productive members of society forever strive to look youthful and sexy. Lifton's argument, backed by psychiatric case-studies and anthropological evidence, goes far beyond the usual moral condemnation of putting away the old. He shows both a social and a psychological link between death-denial or death-avoidance and violence. In Lifton's view, backed by extensive evidence, the fear, pain, and anger in the experience of the death of loved ones badly or only partially experienced and faced, are displaced into aggressive behaviour targeted at enemies which psychologically are made to bear the taint of death. These emotions are projected on to the outside, upon an enemy to be ruthlessly hounded out and destroyed. If disease can be targeted for destruction, death also can be targeted for destruction.

Lifton argues that the scientific medical system makes it singularly difficult for individuals and communities to integrate and confront death. Death is absolutely separated from life. It is the absence of life. This modern construction of reality contrasts with those of so-called primitive societies whose initiation, funeral, and renewal ceremonies abundantly attest to their knowledge of the fact that new life can only be had through immersion in death. In Lifton's view, the broken connection between life and death is at the root of the most spectacular catastrophes of modern times: nuclearism and genocide. The dangers of logocentrism are here shown to be of apocalyptic proportions.

In a system of knowledge where disease cannot be so isolated, objectified, and targeted, death also is constructed very differently. For a more detailed exploration of the place of death in that system of knowledge, I will use the ritual of state discussed in Section 3 of this chapter. This yearly ritual is also a smallpox healing ritual, but every twelve years it becomes a death ritual. Disease and death are here used—a better word would perhaps be 'recycled'—to achieve the regeneration of self, community, and cosmos. A communal immersion in disease and death becomes, precisely, the key to renewal. This corresponds exactly to Lifton's claims, namely that full confrontation and integration of death both psychologically for the individual and communally for the society produces an increase in vitality and well-being.

3   A Non-Logocentric System of Thought and Action

This section discusses a ritual of state performed annually in Puri, in the eastern province of Orissa. As a preliminary, it will be necessary to state briefly the fundamental principles of the system of thought implicit in such symbolic action. What is highlighted in the following section is the continuity between agricultural processes, bodily processes, and socio-political processes. The person is integral to a natural environment and to a social environment. The individual is not viewed—as in the modern West—as pitted against nature in an effort to conquer and dominate it, nor in opposition to society. In this system of thought, the person's very being derives from his or her integration into nature, society, and cosmos.[12]

---

12. The cultural sketch of a local tradition offered in this part of the paper departs markedly from an earlier scholarly tradition culminating in Louis Dumont's *Homo Hierarchicus* (1980; 1st French edn. 1966). In that tradition the exclusive dichotomy of the pure and

3.1 The Land, the Body, and the Body Politic

In Orissa, smallpox, along with many other diseases, is referred to most colloquially and most often simply as 'mother' or as *ṭhākurāṇī*, i.e. 'lady' or 'goddess'. As such, every village or more generally every territory's goddess is a variant of Śītalā who herself is a variant of Durgā or Kālī, the Great Goddess. As the village mother, she is the particular earth within that village or territory's boundary. The following description of Mariamman, the Tamil goddess of smallpox, by Margaret Egnor could apply precisely to the Orissan *ṭhākurāṇīs*:

Mariamman 'took her birth in earth' . . .; she is represented as the head of a woman lying on the ground—or rising from it—and her statue, in the earthen huts which are most of her temples, is of earth. People are born in earth; the home land is 'the earth I was born of' . . . 'Every child is a good child in his birth from earth' (1978: 162–3).

Those born on the same portion of earth, the same village territory, share the same mother, namely, the village goddess. As her children they are all one and form a kin-like community. The village goddess, that is, the goddess of that particular piece of earth, is yearly propitiated by the entire community. She is propitiated to avoid misfortune from occurring to her children, namely, to the community; these misfortunes are mostly crop failures and epidemics. In South-Western Bengal the village goddess propitiated by the community as a whole is Śītalā (Nicholas: 1982). In the plains region of Orissa the village goddess has different names, often names related to the name of the locality, but everywhere she is referred to simply as 'goddess', *ṭhākurāṇī*. In the South-Western region of Sri Lanka discussed by Gananath Obeyesekere she is called Pattini. In South India, similarly, the village goddess, whether she is Mariamman or known by a local name, is worshipped by the community for the avoidance of misfortune (Brubaker: 1978). The very failure to propitiate the local goddess causes her anger, which gives rise to an excess of heat which may cause both drought and illness (Obeyesekere 1984: 42). To propitiate the local goddess, the whole community shares the economic and organizational burden of the festival. Whatever factionalism and conflict may be dividing the community must be at least temporarily set aside so that every segment

the impure plays a fundamental role. Arjun Appadurai has written the following about this book: 'Yet, like many great works, it appears now not to have been the inspiration for a new way of thinking but the swan song for an older one' (1986: 745). Romila Thapar (1985) sounds a kindred note in speaking of a plurality of indigenous Hindu religions. Thapar asserts that there is no single structure of Hinduism, that a notion of a unified religion or culture (Dumont saw the unification in the opposition of the pure and the impure) is a creation of orientalist scholarship. Such orientalist scholarship portrayed Indian culture as essentially logocentric. Whether the logocentrism is wholly the creation of such scholarship or whether such scholarship blew out of all proportion one element among many others from the Indian cultural landscape remains to be established.

of the community may co-operate with every other. No one can be omitted, from the humblest untouchable sweepers and carrion removers to the wealthiest landowner, including the local Brahmin(s). As in the organization of the daily ritual in the central cult of Jagannātha, the sovereign deity of Orissa, no link however small and humble in the vast chain of tasks necessary to carry out the worship may be left out. Everyone has an equally valid share in the ritual. The model can be extended to include the whole kingdom, along with the feudatory principalities: in sharing in the ritual task of worshipping the village goddess, mistress of the local territory, or of Jagannātha, sovereign of the whole territory of Orissa, the people pool their resources and co-operate as functional equals in this task (Rösel 1980: 89). The ritual requires social co-operation, which amounts to social congruence. The most frequent reason for postponing by a year or more the celebration of the village goddess festival is factionalism, and conflict in general, in the local community (Nicholas: 1982). Thus the failure to propitiate the goddess is a political failure. The anger of the goddess arises from anger and conflict in the community which cannot put its fighting aside for the purpose of co-operating in the village festival. The goddess is the earth of the community and when the various parts of her body are at war with each other, are out of congruence with each other, disease—misfortunes due to lack of congruence—is the outcome. Regularly worshipping the village goddess or the territorial sovereign assures that conflict will not be left to grow indefinitely, unchecked, finally to erupt into a major conflagration. Every year some measure of political congruence is necessary in order to carry out the territory's yearly festival and assure the coolness of the goddess and the welfare of the community.

The relationship between agricultural activities, bodily processes, and political processes is one of continuity. All these processes of draining, irrigating, and working the land, feeding and draining the body, and sustaining and ordering the body politic are seen as being of the same kind and continuous with one another. As Zimmermann has put it, Ayurveda (medicine) and Arthaśāstra (the science of political management) are one and the same discourse split into two different branches of knowledge (1978: 101). Using the specific example of the temple of Jagannātha in Puri and its monumental yearly festival (Ratha Jātrā), I will attempt to understand how and why healing and politics are indeed part of the same discourse. Ratha Jātrā is a good candidate for this exercise since it is at once a major state ritual—reminiscent of those in nineteenth-century Bali which Geertz has called 'the theatre state' (Geertz 1980)—in which all representative segments of the Orissan polity participate, and a smallpox healing ritual. The ritual process centres on the illness, treatment, and recovery of the three deities in the temple of Jagannātha (see Apffel Marglin 1985: ch. 9). A good place to begin is the paradigmatic notions of the identity between the draining of the body and the putting into cultivation of lands (Zimmermann 1982: 9). The two are involved in the parallel and similar activities of irrigation/nutrition and of drainage/depletion of land/body (ibid. 242). The agricultural metaphor, in Zimmermann's terms, has a central place in Ayurveda.

The continuity between agricultural activity, bodily processes, and socio-political processes in this system of knowledge may be described briefly in the form of an ideal-typical traditional Hindu kingdom, as this was conceived in Orissa. This description is *not* a historical reconstruction but the description of an ideal type used for the purposes of clarifying certain principles of a system of knowledge. An actual historical description of any given Hindu kingdom would be quite different.

Converting uncultivable into cultivable land is the task of the king. According to Orissan inscriptions the ideal king conquers a kingdom, builds a temple, and then constructs reservoirs to irrigate the land. Then he proceeds to give these territories, newly valuable because of drainage and irrigation, to the deity of the temple and to the Brahmins. The ideal kingdom is illuminated by the sacrificial fires of Brahmins, is full of temples reaching toward the heavens in whose lands reservoirs guarantee plentiful harvests, and has a king who generously gives land to the Brahmins (Rösel 1980: 99). But agriculture is more than a metaphor since 'food is the root of all living beings . . .' (Suśrutra Saṃhita i. 28, in Zimmermann 1982: 221); food is the fount of all human activities (ibid. 224, also Khare 1976). The chain of being in the universe is the production and consumption of food through repeated transformative processing from the cooking in the earth by the sun and by water to the kitchen fires and cooking water. But all kitchen fires are also sacrificial fires and all food is first offered to the deities. The food will be truly nourishing and sustaining of health, well-being, and happiness only through the blessings of the gods. These blessings can be obtained by making offerings to the gods. The gods, being sustained through human food offerings, in return shower blessings on humans. In temple ritual these blessings of the gods are received concretely through the ingestion of consecrated food: *mahāprasād*. Temple Brahmins, priests, first offer this food to the deities, who consume its fragrance borne upwards on the air. After this ritual food offering, the food, which has become the left-over of the deities, is still capable of sustaining and blessing humans. In Rösel's words, 'this divine kingdom maintained itself with the help of a sacred food-chain, . . . it recycled divine pleasure. It was along this matrix of nectar-feeding lands, service, pleasure [*bhoga*, also meaning 'food'], and grace that the God and his palace town increased and decreased . . .' (Rösel n.d.: 17). The expression 'nectar-feeding lands' is applied to lands donated to the temple or to sectarian monasteries for the specific purpose of providing food for the temple kitchen in the form principally of rice (the staple), coconuts, and sugar-cane.

The ecological language of recycling seems particularly felicitous. The food-chain forms a complete cycle in which the deities are the linchpins. From the earth rises the sap into the plants, harvested and variously processed by humans who offer it to the gods, who inhale the food's fragrance. At this end point of a continuously ascending and progressively refining process from the earth to the heavens, the food returns and begins a downward path as the left-overs of the gods, eaten by humans, who are sustained by it and whose bodies drain themselves of the impure left-overs—the non-incorporated or non-used parts of the food, i.e. faeces, urine, sweat—which return to the earth (see Egnor 1978: 50; Daniel 1984: 85).

This chain of life necessitates for its implementation a certain type of socio-political organization: a king to conquer 'virgin' lands and to drain and/or irrigate them and thereby make them cultivable. Some of these lands must then be given to Brahmins steeped in Vedic knowledge, who alone can 'establish' (*pratiṣṭhā*) a deity and install it in a temple (Apffel Marglin 1985: 135).[13] The king must also give some of this newly cultivable land to the temples to provide the food for the gods. The temples must be staffed by temple servants, some Brahmins and some non-Brahmins, who will carry out the tasks involved in preparing the offerings for the deities, the most important one being food. The cooking must be done by Brahmins who are of a lesser status since they are involved in physical service (*sebā*), even though it is service of the deity. Besides Brahmin cooks there will also be need of various other castes such as artisan castes necessary to the cooking process—potters, cowherds, and many others, as well as cultivators.

The king is an earthly incarnation of the divinity, Jagannātha; for this deity is the real sovereign of Orissa. Whatever sovereignty an earthly king possesses can only come from the divinity. This divine sovereignty is established in the king by the landed, Vedic Brahmins at the time of his coronation. The king is also a temple servant, the first among all temple servants. His relationship to the sovereign divinity is one of service and he carries out certain types of ritual service in the temple, the most important of these being at the time of the yearly festival of state when his position of humble servant to the divinity is displayed to the thronged population who have come to participate in it (Apffel Marglin 1985). This idealized and simplified political and social implementation of the chain

---

13. In practice gifts of land by Orissan kings to high-status Brahmins imported from Kanauj in North India established the category of *śāsan* Brahmins and *śāsan* villages. They were indispensable in the chain of being that we are discussing because their Vedic knowledge and pure manner of living entitled them alone to establish temples and deities to dwell in them. The *śāsan* lands enabled the high Brahmins to sustain themselves.

of life leaves out many things, of course,[14] but it serves the purpose of clarifying the structure of a particular system of knowledge.

The maintenance of this chain of life necessitates the whole spectrum of Hindu society; the warriors whom the king needs to conquer and then protect the land; the two main classes of Brahmins and all the other castes necessary to agricultural production, food processing, the disposal of bodily wastes, the construction of temples and human housing, etc. The deities enable the ascending chain of food to begin its return journey to sustain human life. They stand at the apex and the turning-point. Since the gods will only accept pure food cooked by pure hands, temple Brahmins are indispensable. Vedic Brahmins of course can be said to be the most indispensable of all since without their knowledge of the powerful words the deities would not even dwell among humans and could not be fed in the first place. The king by his conquering and agricultural development activities makes it possible to begin the chain of life and, once begun, to protect it. But he is only one enabler among others. As a warrior and a hunter (a royal prerogative) who sheds blood—an impure activity—he is disqualified from being able to offer food to the gods. His very sovereignty is acquired through the powerful words of the Vedic Brahmins. He is totally dependent on the two classes of Brahmins, as they are on him—without him they would have no land and therefore could not sustain themselves.

3.2 A System of Thought in Practice

For this particular cultural construction to have any reality, or in other words for it to become a lived experience, the existence of a particular social and political organization is necessary. Let me attempt to sketch in an ideal-typical way what these socio-political requirements are. The existence of deities who require offerings of pure cooked food as a necessity for human beings to be nourished means that one cannot sustain oneself merely by one's own efforts and feed oneself directly. One needs different types of Brahmins, and the Brahmins need different types of castes to carry out those activities which would pollute them and therefore render them unable to establish and feed the gods. Everyone needs to be protected; the protector because of his activities is also unable to feed the gods himself, and therefore to sustain himself. In other words, this cultural construction demands a social and political order in which everyone is interdependent; everyone needs everyone else because of the deities and their particular requirements. Each function is necessary to maintain the chain of life. This is best seen in the organization of a large temple like

---

14. One of these elements which must be mentioned is the sects and their monasteries (*mathas*) which have also been given lands whose produce is reserved for the deities. The heads of the monasteries (*mahanta*) also perform services in the temple (Rösel 1980: 90 and *passim*).

that of Jagannātha in Puri, where 108 different functions are carried out by some 7,500 temple servants (Rösel 1980: 4–7, 71), who provide for the bodily requirements and pleasure of the deities—food, bathing, clothing, fragrances, cooling, singing, dancing, sleeping, and others. The omission of one single link in the vast chain of actions which constitute this daily ritual either brings the whole operation to a halt (Apffel Marglin 1985: 94) or renders it invalid. Each function, however humble, is absolutely necessary.

There is a functional equality between the various services rendered in the temple; this equality is given by the deities who create the services in the first place by their bodily requirements (Rösel 1980: 87). This functional equality between all the varied services rendered to the deities does not mean that they are all equally esteemed or prestigious, only that they are all equally necessary. Those who can come closest to the deities are much more esteemed than those who are low on the return path of the chain of life, closest to its end point, the earth as the receiver of life's left-overs, which of course is also its beginning.

The number 108 is magical, and has grown from the original 4 in the eight centuries of the temple's existence. Each named service can be carried out by several persons. The number of persons the temple could support was, before the advent of a cash economy, totally dependent on the amount of land possessed by the temple or given to other institutions specifically for the purpose of offering food in the temple. All persons carrying out some service in the temple were fed by the temple. Access to temple service was achieved through heredity. In the case of the creation of new services, or the addition of persons entitled to perform an already staffed service, access was through competitive and conflictual manœvering. Rights to perform certain services could and still can be bought and sold among temple servants. It is important to realize that the various services do not correspond necessarily or even typically with caste divisions. Three-fourths of all temple priests are Brahmins and they share among themselves the great majority of services (see Apffel Marglin 1985: 46). Judicious marriages are another way of gaining access. Rösel summarizes his description of the jostling and competitive behaviour by saying that it amounted to an ordered disorder (1980: 80), the disorder being kept in bounds by the absolute necessity of co-operation. Order is maintained mostly in a decentralized manner since each service group has at its head a 'general' (*bisoi*) in charge of law and order within its own group. There was a person responsible for the overall smooth running of temple activities, the *parikshā*, a *śāsan* Brahmin (that is, a landed Brahmin of the highest status. See note 13). But for the most part he delegated his powers among several temple servants (Rösel 1980: 81). The temple both grew and functioned in a decentralized and somewhat anarchic manner.

New services or new entitlement to existing services were carefully recorded by temple Brahmins in special documents since each service consisted of the privilege of receiving support from tax-free temple lands (these privileges are called *mahal*). The role of the king as first servant of the deity was not one of being able to create or even allot these privileges but only of confirming them through official royal recognition. This is how Rösel describes the situation:

This process of differentiation was at the same time one of diversification. It was not the evolution of a deliberately devised, efficient system of division of labor; instead the present diversification represents more the outcome of eight centuries of mutual alliances, intrigues and suspicion of different, often antagonistic priest groups, eager to intrude into new services and jealously guarding their own against the interference of others. Normally an already internally accomplished system of division of labor was reconfirmed by a king, through the official recognition and installation of a new service, with the subsequent allotment of new shares of holy food and clothes (Rösel n.d.: 6–7).

The king's official recognition came in the form of the granting of titles and was publicly displayed in the ritual of 'tying the sari', that is, tying a piece of the deity's clothing on to the head of the honoured persons. The king could grant such honours (*maryādā*) not only to temple servants but to members of the many monasteries in Puri[15] as well as to feudatory rajas.[16] These honours entitled their receivers to carry out some service in the temple or during certain festivals and to the display of certain paraphernalia symbolizing their honorific status.

Furthermore, and very important to my argument, these honours conveyed upon their recipient some portion of the divine sovereignty. This was expressed in the tying of the cloth of the deity on to the recipient's head. Thus even though the king of Puri is called the 'moving Vishnu' (*calanti viṣṇu*), he is only the first among others; sovereignty is not an exclusive royal monopoly. The king is only one link in the chain of life even though he is a very important link. In fact, all those living in the kingdom were part of the chain of life but some were recognized, through the receiving of royal temple honours, as more important than others. Of course there was competition and conflict over the conferring of these privileges, but in managing these conflicts when they erupted beyond the capacity of groups to arbitrate them themselves, the king's actions, according to the South Indian model elaborated by Appadurai,

were not legislative, insofar as they were always addressed to specific groups and individuals, were not of general applicability, were subject to alteration or repeal according to current needs of kingship, and could not fix the law or even strictly serve as an illustration. Furthermore, the administrative actions of the Hindu king in respect to the South Indian temple were context sensitive and context

15. Rösel gives two separate estimates of the number of *mathas* in Puri, 91 and 70 (1980: 92).
16. See Appadurai 1981 for an illuminating treatment of the topic of honours.

bound in an organizational sense as well. Thus, there does not appear to have been at any time a single, centralized, permanent bureaucratic organization (on the Weberian model). Instead, there was a temporary affiliation of a number of local groups, constituted by, or in the name of, the king and empowered to make public decisions on specific matters (Appadurai 1981: 214–15).

As Appadurai's careful historical study of a South Indian temple shows, this organic state of affairs was fragmented during colonial rule. For example, the competition between two sectarian groups for control of temple affairs was legislated by the British into *two mutually exclusive groups*, the winner being the Tengalai sect, the loser the Vatakalai sect, the latter being legislated forever out of involvement in this particular temple. This legislative action bases itself on universally valid, as opposed to context-sensitive, rules. It inaugurates a new socio-political landscape embodying a logocentric mode of thought. These findings of Appadurai in the context of a South Indian temple seem to fit perfectly with the historical study of the Jagannātha temple made by Rösel.

For the purposes of the present argument, what is essential to note is that the structure of authority in the temple, and beyond the temple in the kingdom, was not a pyramidal, centralized one. Everyone's position was determined and recognized in terms of one's relationship or rather service to the deities. The deities are the only source of absolute authority. The existence of a deity who is the actual owner of the land, who requires to be fed pure food, and who is the fount of all authority and all blessings, enables the existence of non-pyramidal, multi-centric socio-political landscape. At one empirical, positivist level, such a deity is a fiction; at another level, that of lived experience and human social and political life, it is very much real in the sense that without it, the whole tangible edifice of the way people act would collapse (cf. Chapter 1, Section 5, above).

In the chain of life as exemplified in the functioning of a great temple such as that of Jagannātha, conflict or disorder disrupts the vast co-operative task of worship. If any one group or person in the many services required for the ritual to proceed is out of phase, the whole process stops or becomes invalid. Similarly in medicine, 'sickness is a kind of being-out-of-phase, and medicine an art of good conjunction' (Zimmermann 1980: 100), an art of restoring congruence between various elements of the body, the environment, and time; it is an art exquisitely context-sensitive. The king, like the physician, must maintain good conjunction between all the elements of the kingdom so that the chain of life may continue: this, the royal activity of 'protection', is an activity which must by necessity be context-sensitive.

3.3 The Body and the Body Politic in Ritual

Let us shift our focus to Ratha Jātrā, the grand ritual of state enacted yearly in Puri in which the king's ritual action has both medical and political meaning. Furthermore, the whole festival is a political event, the very demonstration of political health and vigour in its ability to orchestrate smoothly (if it is successful) the co-operation of all temple servants, monasteries, and other representatives of the society at large. In pre-Independence days the heads of the various tributary minor kingdoms, and since Independence various representatives of the state government, also participate. This monumental endeavour requires enormous pooling of both economic and organizational resources. It is also the occasion when the current configuration of honours and privileges is publicly displayed.

I have previously described in detail the sequence of this festival and how its processual structure is organized around the illness, treatment, and recovery of the deities (Apffel Marglin 1985). But it is only since then, while conducting field research on traditional methods of dealing with smallpox, that I have gathered enough information to make it clear that the deities' illness was specifically smallpox.[17] Śītalā plays a key role in this festival and is popularly credited with making the deities ill. Perhaps it is the case that everyone implicitly knows that the disease Śītalā sends is smallpox, although Śītalā is the goddess of other poxes and infectious diseases such as chicken-pox, measles, rashes, cholera, plague, gastro-enteritis, diarrhoea, and typhoid.[18] The treatment the deities are given after they have been drenched by the water from Śītalā's well in the outer compound of the main temple parallels the treatment given to a sufferer of smallpox at home. The kitchen fires in the temple are extinguished; only cold foods are offered to the deities; no strangers are allowed in the temple, which is closed to pilgrims during the fortnight of illness. No singing and dancing takes place and no shouting or quarrelling should be heard.

This regimen is similar to the regimen imposed on someone ill with smallpox: no frying, no hot food, no singing, no shouting within the house; daily worship of Śītalā in her temple. Generally, the family behaves with gentleness and compliance toward the patient, who is addressed as Mā. The wishes of the patient can be understood to be those of goddess

17. That this realization did not surface during my previous field-work when smallpox was not of primary concern to me probably indicates that, with the progressive decline and final disappearance of this disease from the region, this part of the significance which the ritual had has receded from people's awareness. However, it may also be a function of my lack of sensitivity or of not asking the right kinds of questions. It is hard to know which.

18. I am deeply grateful to Oopalee Aparajita Kennedy for her invaluable help in introducing me to a knowledgeable relative who provided me with much information on this topic. Other informants identified each disease by its name plus *mā* (mother); others simply called any disease, including smallpox, *ṭhākurāṇī*, meaning simply goddess; others identified smallpox as *basanta* or *basanta mā*. *Basanta* also means spring, for the disease became epidemic in this season which in India is the hot season (see Nicholas: 1981). Another informant said that Śītalā, Mangalā, Bimalā and Buḍhimā were all of the same family and all connected with disease.

Śītalā. Confrontation and aggression, as well as great joy and celebration, are avoided; in general extremes are avoided and gentleness is emphasized. To act otherwise would offend the goddess and bring on her anger in the form of an intensification of the disease. No strangers—non-family members—are allowed in the sick-room. All food—only boiled, unseasoned foods are consumed along with cooling drinks such as green coconut water and sweet milk with banana—is first offered to the sick person and then consumed by family members, as would be done in the worship of a deity.

To return to the Ratha Jātrā. On the last day of the fortnight of illness the deities have recovered and the public can enter and see them. This is called the 'viewing of the new youth'. Two days later the deities are carried in great pomp outside the temple and placed each on one of the three huge wooden chariots (ratha) specially prepared for the occasion. The king then emerges from his palace a few yards across from the temple, carried in a chair, surrounded by his śāsan Brahmin preceptors, ex-feudatory rajas, and some male agnates. He ascends the temporary ramp of each of the chariots in turn and proceeds first to sweep the platform around the deity; he circumambules it, using a gold-handled broom. Then he repeats his steps and sprinkles water fragrant with sandal paste from a pot. Lastly he does a third circumambulation sprinkling powdered sandalwood. This ritual, referred to as the 'sweeping ritual', is one of the dramatic highlights of the festival.

The chariots are then, one after another, pulled by the mass of pilgrims and dragged to the north-east some two and a half kilometres away to a temple called Guṇḍicā where they will reside for seven days. The whole process from the end of the king's sweeping to the end of the deities' temporary stay in Guṇḍicā's temple takes nine days and the period is referred to as the 'nine days festival' (naba dīna jātrā), on the tenth day the deities are replaced on the chariots. The king repeats his sweeping ritual and the chariots are pulled back to the main temple. This is called the 'return festival' (bahuḍa jātrā). On the eleventh day the deities are returned inside the main temple.

Focusing on Śītalā, I became aware that the king's actions of sweeping and sprinkling, besides making him an untouchable sweeper (a fact much emphasized and discussed by informants), were also the actions which the goddess Śītalā is said to carry out when she wipes away the disease. The most commonly found iconography of Śītalā shows her sitting on a donkey, holding in one hand a broom and in the other a pot full of water. On her head she carries a basket or a winnowing fan full of pulses. (As already noted the Sanskrit masūrikā, 'smallpox' comes from a word meaning pulse.) When she shakes her head in anger, she spreads the pulses and gives the disease. When she sweeps the scattered grain away and sprinkles cool water from her pot, she removes the disease. The king's action, punctuating the movements of the deities to and from the temple of Guṇḍicā, parallels exactly the goddess's healing actions.

The temple of Guṇḍicā is empty for the rest of the year, having no installed deity. The name Guṇḍicā is that of the wife of the legendary founding king of Jagannātha temple. However, one of the more obscure meanings of the word *guṇḍi* is 'pox' in Oriya, even though this is not a currently used word. According to Nicholas (personal communication) the Bengali Guṭikā becomes the Oriya Guṇḍicā. Guṭikā is another Sanskrit word for smallpox and is the name of the smallpox goddess mentioned in 1767 by Holwell. The identification of Guṇḍicā with smallpox has since been confirmed to me by Puri informants.

Two informants talked about smallpox itself as the 'nine days festival' and called the tenth day 'the return festival'. That is, the goddess departs and the patient recovers. This terminology is the very same one used to refer to the journey, stay, and return of the deities to and from the Guṇḍicā temple. It now seems to me that the peculiarity of visiting an empty temple may express the fact that the goddess visits people (i.e. they suffer from smallpox) and then returns to where she usually dwells, leaving them empty of the goddess, i.e. recovered. The deities' temporary visit to Guṇḍicā's temple may signify the fact that they have removed the disease from the main temple and left it in Guṇḍicā's temple.

Let me now shift to the political meaning of the king's sweeping ritual. As people often said to me, the king displays here his relationship to the deities; he is to them as the humblest of servants, an untouchable sweeper (*hāḍi*). Even though he is hailed as he emerges from the palace by shouts of 'Victory to the Moving Vishnu!', his role as sweeper emphasizes that the king is a partial emanation from the ultimate sovereign, Jagannātha. In performing services for Jagannātha other persons share in divine sovereignty; speaking of the situation in the late seventeenth and the first half of the eighteenth century, Kulke describes one instance of this 'sharing': 'The Rajas . . . tried to gain and to assure the support of their feudatory rajas . . . by "sharing" their own position in the state cult with them' (Kulke 1978: 339), and granting them honours and privileges such as having a big drum beaten for them (a symbol of sovereignty) during their visit to Puri on the occasion of the great festival (ibid. 342). Being the sweeper of the divinities expresses at once the king's absolute subordination to the deities, his relationship of service to them, and also the fact that he is not the ultimate, absolute source of sovereignty. He performs a service for them and shares this activity with many other persons. The king is called Jagannātha's first servant (*adya sebāka*); as a servant he is one among many. The king is the foremost among several 'mobilizing actors', to use Appadurai's term:

Authority is the capacity to mobilize collective ritual deference to a sovereign deity in such a way that the mobilizing actor partakes of divine authority in relation to those human beings who are either the instruments or beneficiaries of such worship. More simply still, authority is the capacity to command collectivities in the homage of the deity. Of course, given the sociological complexities of the ritual process and the incomplete jural capacities of the deity . . ., such authority *can never be monopolized* by any one individual or group and must always be shared (Appadurai 1981: 226; my emphasis).

What links together the medical and the political meaning of the king's sweeping ritual is that the king, as the physician of the body politic, is part of what I would like to call an 'ecological socio-political system' where congruence, mutual adjustments, and context sensitivity are the order of the day, as they are in healing. Such an ecological socio-political system is the concomitant of a non-logocentric system of thought. To the Western observer it appears as rather anarchic. Another way of putting this is to say that the inability to monopolize authority means that political authority is shared and diffused among many persons and groups. Congruence is brought about by mutual adjustments through conflict and competition, as Rösel describes the relationships between the various service groups in the temple of Jagannātha. This congruence is necessitated by the absolute need to co-operate in the service of the gods. Order is not imposed by an external authority through a chain of command working down a pyramidal hierarchical organization. Rather, order is the result of a conflictual competitive process which has to result in co-operation.

The hierarchy in the microcosm of Hindu society which this temple represents is what I would call, following Gomes da Silva (1986), a circular hierarchy. Let me clarify: the group of temple servants who are in charge of the deities during their illness are a low-caste group said to be descendents of tribals (the *daitās*). During this ritual of state, they play a prominent and irreplaceable role. They are the ones who carry the deities in great pomp from the temple to the chariots. Outside this time, their touch would pollute the deities. During the twelve-yearly enlarged version of this festival, when the deities die after their illness and their wooden images are hacked to pieces and buried, it is these low-caste servants who observe the funeral taboos and rites. They are considered to be blood-kin of the deities.

Similarly, during the yearly festival of the best-known goddess of healing in Orissa (Mangalā), the goddess appears in untouchable men who play the prominent role in her festival, healing the sick and admonishing the powerful. During these times—namely the festival of the chariots in Puri and the goddess festival in villages—those at the apex of the hierarchy, the Brahmins, are useless and become secondary to untouchables or low-caste persons who take charge of things and are in centre stage. The Brahmins are totally helpless to heal and therefore to renew the community. Even the king, if he is to participate in removing the disease, must become an untouchable sweeper. Thus, healing and renewal is in the hands of those low in the hierarchy, those close to the earth on the return path of the chain of life from the deities to the earth. It is in the earth that the impure left-overs such as the dead parts shed by the body are recycled into new life. The earth is the transformative matrix with the power to regenerate. The social hierarchy corresponds to the chain of life discussed above. Those closer to the deities on the upward ascending journey from the earth to the heavens are more esteemed and higher; those on the downward, return path of the deities' left-overs are less esteemed and lower; they are the ones, however, who sustain, renew, and recreate life. The hierarchy is circular for at nodal points, the lowest become the highest; it corresponds to a non-logocentric system of thought where order is attained through disorder, health through disease, renewed life through death. The circularity of the hierarchy is the socio-political embodiment of a non-logocentric mode of thought.

In a pyramidal hierarchy, the organizational form of rational modern bureaucracies, the chain of authority is unidirectional from the top to the bottom, and the separation between those in authority and those upon whom authority is exercised is absolute. The ethos is not ecological, the intent not regeneration. The ethos is one of control and domination—of nature, of disease, of people; the intent is conquest and mastery.

In this Orissan ritual we are faced with a reality in which agricultural, medical, and political processes are seen as being of a kind. The political process consists of a balancing or a harmonizing between various parts of the society. The bodily processes also consist of a harmonizing between hot and cold intakes which itself consists of a harmonizing with the land and its products as well as with the seasons. The variations in heat and cold during the seasons dictate the appropriate countervailing diet in terms of hot and cold in order to balance these two poles. The land, the body, and the body politic are all part of a single great chain of life.

In the eradication approach to epidemiology as exemplified in the smallpox eradication campaign of the World Health Organization and the Government of India in the 1970s, the disease was viewed as the enemy which had to be searched out and destroyed. Disease and ultimately death itself are to be conquered. Such an approach contrasts with the way illness and death are dramatically performed for a collective experience of regeneration in the ritual of state in Puri.

This alternative view of relating disease and health or life and death is very similar to the vision detailed by Ashis Nandy in *The Intimate Enemy* (1983) in which the self and the anti-self are part of each other. He contrasts this indigenous Indian view to that of the Nazis who created an anti-self which they proceeded to externalize and then to exterminate.

4 Conclusion

This chapter has attempted to establish that resistance to vaccination in India both in the nineteenth and in the twentieth centuries was not due to superstition and blind faith in tradition. It is clear that when a vastly more effective method of smallpox control—namely variolation—appeared on the scene in the subcontinent, probably towards the end of the seventeenth century, it was readily incorporated into the existing humoral treatment of smallpox and into the existing worship of goddess Śītalā. When a yet more effective method of smallpox control was introduced over a hundred years later, namely vaccination, it was not similarly accepted and incorporated into existing practices. I would argue that vaccination, both because of its spectacularly low iatrogenic rate, about 1 death in 1,000 compared to about 1 in 100 for variolation, and because of its great technical similarity to variolation—the procedure is practically identical—could have been expected to be readily accepted. The reason it was not was because of the political and cultural entailments of this superior technique. The manner in which vaccination was brought to the people of the subcontinent both by the British in the nineteenth century and by the Government of India in the 1950s and 60s, not vaccination itself, caused resistance.

The fact that the colonial government outlawed variolation only fifteen years after a survey conducted by British physicians in the Eastern Provinces had revealed the effectiveness of variolation there must be interpreted to mean that the government meant to impose its form of prophylaxis by fiat. Notwithstanding the fact that many individual Europeans respected and perhaps even admired the indigenous system of variolation, the message from the government and its authorities must overwhelmingly have been one of authoritarian superiority. Clearly, from the rumours current in the nineteenth century, vaccination was perceived by the people as just another way for the government to impose more taxes, conscript more coolie labour, or in some other way exercise its autocratic power.

The language of the vaccinators is a logocentric language. To it corresponds logocentric behaviour, specifically, repressive political actions such as the outlawing of variolation by the British colonial government and the paramilitary vaccination campaign in post-Independence India. These are not isolated instances but part of a larger totality of repressive or authoritarian political institutions. Even when vaccination was presented to the people in a fashion that was not overtly repressive, the language of eradication violated the people's non-logocentric modes of thought. To speak of smallpox as an absolute evil that can and should be totally eradicated forever was an insult to Śītalā, goddess of smallpox. Śītalā is a concrete symbol or manifestation of a non-logocentric mode of thought and action. To dismiss belief in Śītalā as simple superstition amounts to simple ignorance.

If development means fewer people dying of disease or starvation, such development could have been furthered had vaccination been decoupled from its political and cultural entailments. Variolators could have been informed of the superiority of vaccination: its lower mortality rate and the fact that vaccinated persons are not contagious, unlike variolated persons. Such education, to be successful, should of course have taken place in an atmosphere of genuine respect and understanding towards the worship of Śītalā. Variolators could have retooled and become vaccinators, chanting hymns to Śītalā as they vaccinated. Vaccination could then have been a cheap and grass-roots method of epidemic control. The aim of vaccinating 80 per cent of the population could have been attained if the indigenous system of variolation had not been destroyed. Such a level of immunization—as the medical experts of the 1960s had concluded—would have been sufficient to prevent devastating epidemics from occurring. Smallpox need not have been eradicated; it could have been contained.

But of course all this did not happen. Development as greater control by man of his environment (W. Arthur Lewis 1955: 421) rests on a logocentric mode of thought. In this definition of development is embedded the opposition between man and his culture on the one hand and the environment on the other hand. Nested in Lewis's widely shared view of development is the exclusive, hierarchical, binary opposition of nature and culture and with it all the entailments of a logocentric mode of thought and action. Today's post-colonial governments have made the colonial governments' mode of thought their own. Decolonization has taken place on the land but not in the mind.

If development means fewer deaths from diseases and starvation, superior technologies such as vaccination must be used to alleviate the suffering of the masses. However, to be successfully diffused and transplanted they must be decoupled from their negative political and cultural entailments. This is seldom if ever done, probably because of the widespread perception that more efficacious techniques reflect superior forms of knowledge. This superior knowledge must supplant older, backward, obsolete forms of knowledge. However, forms of knowledge are not graded on an evolutionarily inclined plane with the Western sciences at the upper end and the non-Western forms spread on the lower end. To use Ashis Nandy's phrase, there is no inclined plane of history.

REFERENCES

Apffel Marglin, Frédérique (1985) [catalogued under Marglin, Frédérique Apffel] *Wives of the God-King: The Rituals of the Devadasis of Puri*, New Delhi and Oxford: Oxford University Press.

Appadurai, Arjun (1981) *Worship and Conflict under Colonial Rule: A South Indian Case*, Cambridge: Cambridge University Press.

—— (1986) 'Is Homo Hierarchicus?', *American Ethnologist* (Nov.), 13/4: 745–61.

Babb, Lawrence A. (1975) *The Divine Hierarchy: Popular Hinduism in Central India*, New York and London: Columbia University Press.

Bang, B. G. (1973) 'Current Concepts of the Smallpox Goddess Sitala in Parts of West Bengal', *Man in India*, 531: 79–104.

Basu, R. N., Jezek, Z., and Ward, N. A. (1979) *The Eradication of Smallpox from India*, New Delhi: WHO South East Regional Office publication, 79.

Beck, B. E. F. (1969) 'Colour and Heat in South Indian Ritual', in *Man*, 4 9: 553–72.

Bhattacharyya, A. (1952)'The Cult of the Goddess of Smallpox in West Bengal', *The Quarterly Journal of the Mythic Society*, 43: 55–69.

Brilliant, Lawrence, and Brilliant, Girija (1978) 'Death for a Killer Disease', *Quest* (May–June), 3–10, 98–101.

Brubaker, Richard (1978) 'The Ambivalent Mistress: A Study of South Indian Village Goddesses and their Religious Meaning' (unpublished Ph.D. dissertation) Department of Religious Studies, Chicago University.

Canguilhem, Georges (1978) *On the Normal and the Pathological*, trans. Cawly Fawcett, Dordrecht: Reidel.

Charles, T. E. (1870) *Popular Information on Smallpox Inoculation and Vaccination*, Calcutta: Bengal Secretariat Press.

Culler, Jonathan (1982) *On Deconstruction: Theory and Criticism after Structuralism*, Ithaca, New York: Cornell University Press.

Daniel, E. Valentine (1984) *Fluid Signs: Being a Person the Tamil Way*, Berkeley: University of California Press.

Derrida, Jacques (1976) *Of Grammatology*, Baltimore: Johns Hopkins University Press.

—— (1979) *Spurs*, Chicago: Chicago University Press.

Dharampal (1971) *Indian Science and Technology in the Eighteenth Century: Some Contemporary British Accounts*, Delhi: Impex India.

Dubos, René (1972) *A God Within*, New York: Charles Scribner's Sons.

Dumont, Louis (1980) *Homo Hierarchicus: The Caste System and its Implications*, 2nd edn., Chicago: University of Chicago Press.

Eagleton, Terry (1984) *Literary Theory*, Minneapolis: University of Minnesota Press.

Egnor, Margaret Trawick (1978) 'The Sacred Spell and Other Conceptions of Life in Tamil Culture' (unpublished Ph.D. dissertation) Department of Anthropology, University of Chicago.

—— (1984) 'The Changed Mother, or What the Smallpox Goddess Did When There Was No More Smallpox', *Contributions to Asian Studies*, 18: 24–5.

Foster, George M., and Anderson, Barbara G. (1978) *Medical Anthropology*, New York, Chicester, Brisbane, Toronto: John Wiley & Sons.

Foster, Stanley O. (1977) 'Smallpox Eradication: Lessons Learned in Bangladesh', *WHO Chronicle*, 31: 245–7.

—— (1978) 'Participation of the Public in Global Smallpox Eradication', *International Health*, 93/2: 147–9.

Foucault, Michel (1975) *The Birth of the Clinic: An Archaeology of Medical Perception*, New York: Vintage Books.

Geertz, Clifford (1980) *Negara: Theatre State in Nineteenth Century Bali*, Princeton: Princeton University Press.

Gelfand, Henry M. (1966) 'A Critical Examination of the Indian Smallpox Eradication Program', *American Journal of Public Health* (Oct.) 56/10: 1634–51.

Gomes da Silva, Jose Carlos (1986) 'Le Pouvoir et la hiérarchie' (unpublished MS) Paris.

Greenough, Paul R. (1980) 'Variolation and Vaccination in South Asia, c. 1700–1865: A Preliminary Note', *Social Science and Medicine* 14D: 345–7.

—— (1987) 'Smallpox Immunization in South Asia Before Vaccination—An Overview' (unpublished MS).

History of Inoculation and Vaccination, lecture Memoranda, American Medical Association, Minneapolis 1913; London: Burroughs Wellcome & Co.

Hopkins, Donald R. (1983) *Princes and Peasants: Smallpox in History*, Chicago and London: University of Chicago Press.

Ileto, Reynaldo C. (n.d.) 'An Alternative to Developmentalist Historiography in the Philippines', Manila: De La Salle University (mimeo).

Illich, Ivan (1976) *Medical Nemesis: The Expropriation of Health*, London: Calder & Boyars.

Junghare, Indira Y. (1975) 'Songs of the Goddess Śītalā: Religiö-Cultural and Linguistic Features', *Man in India*, 55/4: 298–316.

Khare, R. S. (1976) *Culture and Reality*, Simla: Institute for Advanced Studies.

Kolenda, Pauline (1982) 'Pox and the Terror of Childlessness: Images and Ideas of the Smallpox Goddess in a North Indian Village', in James J. Preston (ed.) *Mother Worship*, Chapel Hill: University of North Carolina Press.

Kulke, Hermann (1978) 'The Struggle between the Rajas of Khurda and the Muslim Subahdars of Cuttack for Dominance of the Jagannātha Cult', in A. Eschmann, H. Kulke, G. C. Tripathi (eds.) *The Cult of Jagannāth and the Regional Tradition of Orissa*, Delhi: Manohar.

Kunitz, Stephen (1987) 'Explanations and Ideologies of Mortality Patterns', *Population and Development Review*, 13/3: 379–408.

Lakoff, George (1987) *Women, Fire and Dangerous Things: What Categories Reveal about the Mind*, Chicago: Chicago University Press.

Lewis, W. Arthur (1955) *The Theory of Economic Growth*, Homewood, Ill.: Irwin.

Lifton, Robert Jay (1983) *The Broken Connection: On Death and the Continuity of Life*, New York: Basic Books.

Mather, R. J., and John, T. J. (1973) 'Popular Beliefs about Smallpox and other Common Infectious Diseases in South India', *Tropical and Geographical Medicine*, 25: 190–6.

Meulenbeld, G. Jan (1984) 'Proceedings of the International Workshop on Priorities in the Study of Indian Medicine', held at the State University of Groningen, 23–7 Oct. 1983, Groningen: Rijksuniversiteit Te Groningen.

Mertz, Elizabeth, and Parmentier, Richard, eds. (1985) *Semiotic Mediation: Socio-Cultural and Psychological Perspectives*, Orlando: Academic Press.

Morinis, E. A. (1977) 'Smallpox Eradication in India: Its Lesson for Applied Anthropology', *Man in India*, 57/4: 357–62.

—— (1980) 'Brief Communications: Tapping the Flow of Information in a Rural Region: The Example of the Smallpox Eradication Program in Bihar, India', *Human Organization*, 39/2: 180–4.

—— and Brilliant, G. E. (1981) 'Smallpox in Northern India: Diversity and Order in a Regional Medical Culture', *Medical Anthropology* (summer) 341–64.

Nandy, Ashis (1983) *The Intimate Enemy*, New Delhi: Oxford University Press.

Needham, Joseph (1980) *China and the Origins of Immunology*, Hong Kong: University of Hong Kong Center for Asian Studies.

Nicholas, Ralph W. (1981) 'The Goddess Śītalā and Epidemic Smallpox in Bengal', *Journal of Asian Studies* (Nov.), 41/1: 21–44.

—— (1982) 'The Village Mother in Bengal', in James J. Preston (ed.) *Mother Worship*, Chapel Hill: The University of North Carolina Press.

Obeyesekere, Gananath (1984) *The Cult of the Goddess Pattini*, Chicago and London: University of Chicago Press.

Radwanski, Stanislaw (1977) 'The Neem Tree', *Journal of International Agriculture*, 29: 2–5.

Razzell, P. (1977) *The Conquest of Smallpox*, Firle: Caliban Books.

Rösel, Jacob (n.d.) 'The Economy of an Indian Temple: Landed Endowment and Sacred Food' (unpublished MS).

—— (1980) *Der Palast des Herrn der Welt: Entstehungsgeschichte und Organisation des Indischen Tempel und Pilgerstadt Puri*, Munich: Weltforum Verlag.

Rosenberg, Charles (1979) 'The Therapeutic Revolution: Medicine, Meaning, and Social Change in 19th Century America', in M. J. Vogel and C. E. Rosenberg (eds.), *The Therapeutic Revolution*, Philadelphia: University of Pennsylvania Press.

Roy, Satindra Narayan (1927) 'Popular Superstitions in Orissa about Smallpox and Cholera', *Man in India*, 7: 217–26.

Sinha, N. K. (1967) 'Administrative, Economic, and Social History, 1757–1793', in id. (ed.) *The History of Bengal (1757–1905)*, Calcutta: University of Calcutta.

Thapar, Romila (1985) 'Syndicated Moksha?', *Seminar* (India), 313: 14–22.

Turner, Bryan S. (1984) *The Body and Society*, Oxford: Basil Blackwell.

Wadley, Susan S. (1980) 'Śītalā: The Cool One', *Asian Folklore Studies*, 39/1: 33–62.

Wise, T. A. (1867) *Review of Hindoo Medicine*, 2 vols., London: Churchill.

Worsley, Peter (1984) *The Three Worlds: Culture and World Development*, Chicago: University of Chicago Press.

Wujastyk, Dominik (1988) ' "A Pious Fraud": The Indian Claims for pre-Jennerian Smallpox Vaccination', in G. J. Meulenbeld and D. Wujastyk (eds.) *Studies on Indian Medical History*, vol. ii, Groningen: Groningen Oriental Studies.

Zimmermann, Francis (1978) 'From Classic Texts to Learned Practice: Methodological Remarks on the Study of Indian Medicine', *Social Science and Medicine*, 12: 97–103.

Zimmerman, Francis (1980) 'Ṛtu-Satmya: The Seasonal Cycle and the Principle of Appropriateness', *Social Science and Medicine*, 14B: 99–106.

——(1982), *La Jungle et le Fumet des Viandes: Un Thème Écologique dans la Médicine Hindoue*, Paris: Gallimard-le Seuil; Hautes Études.

5

Modern Medicine and Its Non-Modern Critics: A Study in Discourse

ASHIS NANDY AND SHIV VISVANATHAN

1 Development, Medicine, and Language

The idea of development has served many purposes in our times. It has served as a reason of state, as a legitimizer of regimes, as part of the vision of a good society, and, above all, as a shorthand expression for the needs of the poor. It has produced a new expertise and created a new community of scholars, policy-makers, development journalists, readers of development news, development managers, and activists—who together can be said to constitute the development community.[1]

One purpose, however, development has served less conspicuously: it has endorsed the claims to power over the human body, as a domain of social knowledge and social intervention, ventured by organized centres of power in a society. These are centres inaccessible to the citizen and often even to the community to which he or she belongs. Taken away from the individual and handed over to the organized centres of power in the society, the body politically becomes and is redefined as a carrier of hedonistic pleasures or as a vehicle of diseases and suffering.

If the body can be separated from a person's selfhood and controlled, it can also be corrected and improved. Also, the body can be controlled only if it can be corrected and improved. Either way, another domain of individual choice becomes a part of public life, directly subject to the society's power–knowledge nexus and to the typical format of expertise which goes with the nexus. What was once a matter of personal suffering and personalized healing thus becomes subject to the demands of large-scale engineering, planning, and intervention. Medicine becomes a proper theme in development.

Development in its halcyon days was economic development. Other disciplines entered the area apologetically or stealthily—as supplementary knowledge of social structures facilitating or hindering economic growth, as insights into the psychological factors motivating or discouraging

---

1. Readers will of course notice the similarity between Henry Kissinger's concept of the foreign policy community and our concept of the development community. This is not accidental: both communities perform roughly analogous functions.

economic growth, as information about the political factors influencing economic decisions. As the scope of the idea of development has expanded, development has become a larger area. We talk now not merely of the science of development but also of the development of science, not merely of the technology of development but also of the development of technology.

As a consequence of such reversals in speech, development is no more a mere treatment of the economic ills of a society; the development of healing as a science has become an important plank in the ideology of development. Development is no longer development unless it takes the benefits of modern medicine to the traditional, underdeveloped parts of the society, unless diseases and pestilences are removed by modern knowledge from the lives of the citizens, and unless the entire population of a country is brought within the ambit of the modern doctor and taken out of the dominion of folk wisdom, domestic remedies, and the non-modern healers.

Such a development was probably inescapable. For the last five decades, since the social sciences came into their own after World War II, the language of modern medicine has contributed handsomely to the language of development. Pathology, sickness, treatment, diagnosis, and cure have all been important terms in that part of the language of the body politic which has constituted the main discourse on development. Thus the now receding enthusiasm for the psychological sources of economic growth has often used the language of *injecting* the entrepreneurial spirit in underdeveloped cultures and of *curing* the pathology of non-entrepreneurial persons by introducing the *virus* of the achievement motive into them under quasi-therapeutic conditions.[2] The non-enterprising person has been seen, regularly enough, as falling short of full psychological health and negating the organizing principles of the fully functioning personality, at least in the popular culture of development studies.[3] Development is good, the argument goes, because it brings true health to everyone; development is health because healthiness takes you towards or gives you development; and finally, development is healthy because the language of development extends the modern language of healing not only to the individual but also to the society.

Long before Michel Foucault and Ivan Illich became eponymous figures in contemporary social criticisms of modern medicine, there had existed a certain scepticism towards doctors in traditional systems of thought and ways of life. The scepticism extended not merely to foreign or non-rooted

2. See for instance the description of the group-therapy-like situations in which it was sought to introduce the achievement motive to Third World societies (McClelland and Winter 1969).

3. If one offsets against this Everett Hagen's (1963) description of the non-enterprising person as the authoritarian person, *à la* Theodor Adorno and his associates, one is left with little doubt that some sought to medicalize the problem of development.

systems of healing, including what is called modern medicine or allopathy, but to traditional systems too, including the systems to which the sceptics gave their allegiance. It was this element of 'self-destructiveness' which paradoxically gave the traditional systems of medicine their viability and humanness.

It is possible to argue that modern medicine, which was one of the last sciences to grow out of the traditional sciences in Europe and consolidate itself as a 'proper' science in the nineteenth century, was the first major system of healing to try to do away with this element of scepticism and self-criticism. Some amount of scepticism and criticism survived in the popular culture, but it did not easily translate into philosophical doubt within the system. The Popperian principle of falsifiability, so central to the positivist self-concept of science, does not include within its scope any scepticism towards the basic philosophical assumptions or culture of post-seventeenth-century science. Once medicine became a positivist science, it also became philosophically and culturally less self-critical. The self-doubt of the modern doctor is essentially a personal self-doubt; so is the doubt of the patient expressed in medical litigation, or in the increasingly contractual relationship the patient enters with the doctor. The doubt almost always centres around the doctor's skills or around empirical medical knowledge, rarely around the philosophical and cultural assumptions of modern medicine.

In fact, it is possible to argue that the principle of falsifiability itself has suppressed many forms of critical consciousness within modern medicine. Certainly the principle has not allowed the kind of folk wisdom which many traditional systems of healing have often used as a baseline of criticism (expressed for instance in the Sanskritic saying quoted in many parts of India, of which a free translation is 'one who kills a hundred becomes an ordinary doctor, one who kills a thousand becomes a great physician' (Kakar 1986: 18–21). Clifford Geertz has talked of common sense as a cultural system (1983: 73–93). By disconnecting itself from the community life which organizes common sense as a culture, modern medicine has disconnected itself from the common sense which endorses scepticism in many traditional cultures of medicine.

In this chapter we review the implicit visions of health and knowledge which scaffold modern medicine in India and in the process provide an outline of the world-view and the concerns of some of the more explicit criticisms of modern medicine produced here. This review is informed by the awareness that the Indian debate on modern medicine is organized around two philosophical positions. On the one side are groups such as Medico Friends Circle, Delhi Science Forum, Kerala Sashtra Sahitya Parishad, Consumer Education and Research Centre, and some others associated with the Drug Action Network, as well as by activist-scholars like Abhay Bang, Anil Sadgopal, Narendra Mehrotra, Dhruv Mankad,

and probably even the redoubtable Zafrulla Chaudhuri. On the other side
are activist-scholars like Ziauddin Sardar, Claude Alvares, Mira Shiva of
the Voluntary Health Association of India, and many in the Patriotic
People's Science and Technology group. (Manu Kothari and Lopa Mehta,
two of the best-known social critics of medicine in this part of the world,
take a more eclectic position, though they are obviously more in sympathy
with the second position philosophically.[4]) For the former, a critique of
modern medicine has to be primarily contextual; for the latter, it has to
be contextual *and* textual. We locate our analysis in the space defined by
these two groups and try to expand the scope of the debate by
reconstructing in this chapter some of the debates on the subject which
took place earlier in this century.

We should clarify here that we are aware of the excellent work done
on traditional systems of Indian medicine by academics such as Charles
Leslie, Paul Brass, Roger Jeffery, and Francis Zimmermann. However,
we are also aware that these works bypass the continuing intellectual
attempts in India to grapple, often from outside academia, with the social
relations and political content of modern medicine in contemporary India.
And we, living in a post-Bhopal world, are forced to define our intellectual
responsibility mainly in terms of the politics of knowledge with which
the social critics and political activists working in the domain of health
in India today must live.

1.1 Manifest Critiques

There are some identifiable foci in the public debate on modern medicine
the world over, and there are two distinctive approaches. The dominant
idiom is that of the critics who stress *implementation*—the social responsibility of the modern doctor, the inequity in medical delivery
systems, and the pros and cons of socializing medicine. The other approach
tries to bring the *content* of modern medicine under critical scrutiny. Its
baseline of criticism is outside modern medicine, often outside the modern
world-view.

Thus, the second approach gives the example of the major killers in
human history—pestilences ranging from plague to cholera—which have
been eliminated from many countries not by modern drugs but by
improved public health systems. Plague went out of Europe long before
its nature was identified and a medical antidote was found for it.

The study of the evolution of disease patterns provides evidence that during the

4. See for instance Jayarao and Patel 1986; Bang and Patel 1985; Sathyamala, Sundharam,
and Bhanot 1986; Sardar 1986; Madras Group 1984; Alvares 1988; Kothari and Mehta
1973, 1979; and also various issues of *Information* and the *PPST Bulletin*.

last century doctors have affected epidemics no more profoundly than did priests during earlier times. . . .

The infections that prevailed at the outset of the industrial age illustrate how medicine came by its reputation. Tuberculosis, for instance, reached a peak over two generations. In New York in 1812, the death rate was estimated to be higher than 700 per 10,000; by 1882, when Koch first isolated and cultured the bacillus, it had already declined to 370 per 10,000. The rate was down to 180 when the first sanatorium was opened in 1910, even though 'consumption' still held second place in the mortality tables. After World War II, but before antibiotics became routine, it had dropped into eleventh place with a rate of 48. Cholera, dysentery, and typhoid similarly peaked and dwindled outside the physicians's control. . . . nearly 90 per cent of the total decline in mortality between 1860 and 1965 had occurred before the introduction of antibiotics and widespread immunization (Illich 1976: 115–16; see also Illich 1986: 3–8).[5]

Even if one does not fully accept such arguments, it is possible to see the major elements in the present crisis in medicine as the points of convergence of both textual and contextual—content and im-plementation—problems. As the 'hard realities' of this crisis are not our concern in this paper—this is a study in discourse, not an empirical stock-taking of modern medicine—we shall, however, only enumerate the problems to set the stage for our analysis.

The first is the recently much-discussed problem of clinical iatrogenesis. There are now societies where nearly one-third of all medical referrals are reported to be iatrogenic. In specific areas the data look even more disturbing. For instance, in Massachusetts, the home of the editors of this book, the number of children disabled by the treatment of cardiac non-disease exceeds the number of children under effective treatment for cardiac disease (Illich 1976: 24). The situation attains a certain poignancy in many Third World societies where entire populations are often herded like cattle, through coercive legislation or with the help of massive propaganda by state-owned media, towards accepting medical or surgical interventions or drugs which are unacceptable to many First World societies. Millions of plastic loops distributed for contraception without proper medical supervision, heavy use of useless but harmful choloroquinol-based anti-diarrhoeal agents, indiscriminate prescription of concentrated vitamin preparations (which have dramatically improved the health of ants and earthworms in many societies because they are excreted

---

5. The only apparent exception to the rule has been smallpox. This exception can be viewed in two ways. First, one may argue that the 'irrational' resistance to smallpox vaccination in many societies is partly a result of a 'rational' generalization made by the public from their experience with other epidemics. By contrast the use of the example of smallpox by the élites and the Westernized middle classes of the Third World to illustrate irrational resistance to modern health care can be seen as an interested attempt to generalize from a single exception. Second, it is doubtful if the theory of smallpox as an exception can be fully sustained, for traditional methods for combating the disease were effective but were eliminated for political reasons. See Chapter 4 above.

by the human body within a few hours), useless surgery ranging from unnecessary tonsilectomy and removal of impacted molars to cardiac bypass and Caesarean section, over-intervention in cases of cancer—they can all lead to forms of suffering against which there usually is little check, medical, social, or legal, in Third World societies.

Second, there are the mutant organisms or the drug-resistant strains of bacteria which have 'learnt' to live with drugs. As the drugs multiply, so do the strains of common organisms. These new strains are often more virulent and less manageable than the original organisms with which the humans have learnt to live for thousands of years. Typhoid vaccination, according to some, is now effective in less than 50 per cent of cases; the Widal test, till recently a reasonable laboratory 'proof' of typhoid, is effective in a smaller and smaller number of cases. Meanwhile, typhoid has become more difficult to identify through clinical observation, for the contours of the disease have changed in many countries, and chloramphenicol, the antibiotic routinely used in typhoid, now fails to give results in a large proportion of patients, due to its heavy and indiscriminate use over the last three decades for even minor ailments.

Third, there is the growing cost of treatment. Medical research now costs more not merely because of inflationary pressures, but also because of the growing demands on the medical R. & D. systems to produce drugs to cope with iatrogenic complications and mutant organisms. Americans now spend more on health every year than on food or shelter. This cost becomes prohibitive for the poorer parts of the world which are often unable to keep up with modern medical R. & D. but have to bear a major share of the burden, by paying high prices for drugs and new medical technology. Not only have the new drugs begun to reflect the galloping R. & D. costs, but just when some of the Third World societies acquire the technology for one of the wonder drugs and bring down its price through mass production, the effectiveness of the drug begins to decline. Thus, by the time it had been made cheap and easily accessible to Indians, the effectiveness of penicillin had declined in India from 92 per cent in the 1950s to 8 per cent in the early 1980s, and doctors have had to shift to costlier and more effective alternatives.

Fourth, there are now health problems created and sustained by the urban-industrial life-style. Modern medicine finds it difficult to cope with environmentally induced health disasters because it operates on the basis of Baconian inductionism, somewhat in the fashion of the detective in a Victorian crime thriller pursuing a single criminal who seemingly has nothing to do with the rest of the society and whose elimination from the society leaves the society healthy and whole. One example will suffice:

Some years ago, large quantities of DDT were used by the World Health Organisation in a programme of mosquito control in Borneo. Soon the local people, spared a mosquito plague, began to suffer a plague of caterpillars, which devoured the thatched roofs of their houses, causing them to fall in. The habits of the caterpillars limited their exposure to DDT, but predatory wasps that had formerly controlled the caterpillars were devastated.

Further spraying was done indoors to get rid of houseflies. The local gecko lizards which previously had controlled the flies, continued to gobble their corpses—now full of DDT. As a result, the geckos were poisoned, and the dying geckos were caught and eaten by house cats. The cats received massive doses of DDT, which had been concentrated as it passed from fly to gecko to cat, and the cats died. This led to another plague, now of rats. They not only devoured the people's food but also threatened them with yet another plague—this time the genuine article, bubonic plague. The government of Borneo became so concerned that cats were parachuted into the area in an attempt to restore the balance (Ehrlich and Ehrlich 1982, quoted in Goldsmith and Hildyard 1984: i. 79).

Finally, giving these four elements of the crisis a sharp edge is what Mira Shiva (1985) infelicitously calls the pharmaceuticalization of health. In societies where modern medical technology is available only in a few pockets, where the number of modern doctors and hospital beds are few, and where the capacity to pay for modern medical facilities is poor, medicalization has built-in limits. But the penetration of drugs into all spheres of life, including medicine, becomes for the same reasons deeper and more dangerous. Often one finds in such societies that drugs, with their easy and wide reach, are expected to take over the responsibility for public health from the doctor and health care agencies, in fact from the society itself. And the drugs, in the context of these expectations, become an end in themselves. According to at least one estimate, the proportion of useless drugs in India is as high as 70 per cent and there are 4,000 drugs in circulation in the country which could be banned or are already banned in other countries (Shiva 1985; see also Alvares 1986).

These five crises of modern medicine can be studied in many ways: as problems of medical R. & D., as problems of medical training and hospital management, and even as indicators of a paradigmatic crisis in modern medicine. In this paper we seek to grapple intellectually with the crises at the plane on which the dominant philosophy of healing constructs the patient as a scientific reality and defines the doctor and his therapeutics as a scientific enterprise.

1.2 Latent Critiques

Underlying the manifest crises of modern medicine are two basic and related issues: (1) the reconstruction of the reality of the patient through the standardization of the two-person relationship within which a therapeutic encounter takes place, including the specific forms which the principles of experimentation and operationalism assume within modern medicine, and (2) the reconstruction of the doctor as a specialist or professional and the redefinition of the doctor as an applied scientist rather than a healer. Those providing a critique of modern medicine with an awareness of these latent issues assume that the core of medical practice is not the cumulating knowledge of physiology and drugs but the dyadic interpersonal relationship between the doctor and the patient.

The relationship between the modern doctor and his patient, one part of the critique says, is increasingly characterized by attempts made through the methodology of modern medicine to decompose the patient as a person. True to the traditions of positivist sciences, medicine tries to change the patient from an experiential reality to an experimental one, move him from his life-world to the laboratory, reduce him from a molar to a molecular reality, and reinterpret his disease as somatic or psychological rather than psychosomatic.

The expression 'experimental' here does not mean that the doctors experiment on the patient, though some doctors do and most doctors unwittingly endorse the vivisectionist base on which the consciousness— and the unconsciousness—of the experimental machine is built. Nor does 'experimental' mean that the patient ceases to be human to the doctor, though something of that too is involved in the change.[6] The expression refers to the reconstruction of the patient and his suffering into a set of variables and readings as in a laboratory process. It means that modern medical practice, even if temporarily and for the purposes of the clinic, *has* to give primacy to the laboratory reality of the person in preference to his personal and, as it happens, clinical realities. It is by suppressing the last two realities that the scientific enterprise called medical practice can be sustained. The process of suppression (see Chapter 3) is socially imposed by a particular form of expertise which bases itself on the dualist world-view of modern science, a view which involves a transition from objectivity to objectivification (Nandy 1987: 95–126).

To give an example of another kind of reductionism involved here, the transformation of a psychosomatic reality to either a purely somatic case or a purely psychiatric one (usually the former) does not mean that modern medicine does not have any space for the psychosomatic: it has. However, this space is reserved for a specialization. In modern medicine, there are three forms of illness—somatic, psychological, and psychosomatic—each one requiring a different kind of professional expertise, whereas for some other visions of health there is only one form of illness: the psychosomatic. Some of the latter, such as homeopathy, are discerning enough to add that while all illnesses are psychosomatic, some are more somatic and others are more psychological. That which is a classification in one system becomes a scale in others.

The main point is that the doctor who trusts the voice of the patient

6. See for instance Robert Lifton's deeply disturbing studies of concentration camp doctors (1982, 1986).

more than pathological test results in his own clinical work is perceived as less scientific in his practice, even though he may be perceived as a more gifted healer and more respected as a practitioner. He may be respected as a doctor but not as a scientist and, though he may be considered successful by his community, professional honours and fame are likely to pass him by.[7]

This is because laboratory test results provide a series of readings from which it is possible to reconstruct the patient as a clinical body in which the doctor therapeutically intervenes. The readings, when seen as operational definitions of the reality of the patient, must have priority over the doctor's personal impression of the patient as a person and the doctor's clinical impressions of the patient as a patient. The latter are parts of a trans-science, as defined by Alvin Weinberg (1972); their vicissitudes fall outside the science of modern medicine and they are sometimes called, in half-contempt, 'bedside manners'. Readings, on the other hand, allow for control and prediction and are therefore seen as the heart of the science of medicine.

The shadow patient, the patient reconstructed from the pathological test results, then acquires a medical reality and autonomy of its own; it is with that shadow that the modern hospital is primarily concerned. The rest, that is the patient's personal and clinical realities, are seen by the medical system as variables which induce compromises—often major and necessary compromises—with the science (as opposed to the art) of medicine. They are not seen as variables with an intrinsic scientific status. And because modern medicine is constantly trying to be a better science rather than a better art, the logic of the process pushes the discipline further towards viewing the human body as a complex machine.

The second part of the critique says that modern medicine *has* to conceptualize the patient as the sum of a finite set of subsystems which, in turn, have to be seen, for therapeutic purposes, as relatively and functionally autonomous of each other. One or more of these subsystems, when affected by a disease, has to be separately treated according to the needs created by the disease process, in turn seen as an external encroachment into one or more subsystems.[8] The treatment usually consists in entering the affected subsystem(s) with a 'counter-agent' or in intervening in the subsystem surgically. If in the course of this battle against ill health—the use of the term is common in the modern medical

7. There is a shift in this respect from the earlier phases of modern medicine in India, dominated by larger-than-life physicians like Nilratan Sarkar and Bidhan Chandra Roy, and the present phase when the most prominent figures in the world of Western medicine in India are primarily researchers. See also the plague episode and Haffkinism discussed below.

8. This view of disease as an external process finding a habitat in the body could itself be an interesting subject of enquiry, because many other systems see disease as basically an internal process triggered by external factors. See Section 4 for an example.

discourse—other subsystems are affected, they are handled through another set of interventions, in the form of another set of drugs or another form of surgery. Previously such effects were called side-effects of drugs, now they are called clinical iatrogeny.

It is possible to argue that the entire range of specializations in modern medicine is a direct outcome of this perception of the patient. Specialists are increasingly seen in modern medicine not as a tangential development or deviation from the primary agent of medicine in action, the general practitioner. The general practitioner is seen as a residual category—that which is left behind after the specialists and the specializations are taken out of the field. In the medical Utopia, therefore, there is no place for the GP. He or she is there today as a temporary compromise with the truly scientific and fully developed medical fraternity. For the truly scientific and fully developed medicine, as an area of knowledge and action, is viewed as by definition the sum of the medical specializations. Ideally such a medicine should not have any place for the generalist. Obviously, this way of looking at things is a far cry from the work cultures of many non-modern medical systems in which, because the patient/client is seen in holistic terms, the doctor is also expected to be a generalist first and specialist second. In fact the specialist, when operating in a non-modern system (for instance, the osteopath in Ayurveda), is often of a lower status than the generalist.

The obverse of this issue is the problem of operationalism. If the patient's scientific reality is conterminous with the patient's operational reality, as modern medicine seems to assume, then it is only the patient's operational reality which allows the doctor—and through him the society—'true', controlled intervention. It allows one to predict (prognose), test the prediction, reformulate the diagnosis, and alter the course of intervention. The individual patient's health, too, becomes assessable mainly from the central tendencies of a series of statistical distributions. And the two-person dialogue between the doctor and the patient gets redefined as another input into a quasi-man-machine system constituted by the doctor and the laboratory. The limits to the system are set by the existing level of medical technology and the 'contract' between the doctor and the patient.

Such a conceptualization leaves scope in the medical discourse only for a monologue from the doctor and for either silence from the patient—the best patient is probably the one who considerately allows the doctor to do a *post mortem*—or for 'noise', the language of suffering used by the patient during consultancy, a language only fit to be interpreted with the help of the standardized categories of medical symptomatology.

In such a world of healing, the doctor's sense of security no longer depends on his clinical, empathetic understanding of two sets of data, one derived from the clinical examination of social reality of the person and the other derived from the operational measures of the patient's body functions or dysfunctions: it begins to depend almost exclusively on the latter. Thus, for those interested in the art of medicine or in a holistic understanding of healing, cholera has two sets of causes—(1) poverty and the associated collapse of public health measures and (2) cholera germs finding a habitat in an individual's body. For those seeing medicine from within the world-view of modern science, cholera is caused only by the germs and can be eliminated by vaccination or, after one has been stricken by the disease, through rehydration and maintenance of the body's fluid composition. The social context enters only the epidemiology, not the therapeutics. In the first case, the 'voice' of the victim is important; in the second case it is not.

2   Three Languages of Criticism

There are two ways of taking stock intellectually of the criticisms of the modern medical system in the savage world. The first is through an empirical analysis, cataloguing its efficiency through an audit of birth, death, and health. Such an analysis allows one to uphold some criticisms and reject others on 'scientific' grounds. However, such an analysis also tends to become 'external' and to focus on the political economy of medicine, on the sociology of hospitals, or on the medical profession. The second way is to approach the task of stock-taking in terms of what may be called an ecology of knowledge. In this approach the modern medical system, as a collective representation, is made to confront the possibility of its 'other'. To elaborate this simple point we shall now shift our focus to the dialectic between the 'self' of modern medicine and its 'other', laying particular stress on the availability of alternative imaginations within which the dialectic works.

More specifically, we shall examine the intellectual critiques of modern Western medicine within the Indian national movement. The particular period we shall consider is the post-Swadesi period, the two decades after the Swadesi movement of 1904, which led to attempts to indigenize industry and education in India, but our analysis will be a free-wheeling description drawn mainly from four 'archives': the feminist-theo-sophist-occult writings of Helena Blavatsky (1831–91), Lind-Af-Hageby, and Annie Besant, the neo-vitalist biology of Patrick Geddes, Gandhi's Hind-Swaraj, and G. Srinivasmurthi's 'modernist' construction of an Ayurvedic critique of allopathy. These constitute what we like to call the archives of dissenting Western imagination in alliance with indigenous knowledge systems in India.[9]

9. The most important element in these archives is theosophy. Theosophy played a significant role in the Indian national movement. Allan Octavian Hume, generally regarded as the founder of the Indian National Congress, was a theosophist. Annie Besant

We choose such a period and its archives for three reasons. First, the debates in this era were pluralist. Parallel to the opposition between white and black, the colonizer and the colonized, was a deeper dialogical encounter in which the Western participants saw in India a possibility to be lived out. India to them was a place within which the other West of William Blake and Paracelsus could be revived. India in turn, seeking liberation from the West, nevertheless saw in the West an addition to the pool of alternatives in knowledge available within India.

Second, the era anticipated the disrepute into which later critiques of Western science have sometimes fallen. Today, such critiques are often seen as being associated either with passing fads or with obscurantism and authoritarianism. The possibilities of alternative medicine or science immediately bring to mind the years of Lysenko, the fact that Adolf Hitler was a great advocate of nature cure, that Mussolini was an anti-vivisectionist. We shall however argue that, instead of being eclectic fads as are some critiques of modern medicine today, the debates of the post-Swadesi era had a civilizational tenor to them. Also, there was in the debates a certain *naïveté*, a nakedness of intentions which makes it easier for us to elaborate their strategies and consequences.

Third, we feel that in any reconstruction of a critique of a knowledge system, an emphasis only on the nature of power encoded in the system is inadequate. One must concentrate on the content and strategies of dissent. All too often dissenting groups have sought the replacement of those in power without challenging the nature of the discourse. The critics become contextual and emphasize the social misuse of medical science; they fail to grasp the intrinsic nature of the science as a mode of cognition. The exoteric history of science, too, has concentrated on such overt processes, failing to show how esoteric critiques have provided ethical spaces from within which one can confront the hegemony of modern medicine.

2.1 The Theosophy of Alternatives

One of the most obvious illustrations of this is the feminist movement and its critique of medicine. Official feminism has often stressed equality, without an adequate, built-in cultural critique of uniformity and standardization. It has not been a celebration of difference, of reciprocity. Such a feminism has at a basic level left unchallenged the official medical discourse. As a result, such critiques have merely enlarged the scope of

(1847–1933), President of the Theosophical Society, was elected President of the Indian National Congress. She was also, as we know, a leader of the Home Rule Movement. Patrick Geddes (1854–1932), the Scottish biologist, came to India in 1914 to prepare a town planner's report on Madras. He was the first professor of sociology at Bombay University and the first English biographer of the botanist J. C. Bose (1858–1937). Maria Montessori (1870–1952), who played such an important role in shaping the nationalist education policy in India, also had strong theosophical leanings.

the scientific gaze. We shall make this point by taking the reader through the works of Lorna Duffin and Jacques Donzelot, then contrasting them with the efforts of occult feminism in the works of theosophically inclined writers who influenced the Indian national movement.

Duffin's 'The Conspicuous Consumptive: Woman as an Invalid' (1978) is a remarkable study which shows that the perfect lady in upper-class Victorian England was a perpetual invalid. Duffin argues that the social construction of woman-as-perpetual-invalid could not have been maintained without the aid of the medical profession. Using the *Lancet* from 1850 to 1890, Duffin describes the different strategies by which the medical profession, through the scientific definition and control of the woman's body, helped maintain the social inequality of women.

The picture that emerges is one of a classic double bind. First, women were regarded as ill because they were women and, second, women became ill when they attempted to do anything outside the conventionally accepted feminine role. Both nature and culture were conscripted to maintain the status of the woman as invalid.

By defining the woman as ill, all specifically female functions were treated as pathological. Puberty, menstruation, pregnancy, labour, lactation, and menopause, all became conditions that 'invalidated' the woman, rendering her incapable of mental or physical labour. 'The entire animal economy of woman', as one doctor put it, 'is linked to the gigantic power and influence of the ovaries' (Duffin 1978: 34). There was a corollary to this. All nervous disorders of women were linked to disturbances in the reproductive system. Robert Barnes in his Lumleian lectures of 1878 claimed that the convulsions of childbirth were indistinguishable from those of epilepsy. He added 'at menopause, the nervous force no longer finding useful function goes astray in every direction' (ibid. 36).

Duffin notes that by defining all normal female functions as pathological, doctors also removed the control and management of pregnancy and childbirth from the hands of women and midwives, and placed them in the hands of male medical practitioners. It is easy to understand, in terms of these social processes, the responses of the medical profession to the entry of woman into it. It involved another double bind. If women themselves become ill by transgressing the boundaries of the feminine role, protecting women from the hazards of medical profession is a medical responsibility. Neurasthenia, Duffin shows, became a women's disease because it was allegedly caused by increased mental activity; she notes the increase of clitoridectomy and ovarectomy as cures for epilepsy, hysteria, sterility, and insanity in woman. Herbert Spencer in his *Principles of Biology* claimed that 'flat chested girls, who survive the high pressure of education' would be unable to bear a well developed infant or feed it (cited in Duffin 1978: 33). On the other hand, reverting to the pristine purity of womanhood was reverting to illness, too.

The history of the feminist movement chronicles the various attempts by women to liberate themselves from the circumscribed sexuality that medicine imposed on them. Particularly important in this context were the efforts of Marie Stopes, Margaret Sanger, and Annie Besant in her pre-theosophy days. Yet one senses that while they allowed for a greater role for woman in the economic and political systems, they left the content of medical science intact. One could go further and say with Donzelot that the redefinition of the mother–child bond, so central to the feminist movement, was extracted at a heavy price (Donzelot 1979). For instance, the new medical sciences like eugenics and psychotherapy used the feminist movements to widen the power of modern science, particularly that of the scientific 'gaze', as Foucault might put it. As a result, psychology escaped 'from the insane asylum' and obtained tutelage over the grid of social health so central to contemporary medical hegemony. The process is similar to what Foucault describes in *the Birth of The Clinic* (1963). Foucault argues that the patient, particularly the poor patient, could avail himself of medical facilities only by opening himself up to scientific observation and intervention, by becoming the object of the new science of medicine.

In sum, the possibility of a feminist style in science was ignored in these attempts. Geddes and Thomson (1914) make this point clearly. They emphasize the need to make the most of the complementary qualities of women.

It is important that medical schools and medical posts should be open to women of special aptitude. But from our general biological point of view, it seems that the most promising line of experiment would be that of providing specialized education for medical women—not 'easier' or 'lower' or any nonsense of that sort, but different—so that there might arise not duplication of one type of medical servant in the state but two distinct types of medical servant. It must be urgently emphasized, however, that the fittest medical education is not likely to be that which men in their wisdom prescribe, but that which women with a free hand, work out for themselves. . . . As Ellen Key has declared, 'to put women to do men's work is as foolish as to set Beethoven or a Wagner to do engine driving' (pp. 233–4).

Geddes did not specifically talk of an alternative feminist science of medicine, but the possibility was entertained by some women at the time. There was a realization that the hegemony of medical science arose from the suppression of the 'other' as a patient, madman, child, woman, and animal, that the liberation of women from medicine could only be brought about by liberating these suppressed others. We shall now turn to the strategies theosophist feminism employed in formulating this awareness.

To understand occult feminism, one must remember three facts. First, there was a realization among the theosophist feminists that while liberty for women at one level was a result of secularization and rationalization, this liberty had a cost. Woman's participation in the eugenics and family planning movements had led to what may be called the semantic impoverishment of the feminine body, that is, the availability of signs, symptoms, and symbols centring around the body diminished in the new social contract between the feminists and the medical establishment. The asexualism of the industrial life was already eroding the essentially feminine and, by 1917, there were already anxious reports about the decline of breast-feeding among working women (Srinivasmurthi 1917).

Second, the occult feminists realized the importance of treating the patient as a woman of knowledge. They realized (1) that the mechanomorphic body of vivisectionist medicine, the élitism of eugenics, and IQ psychology gave little scope for the free play of the patient's knowledge or self-expression, and (2) that the oppositions between nature and culture, woman and man, and the domestic and the professional had to be redrawn, and to do so they had to reshuffle the relationships between man, nature, and God. The occult provided the space for both sets of activities; it pluralized the materialist concept of the body by multiplying the number of bodies. The sheer availability of other bodies—the causal body, the astral body, the etheric body—created multiple realities, spaces within which new possibilities could be worked out. The reductionism of the materialist body was no longer able to account for the emergence of forms of consciousness and psychic powers that the presence of the astral and etheric body provided for.

Helena Blavatsky remarked that it never occurred to the physician that it was in the physiology of the mind—in the relationship of the conscious self and the body—more than in the material body that the causes of many maladies were to be found. According to her, it was in that relationship that the secret of medicine was to be sought rather than in the molecular structure on which generations of doctors had toiled with little success (Blavatsky 1966: iii. 189).

Third, with the multiplication of bodies and the forms of consciousness, the innumerable nervous disorders associated with women were reread. Hysteria, spirit communication, telepathy, and clairvoyance became spaces for a new freedom, spaces where the rules and the regimentation of the official medical body were irrelevant. Simultaneously, an attempt was made to remove the various nervous disorders associated with woman from the domain of pathology to the domains of the normal and the supra-normal. Charles Leadbeater (1904: 30) cites one of the earlier instances, that of Anton Mesmer. He says,

throughout his early experiments, he (Mesmer) was under the impression that magnetic sensitiveness was always a symptom of ill health; and it seems to have been a great surprise to him when he found that one of his patients retained her power after recovery. Further investigation led him to understand that it was not a question of health but a psychic faculty; and he conjectured correctly enough, that all in reality have the power to a greater or lesser degree; but in some it is only able to come to the surface when ordinary physical faculties are weakened by sickness.

Partly as a result of such formulations, there was a virtual epidemic of occult and spiritualist happenings, in which women were the primary medium of occultism and spiritualism. There was a celebration of telepathy, spirit healing, reincarnation, and clairvoyance. It was one of the few surrealistic periods in the annals of medical science.

This period also emphasized the importance of language and communication in the doctor–patient relationship. As Blavatsky remarked, not all prophecies and communications 'could be reduced to the same level with the hallucinations of the ventroloquist Mlle. Amonda, whose delusions were due to vapours caused by the hysterical swelling of the large intestine' (Blavatsky 1910: 119). The statements of mediums and the language of hallucinations became important. Blavatsky did however add in a wry aside that

the great majority of spiritual communications are calculated to disgust investigators of even moderate intelligence. Even when genuine, they are trivial, commonplace and vulgar. During the past twenty years we have received messages purporting to come from Shakespeare, Byron, Franklin, Napoleon, Josephine and even Voltaire. The general impression made upon us was that the French conqueror and his consort had forgotten to spell words correctly; Shakespeare and Byron have become inebriates and that Voltaire had turned into an imbecile (1968: 41).

Yet, occult medicine was a genuine effort to restore the importance of speech in the doctor–patient relationship. In attempting this, it did add a truly semiotic dimension to modern medicine. It went beyond the reductionism of cause and effect, and stimulus and response, to the world of signs, symptoms, and symbols.

In such an exercise, the patient and the world of the patient became central. As important was the reconceptualization of the mother–child bond and the way it linked with the doctor–patient relationship. Figure 1 gives an idea of the alternative visions of childhood, so central to the theosophical exercise and the concept of medicine which went with it.

The concept of the patient in such a framework gave free play to a number of basic selves of woman—the pregnant woman, the patient, the mother seeking to understand childhood outside the narrow world of eugenics and modern medicine. The framework raised questions like: What is a foetus? What makes some foetuses become 'monstrous' and others angelic? How does one cope with or explain prodigies and morons? Does the foetus have rights?

The emphases in these questions shift from the demands of the scientific-medical world to the systems of meaning that women find

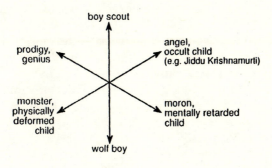

Fig. 1

relevant as women, mothers, patients, and as parts of the folk imagination. The questions cut across nature and culture, and across the human, the subhuman, and the animal. It is ethnoscience at its most autonomous, formed not by rejecting medical science but incorporating some aspects of it into a more meaningful bricoleurian world.

The problem of the monster—the entire teratology of deformed babies, those born with little tails, excess hair, withered feet, strange birthmarks, and other forms of stigmata—was something that had always boggled the folk imagination. Theosophy, when it concerned itself with the problem, found evolutionist teratology neither sufficient nor convincing. The evolutionist account had no place for reincarnation, which was so important to the folk imagination. For the theosophists, only the cycles of birth and rebirth endowed biology with any sense of natural justice.

The re-emergence of the monster was accompanied by the resurgence of stories about the wolf boy, about children who had lived so close to animals that culture seemed minimal in them. The wild boy of Aveyron was a part of both the folk and the scientific world. The attempts to treat him by doctors like Jean Itard were later to inspire Maria Montessori, the well-known educationist and the first Italian woman to receive a medical degree (Lane 1979). While working at a psychiatric clinic in Rome she frequently visited the city's asylums, where she found idiot children grouped indiscriminately with the insane. The early work on the wolf boy had convinced her 'that mental deficiency presented chiefly a pedagogical rather than medical problem' (Lane 1979: 280).

If Montessori's first radical step was to demedicalize the problem, her second move, as many theosophists observed, was to alter the interventionist frame of mind. For Montessori, education was not 'something we do for the child, but largely something we refrain from doing, so as not to interfere with its growth' (Jinarajadasa 1938: 129). The child to Montessori was a little messiah (ibid. 134). Finally, according to her, account had to be taken not only of the child's physical but also its psychic life—which for the theosophists included the spiritual life. Partly as a result, for Montessori every parent, especially the mother, became a true scientist caring for the child. This spiritual humility, too, was radically different from the interventionist eugenics of the time.

The radical imagination of Montessori as a doctor captured the spirit of the theosophists with remarkable sensitivity. There was no distancing of the professional from the non-professional here, for every woman could feel there was a Montessori in her. Montessori's science was one of demedicalization and deregimentation. It was not a medicine that preached the surveillance of the body in a barrack-like school. It did not pathologize the child in order to objectify him and thus legitimize further intervention. And though there was innocence here and though the retreat of power was temporary—for her teachings were soon incorporated in courses of home *science* and *scientific* social work—for a while she represented the ideal medical scientist working as a participant observer.

The feminist-theosophist imagination also counterpoised the wolf boy against the boy scout. If the former represented nature which had to be recovered for culture, the other represented culture reaching back to nature. However, theosophists had little sympathy for Baden-Powell's concept of scouting, which was steeped in social Darwinism and coloured by imperialism (Springhall 1977: 57). To Baden-Powell scouting was a form of social hygiene established to counter the threat of English national decadence and the lack of enthusiasm for the empire. He was against free feeding, old age pensions, and strike pay, 'for they did not make for the hardening of the nation' (ibid.).

What theosophy sought to do was to recover the other part of Baden-Powell and integrate it in an alternative frame—the ecological consciousness, the romantic woodcraft naturalism of Ernest Thomson Seton, who had inspired the sections on woodcraft in Baden-Powell's book. Central to Besant's dissident idea of the boy scout, embodied in the Hindustan Boy Scout movement, was that the boy scout was kind to animals. The child thus became part of the anti-vivisectionism so central to the theosophist critiques of medicine as well as part of the movements for the rights of animals and women in the West. The debate on the intelligence of animals, such as reports on horses able to count, were frequent in theosophist journals. The scouting lore, too, was full of anthropomorphic anecdotes. Gerald Carson has remarked that 'the zoologists may shudder but the anthropomorphic anecdote has made more friends for the animal kingdom than they have' (1972: 121).

One last observation. As we have already said, there was an air of surrealistic biology about the theosophical framework. The theosophists produced a picture of a circus rather than that of a museum. The museum as a representative of modern science classifies defeated systems and alien bodies into the rigidity of a linear-evolutionary framework. The circus domesticates such alien bodies but allows for free-wheeling imagination. The surrealistic bricoleur of bodies in theosophy challenged the conventional ideas of the normal and the pathological. It was reminiscent of the role of the carnival in medieval times. To mix metaphors, Blavatsky and other feminists were like intellectual Barnums who had turned the world of medical knowledge into a circus juxtaposing folk jugglers and psychologists, Paracelsus and Darwin, the magician and the scientist, so that formal medical science lost its priority. Condemning this as quackery, fraud, or pseudo-science misses the point. It is like saying Salvador Dali could not see straight. Theosophist attacks were like sociological stances, tactics against the hegemony of a domineering medical science. The strategy was simple: pluralize the number of bodies and modern medicine would find it more difficult to regiment them. And this strategy had to involve India; the theosophists had to discover their circus in India. For India, according to them, showed all the signs of being the site for an alternative medical imagination.

But the Swadesi movement in India was already finding scientific medicine seductive. Lala Har Dayal had already said, 'a little science confers more happiness on mankind than all the piety of the middle ages' (1912: 48). He noted that while Pasteur and Koch were not saintly ascetics, they were still greater benefactors of humanity than all the nurses of the religious organizations. For Har Dayal, modern science had to become the Vedas of the resurgent India, and the scientist the model for the *rishi*hood of the future. 'Do not . . . follow the old footsteps of the rishis. Benares and Puri have had their day. What is there in Benares but . . . fat bulls and fat priests. What is there in Puri but cholera . . .?' (p. 49). The theosophists, on the other hand, were afraid that Indian nationalism, in its quest for liberation, might internalize the violence of a desacralized Western science. In fact, in the specifics of its critique of the Swadesi movement, theosophy also became a critique of the Swadesi internalization of vivisectionist medical science.

2.2 Theosophy and the Violence of Vivisection

Vivisection has been defined as the justified infliction of pain on animals in the pursuit of science. As a scientific ritual it includes starving, baking, crushing, beating with mallets, fracturing bones, varnishing with pitch, subjecting to varying atmospheric pressures or to none, blowing up the body by forcible inflation, poisoning, amputating, burning, and irradiating. The anti-vivisection movement in the early part of this century attempted to show how modern science legitimized the violation of the integrity of the other when that other could be defined as animal or, for that matter, as criminal, black, monster, poor, or colonial subject.

This attack on vivisection has to be understood in terms of the career of public health in India. The introduction of vivisection in India involved what a gathering of Jains once called the rise of Haffkinism and Pasteurism in India. We borrow an example from Helen Bourchier's classic paper at the 1907 Anti-Vivisection and Animal Protection Congress. Bourchier contrasts the Hippocratic view of medicine as an ethical art and the modern laboratory view of medicine. She shows the contrast by examining two distinct empirical approaches to plague, the first evident in the case of the plague in Egypt in the late nineteenth century and the second in the Great Plague of Bombay, which began in 1896 and lasted twelve years.

When plague struck Egypt, Sir John Rogers, who was then Director General of the Sanitary Department, immediately instituted a series of measures. Persons found infected were isolated and those who came into contact with the patients were quarantined, where they were fed and compensated for the loss of their time. These measures were supplemented by others, such as lime-washing of infected houses and the disposal of garbage away from the city precincts. As a result, the epidemic subsided within six months, the eventual death toll being a mere 45. Today, the Egyptian case is hardly remembered in the annals of science, while the Bombay plague is cited as an example of the success of medical science (Bourchier 1907: 84–5).

Bourchier shows that when the epidemic was raging in India and millions were dying, a group of doctors brought to the notice of W. M. W. Haffkine, the well-known medical researcher, the importance of introducing sanitary measures similar to the one employed in Egypt. But Haffkine represented what they called 'the laboratory point of view'; he had come 'to test on man the remarkable results which he had obtained on animals in the laboratory with the cholera bacillus' (Bourchier 1907: 85, 78). He rejected their suggestions and ensured that no sanitary measures were undertaken while his vaccine was being tried out. He had his own ideas about experimental and control groups and about how far people in a colony could be used as guinea-pigs for the sake of the progress of science. It tells one something about the culture of modern medicine that not only has the modern medical profession half-forgotten the Egyptian plague; it has deified Haffkine as a great healer and benefactor of the non-Western world.

Theosophist editorials warned that the vivisectionist rituals of the laboratory state would soon envelop a whole series of 'others'. They referred to the proposed measure to legalize the vivisection of criminals sentenced to capital punishment in Ohio, in the United States. They warned that the logic of vivisectional science was such that the

capitally sentenced criminals would be utterly insufficient to meet the demand for living human subjects and accordingly paupers, lunatics, hospital patients would have to be utilized. In short time, no poor and friendless person would be safe and at length all classes would find themselves exposed to this danger ('Cuttings and Comments', Mar. 1903: 382).

Already hospitals had become so blatant that opportunities for vivisection were widely advertised in medical directories. Lind-Af-Hageby cites the example of the Charing Cross Hospital at London which advertised in 1907:

from the extensive outpatient department, the most instructive cases were drafted into the wards for the benefit of the pupils and the outpatient practice as well as the special departments for female disorders, childrens diseases, eye diseases and skin diseases are similarly utilized . . . a large number of casualities are annually admitted, affording valuable opportunity for surgical practice (1907: 95).

St Bartholomews Hospital recommended itself in the following words: 'The Hospital contains 670 beds, in addition to 70 beds for convalescent patients at Swanley, in Kent. There is therefore an abundance of clinical material' (ibid.).

The theosophist campaign against vivisection thus became a virtual charter of civil rights for the victims of medical violence, a violence which was now increasingly backed by the state. The theosophists insisted that the violence of modern medicine was not merely directed against distant or pathological others; it was also the banal violence of everyday science. Thus, Annie Besant warned Swadesi pedagogues against unnecessary dissections in science classrooms. Referring to schools in Europe she said,

they repeat experiments of advanced scientific men in order to watch with their own eyes the results which they read in their text books. This is not done for the gaining of new knowledge, but is merely idle repetition of facts well established. For instance, a dog will be taken and laid upon the dissecting table, then the nerves will be exposed along the neck and under the skin of the legs, and while strapped in this condition, a sudden injury may be caused by the application of a red-hot iron, to a particular part of the brain and the dog will bark and the professor will brutally say to the public, 'See how we make the dog bark by stimulating this position of the brain' (Besant 1896: 7).

Besant warned against such early brutalization in schools, and other theosophists argued that the entry of such a science into society could be dangerous. It was in this context that they opposed the inauguration of the Pasteur Institute in India ('Cuttings and Comments', June 1903: 565–68).

The advocates of vivisection, on the other hand, first propagated the fear of a disease, rabies in the case of the Pasteur Institute, and then offered science as a solution. Of this a theosophist said, 'Westerners are awfully afraid of hydrophobia. It means death to them. Pasteur's Institute is supposed to be the only saviour and those that cannot bear the expense of going to it, must succumb to it sooner or later' (Perraju 1902: 23). 'Yet in Indian villages', the essay pointed out, 'there are always pariah dogs which bite villagers. They can never hope to get to Kasauli and yet are cured and live' (ibid.). The theosophists emphasized the importance of vegetable therapeutics, of herbs from other systems, of alternative systems of medicine in general, particularly in the context of resisting vivisection. For instance, they pointed out that, in the care of rabies, the usual prescription was the juice of the *ummetha* plant mixed in jaggery. They seemed to feel the need to create life-giving myths or, if that was not possible, to give to the dominant medical system what, loosely following Arne Naess (1972), we can call 'postulates of impotency'.

The ideas of homeopathy were often used by the theosophists as examples. Samuel Hahnemann and his collaborators had experimented on themselves with about 97 drugs. The results had been 'astonishing'. The symptoms caused by the drugs had produced faithful 'pictures' of everyday illnesses. Hahnemann's 'provers', in expressing their abnormality, had used the exact phrases encountered in interviews with patients. Hahnemann had also found that nine-tenths of the symptoms produced were subjective, that is, they required human speech to articulate them. He had these classified, a classification which has survived in homeopathy till today. All this would have been impossible had he employed animals (Petrie Hoyle n.d.).

There is one other reason why the theosophists might have found homeopathy attractive. We have already noted that one criticism of modern medicine is that it sees the patient not as a person but as a table of symptoms. Homeopathy shares this critical view and, to counter what may be called the impersonalization of sickness, advocates the individualization—and repersonalization—of the patient's symptoms. For the homeopath, every case is unique. The disease for which different patients may be consulting him may be the same, but the treatment should be different in each case. The physician has to consider the mental, emotional, and physical pathology of each individual and the unique way in which the individual reacts to his illness. The clinical interview, therefore, becomes crucial for the homeopath's work.

2.3 Western Medicine and the State

Let us now turn to another major, if indirect, theme in theosophical critiques of modern medicine. To articulate the theme we shall first have to recognize that the history of power has become in many ways the history of the body as well as a historical catalogue of the various forms of body technique and discipline devised to control the body in a laboratory, barrack, hospital, or school. To the theosophists, as to other dissenters of their times, medicine was becoming a legitimizing principle of the state. It allowed the state to inspect, survey, and classify people in terms of medical categories—as insane, criminal, or sick (Foucault 1980). Sometimes the state even used these categories to exterminate or liquidate individual communities and races. The grand traditions of political theory have ignored this 'mundane' politics of everyday life. The abstract celebrations of market, state, and sovereignty have time and again suppressed the awareness that medicine is politics, that it has provided the dominant metaphors of control and collectivization. Alfred Wallace once remarked that one required certificates from only two registered doctors to send a feminist to an insane asylum (Wallace 1908: 456–7).

This compact between Western medicine and the nation-state worried dissenters of the era. They realized that if health was power and the state a form of hygiene, the civil society must contain alternative notions of health, pathology, and cure. The availability of such alternative notions was fundamental to contain, ecologically, the hegemony of the medical state. In the next section we shall return to this issue.

On a less ambitious level, there were the works of Wallace, a British advocate of the Swadesi movement, and Geddes. Wallace exerted a great influence on the theosophists in India. To Wallace, the very success of science as a mode of being was a sign of concern, because science could be cognitively coercive but could not be domesticated within its concept of method. The heretical impulse behind nineteenth-century mesmerism and homeopathy was, to Wallace, an ethico-scientific imperative, which some scientists must follow to prevent the dominant system of science from becoming hegemonic. Wallace's book *The Wonderful Century* (1908), a history of nineteenth-century science, has an intriguing second half. There, after outlining the triumphs of Western science, he develops the ideas which were regarded as heretical by the scientifically minded: psychic research, phrenology, critiques of vaccination. (The heretical impulse also found expression in the theosophical movement's paradigmatic scientist, Jagdis Chandra Bose. Bose introduced into modern plant physiology totally disjunctive ideas of life and matter which unfortunately were to be domesticated and eventually absorbed into the dominant structure of science (Nandy 1980: Part I).)

The effort of Geddes was more collective. A maverick biologist, Geddes believed that the hegemony of a mechanistic science had coloured major areas of Western thought—physical sciences, economics, pedagogy, health, and even the Haussmanic city with its celebration of linear planning and mechanical grids of roads, disguised to cut across vital communities merely because they were poor or disease-prone. Geddes saw in his neo-vitalist biology the possibilities of a dialogue the West had suppressed, both within itself and in other traditions. It was in this context that he felt that India would be the site for a post-Germanic university (Geddes 1904).

For Geddes, no university system was complete without its dissenting academies. The career of the university as an organism often reflected a violent dialogue with competing notions of knowledge and pedagogy resident in its environment. The success of a university lay in its ability to provide a working synthesis. For instance, the medieval university itself arose out of an attempt to reconcile the doctrines of Christian church with the recovery of Aristotle. Parallelling this, he argued, the ideal culture of medicine should have physicians of many faiths, comparing not only their drugs but also their doctrines.

India, Geddes felt, could start such an exercise. He hoped that the exercise would lead to the revival of a rural view of science. He claimed that the economics of the leaf colony and the economics of metals were coming into conflict and that the first would once again have a larger significance, as it once had in the rural world of the old. He hoped that the young doctors from Edinburgh, London, or Paris would go to study Indian diseases and interpret India's diverse cultural context to throw new light on European bacteriology, as Calmette had brought back to the Pasteur Institute at Lille, to its brewers and bakers, a new yeast from old China, thus taking an industrial and a chemical step in one (Geddes 1904: 1). In pursuit of such an idea of the university Geddes wanted Shantiniketan, the alternative rural university founded by the poet Rabindranath Tagore (1861–1940), to embody both a scientific and aesthetic encounter with the West, but the concept lost out in Tagore's final blueprint for the university. The Swadesi nationalists, on their part, defeated Geddes's hopes of designing the new university at Benares.

The other strategy to work out new relationships among various medical systems was political. In England, during the debate over the registration of medical practioners in the 1920s, Lind-Af-Hageby convened a conference on medical liberty and declared the right to medical freedom as a civil right. It included the right to choose one's treatment, the right to do without a doctor, and the right to resist the fashions of orthodox and unorthodox medicines (Geddes 1904: 16; Hageby *et al.* 1934: 2). In fact she forwarded a scheme for a Parliamentary party on medical liberty with some of the following objectives:

1. To resist legislation by which the right of the individual to reject orthodox treatment could be abrogated and by which the prevalent theories of allopathic medicine would be identified with the state.
2. To spread knowledge of the various schools of nonconformist medicine and to demand for them the same liberty and independence as has been obtained by nonconformists in religion.

3. To work for the extended recognition of unregistered medical practitioners and thereby give facilities for the demand for systems of healing which were in advance of the accepted modern school of medicine.
4. To safeguard the public against fraud by encouraging the various societies and bodies concerned with unorthodox practice to qualify and register their own practitioners and to promote an act of Parliament by which such qualified practitioners would be able to exercise their powers of healing without being molested and subject of criminal charges (Hageby *et al.* 1934: 7).

Hageby felt that, given the power of the state, these rights had to be built into the social contract between the citizen and the state.

When the same question of registration and recognition of medical systems was debated in India, the emphasis was not only on contract but on the idea of the medical system as a commons. The practitioners of traditional medicine argued that it was a system of cure suited to the environment and life-style of the community both in terms of economics and culture. They presented these arguments in a series of reports, the most famous of which was the report of the Madras Committee under the chairmanship of Mohammed Usman (1923, cited in *PPST Bulletin*). What was revealing about these reports was the nature of questions asked and the answers offered. The responses of the traditional practitioners was similar to craftsmen facing the political hegemony of the factory. It was not that the modern factory was more efficient; efficiency after all can be judged along myriad dimensions. But, as Stephen Marglin argues in Chapter 7, the modern factory facilitated greater control and surveillance of workers.

The basic question the traditionalists had to confront was whether traditional systems of medicine were scientific. The practitioners realized that what was being challenged was not the efficacy of the system but an alternative civilizational style.

When we speak of our medical science they ask us with great wonder if there is indeed such a thing. Instead of posing such a question, if we first agree that there is such a thing as a Hindu people and they also like others have a religion, a language and a science and a great ancient civilization ('Responses', 1984: 92).

The traditional doctors tried to show that their medicines were suited to the genius of the Indian people. They argued for instance that the Ayurvedic system was particularly suited to the poor, that the food they prescribed was as cheap as their medicines. They did not require 'ice, icebags, thermometers, or even Pearl Barley, malted milk, essence of chicken, but could manage with herbs available right in their back-yards' (ibid. 71).[10] Only gradually did the traditional doctors realize that the efforts were futile, for what was being built was an industrial grid.

10. For an elegant parallel description of the same tragic process from the point of view of the Unani system see Sardar 1986. See also Madras Group 1984.

The report of the Industrial Commission (1918) had just appeared and although it had been shelved by the colonial government, it provided the rudiments of the classificatory grid that was to underwrite the modern society in India. Dissent or difference would have a different value in such a system.

Central to the emerging discourse on development, represented by the report of the Industrial Commission, was the classification shown in Fig. 2. In it industry, science (medicine), and the nation-state were to be parallel rubrics. Under each of these rubrics, the first category encompasses all those below it. It is primary, allegedly more stable and efficient, more bureaucratizable; it is literally paradigmatic in the sense in which Kuhn (1970) defines the term. The lower forms represent not the 'other' as a possibility, but defeated, 'unscientific' structures, to be absorbed, assimilated, or marginalized. Thus ethnicities and local cultures were to be homogenized through the school, marginalized in the reservation, or put in the museum if disappearing. The logic of the intermediate or craft traditions could survive in the short run but would eventually yield, the argument went, to the all-absorbing power of the multinational industrial empires. It was not that modern medicine was not sensitive to folk or traditional forms of medicine, but it did not see them as parties to a dialogue or as an 'other' to be preserved; it saw them as a bag from which products had to be taken out.

Modern industry	Western medicine	Nation-state
Intermediate or medium-scale industry	Traditional medicine	Major religious or ethnic grouping
Cottage industry, Craft	Folk medicine	'Little culture'

Fig. 2

3   Gandhi as a Medical Scientist

Two issues remained to be discussed: the possibility of every man or woman becoming a doctor and the survival of a society without Western medical doctors. Both were forcefully articulated in Gandhi's *Hind Swaraj* (1963).

Gandhi's contribution to the debates on science and technology is usually described as a strange, anti-industrialist amalgam of an oriental Lud and Ruskin. But the *Gestalt* looks radically different if one looks at

Gandhi through his own eyes. Gandhi thought of himself as a scientist and looked at others as such. His autobiography, *My Experiments with Truth* (1927), was just what it claimed to be, the life and experiences of a scientist. Viewed thus, his *Hind Swaraj* becomes a fascinating science policy document of the post-Swadesi era, trying to resolve many of the problems that nagged the debate on science and technology. This section will focus briefly on the two texts to examine the alternative view of medical science they project.

Hind Swaraj has all the immediacy of a contemporary statement on science policy. Like all science policy statements, it presumes a relationship between truth and power. However, it grounds that relationship not in a political economy but in an ecological politics organized around a set of ethico-religious principles. Overtly, *Hind Swaraj* includes only a brief, trenchant critique of modern doctors, to parallel its critique of modern lawyers. Implicitly, it takes on the principle of the professionalization of modern scientific disciplines and the fact–value dichotomy which prompts modern society to locate the ethical controls on science outside scientific knowledge (cf. Sahasrabudhe 1985: 99–105). In this respect, the aphoristic essay resembles a Euclidean list of axioms. It holds that:

1. All critiques of technology must be ecological (oikos = house). (For Gandhi ecology, like charity, began at home. The household and neighbourhood were the prime units of concern.)
2. All notions of ecology are eventually ethical.
3. All ethics are eventually religious.
4. All religions are civilizational and, therefore, a critique of science and technology has to be a civilizational critique, encompassing the ideas of polity, economy, and consciousness. (For Gandhi, however, civilizations could be both baselines for and subjects of social criticism.)

The Gandhian concept of modernity encompassed more than the fact of British colonial rule; modernity was the principle of modern Western civilization. The British were the vehicles of oppression, carriers of a disease called modernity, and just as captive to its technological power. Thus, the Swadesi analysis was inadequate for him because it failed to unravel and cope with the logic of modernity.

Underlying the argument of *Hind Swaraj* is the metaphor of the body, relating the human body to the body politic. Bodily scale defines not only the nature of activity, but prescribes its limits. Modern mechanistic civilization is a disease because it violates the integrity of the body. The real tool, argues Gandhi, should be a natural extension of the body, not disjunctive with it. From these simple premises he outlines a critique of modernity, arguing that like colonialism, it is a self-inflicted disease, reflecting the dissipation of both the colonizer and the colonized. He illustrates it through his criticism of the railways in India. The simple fact of two styles of locomotion, by foot and by train, becomes a parable of modernity:

God set a limit to man's locomotive ambition in the construction of his body. I am so constructed that I can only serve my immediate neighbourbood, but in my conceit I pretend to have discovered that I must with my body serve every individual in the universe. In thus attempting the impossible, man comes into contact with different natures, different religions and is utterly confounded. According to this reasoning, . . . railways are a dangerous institution. Owing to them man has gone further away from his maker (Sahasrabudhe 1985: 28).

The railways disrupted the Indian body politic, which Gandhi saw as a huge body digesting and assimilating different cultural strands. He then showed how the two styles of technology, reflected in pilgrimage on foot and rail travel, represented memory and erasure respectively. The pilgrim's progress was an act of faith. The arduous act of pilgrimage to different corners of India gave the pilgrim both a sense of neighbourhood and of nationhood, helping him to internalize both similarities and differences. The mechanical negotiation or 'ingestion' of territory through rail travel erased the sanctity of places and turned them into physical spaces. For Gandhi, the modern machine set off a decline into the pathology called history, which was a movement away from nature. A return to nature presupposed a spiralling back to body time and body scale, to bodily discipline. According to him, Indian civilization reflected the social construction of such spirals of conduct.

Gandhi also argued that the modern machine reflected unbridled appetite. Modern civilization was hedonistic, gauging progress in terms of calories and comforts. Such a civilization had to be hostile to the Indian concept of good conduct. He said,

Our ancestors saw happiness as largely a mental condition. It is not that we did not know how to invent machinery but our forefathers knew that if we set our hearts after such things, we would become slaves and lose our moral fibre. They, therefore, after due deliberation decided we should only do what we could with our hands and feet. Real happiness consisted of the proper use of hands and feet (Sahasrabudhe 1985: 37).

In a fundamental sense, Gandhi, J. C. Bose, and P. C. Ray were the critical scientists of the Swadesi and post-Swadesi era. For each, the encounter with the colonial West was a crisis in identity. Each had to construct a social self in which modern science and technology were crucial targets of love and/or hate. Very self-consciously, each contributed to the social development of the scientist's role in India: Ray the chemist as the ascetic savant-entrepreneur, Bose the physicist turned plant physiologist as the scientist who used native ideas of vitalism to confound scientific classifications of life and non-life, and Gandhi by defining the role of the dissenting scientist in modern India and by reaffirming the scientific role of the humble craftsman embedded in the folk traditions. However, Gandhi managed to do something more. He challenged the deeper axioms of science: the dualism of knowledge and power, religion and science, and the laity and the expert.

As a part of this challenge, Gandhi chose a medical science which was everyday in its immediacy, dietetics, and hygiene. There was a certain playfulness to him, a certain 'cognitive indifference' to the products of modern science, as his grandson, Ramchandra Gandhi, informally puts it. Science, like Western manners and dress, became something to be tried on, modified, even discarded. After all, borrowed etiquettes ultimately have to yield to the demands of hygiene and *svadharma*, one's own specific code of conduct. At another plane the project was more serious and holistic. Dietetics, sexuality, technology, all were for him exercises in the pursuit of truth. The autobiography became an account of a continuing experiment, with the body as the test-tube; the discipline of the body served as a model for the civics of the body politic. For he was concerned about how to embed science in everyday life and yet save everydayness from becoming banal, non-critical, and coercive.

The answer Gandhi tried to give, according to his account of his formative years, involved a split-level encounter with the West. At one level, he was the young man from the colony playing the Anglicized dandy, with his double watch chain of gold, Gladstone collars, flashy ties, leather gloves, violin lessons, and speech lessons from Bell's *The Standard Elocutionist*. At another, he was a staunch vegetarian whose vegetarianism was originally only a promise to his mother but was slowly becoming a philosophy. One of his friends, trying to dissuade him from it, suggested that he read Bentham on utility. Instead he picked up at a restaurant Henry Salt's *A Plea for Vegetarianism* (1886), which he read and reread.

Vegetarianism in Gandhi's youth was not always a fad; it was a site for the location of alternative world-views. It introduced him to the other West of occult philosophy, theosophy, various versions of socialism, and anti-vivisectionism; to Blavatsky, Anne Kingsford's critique of diet (1889), and Louis Kuhne's naturopathy (1892). All of them combined with John Ruskin and Leo Tolstoy to provide not only an alternative view of the West but also to help him anchor his own identity in traditions. Vegetarianism linked a traditional religious view of health to an alternative Western philosophy of medicine. The writings of the vegetarians, the theosophists, Ruskin, and Tolstoy had in common not only a hostility to mechanistic-vivisectional science but also the concept of the patient as his own doctor. Instead of experimenting on others, one experimented on oneself. Above all, as Salt put it, it was in the science of diet and hygiene that the opposition between Western science and religion was resolved, creating the possibility of a moral science. Salt's work convinced Gandhi that food reform could lead to social reform. Indeed, vegetarianism not only equipped the Mahatma with particular kinds of political-ideological skills; as a number of his biographers note, it enabled him to work out the outlines of a critique of modern medicine.

The critique was underpinned by a philosophical sensitivity to three political-ethical issues. First, Gandhi's vegetarianism sought to recover the body for the individual as part of a search for individual autonomy, in turn representing a community-based search for autonomy of small human aggregates—the Gandhian village republics. For this the vegetarian had to practise poverty, chastity, and other forms of discipline, to accept the ethical and cognitive responsibility for his body and, thereby, reject medical processing by the state and by the state-licensed medical practitioners.

Second, Gandhi identified in the body politic the pathological expression of three forms of violence: racism, prostitution, and vivisection. They were not arbitrarily put together. Each form reflected a particular violation of the body and all three interpenetrated in the parasitism of the city. The city was home of censuses, epidemics, and medical science. His experiences in South Africa had led him to connect racism, urban life, and medicine. In both Natal and Transvaal, objections to the presence of Indians in towns were raised on sanitary and medical grounds, and the doctors had helped drive the Indians out of the towns into 'locations'. In response to this ultimate form of medical surveillance, and to confront the triangle of violence in a mechanical city, Gandhi encoded within his idea of a non-industrial way of life, along with vegetarianism and anti-vivisectionism, traditional agriculture, *khadi* (hand-spun and hand-woven cloth), and *charkha* (the traditional spinning-wheel). For him they signposted the road to the recovery of the body.

Finally, Gandhi's thought incorporated the idea of iatrogeny but went beyond it. *Hind Swaraj* not only located the science of medicine in the colonial structure—'to study European medicine is to deepen our slavery', it says—this tract also held the patient responsible for the persistence of the iatrogenic regime. Modern doctors helped perpetuate the urban-industrial civilization by disconnecting overconsumption from its bodily consequences. As a result, they—the doctors—destroyed the 'natural' resistance to an expropriatory system, apart from helping the patient to lose control over himself. For such a world-view, the immorality of modern hospitals was axiomatic and the recovery of the body from the medical expert by the laity both a moral statement and an affirmation of political-moral autonomy.

This was a more radical set of proposals than theosophy offered. Theosophy rejected birth-control and vaccination intuitively because they militated against its vision of childhood. Gandhi rejected the citizenship of a polis where to be inoculated was to be. The clash between Gandhi and Besant is often interpreted as the struggle between Home Rule and Swaraj. Actually it was also a clash between the occult body and the mystic body. Gandhi's radicalism lay in offering a more playful, though less Borgesian, critique of science. In it not only does every man become a scientist and every village a science academy, but there is a demand for a cognitive resistance to the gross appetite of modern science.

Few accepted his offer. The *satyagrahi* remained a political resister, too sedate to accept this invitation to an alternative vision of science.

4 A Traditional Critique

The theosophists, despite all the fascination the mysterious East had for them, were primarily the carriers of the underground traditions of Western science. Their critique of modern science had sometimes to be a play on the absurd, given the near-total dominance of the target of their criticism. Gandhi's critique, on the other hand, was a more down-to-earth attempt to represent both the dissenting traditions of the West and the surviving traditions of medicine in his own society. Because he linked his theory of the body to the theory of politics on the one hand, and the politics of culture on the other, his resistance to medicalization had to become, in practice, part of a larger theory of resistance.

A third possible baseline of criticism still remains to be marked out. We have not asked till now which way a critique of Western medicine will go if the point of view is that of a traditional Indian medical system, unaided by critical Western thought.

In this last section we shall try to answer this question by describing briefly what in many ways was a brilliant critical response to Western medicine, given in the post-Swadesi era by G. Srinivasmurthi on behalf of Ayurveda. A remarkably versatile figure, Srinivasmurthi was an outstanding Sanskrit scholar and litterateur who had translated *The Merchant of Venice* into Telugu. Though he preferred to describe himself as a 'humble votary' of Western medicine, he was a trained modern doctor, fashionable enough to become a personal physician of John Barrymore, the actor. But while he respected Western science, Srinivasmurthi was not awed by it. In fact, he was prescient enough about modern science to say of atomic energy in 1923, 'fortunately for the world, Western scientists have not been able to release this energy' (p. 20). He had the bilingual's confidence that a dialogue between different medical systems was possible. His minute on indigenous systems was a part of the Usman Committee Report but can be read independently as an argument for a more plural encounter among medical systems.

Srinivasmurthi realized that the official history of Western science acted as a filter, preventing the possibility of such an encounter. For the official history saw the authorities derived from the scriptures and from science as antithetical. Such a history could not be sympathetic to a medicine which cited the authority of scriptures as one of the guides to right knowledge. Western science, he realized, would read such an appeal to authority as a 'petrified dogma', which denied the freedom of individual action so essential to the pursuit of science.

The idea of scriptural authority in indigenous knowledge, however, was radically different from that in the West, Srinivasmurthi argued. Scriptural authority in India did not have 'the sterilising touch . . . that sought to burn away the tender seed of science which Galileo planted at the risk of his life'. The minute says,

no one who has not entered into the very soul of Hindu thought can appreciate what scriptural authority means to the Hindu and how two persons paying the profoundest possible veneration to the same scriptural texts can yet interpret them in ways as diverse as the poles; a classic example that occurs to my mind is how all schools of Vedanta—from uncompromising duality (Dwaita) to absolute non-duality (Advaita)—purport to be based on the same scriptural text (p. 11).

The minute observes that no orthodox pundit would admit that the Vedas were in error, but one pundit could claim that his commentary was more in conformity with the truth of the texts than that of others. 'In other words, differences of views were expressed through commentaries on texts rather than by altering the texts themselves' (p. 11). This absence of dogma, and this playful invitation to a festival of interpretations, allows for as many commentaries and editions of the scientific method as of a religious text.

Srinivasmurthi notes that there are historical precedents for similar exercises in the West. He quotes William Osler's observation,

the quarrels of doctors make a pretty picture in the history of medicine. Each generation seems to have had its own . . . The Arabians and the Galenists, the Brunonians and the Broussonians, the Homeopaths and the regulars have in different centuries rent the robe of Aesculapius (p. 8).

Such differences, Srinivasmurthi feels, could lead to 'not unhealthy disputations'. And he invites one to a dialogue of medical systems similar to a dialogue of religions. The dialogue would not be a search for uniformity through a search for similarities. Nor would be there an attempt to translate mechanically terms such as *vayu*, *pitta*, *kapha* into wind, bile, and phlegm, thus reducing Ayurveda to the old abandoned humoral theory of the Greek physicians (p. 16). It would rather be an attempt to grapple with systems and systemic differences, without reducing indigenous systems to the procustean bed of Western medicine. It would not even be a search for equality between the intellectual systems of the colonizer and the colonized but a fraternal disputation on differences.

The minute stresses the differences in the construction of two systems, allopathy and Ayurveda, and specifically mentions the mix of science, philosophy, and religion in the native system. It points out that in Madhavacharya's *Sarva Darśana Sangraha*, which is a discussion of roughly sixteen religio-philosophical faiths of India, each discussion constitutes a chapter. One finds here, along with discussions of Buddhism, Jainism, and Advaitism, a full chapter on *Raseśvara Darśanam* or chemistry (p. 13).

To the Western mind such an arrangement of chapters would mean a confusion of the categories of science, philosophy, and religion. A Hindu perceives it differently.

The one supreme object of life is to attain the state of self realization or *Mukti* . . . now the study of Chemistry helps me to achieve this object by intelligently using mercury and other chemicals in the healthy regulation of my physical and other bodies; here we see at once how the philosophy . . . of chemistry is indissolubly associated with the science of chemistry and with certain ethical and physical practices broadly included under the name of 'Religion'—the religion if you please of Chemistry. As in chemistry so it is in Mathematics, Grammar, Exegetics, Ayurveda, or any other branch of study . . . (p. 13).

We must mention in this connection the recommendation of the Usman Committee that support to native systems of medicine should not be left only to the state but also be the responsibility of temples. The report recommended that some of the great south Indian temples take on the task of encouraging Ayurvedic and Siddha systems. This obvious attempt to move beyond the secular idiom of the modern public realm reminds one of A. L. Basham's observation on the relationship between the Ayurvedic and Unani systems: 'The practitioners of the two systems seem to have collaborated, because each had much to learn from the other and whatever the *ulama* and the brahmans might say, we have no record of animosity between Hindu and Muslim in the field of medicine' (in Leslie 1976: 40).

It is in this spirit that Srinivasmurthi ventures a critique of Western medicine from an Ayurvedic vantage-point. An elaborate exercise, it centres around three related sets of ideas: (1) the opposition between external and internal conceptions of disease, (2) the relationship between the disease and the patient, and (3) the relationship between the clinical and the laboratory conceptions of disease.

Sociologically one of the major oppositions between Ayurveda and allopathy has centred around the germ theory of disease. While the modern Western theory has generally looked at disease in terms of the diverse objective agencies that invade the body, Ayurveda has looked at disease in terms of internal processes, triggered by external factors. Srinivasmurthi notes that while Ayurveda recognizes the role of micro-organisms, it does not grant them the centrality they possess in allopathy.

They [the Ayurvedis] merely looked upon the germ as one among the many causative factors, capable of producing disease, if the soil or field (*Kshetra*) was suitable for the growth of the germ seed. It is when the bodily constitution was undermined by the non-observance of the laws of health such as *Ritucharya* (hygienic rules for various seasons of the year), *Dincharya* (hygienic rules for daily conduct) *Bramhacharya* (hygienic rules for celibacy or regulated social life) and so on, that the *Kshetra* becomes suitable for the growth of germ seeds, which were powerless to do mischief in the case of people who lead pure and healthy lives . . . (Srinivasmurthi 1923: 42).

Srinivasmurthi goes on to ask,

Can the germ enthusiast say definitely that the cholera vibrio or the tubercle bacillus is *everything* in the causation of cholera or tuberculoses? . . . Certain germs may be living for years in our intestines on terms of neutrality or even of harmonious helpfulness; but the moment something untoward happens to the intestines, they may at once grow unfriendly and declare war. Now all these years the so called exciting cause was there but powerless to excite . . . Why should we not call the injury to the intestines the exciting cause and the bacterium the predisposing cause. They are apparently like seed and soil. . . . It seems the *tridosha* theory looks at the question from the standpoint of the soil, while the germ theory looks at it from the standpoint of the seed.

'Keep out the seed—away with all germs and you are safe'—that is the slogan of the germ enthusiast. 'It seems impracticable to keep out germ seeds which are ubiquitous. Therefore keep the soil in such a condition that no seed can grow, even if it gets there.' So urges the Ayurvedist (ibid. 43).

The question, Srinivasmurthi points out, is whether one should regard bacteria as the result or the cause. He asks as an example whether the term influenza denotes merely a group of clinical signs and symptoms or whether it signifies that influenza is caused by a specific germ. The answer, he believes, is unclear and unsatisfactory, and leaves one wondering why the germ theory has become such a fetish.

Ayurveda's 'agricultural view' becomes relevant in this context. Srinivasmurthi notes that Western medicine has been more prone to classify bacteria by their morphological characteristics, ignoring the wisdom of the agriculturalists who insist on paying more attention to what the bacteria do than to what they are. For example, whether an attack of Shiga dysentery or cholera will be mild or severe depends upon intestinal contents. If an abundance of amino-acids is present, Srinivasmurthi points out, toxic amines will be produced, and the attack will be severe. If the diet has left little protein residue in the intestine, the bacteria will produce little toxic amines, and the attack will be mild (ibid. 46).

Srinivasmurthi goes on to say that even Western medical theory has been moving away from the germ theory and assuming a more Ayurvedic position, attending to the soil, keeping it such that the germ seeds cannot thrive on it. Even the informed laity, according to him, are realizing that the active campaign to abolish bacteria is futile. He quotes in this connection a comment of *The Times* of London: 'the control of human resistance offers a brighter future than the direct attempts to eliminate disease' (ibid. 44).

Beyond the possibility of a dialogue on the conceptual difference between external and internal concepts of diseases lies the scope for a dialogue on the styles of diagnosis. Srinivasmurthi cites Yamini Bhusan Roy to make the point that 'western doctors do not possess the key to the proper diagnosis of the patient though they were correct in their diagnosis of the disease' (ibid. 59). Allopathy pays little attention to the *prakriti*, the inherited constitution and idiosyncrasies of the patient. The system does not care for ideas such as *jati* (race), *kula* (tribe), *desa* (place), *kala* (time), *vayas* (age), or the *pratyama niyata* (individual peculiarities) of body temperament.

On the basis of Gananath Sen's observations, Srinivasmurthi discusses the possible consequences of such a bias:

While western medicine cannot help us to tell beforehand which of our patients is likely to suffer from quinine idiosyncracy, and which not, we are able, if we know how to diagnose our patient (especially his *prakriti*), according to Ayurvedic methods, to avoid making any mistakes about quinine administration . . . Western medicine has at present no means of recognising the patient's *prakriti* . . . It has to act more or less blindly, and learn from the bitter experiences of its patients (ibid. 60).

The stress on disease rather than on disease-and-patient is identified as a by-product of the shift from the clinical to the laboratory view in Western medicine.

The laboratory worker obtains his result by a delicate mechanical contrivance, but the physician has to train his senses to recognise these different sensations. As a consequence of his inability to acquire this knowledge, he ignores information which it reveals particularly about the early signs of disease (ibid. 54).

Prognosis, according to the Ayurvedis, has been given inadequate significance in allopathy, even though much information exists about the stages of a disease. To the Ayurvedi, the importance of interrogation, the elaborate liturgy of procedures by which the doctor interrogates the patient, seems conspicuous by its strange absence in allopathy.

The laboratory view of treatment is found objectionable not merely morally, as an instance of óbjectification, but cognitively. Srinivasmurthi puts this succinctly:

experiments on healthy animals may easily lead us astray; and it is fallacious to judge the effect of a drug on a human being by the effect it produces on animal; . . . it is also fallacious to judge the effect of a drug on a diseased human being by the effect it produces on a *healthy* animal; . . . then again there is the clinical fact that two persons may not react to the same drug in the same way in two different conditions of ill health; in a very real sense then, every dose of a drug that we administer to a patient is a new experiment (ibid. 69).

The author therefore wonders, given the discoveries of the botanist J. C. Bose, if one may someday obtain from plant experiments the sort of help presently derived from experiments on animals (ibid. 69).

Srinivasmurthi makes one final point about the cognitive capacities of the two systems of medicine. The Ayurvedic classification of diseases and treatments seems elaborate enough to provide 'ready-made niches' for other forms of treatment such as allopathy, homeopathy, osteopathy, Kuhne cure, vaccine therapy, psychotherapy, etc. This has saved it from the two perils of Western medicine, namely faddism and hyper-specialization. In Ayurveda, as in Hindu thought, there is no need for anyone to set up a closed or over-defined sect of his own and proclaim it from the housetops as offering a panacea. On the other hand,

With our western brethren the case seems to be quite different. There, we have an ever-increasing number of medical sects, each with a special nostrum or formula wherewith to cure or charm away all the ills that flesh is heir to. Each may undoubtedly have a limited field of usefulness and applicability, but the danger lies in the attempt to transform it into a universal panacea . . . One would cure all ills by osteopathy, another by chromopathy, yet another by homeopathy, a fourth by allopathy, others by electricity baths, food reform, vaccine therapy, charms, incantations, miracle workings, magnetic healing, faith cures, denial of diseases, affirmation of health, and so on, till one fails to see the forests from the trees.

Then, tongue in cheek, the author quotes Bernard Shaw's caricature of the heart-break house of Western medicine.

Now Heart Break house was a hypochondriacal house, always running after cures. . . . It was superstitious, and addicted to table rapping clairvoyances, materialization, seances, palmistry, crystal gazing and the like to such an extent that it may be doubted whether ever before in the history of the world did soothsayers, astrologers, and unregistered therapeutic specialists of all sorts flourish as they did during this half of the century. . . . The registered doctors and surgeons were hard put to compete with the unregistered. They were not clever enough to appeal to the imagination and sociability of the heartbreakers by the acts of actor, the orator, the poet, the winning conversationalist. They had to fall back on the terror of infection and death. They prescribed innoculations and operation. Whatever part of the human being could be cut out without necessarily killing him they cut out and he often died (unnecessarily of course) in consequence. From such trifles as uvulas and tonsils, they went on to ovaries and appendices until, at last, no one's inside was safe . . . (ibid. 63).

5 Knowledge, Consciousness, and Dissent

We have in this paper told the same story twice, once in our own language and then, at greater length and more colourfully, with reference to three strands of consciousness which emerged during the first three decades of this century in India. The second telling of the story has some specific implications. We now find we have, in the process of telling our story, described three modes of dissent from modern medical philosophy in this part of the world. Each of these modes is simultaneously an attempt to understand modern medicine and to cope with the typical clinical, social, and philosophical problems this mode of healing introduces into the world of applied knowledge.

These constructions of modern medicine in non-modern terms are, therefore, three forms of seeking meaning when confronting a politically powerful knowledge system which shows immediate practical results in some areas but is intellectually, socially, and morally disorienting. From the 'irrationality as defiance' of some of the theosophists to the 'culture as resistance' of Gandhi to the 'indigenous as the theory of the exogenous' of Srinivasmurthi, each construction revalues the past in the light of the present, to keep possibilities open for the future. Each construction also in turn produces its own set of problems which is no less formidable than that produced by modern medicine. It is however an indicator of the power of the empiricism of life, as opposed to the empiricism of academia, that the three responses among them almost fully anticipate our summary description of the contemporary critiques of modern medicine in the first part of the paper. Admittedly this anticipation is only sometimes self-conscious; admittedly it often uses specific formulations which verge on the absurd; admittedly too, the anticipation is mostly a product of a self-exploration which sometimes tells more about the attempts to restore self-esteem in the Indian middle classes than about the inner logic of modern medicine. Yet the fact remains that, in some mutually potentiating way, the critiques converge. They converge because even though they diagnose the illness of modern medicine differently, the clinical acumen which informs them helps the critiques to identify the broad contours of the problem similarly.

Beyond this convergence lies a paradox. Six decades ago, modern medicine was already triumphant in the West. But it was yet to become fully hegemonic in the Indian medical scene. What is easy to identify today, when the crisis of modern medicine has 'matured', had then to be the concern mainly of cranks and visionaries. And the two categories, as we well know from the growing literature on the nature of scientific creativity, are rarely if ever exclusive categories. Yet we have shown in this chapter that, to judge by the responses to modern medicine, the 'demented' and the other-worldly 'sages' diagnosed the crisis of modern medicine with greater clinical and philosophical perspicacity than did the specialists and the 'normal' scientists. Perhaps it is in the nature of a 'successful' modern knowledge system to push to the periphery all criticisms of the system and to ensure that these criticisms survive only in the form of artistic or fantastic imagination.

That these criticisms can sometimes return as the unconscious of the modern world is a part of the same story. You have to tell the story twice only to reaffirm that even criticisms with limited access to empirical data, even criticisms couched in the language of anti-empiricism, can, if the critic's moral sensitivities are not blunted, show greater empirical sensitivity than those wedded to empiricism but unwilling to confront the problems of suffering without reifying it.

REFERENCES

Alvares, Claude (1986) 'The Dangerous, the Useless and the Needy', *Afkar Inquiry* (Oct.), 3: 26–33.

—— (1988) 'Science, Colonialism and Violence', in Ashis Nandy (ed.), *Science, Hegemony and Violence*, New Delhi: Oxford University Press.

Bang, Abhay, and Patel, Ashvin J., eds. (1985), *Health Care, Which Way To Go*, New Delhi: MFC.

Basham, A. L. (1976) 'The Practice of Medicine in Ancient and Medieval India', in Charles Leslie (ed.), *Asian Medical Systems*, Berkeley: University of California.

Besant, Annie (1896) *Against Vivisection*, Benares: Theosophical Publishing House.

Blavatsky, Helena P. (1910) 'Three Months in the Blue Mountains near Madras', *The Theosophist* (June), 31: 113–20.

—— (1966) *Collected Writings* (1879–80), Illinois: Theosophical Publishing House.

—— (1968) *Isis Unveiled* (1877), Los Angeles: The Theosophy Company.

Bourchier, Helen (1907) 'The Use to Which Men and Animals Alike are Put to by Men of Science', in Lind-Af-Hageby (ed.), *The Animal's Cause*, London: Animal Defence and Anti-Vivisection Society.

Carson, Gerald (1972) *Men, Beasts and Gods*, New York: Charles Scribner.

'Cuttings and Comments' (Mar., June 1903) *The Theosophist*, 24.

Donzelot, Jacques (1979) *The Policing of Families*, London: Hutchinson.

Duffin, Lorna (1978) 'The Conspicuous Consumptive: Woman as an Invalid', in Sarah Belamont and Lorna Duffin (eds.), *The Nineteenth Century Woman*, London: Croom Helm.

Ehrlich, Anne, and Ehrlich, Paul (1982) *Extinction*, London: Victor Gollanz.

Foucault, Michel (1963) *The Birth of the Clinic: An Archaeology of Medical Perception*, London, Tavistock.

—— (1980) *Power/Knowledge: Selected Interviews and Other Writings 1972–1977*, trans. Colin Gordon *et al.*, Brighton, Sussex: Harvester Press.

Gandhi, Mohandas Karamchand (1927) *The Story of My Experiments with Truth*, Ahmedabad: Navjivan.

—— (1963) *Hind-Swaraj*, Collected Works of Mahatma Gandhi, iv. 81–208, Delhi: Publications Division, Government of India.

Geddes, Patrick (1904) *On Universities in Europe and India, Five Letters to an Indian Friend*, Madras: National Press.

Geddes, Patrick, and Thomson, Arthur (1914) *Sex*, London: Williams and Norgate.

Geertz, Clifford (1983) 'Commonsense as a Cultural System', *Local Knowledge: Further Essays in Interpretive Anthropology*, New York: Basic Books.

Goldsmith, Edward, and Hildyard, N. (1984) *The Social and Environmental Effects of Large Dams*, Powys, Wales: Wadebridge Ecological Centre.

Hageby, Lind-Af (1907) 'Vivisection and Medical Students: The Growing Distrust of Hospitals and Their Remedy', in ead. (ed.), *The Animal's Cause*, London: Animal Defence and Anti-Vivisection Society.

—— et al. (1934) *Progress and Freedom in Medicine*, London: Animal Defence and Anti-Vivisection Society.

Hagen, Everett (1963) *On the Theory of Social Change*, Homewood, Ill.: Dorsey.

Har Dayal (1912) 'The Wealth of the Nation', *Modern Review* (July), 12: 43–9.

Illich, Ivan (1976) *Medical Nemesis: The Expropriation of Health*, New York: Pantheon.

—— (1986) '12 Years After, Ivan Illich Revisits Medical Nemesis', *IFDA Dossier* (July–Aug.), 54: 3–8.

Indian Industrial Commission Report (1918), reprinted 1988, Delhi: Agricole Publishing Co.

Information (newsletter of Voluntary Health Association of India).

Jayarao, Kama, and Patel, Ashvin, eds. (1986) *Under the Lens, Health and Medicine*, New Delhi: MFC.

Jinarajadasa, C. (1938) *The New Humanity of Intuition*, Adyar, Madras: The Theosophical Publishing House.

Kakar, Sudhir (1986) 'Doctor at Large', *The Illustrated Weekly of India* (6 July), 18–21.

Kingsford, Anne (1889) *The Perfect Way in Diet*, London: Kegan Paul, Trench, Trubner.

Kothari, Manu L., and Mehta, Lopa (1973) *The Nature of Cancer*, Bombay: Kothari Medical Publications.

—— and —— (1979) *Cancer, Myths and Realities*, London: Marion Boyars.

Kuhn, Thomas (1970) *The Structure of Scientific Revolutions*, International Encyclopedia of Unified Science, vol. 2, no. 2, Chicago: University of Chicago Press, 2nd edn. (first published 1962).

Kuhne, Louis (1892) *The New Science of Healing*, Leipzig: Author.

Lane, Harlan (1979) *The Wild Boy of Aveyron*, London: Paladin, Granada.

Leadbeater, Charles (1904) 'The Rationale of Mesmerism', *The Theosophist* (Oct.), 26: 29–40.

Lifton, Robert Jay (1982) 'Medicalized Killing in Auschwitz', *Psychiatry* (Nov.), 45: 283–97.

—— (1986) *The Nazi Doctors*, New York: Basic Books.

McClelland, David C., and Winter, David G. (1969) *Motivating Economic Achievement*, New York: Free Press.

Madras Group (1984) 'What is the Role of Indigenous Medical Sciences in our Health Care System?', *PPST Bulletin* (June), 4: 64–95.

Naess, Arne (1972) *Pluralist and Possibilist Aspect of the Scientific Enterprise*, London: Allen and Unwin.

Nandy, Ashis (1980) *Alternative Sciences: Creativity and Authenticity in Two Indian Scientists*, New Delhi: Allied.

—— (1987) 'Science, Authoritarianism and Culture: On the Scope and Limits of Isolation Outside the Clinic', in *Traditions, Tyranny and Utopias: Essays in the Politics of Awareness*, New Delhi: Oxford University Press.

—— ed. (1988) *Science, Hegemony and Violence*, New Delhi: Oxford University Press.

Perraju, K. (1902) 'Extraordinary Virtues of Indian Plants', *The Theosophist* (Oct.), 24: 23–7.

Petrie Hoyle, E. (n.d.) *Homeopathy and Vivisection*, London: Animal Defence and Anti-Vivisection Society.

PPST Bulletin (published by the Patriotic People's Science and Technology Group).

'Responses of Indigenous Medical Practitioners to the Madras Enquiry Sixty Years Ago' (1984) *PPST Bulletin* (June), 4: 64–95.

Sahasrabudhe, Sunil (1985) 'Hind Swaraj and the Science Question', in Nageshwar Prasad (ed.), *Hind Swaraj: A Fresh Look*, New Delhi: Gandhi Peace Foundation.

Salt, Henry (1886) *Plea for Vegetarianism and Other Essays*, Manchester: The Vegetarian Society.

Sardar, Ziauddin (1986) 'Medicine and Metaphysics: The Struggle for Healthy Life-Styles', *Afkar Inquiry* (Oct.), 3: 40–7.

Sathyamala, C., Sundharam, Nirmala, and Bhanot, Nalini (1986) *Taking Sides: The Choices Before the Health Worker*, Madras: ANITRA.

Shiva, Mira (1985) 'Towards a Healthy Use of Pharmaceuticals: An Indian Perspective', *Development Dialogue*, 2: 69–93.

Springhall, John (1977) *Youth, Empire and Society*, London: Croom Helm.

Srinivasmurthi, G. (1917) *The Slaughter of the Innocents*, Madras: Author.

—— (1923) 'Secretary's Minute', *Report of the Committee on Indigenous Systems of Medicine*, Madras: Government Printing Press.

Wallace, Alfred (1908) *The Wonderful Century*, London: George Allen and Unwin Limited (first published 1898).

Weinberg, Alvin (1972) 'Science and Trans-Science', *Minerva*, 10: 209–22.

6

Technology and the Reproduction of Values in Rural Western India

ARJUN APPADURAI

1 Introduction: Morality, Politics, and Technological Change

The problem of assessing the costs of economic change in any society is simultaneously moral and political. It is moral because it involves problems of autonomy and coercion, and because it involves cross-cultural and intra-social debates about value. It is political because it entails decisions about *whose* preferences count, *what* criteria to use in assessing such preferences, and *how* to establish acceptable grounds for a genuine debate about development.

The body of this chapter is devoted to the presentation of a highly specific setting—a village in Western India—and a highly specific technological change—the electrification of traditional open-surface wells. But embedded in these specifics are a host of larger processes and more general issues. Though my argument depends, in part, on my interpretation of the commercialization of agriculture in Maharashtra in the last century, its general assumptions are anticipated in this introduction.

Any moral and political assessment of technological change encounters the following major dilemma: is there any reasonable middle ground, in assessing the pros and cons of technological change, between using some variety of Euro-American utilitarianism and succumbing to some radical form of relativist cultural protectionism? My own approach to this dilemma is as follows. I am firmly opposed to *any* technical calculus of welfare which operates on criteria that are wholly external to the moral and cultural values of the community whose future is at stake. This position rests on the notion that imposed change (and, by extension, imposed criteria for the assessment of change) is on a priori grounds unacceptable because it is, in the most general sense, anti-democratic. But in a world in which at least some members of rural communities appear to desire and seize the opportunities offered by new technologies, how shall we assess the worth of technological change?

One class of answers to this question is fundamentally distributional in its orientation and takes as a key consideration the matter of how widely and deeply the gains of technological change are distributed. The trouble with this solution is that it is a version of the utilitarian solution, and contains no provisions for taking into account the moral and cultural fabric of the community as a value in its own right (in my terms, as a prime value). Instead it relies on some explicit or implicit aggregation of preferences, whose ultimate ground is *individual* choices, preferences, and benefits. I shall return to the problem of individualism shortly.

I am also opposed to what I have called the position of radical cultural protectionism, which would suggest that the preservation of any coherent cultural system is a prime value, which requires no further justification. Here I have two objections. The first is that this argument relies on an implicit valuation of cultural difference as an end in itself. This valuation comes out of a relatively recent Euro-American orientation, which is often used to enslave other communities in invented ideas about their own authenticity. That is, one product of the encounter between the West and the non-Western world in the post-Renaissance period has been a series of anthropological and proto-anthropological efforts to create ideas about 'authentic natives', as opposed to those who are somehow believed to have been corrupted by contact with the outside world. This generally invidious contrast frequently forms the basis for discussing the relative authenticity of other cultures on the basis of criteria in the control of the Western observer. Authenticity is, in any case, a Western concern with a relatively short history.

Second, this argument can be (and is) often used to justify a variety of inhumane and undesirable cultural practices, along with whatever is valuable within a given cultural system. What Lévi-Strauss once said about functionalism can usefully be pirated in the following form: to say that any culture is valuable is a truism, but to say that everything in a culture is valuable is an absurdity. How then are we to assess change from a moral point of view?

One step towards an answer involves the relationship between relatively narrow, 'economistic', criteria for assessing technological change and broader, more 'holistic' ones, centred on the reproduction of the core cultural values of a community. Although the distinction between these two sorts of criteria is analytically fairly clear, there are situations where the two criteria not only lead to similar assessments, *but must necessarily do so*. This convergence of assessments is likely to occur when technological change is accompanied by losses of indigenous knowledge. My empirical case represents just such a situation.

To identify the conditions for such convergence, it is necessary to specify the critical differences between 'economistic' and 'holistic' criteria for the assessment of technological change. Let us note the important similarities between these two kinds of criteria: both are value orientations towards technical change; both claim to be oriented, in the last analysis, to collective well-being; and both are grounded in some sort of moral

universalism. The crucial difference, however, lies in the relative importance of the individual in each of them. In all varieties (however broadly
based) of economistic assessment, the individual is seen both as the crucial
locus of agency and as the prime moral value. In more holistic frameworks,
the prime value is the reproduction of communities and the important
loci of agency are usually various kinds of groups and collectivities. The
emergence of individualism as a moral orientation in European thought
(and its cross-cultural implications) constitutes a very large subject which
can hardly be fully engaged here. For one thing, the links (and distinctions)
between ideas about the self (which have a long history), the rise of the
individual, the formation of a commercial ethos, and the rise of a market
culture, even in the West, have hardly been fully worked out.

The situation is murkier still when we look at this matter from a
comparative perspective. While we have good grounds to believe that the
relatively recent Euro-American valuation of the individual runs against
the moral grain of many other societies, we can hardly deny that in many
of these other societies complex commercial cultures have existed (even
prior to Western contact), as have complex, gain-oriented, patterns of
calculation. Sorting out this labyrinth of issues, which involves carefully
distinguishing between different ideas about the self or person, different
formats for the cultural organization of commerce, different modalities
for calculation, and different patterns of market-orientation, is an important
task which is still very much in its infancy. For my purposes, I shall be
concerned with the *sort* of individualism that arose in the Western Indian
experience of commercialization in the last century. This does not preclude
the possibility that other forms of individualism may have pre-existed in
Western India or risen in the last century; nor does it deny the fact that
in Western India, and elsewhere in the world, there were very important
links between markets and the countryside long before this past century.
My concern here is with one such articulation of the 'individual' and one
such experience of commercialization.

Since my axiomatic starting-point is the *value of reproduction* (as an
entitlement of all human communities) it is important to specify what
exactly the reproduction of a community entails. It entails the reproduction
of its central social forms, as expressions of its core values. This
commitment to the value of reproduction does not contradict my earlier
statement of opposition to radical cultural protectionism, since the latter
is usually built around values and principles imposed on the community
by some external agency, usually with some exogenous perspective, while
the former is based (at least in principle) on an effort to discover
endogenous criteria for the reproduction of community. Nevertheless, in
practice, there is a danger that the more desirable of these two positions
(from my perspective) might lead one into the less desirable one. But that
is a risk that must be run.

In the case of the rural community in Western India which constitutes my main source of data, the core values, and thus the central social forms, revolve around *sociality* itself. This is not simply yet another instance of Durkheim's general theory about the primacy of society over the individual, which probably holds for all societies, and whose genealogy goes back to Aristotle. Rather, I intend to suggest that in this community (and others of its type) much of what is seen as valuable by members of the community, and much of what appears to underly the central traditional forms of social life, are linkages between persons and groups, taken for granted not only as means but also as ends. If it can be shown, in such a situation, that the *prime value of sociality* is eroded by a particular process of technological change, we have grounds to regard the change in question as inimical to the reproduction of the community.

The convergence between this ('holistic') reason for criticizing technological change, and any one of a number of narrower, more 'economistic' reasons for criticism, lies in the relationship between knowledge and technological change. In many traditional agrarian societies (and probably in some non-agrarian ones as well) it is difficult to distinguish technical knowledge very clearly from knowledge which is tied to larger normative and social ends. In such societies, *techne* and *episteme* (to borrow Stephen Marglin's use of the Greek terms) are both embedded in wider social, religious, and epistemological grounds and contexts. In turn, this leads me to suggest that the question of the 'decoupling' of various technologies from their primary cultural settings and entailments to new cultural settings (see Chapter 1) may best be attacked, in the first instance, at the level of knowledge, rather than at the level of practice or organization.

From this perspective, the critical fact about the commercialization of agriculture in Western India in the last century is that it *creates* a new distinction between technical knowledge and its larger epistemological context. The emergence of an *agronomic episteme*, divorced from a wider *agrarian* discourse, represents just such a separation of knowledge from context, in the process of which the corresponding *techne* is rendered obsolete. In this process, the very epistemological fabric of the community is also rendered obsolescent and survives only in the diminished form.

This is the epistemological precursor of the corrosion of the prime value of sociality. It is in such situations, where technological change creates a (previously meaningless) distinction between technical knowledge and broader modes of knowing, that utilitarian criteria for assessing such change lead to the same conclusions as broader criteria involving cultural reproduction. For change of this sort tends simultaneously to involve a reduction of options (and an increase of risks) for individuals and groups, and lead to a corrosion of core cultural values. It is this sort of double jeopardy which I will seek to illustrate in my account of the process of commercialization of agriculture in Western India.

2 Agriculture in Maharashtra

The state of Maharashtra in Western India was formed in 1960, after the Bombay Presidency of British India was split into the linguistic states of Maharashtra and Gujarat. But Maharashtra, as a linguistic, religious, and cultural region, has an identity going back at least 800 years which undergirds current conceptions of the cultural unity of the state. Maharashtra is an interesting state because it combines a relatively advanced industrial sector (producing fertilizers, heavy machinery, drugs, textiles, and motorized transport) and a sophisticated financial and commercial sector, centred on the city of Bombay, with a relatively impoverished agricultural sector.

The agricultural sector in Maharashtra has a profile which is deeply rooted in its ecological and historical circumstances. The state can be roughly divided into a narrow coastal strip, which is very densely populated, has a very high rainfall, and is massively involved in rice-production, and a very large plateau (part of the Deccan plateau), on the other side of the hill-range known as the Western Ghats, which is characterized by low rainfall, low population densities, and a production profile dominated by millets (sorghum and pearl millet) and pulses. This very gross ecological contrast, of course, conceals finer distinctions, particularly in the plateau region, where there are differences in the degree of urbanization, the number and accessibility of market centres, the quality of soil, and the amount of rainfall. In keeping with these, and other, differences, the history and nature of penetration of rural communities by the forces of commercialization is also varied.

The village in which I worked (described in detail in a subsequent section) is located at the western edge of this dry agrarian region, near the city of Poona, and is only 6 hours (by bus and train) from Bombay. It is part of Poona district, which in terms of the intensity of irrigation, the amount of land devoted to commercial crops, the numbers of males who work in cities (while their families remain in the villages), etc., represents a more diverse profile than many of the other dry districts. Poona district, though it contains subregions which are rain-deficient and largely devoted to subsistence cereal cropping, also has many pockets of intensely commercialized agriculture. In particular, this district is responsible for a large share of the sugar-cane production of Maharashtra state, which is in turn a very significant proportion of the sugar-cane production of all of India. It also has a very important share in the production of vegetables and pulses for regional markets, as also of wheat and rice production in the state. Poona district thus represents a complex agrarian profile, with a fairly substantial history of commercialized agriculture. As we shall see, the village I studied reflects this history in important ways.

The intensity of commercial agriculture in Maharashtra, as in many other rain-deficient parts of South Asia, is critically determined by access to man-made irrigation techniques, principal among which are canals and wells. It is my impression that the relative importance of wells to commercial agriculture is greater in Maharashtra than in any other Indian state. But wells, as we shall see, are a very complex and intricate part of the total agrarian world of rural Maharashtra. Changes in their technology have a historical context which transcends the technological dimension, and which involves the emergence of an agronomic discourse in Western India in the last century.

3   Commercialization and Agricultural Discourse

It is notoriously difficult to get reliable historical information at the village level, especially regarding the sorts of epistemological and moral shifts that accompany technical change in a domain such as agriculture. The bulk of the historical sources are colonial records and reports which have a particular epistemological and rhetorical structure (Saumerez Smith 1985), one that does not encourage the sort of cultural analysis in which I am engaged. But there is a type of document which can be used to chart, at least in a very rough way, shifts in indigenous ideology which instantiate the conceptual costs of technical change. In the Maharashtrian case, I have been fortunate to discover certain nineteenth-century tracts concerning agriculture which provide a bench-mark against which I can compare current 'official' discourse concerning agriculture contained in such sources as farmer's magazines, diaries produced for farmers, texts produced by and for agricultural universities, and so on. What a sampling of these texts (all of which are in Marathi) permits is some rough approximation of the contours of epistemological change in agricultural thought in Maharashtra.[1]

It is important to understand that these sources constitute varieties of 'official' ideology and they do not by any means bring us the direct voice of the farmer, particularly the small farmer. Indeed, they all constitute efforts to persuade farmers in Maharashtra to undertake new kinds of agricultural practices. They are thus rhetorical in structure, and reflect the forces of commercialization as they linguistically and conceptually impinge upon farmers. It is difficult to know exactly how many farmers read (or had indirect access) to such texts—either in the past or in the present—and it is therefore hazardous to infer much about their effects on farmers. What they do permit is a picture of the changing assumptions of official agricultural ideologies, and of the way in which an indigenous agronomy is formed that reshapes, selects and eliminates important parts

1. The Marathi texts I have used are all to be found in the India Office Library (London) and are the following: Amruttungal 1852; Khare 1892; Apte 1890; and Nipunge 1981.

of village-level agricultural knowledge. The analysis of these changing assumptions permits a rough corroboration of the case for cultural change that I have made in the subsequent parts of this paper, and a more precise linguistic sense of how commercialization is made a locally credible and inexorable process.

The bench-mark text that I have used, Amruttungal (1852), is in the form of a dialogue between a learned and widely travelled Brahmin and a Kunbi farmer in the town of Paithan in Aurangabad district, one of the driest and still least modernized parts of rural Maharashtra. Without providing much justification for its main assumption, the text takes for granted that this cosmopolitan Brahmin has much to teach the Kunbi farmer and his four sons, who are portrayed as struggling to eke out a subsistence existence on their holdings. The text constitutes a fascinating glimpse of what, in the middle of the nineteenth century, was seen by some Maharashtrians as the cutting edge of rural commercialization.

The most striking thing about this text is that it confirms the extent to which an extensive commercial vocabulary was already in use in the agricultural sector. The lexicon of commercialization in this text is centred around costs (*kharcha*) and their reduction, increases in yield (*utpanna*), the frequent use of the concepts of profit (*nafā*) and loss (*thōtā*), and the idea of the commodity (*jinnas*). Together, these terms are used in sentences attributed both to the 'expert' Brahmin and to the Kunbi peasants, in ways that express the central rhetorical goal of this text—increased agricultural yield and income. The main chapters are devoted to advertising the commercial virtues and the principal techniques associated with growing new varieties of local cultigens (like sugar-cane); new cultigens from Europe like potatoes and fodder grass; and the value of breeding animals like goats and horses.

What is interesting about this rhetoric of new agricultural opportunities and techniques (firmly couched in the commercial idiom discussed above) is that it does not yet use the concept of the 'progressive' or 'modern' (*ādhūnik*) farmer, but speaks only of the clever or competent (*hushār*) farmer. Further, the agricultural message is couched in terms of a generalized preaching of the virtues of the European regime: separate chapters are devoted to the importance of literacy and the virtues of Christianity (the book was apparently written by a local convert); and there is a fascinating chapter which tries to allay the fears of the farmer regarding the newly introduced coinage of the East India Company, by preaching the associated virtues of standardization, free exchange, elimination of middlemen, and so on. Thus we can see that, at least at this stage, the commercialization of agriculture is seen as part of a general 'rationalization' of rural life, in the domains of education, religion, and commerce.

Yet, when we look closely at the language of commercialization and its accompanying epistemological framework, it is quite different from later 'official tracts'. For one thing, the concept of capital (*bhāṇḍval*) is not used once in the entire text. Though it was probably in use in other commercial contexts in mid-nineteenth-century Maharashtra, it does not appear to have been a critical requirement of the rhetoric of commercializing interests in agriculture. Thus, unlike later texts, in which it is noted that certain improvements pose major challenges in terms of 'capital', in this early text the matter is simply seen as one of 'costs' and associated gains. By extension, agriculture as a whole is not yet seen as a commercial enterprise, in which investment, saving, and capitalization are seen as the critical engines of profit. Rather, profit is seen in proto-capitalistic accounting terms, as a matter of reducing costs and seizing opportunities to make bigger profits largely by increasing yields and by exploiting new cultigens and animals.

Finally, it is interesting to note that a series of things which are problematic for small farmers are here simply taken for granted as unproblematic features of the agrarian landscape. Thus, though the section on sugar-cane makes much of its need for water, wells and their management are simply not mentioned, nor is the problem of water more generally. Land is also treated tacitly as an expanding resource. Finally, though there are brief mentions of problems of labour, on the whole there is a model of family farming in which the problems of hired labour are yet to emerge. Lastly, credit for agricultural investments is not treated as a major problem in the economics of farming. It does appear in the section on currency, where it is seen as part of the evil stranglehold of money-lenders and absentee landlords. Credit is thus still part of the social universe of dependency and debt, rather than a part of the progressive framework of investment and enterprise.

In general, the picture we get from this 1852 text is one of an incipiently commercialized but not an aggressively entrepreneurial agricultural world, which is just being exposed to new cultigens as well as new forms of currency, religion, and literacy. Though it is a discourse which is underpinned by the language of profit and loss, there are only the beginnings of a thoroughgoing ethos of economizing, and it portrays small farmers as averse to risks, subsistence-oriented, and suspicious of new agricultural and commercial techniques and instruments.

The situation is much changed by the latter part of the nineteenth century. The two texts which I have consulted, Khare (1882) and Apte (1890), show a vastly more complicated view of the agrarian process and its commercial dimensions. This is no surprise, given that by 1880, with the impact of the railways and the linkage of many parts of rural Maharashtra to regional and world markets in sugar-cane, cotton, rice, and wheat, great changes were under way. Population growth, the extension of agriculture, the pursuit of commercial opportunities—all of which characterize the period from 1870 to 1920—had already transformed the rural landscape in important ways.[2]

The first of these texts, Khare (1882), is at once a polemic about the sad plight of the Maharashtrian farmer and his exploitation by urban people, money-lenders, and the state, and a manual for progressive farming techniques and objectives. It thus anticipates the anti-urban, activist ethos of the powerful farmers' movements in Maharashtra in the later 1970s and early 1980s. In its critique of external commercial interests, particularly those of *baniyas* (businessmen) and others from the North, it provides a rich glimpse of the ideological ethos of the Deccan riots of 1875.

Although it is ostensibly a powerful plea on behalf of hard- pressed farmers, its central assumption is the ignorance of farmers whose lack of knowledge (*gyān*) is seen as the principal reason for their poverty. This sense that farmers do not know what they need to know (already implicit in the 1852 tract) is now explicit, and it expresses the formal announcement of the gap between 'official' agronomic knowledge and the traditional knowledge of farmers in this region. More generally, by this period we witness the formation of an indigenous agronomic discourse in which the knowledge of farmers is simply absorbed into a larger, more rationalized discourse, framed in information and exhortation concerning new tech- niques and goals. That is, a large part of these new tracts simply consists of the description and codification of existing knowledge, with periodic insertions concerning new alternatives. Thus, in the 1882 tract, a brief section on the use of animal manure notes that farmers, knowing the virtues of cattle dung, already use it as manure, but that they are unaware of the method already established in England (*vilāyat*) for using the urine of cattle to produce fertilizer. But what is important is that the entire scheme of agricultural knowledge is beginning to be transformed into a seamless web of technical information, where the line between what farmers already know (and thus do not need to be told) and what they do *not* know is increasingly obscure. This transformation of practical knowledge into agronomy is the critical symptom, at the level of discourse, of the process of commercialization.

One strand of the tract literature of the latter part of the nineteenth century (exemplified by Khare 1882) is fundamentally populist, anti- money-lender and pro-farmer, in its tone. It is only secondarily technical and agronomic in its rhetoric, and to the extent that the world of commerce

---

2. My general sense of the social, political, and economic transformation of agriculture in South Asia in the last century has been especially informed by the following four collections of essays: Bayliss-Smith and Wanmali 1984; Chaudhari and Dewey 1979; Desai, Rudolph, and Rudra 1984; and D. Kumar 1983. As far as the agrarian transformation of Maharashtra is concerned, I have benefited greatly from the following: Attwood 1984, 1980; Banaji 1977; Catanach 1970; Charlesworth 1985; Fukazawa 1983; Keatinge 1912, 1921; R. Kumar 1968; Mann 1917; Mann and Kanitkar 1921; McAlpin 1983; Perlin 1978.

(*vyāpār*) enters its framework, it is largely in terms of the relationships between money-lenders and farmers. In this model, farmers are presented as toiling, poor, ignorant, and exploited, whereas the landlord/ money-lender (often portrayed ethnically as a *marvadi* or *baniya* members of business communities with their origins in Gujarat and Rajasthan) is seen as avaricious, literate, calculating, heartless. Though the farmer, in this type of rhetoric, is exhorted about the virtues of work (*udyōg*), utility (*fāydā, lābh*), and organized leisure (*vishrānti*), he is still not conceived fundamentally as an entrepreneur. Indeed, in this work, farming (*shēthi karṇyā*) and commerce (*vyāpār*) are contrasting activities, and the farmer (*shētkari*) and the money-lender (*sāvkār*) are seen in a nasty but unavoidable symbiosis. It is in the context of ameliorating, but not transforming, this relationship that the language of commerce enters this tract, in the terminology of loans (*karja*), interest (*vyāj*), amounts (*rakkam*), security for loans (*vasūl*), and so on. The sole use of the term *bhāṇdval* (capital) in this text is with reference to money-lenders. Although this does not mean that farmers in Maharashtra in the 1880s were not involved in commercial agriculture, it does suggest that the conception of farmers as capitalists (*bhāṇdvaldār*) was still alien to much official discourse.

But in the 1890 tract, called *The Best Farmer* (*Uttama Shētkari*), the romantic and populist tone of the earlier tracts gives way to a more businesslike, technical, and specialized treatment. This work is a careful analysis of the relationship between farm size, hired labour, and landowners' participation in agriculture, with a fairly complex conception of the optimization of various forms of owner–labourer relationships.

This text is also a very early index of the emergence of time as a commercialized resource in agriculture. Early in the text, it is asserted that the value (*mōl*) of time (*vēḷ*) in agriculture is matched in very few other businesses (*vyāpār*), and a whole series of examples is provided of how various contingencies tend to interfere with the proper timing of agricultural activities and thus cause loss (*nuksān, thōtā*) to the farmer. Notable in this picture of the exigencies of timing is the failure to mention man-made water problems (though uncertain rainfall is mentioned) and the implication that ritual obligations generally take (and ought to take) precedence over agricultural pressures.

So too, agricultural produce is referred to in the text as *māl* (goods) and there is an implicit sense of the profitability of rural enterprise underlying the examples in the text. Thus a farmer who owns a 'one-pair' holding (i.e. what can be worked by a pair of bullocks, roughly equal to 16–20 acres) by himself with the assistance of careless casual labourers, is likely not to be doing very well, even if he looks to the outside observer as if he is very wealthy. The small farmer (*lahāṇ shēth karṇārā*—itself probably a recent technical category in this official discourse), is seen as lacking cash capital (*paishāchā bhāṇdval*). He is depicted as suffering from being on the wrong side of a series of economies of scale and thus as perennially a victim of the scarcity of cash (*paishāchī taṇchāi*).

This 1890 text represents a strong pitch for partnership and sharing arrangements (*bhāgīdāri, sarkati*) among small farmers, and in this context what emerges is a fully fledged conception of agricultural capital. It is explicitly noted that cash is not the only form of capital (*bhāṇdval*) required for farming, but that the seeds, animal feed, tools for weeding, cultivating, and threshing, etc. are also forms of capital. Partnerships are seen as a way to accumulate larger capital and large capital enterprises are said to involve lower costs (*mōṭyā bhāṇdvalāchē vyāpārāth kharcha kamī lāgtō*). Furthermore, the larger the capital, the greater the profit (*jitkē bhāṇdval mōṭhē titka fāydā mōṭhā*). The virtues of the division of labour (*shrama-vibhāga*) are seen as an adjunct to the idea of partnerships in small-scale farming.

In general, this tract is dominated by a full-blown conception of farming as a capital-oriented business and of the virtues of 'economizing', particularly from the point of view of partnerships among small farmers. What is notable is that even in this tract, wells are not seen as a major focus of co-operative control or ownership, and are largely taken for granted as aspects of the agrarian landscape. The sole form in which problems of water are mentioned is in terms of the uncertainty of rainfall, as in the earlier tracts.

Thus, by 1890, it appears that a mature agronomic discourse in Marathi had emerged, largely formulated by petty officials in the bureaucracy. The samples we have looked at allow us to see the formation of a rudimentary commercial consciousness in agronomic discourse. However, these tracts seem even in 1890 to conceive of agriculture as largely a social process, in which farmers and farming are part of a larger world of relations, groups, and orientations. It is not yet a technical or narrowly scientific discourse, devoid of social analysis, political opinions, or cultural polemics.

Before turning to a contemporary example of official agronomic discourse, exemplified by a farmer's diary from 1981, it is important to note that the period from 1890 to 1980 is obviously one which involved major social, economic, and technical transformations in the rural land-scape of Maharashtra. Though it is far outside the scope of this chapter even to summarize these changes, the most important among them must be noted: the rapid expansion of cultivation in the period from 1880 to 1920, which has some of the marks of a boom period: rising prices for agricultural commodities, increased productivity, absorption of most arable land and water resources. This period was followed by a slump which lasted well into the thirties world-wide, during which there was little significant growth. But starting in the forties, and continuing up to the time of writing (late 1980s), we have had the beginnings of a major technological revolution in agriculture, the key features of which are the availability and spread of chemical fertilizers, new varieties of seeds, mechanized tools for a variety of agricultural operations, and oil and electricity as new sources of power. This agricultural revolution, it must be stressed, has not spread very deeply into rural society in Maharashtra, but it clearly indicates the technological shape of things to come.

The *Farmer's Diary* (*Krishival Dāyiri*, ed. H. L. Nipunge) for 1981 (which combines the features of an American-style farmer's almanac with those of a daily notebook and record) was produced by a publishing house in Poona to be sold at a price of Rs 10, a little over one US dollar at the then current rate of exchange, but a significant sum of money for any but the richest farmers. The content of the diary as well as its price indicate clearly that it was directed at the uppermost stratum of Maharashtra's farmers. It consists of almost 170 pages of small- print text, which precede a rather small number of blank entry- pages for the days of the year. The printed text, which is heavily interspersed with advertisements for seed, fertilizer, and farm machinery companies, is an extremely detailed and technical guide to every important aspect of 'progressive' or 'modern' (*ādhūnik*) farming in Maharashtra. As such, it doubtlessly represents the vocabulary that is shared by agricultural colleges, agribusiness, and agricultural extension workers in today's Maharashtra. Coming almost one hundred years after the 1890 tract I discussed earlier, a century characterized by steady growth in agricultural education as well as in agribusiness, it is no surprise that this text takes the commercial logic and structure of agriculture wholly for granted, and focuses largely on the technical and agronomic specifics of soils, seeds, modern cultivation techniques, water, and fertilizer use for a large variety of commercial crops. It has a chapter each devoted to sugar-cane and to onions, both important commercial crops in Maharashtra, and others devoted to fruits, flowers, modern machinery, seeds, and fertilizer. Throughout, there is an emphasis on the use of newly developed hybrids as well as on the use of a wide variety of chemical fertilizers. Though a great deal could be said about the vocabulary and ethos of the agronomic discourse contained in this text, I will restrict myself to a few points which are salient to the larger argument of this chapter.

The most striking feature of this text is the virtual elimination of rough measurement algorithms, and their replacement by extremely precise (generally Western) measures. Whether it is a question of the depth of the water-table, the amount of fertilizer appropriate to various crops, the number of times a particular crop needs to be watered, the average yields of crops in the state, or anything else, the text generally gives precise numerical measures. It therefore represents the culmination of a process of technical and commercial penetration of indigenous agricultural discourse, which, as I will show in a subsequent section, depended mostly on approximate, relational, and context-bound kinds of measurement. If we look back at the earlier tracts from this perspective, we can see that in 1852 this type of precise idiom of measure was virtually absent; it begins to appear in the 1882 and 1890 tracts, although even in these the more approximate and practice-oriented forms of measure tend to coexist with the new, more technical forms. But by 1981 it is clear that indigenous agronomic discourse has no room for approximate or context-tied forms of measurement.

The second notable fact is that the entire framework of this 1981 text is profoundly individualistic. There is no indication anywhere in it that there are complex forms of co-operation and interdependence in rural Maharashtra, both between wealthier farmers, and between them and poorer farmers. In this sense, not only can we see how the entrepreneurial, individualistic ethos sets the tone of mature agronomic discourse, but also that as such discourse grows more technical, it tends by its nature to become less sociological. Put another way, by 1981 agronomic discourse ceases to have any concern with agrarian relations and sees farming as a wholly technical enterprise.

Similarly, in this text, the rural calendar has become wholly demystified and all sense of the ritual periodicities that frame agricultural activity has been eliminated. Although the tripartite terminology for the climatic seasons (*uṇhāḷā*, *pāvsāḷa*, *hivāḷa*) and the dual structure of the cropping seasons (*kharif*, *rabi*) is still in place, the major change is that the folk organization of major agricultural activities according to the system of *nakshatra*s (lunar asterisms) is completely eliminated; instead the English calendar months and then various numbers of days to characterize the time between operations are used. The earlier tracts all refer to the *nakshatra*s as ways to time major operations, as do farmers in Vadi and elsewhere in Maharashtra today. More important (and anticipating the discussion in the next section of the chapter), the text as a whole clearly sees agricultural activity as the driving force of the calendar, as exhaustive in its temporal claims, and as wholly independent of ritual and other social periodicities. This text truly instantiates what, paraphrasing E. P. Thompson, we might call agronomic time.

In a chapter on bank loans, the text makes it clear that the only loans that are relevant are those that are meant for the improvement (*sudhārnā*) of the farm and for increased production (*utpādan vaḍhisāṭhi*). This is the only context in which the text brings up the digging of new wells or the deepening of old ones, among examples of purposes for which banks are likely to grant loans. The text also makes it clear that banks are not interested in loans for consumption needs, and warns farmers not to divert the money they receive for improved agricultural production to immediate consumption needs. In general, the section on bank loans confirms the overall tone of the text, which is that of a technical manual for the exemplary (*ādarsh*) farmer, committed to new techniques and crops, oriented principally to the market-place, free of the social relations of rural life and the rhythms of the ritual calendar. Such a figure is clearly not yet a reality in rural Maharashtra, but he is the model target (and ideological goal) of the new agronomy.

This brief sketch of change in the discourse of agriculture in Maharashtra was meant to complement our knowledge of changes 'on the ground' in the last century. But it also puts us in a better position to interpret and place in context the very specific shifts in practice and ideology that I shall discuss next, this time in the setting of a single village. Today, as in the past, rural Maharashtra is characterized by extreme *spatial differentiation* (Charlesworth 1985: 142–55), both in ecology and in the resulting patterns of commercialization and social differentiation, so that there can be sharp differences not only between broad regions within the state, within districts, and within *talukas* (subdivisions), but even between villages which are a few miles from each other. One cannot therefore leap easily from macro- to micro-data, but the account I have given of the formation of a regional agronomic discourse can serve as a general backdrop for the specific case I turn to now.

4   The Ethnographic Locus

The village from which I have drawn this data—and to which I have given the pseudonym Vadi—is located about 25 miles south-east of the city of Poona, in Purandhar *taluka* (subdivision), Poona district, about 130 miles inland from the coastal metropolis of Bombay. Its location places it on a gradient of decreasing rainfall in the Deccan Plateau. Rainfall in Vadi probably totals less than 25 inches in most years, and is sharply seasonal. The peak period of rainfall in normal years is in the months of June, July, August, and September, which account for about 75 per cent of this total. October and November usually account for about 15 per cent, the months from December to March for about 3 per cent, and April and May for about 7 per cent. These figures are very approximate, for there can be sharp year-to-year fluctuations from this norm. The village is about 2.5 miles from Saswad, the *taluka* headquarters, which is the principal bus link to Poona and to Bombay. There is a road passing the village which is used by the buses of the State Transport system and by the trucks of the transport companies that move vegetables from villages like Vadi to Poona and to Bombay.

The population of Vadi in 1981 consisted of approximately 900 persons, who were distributed in 193 households. About 30 per cent of these households contained families that were 'joint' (*ēkatra*) in one or another sense, while the remaining 70 per cent were 'nuclear' (*vibhakta*). The total amount of cultivated land was about 880 acres of which about 280 acres (less than 33 per cent) was wet land, i.e. land that has access to water above and beyond rainwater. Mean landholdings were 4.5 acres, with mean dry landholdings being 3.1 acres and mean wet landholdings being 1.4 acres.

Vadi has a very significant set of links with the outside world. Out of the 193 households, 104 had one (and often more) members of the family outside the village, usually earning a living in Bombay or Poona. But this should not give the impression that Vadi is a 'remittance' economy in any simple sense, since many of these wage-earners support dependents in the city, and others, for a variety of reasons, send cash back to the village only in special circumstances. Thus it is no surprise that although 104 households had working members outside Vadi, only 33 of these households described cash salaries as their principal means of subsistence (when compared with income from cash crops, sale of family labour, and the products of their own fields).

The caste composition of Vadi was relatively simple. Out of the total of 193 households, 174 were Maratha, and the rest were distributed among the various lower service castes, including some considered 'Untouchable'. When villagers stated that this was a 'Maratha' village, they were not far wrong. The Maratha households themselves were organized into four numerically dominant lineages (*bhāuki*) and three numerically minor ones. The families in each lineage shared surnames (*āḍnāv*), although there is here an ethnographic curiosity in that two of the dominant Maratha lineages share the same *āḍnāv*. The families of the other castes were similarly identifiable by shared surnames.

I have already noted that mean landholdings were small. Agriculture, to produce crops for household consumption as well as for sale, was the principal economic activity of the villagers. The principal subsistence crops were sorghum (*jowar*) and millet (*bājri*), and most villagers grew at least some of each. In addition, however, there was a very large number of other cultivars. Small amounts of wheat and rice were grown. The principal commercial crops were sugar-cane, onions, and green peas. Also important, but more for consumption than for sale, were a variety of lentils and pulses, peanuts, many kinds of greens, and small amounts of tomatoes, carrots, figs, fodder, grass, and flowers. All the crops grown principally for sale (and here peas and onions are the most important), as well as the vegetables grown for home consumption, required irrigated land.

There are two major cropping seasons: the *kharif* season, from June to October (which relies on the monsoon rains) and the *rabi* (or winter) season, when the bulk of the irrigation- dependent, market-oriented farming is done, which runs from November to February. The hot (*uṇhāḷā*) season from March to May is the most taxing because of the heat and lack of water, but those who did have access to water in this season used it to grow certain vegetables. The hot season is also the season for repair of tools, preparation of the land in anticipation of the June rains, and the celebration of marriages and other village festivities. It is the season of high expenditure and low income for many households.

While the technology of agriculture was largely traditional, its economic framework was no longer so traditional. The bullock and the plough were still the key instruments of agriculture, and the tools used for winnowing, weeding, reaping, sowing, threshing, and harvesting were still largely part of a very ancient material inventory.[3] Yet there had been important changes. The use of fertilizer and of pesticides, particularly for cash crops, had become common, and animal manure was infrequently used. Agricultural labour was paid for almost entirely in cash, and there were clearly understood rates of payment for different tasks, seasons, and genders. Vadi was a labour-surplus village, for though there were very few landless households, the number of land-poor households was quite large. Even the intermittent flow of urban remittances was inadequate to sustain the land-poor households, whose women and men had to sell their labour in addition to using it to manage their own smallholdings. Thus it was not often that the farmers of Vadi needed to hire labourers from other villages.

Vadi, in 1981–2, was in a variety of ways highly monetized. Even the poorest households were deeply tied into the cash nexus and most households, in the opinion of these farmers, would have collapsed without a few hundred rupees per month, at the very least (Rs 9 = US $1 then). One major way to improve one's position in a world dominated by cash transactions was to enter the market in agricultural commodities, not only as a labourer (where the prospects for improvement were dismal) but as a producer. This meant gaining access, however precariously, to irrigated land. Before I can discuss *local* changes in agricultural knowledge in the context of commercialization, it is essential to present the elementary facts surrounding irrigated agriculture in Vadi.

5   The Technology and Sociology of Irrigation in Vadi

The basic technological structure of the 74 wells in use in Vadi in 1981–2 probably goes back at least a millennium and consists of a hole dug in

3. The whole topic of changes in agricultural technology in Western India needs careful examination of a sort that has yet to be given to it. But it is highly probable that the major technological break, prior to the recent increase in heavy machinery, new seed varieties, fertilizer, and irrigation technology, is the incorporation of *metal* into what were previously wholly wooden farm implements. Though this shift doubtlessly began in the 19th century, there is some evidence that it took off only in the early part of this century under the stimulation of agribusiness and rural commercial interests: see Mann and Kanitkar 1921. As far as wells are concerned, the shift from earthen to masonry walls probably occurred in two waves, the first in the 1850s and the second in the period from 1880 to 1920, as responses to commercial opportunities in the first case and to government loan programmes in the second.

the soil to a depth of anything from 20 to 60 feet (about 6 to 18 m.), and with a diameter of anything from 15 to 30 feet (3 to 9 m.).[4] The traditional measure for the depth of a well is a *paras* or *purush*, indicating the height of an adult male, but actually equivalent to about 7 feet (2 m.). Although some wells were probably dug by family or village labour, specialist castes of well-diggers are a well-known part of the historical record in Western and Southern India. In the past, the inner walls of this hole were 'finished' with stone and lime, and there would have been a wooden superstructure. This superstructure would permit the dropping and lifting of a leather water-container. The raising and lifting would have been accomplished by either two or four bullocks.

By the 1970s, wells had acquired some new features, though their basic design persists. Cement had largely replaced lime for the finishing of the interior; steel containers (*mōṭ*) had replaced the leather water-containers; and, in a few cases, rented boring machines had replaced human labour for the actual digging. Most important, animal power had come to be regarded as obsolete, although about 12 wells still used this form of power. The energy source of choice was electricity, although about 5 wells were powered by diesel-engines. This meant that there were about 57 wells that were powered by 3 or 5 h.p. electric motors. Sometimes these modernized wells had varying lengths of pipeline, but often traditional dug channels (*pat*) were used to take the water from the mouth of the well to the fields. Most wells physically pre-dated the arrival of electricity, and were thus simply electrified traditional open-surface wells. The technology of wells may thus better be called mixed than traditional.

Wells were part of the picture of very small and fragmented holdings in Vadi, but were also indicative of a relatively high proportion (33 per cent) of irrigated land to total cultivated land, compared to the figure for the state, which was 11 per cent in 1975–6. In Vadi, in 1981, 142 households shared about 280 acres of wet land. Of these households, about 33 per cent had wet landholdings of less than 1 acre, about 60 per cent had less than 2 acres, and about 80 per cent had less than 3 acres. Only 11 of these households had more than 5 irrigated acres each, and 1 of these had 25 acres, the largest concentration of wet landholdings in Vadi. I present these figures to show that these irrigated holdings are extremely modest, by and large.

Most farmers owned several plots (*tukḍē*) of wet land; these holdings were not usually physically contiguous, which means that the farmers were often shareholders (*hissēdār, vātēkārī*) in more than one well. Although there were 24 single-owner wells, and 13 two-owner wells, even the farmers involved in these had shares in some of the other wells, which had co-sharers ranging in number from 3 to the most involuted case,

---

4. This discussion of wells draws heavily on Appadurai 1984: 3–14.

which involved 31 co-sharers. The scattered picture of individual land-holdings was further layered over by a criss-crossing web of shares in wells. Shares in wells usually remained attached to the pieces of land with which they were associated and, in Vadi, to buy or inherit a piece of land was by definition to inherit a share in the well which allowed it to be irrigated. Yet shares in wells were not entirely tied to pieces of land for wells could fall into disuse; or water from one well (theoretically meant to irrigate a particular plot) could be diverted by the shareholder to another plot not associated with it; or well-shares could lie dormant while the pieces of land associated with them were watered by water from another well to which the shareholder had access.

Nevertheless, as a rule, shares in wells were closely associated with pieces of land, and thus the major way in which shareholders in wells acquired these holdings was through land inherited from their male parents. This is reflected in the fact that many wells had shareholders who were all male agnates (paternal kinsmen) from the same named lineage, and sometimes they were sons of the same father. This picture of patrilineally inherited shares was fairly persistent, so that when one encountered a well which had mixed lineage membership, or in which there was one anomalous surname, it could easily be traced to one of the following three sources: a sale of the land (and the associated well-share) to an outsider by a lineage member in financial difficulty; the acquisition of a piece of lineage land by an outsider because of a loan default in which the land was the security (*tāraṇ*); or, in the few cases where a woman was named as a share-holder, it turned out that she was a widowed member of the lineage, whose husband had received that land as part of her dowry, with the land reverting to her after his death.

Approximately 33 per cent of these wells had between 1 and 4 shareholders and thus did not require complex systems for sharing water. But the remaining 66 per cent, which had between 5 and 31 shareholders, did require complex time-sharing systems. To understand these systems, it is necessary to have some knowledge of the role of wells in agricultural production. Well-watered land is (and has been for the known past) crucial to growing most crops in the winter and summer seasons when the rains are minimal. Very few wells had water through all 12 months, and it is these few 12-month wells (*bārāmāhi*) that allowed their beneficiaries to grow sugar-cane, which requires ample water throughout the year. The bulk of wells were known as 8-month wells (*āṭmahi*), and yielded water from approximately mid-June to mid-February. Such 8-month wells permitted the growing of onions and green peas (the two major cash crops), plus a variety of other vegetables and fruits which were grown both for market and for home consumption, as well as small amounts of rice and wheat.

In wells that had more than four or five shareholders, who were working small plots of land and growing the same cash crops (such as onions) at much the same times, there were fairly complex turn-taking (*pāḷi*) systems. These systems varied depending on the number of shareholders, the water-retention capabilities of the well, especially in the hot weather, the crops being grown by the shareholders, and the amount of land under the well in question. Usually the system was a 12-day or 8-day rotation, and the amount of time (1 day or 2 days or a part of a day) that a particular turn consisted of depended on the amount of land that a particular landholder had in his share. It was in the hot season, when the water level dropped, and when the cash crops needed water in order to yield profits, that these systems came into play. It was also at these times that those farmers who had access to their own wells or to low-membership wells had the greatest advantage.

In general, partly because of the fragmented holdings under wells and the problem of low capital for many of these farmers, few wells involved 100 per cent use of the plots that were described as being 'under' them (*vihīrīkhāḷī*). Frequently, only a third of the acreage nominally associated with the well was actually in productive use. This was a sign of the incapacity of shareholders to afford the labour and other costs associated with full use of their well-linked acreage. In most cases, the under-utilization of these nominally irrigated plots was a function of these disabilities and not of the limits of the wells alone. Consolidation of holdings is the key to the economics of using these wells optimally, but most farmers had holdings that were far from each other in addition to being small. Wealthier farmers were always seeking to acquire, either by direct purchase or by mortgage-defaults, plots near ones they already owned.

All farmers in Vadi who lacked access to shares in wells would have liked to acquire such shares. All farmers with shares would have liked to see these shares electrified. (I speak of electrified 'shares' rather than of electrified wells because there were several cases of wells in which some shareholders had invested in motors which they operated during their turns. The motor was not available to other shareholders who could not afford to participate in the original investment, and who therefore used bullock power during their turns or, in a few cases, rented diesel-engines, which were portable.) And all farmers would have liked to have wells of their own, preferably electrified, without having to co-operate with other farmers in the original investment or in the subsequent turn-taking. The reasons for this antipathy towards partnership, in a community traditionally committed to the value of sociality, are discussed in the conclusion to this chapter.

The motorized wells which had multiple shareholders clearly reflected the fact that the costs of electrification (a 3 h.p. motor cost about Rs 5,000 ($555) and a 5 h.p. motor about Rs 8,000 ($888) in 1981) exceeded the financial capabilities of most farmers. Yet the decision to invest jointly in a new well was even harder than the decision to invest jointly in a new motor for an existing well. The costs of a new well, including digging it, installing a motor, and perhaps installing pipeline, ranged from Rs 20,000 ($2,222) to Rs 40,000 ($4,444). This was a very sizeable investment, since the mean annual cash income of most small farmers (from all sources) was unlikely to exceed Rs 5,000. Given the small individual plots, the chances that some of the co-sharers would not be able to afford the inputs to make the optimal use of the irrigated land, and the chances that economic difficulties would make some of them renege on their share of the bank loan repayments or the electricity bills, it was no surprise that all but one of the new wells dug in the five years before 1981 were entrepreneurial ventures by single farmers. There had been joint efforts to electrify existing wells, but there were several wells where plans to electrify had not come to fruition, and others that, though electrified, were under-utilized, especially by the poorer shareholders.

6   Knowledge Shifts in the Locality

Let us recollect, at this point, the argument about epistemological change which was previewed in the introduction to this chapter. It was suggested that the commercialization of agriculture in the last century has created a new *agronomic episteme*, which renders much of the existing agrarian *techne* obsolete. Through a series of examples, three of which pertain to the content of knowledge, and three others to styles of knowledge, I shall demonstrate how commercialization leads to radical epistemological shifts.

6.1 Knowledge Loss

First, very soon knowledge of how to construct, maintain, and efficiently operate non-motorized wells will become obsolete, just as knowledge about leather water-containers has already largely vanished because of their replacement by metal water-containers in wells. Why should we worry about the loss of this particular sort of knowledge? After all, it might be claimed, animal-powered traditional wells belong to an inefficient and rapidly disappearing mode, and it is likely (as well as desirable) that more and more farmers will acquire shares in motorized wells or in larger modern systems of water-distribution. Is it not simply urban romanticism about rural life to regret the passing of such knowledge?

The fact of the matter is that in many dry parts of rural India, like Maharashtra, a significant number of farmers still eke out their subsistence on the edge of commercial agriculture by their access to bullock-drawn well-water. For them the understanding of the requirements and uses of such wells is by no means irrelevant. Secondly, for many farmers, participation in the ownership of electric motors for well-water is a risky matter, and sometimes partnerships in such wells fail, or, due to economic exigencies, shares in such wells have to be sold. In these cases, those without access to, and knowledge of, traditional techniques are likely to be pushed out of the market in cash crops (which require irrigation) completely. This will make the ups and downs of farm fortunes sharper in the current transitional milieu. Thus, until such time as there is universal and reliable access to electric power for wells, knowledge of bullock-drawn well-water ought not to be pushed into obsolescence. Finally, in so far as bullock-powered wells often involve bullock-sharing systems, which draw poorer farmers into partnership arrangements, the elimination of these systems also means the end of certain modes of co-operation among farmers. Again, until it is perfectly clear that all farmers operate in a world in which household autonomy is a safe and satisfying mode of organizing subsistence, such changes are risky ways of eating into social capital, particularly for poorer farmers.

As for the shift from leather to metal water-containers, the argument is simpler. This shift pushes farmers inexorably towards greater dependence on large-scale markets, and towards greater vulnerability to price shifts and uncertainties in supply. If ever there is a major change in prices for metal goods, a great many poorer farmers are likely to find themselves going deeper into debt in order to afford metal water-containers. Further, since, the making of leather water-containers was an important occupational entitlement of the lowest leather-working castes, this change pushes them into metropolitan markets for their goods and services, thus further compromising the autonomy of rural economies.

Second, with increased dependence on industrially produced fertilizers, even among small farmers, detailed knowledge about how best to use animal manure for agricultural production will become restricted to an older generation and will then disappear. Again, why should we care? First, because in such complex traditional ecosystems, with their delicate relationships between animal manure, agricultural productivity, costs of farming, relative local self-sufficiency, and impact on the soil, there is ample evidence that animal manure can be extremely effective when available. The problem in the part of Maharashtra in which I worked is that in the last serious period of drought, in 1972, a great many cattle were sold, and local cattle populations have never returned to their previous levels. When this situation is combined with the sort of pressure on farmers from government, agribusiness, and outside experts to shift to industrial fertilizers (a part of the growing agronomic *episteme* I described in Section 3 of this chapter), we can see why farmers, even smaller ones, might be tempted to abandon the use of animal manure, and the knowledge of the algorithms traditionally associated with its use. Among many farmers, the pressure to generate sizeable short-term cash incomes (to meet subsistence needs that can increasingly be met only with cash) leads to over-use of chemical fertilizers, with possibly disastrous long-term effects on the soil. In Maharashtra, as elsewhere in India, there is a widespread feeling that chemical fertilizers 'heat' the soil excessively. Thus, in abandoning older fertilizing technologies, farmers are losing the capability to fall back on a technology that might, in certain circumstances, be better for them and their fields. Knowledge lost, in the case of agricultural techniques, is choice foregone.

Third, as reliance on government geologists and other modern experts for locating sub-surface water sources increases, there is going to be reduced demand for the services of water-diviners. In rural Maharashtra, such individuals, called *pānhāḍi*, are frequently drawn upon in the course of decisions to locate new wells. Whatever the objective virtues of their systems for divining the location of sub-surface water (and I, for one, have an open mind on this question), they serve an important role in contemporary decisions to sink wells. Sinking a new well, in the parts of rural Maharashtra with which I am familiar, is a costly, risky, and time-consuming process. It involves the commitment of major household resources, often the contracting of partnership ties with other local farmers, the taking on of debts to banks or co-operatives, and the commitment of a large and indefinite amount of family time for the supervision of whoever does the actual work. Given the nature of the costs and the potential benefits, it is a major decision and one attended with considerable anxiety. A crucial part of the decision is the question of where to locate the well. Farmers themselves have projections, based on village understandings, the location of other wells (old and new), and the advice of friends and neighbours, about where there is likely to be a good vein. Government geologists, who use Western scientific techniques and instruments, have a different conception of the water-table and of the optimal places for a well on any given plot of land. So far, farmers have been able to arrive at what they regard as reliable decisions in this crucial matter by triangulating these three kinds of knowledge and then arriving at a choice which best conforms with the predictions of either two or all three of these modes. As the expertise of water-diviners disappears, it is not just that we lose an important traditional eco-technical skill. We also lose one component in a process which allows farmers to make a complex and risky decision using multiple diagnoses. Here again, a loss in knowledge is a curtailment in epistemological multiplicity and choice.

What is true of material technologies is less true of ecological knowledge. Farmers' knowledge about rainfall, soil, and water as natural systems seems to have survived in many parts of India, but it is only a matter of time before reliance on radio, television, and other metropolitan forms of agrarian expertise pushes indigenous knowledge increasingly out of the picture. What is, of course, most resilient is knowledge about people, deities, cosmological happenings, and ritual calendars and rhythms. In this area the fabric of traditional rural knowledge seems to have been least affected. Still, since knowledge, especially in rural settings, is not tightly compartmentalized, the archive as a whole will probably begin to be structurally transformed, although it is difficult to say how or when.

6.2 Shifts in Ways of Knowing

I have spoken so far about the content or archive of agricultural knowledge. In this regard, I have suggested, change is fairly rapid and fairly extensive. But what about the traditional way of knowing, traditional rural epistemology? In Section 3 above I have already suggested some of the significant ways in which the emerging agronomic discourse of the last century redefined the world of the farmer. In particular, I pointed out ways in which the terminology of measurement and the handling of time were altered by the incipient commercial setting. In what follows, I locate these shifts in the specifics of the farming world of Vadi, and in its *epistemological style*. This style, in any community, has several dimensions, of which the following three are especially important: (1) typical modes of assessing certain phenomena, what we might call *modes of analysis*; (2) typical ways in which knowledge is shared or distributed in the community, i.e. *the political economy of expertise* in that community; and (3) the strategic *relationship between sectors of knowledge* (and thus of experience), which determines what kind of knowledge takes priority over what other kind. This last dimension is where matters of knowledge shade over most visibly into matters of value. I turn now to some examples of each of these dimensions of the epistemological style of farmers in Vadi, and changes to which they provide testimony.

Using material from Maharashtra, I have suggested elsewhere (in a paper on rural technologies of measurement, Appadurai 1989)[5] that the difference between contemporary Western terminologies of measurement and their non-Western, rural counterparts is not simply a difference in vocabularies, calling for care in translation. Rather, rural terminologies of measurement reveal assumptions about the relationship between number and quantity, the relationship between measures and standards, the acceptability of approximation over precision, and the centrality of social negotiation to measurement, which are fundamentally divergent from the abstract, context-free, precise norms to which contemporary scientific systems aspire. Thus, when farmers assess the extent of their lands, their yields, their local populations and sub-populations, their needs, and many other things, they do so in terms which are not just superficially different from our own but which contain and reflect a very different understanding of what measurement is all about.

One example of this important difference will have to suffice here.

5. This extended essay will form one of a set of essays currently in preparation by the author.

Farmers engaged in growing onions (largely for the market) often have to buy onion seedlings from other farmers. When the purchase of these seedlings is negotiated, it is done in terms of a measure called a *vāfā*, a roughly standardized 'bed' in which such seedlings are planted. The buyer bids a certain sum for a particular *vāfā* (or set of *vāfā*) of seedlings, and then there may be a counter-offer by the seller, and then a final resolution. Although this may look like standard haggling over the price (i.e. the value) of a clear-cut amount of something, it is rather negotiation over the amount itself, expressed in the idiom of price. Since these 'beds' vary in size and shape and since the number of seedlings in them has to be guessed at visually, what in effect the buyer and seller are bargaining over is their respective estimates of quantity using the measure of price— offers and counter-offers. Such relationships between quantity estimates, approximation, and value characterize many other sorts of activities in rural Maharashtra.

Yet, in a world which is increasingly defined by money, by markets, and by externally calibrated institutions of measurement, such as clocks, calendars, and measuring tapes, a very different mode of measuring is becoming relevant to more and more contexts in rural life. This new mode is characterized by precise and context-free instruments of measure, non-negotiable results of acts of measurement, and a generalized re-placement of approximation by precision. Signs of this shift are every-where, though the traditional mode of measuring is still the normal one. But every farmer who operates with cash flows, who works in industrial or quasi-industrial settings, and who responds to bureaucratic re-quirements in his search for cash, credit, electricity, or health needs must learn new ways to measure his world, or at least to express his estimates of things. Again this sort of erosion of traditional modes of analysis is not just unfortunate in itself, but reflects the degree to which farmers (often in spite of their preferences) are forced into large-scale, metropolitan interactions, contexts, and modes of thought. To the degree that such incorporation into larger systems is neither pleasant nor freely chosen, its accompanying epistemological costs must, in principle, be deemed high.

As regards the political economy of expertise, it is possible to postulate a growing unevenness in the distribution of agricultural knowledge, both within and across specific agricultural communities and regions. The intensification of agriculture has among its many consequences the spatial and social differentiation remarked on by Charlesworth (1985) and others. Increasingly, there are crops (such as sugar-cane) which demand that plots be given over to them permanently and regions that are constrained to specialize in this or that crop because of market pressures and opportunities. There are farmers who specialize in this or that crop. The crudest example of this last factor is that in more and more communities, there is a clear gap between those wealthier farmers whose lands are completely (or largely) given over to commercial crops and those whose small plots are devoted mainly to subsistence crops.

Of course, this growing differentiation does not have direct implications for the distribution of knowledge, since poorer farmers often work on the commercial plots of richer farmers and richer farmers maintain portions of their land for subsistence crops so as to be free of the vagaries of the market. Yet there is no doubt that knowledge of agricultural operations is now more intricately shared, especially in regard to the overall strategic handling of livelihood. The agronomic discourse discussed earlier is not evenly distributed in Vadi. Wealthier farmers today speak the language of risk (*khatrā*), of investment (*kharcha*), of capital (*bhāṇdval*), and of planning (*vichār*) in ways that reflect directly their exposure to, and interest in, the discourse of fertilizer companies, bank officials, large agricultural traders, and development experts, both public and private. The 1981 farmer's diary discussed earlier epitomizes this type of usage. Poorer farmers, by contrast, though they will occasionally speak of capital, *nafā-thōtā* (profit and loss), and so on, are not active or frequent users of the language of agricultural entrepreneurship.

These linguistic variations reflect deeper and subtler variations in how knowledge is shared. It seems clear that, over a long period of time, the amount, at the level of knowledge, of what Anthony Wallace called the replication of uniformity or Durkheim would have called mechanical solidarity has decreased; and there is more and more of what Wallace called the organization of diversity and Durkheim would have called organic solidarity (Wallace 1970; Durkheim 1960). In short, farmers increasingly know what they know in a piecemeal manner, consonant with technical and environmental segmentation as well as with social and economic stratification. More and more rural communities are held together because of differences—rather than through similarities—in what various persons and groups know about the conduct of agriculture. Needless to say, such unevenness can and does reinforce structures of inequality and domination in rural India. Though this tendency too is not yet dominant, its direction is clear. It is towards that division of epistemological labour which characterizes complex modern communities the world over.

The strategic relationship between sectors of knowledge is the hardest aspect of the epistemological style of rural communities to pin down, but it is perhaps the most important. In any given epistemological universe, some things frame others, some things are regarded as less questionable than others, some issues and perspectives colour the way others are apprehended, discussed, and acted upon. It is this aspect of any particular system of knowing and speaking that Michel Foucault sought to capture in his idea of a discursive formation (Hoy 1986).

One major shift that is under way in the discursive formation of rural

India, again based on my field-work in Vadi, concerns the experience and handling of the temporal dimension of rural experience. Time is a central resource in all agricultural communities, and India is no exception. Time is experienced as the continuing interaction of several kinds of rhythms and periodicities, cosmological, ecological, ritual, and economic. The timing of agricultural decisions reflects very complex negotiations and compromises between these various kinds of periodicities, and I have elsewhere argued that poorer farmers are at a very specific kind of disadvantage in the distribution of time as an agricultural resource.[6]

But I want here to make a more general point. While it appears that in the past ritual and ecological periodicities set the rhythms of production, consumption, and reproduction, and defined the framework of knowledge and of belief within which production goals were set and pursued (all the nineteenth-century tracts discussed earlier support this view), this practical and epistemological priority is in the process of being reversed. Increasingly, as suggested earlier, time itself is subject to the overwhelming pressure of the market-place and the logic of commercialization. That is, more and more of the rhythm of agricultural life is set by the labour, cash, and climatic needs of commercial crops, affecting not only those wealthier farmers who are massively tied to markets in agricultural commodities, but also those poorer farmers who provide the labour and part of the clientele for the products of this intensification and commercialization of agriculture. As I suggested earlier, the logic of agronomic *time* is beginning to make increasingly involved a limited social calendar, to set the pace of life, and to leave ritual and ecological periodicities in a somewhat more marginalized role.

Let me explain by means of an ethnographic example. The main commercial crops in this part of western Maharashtra are sugar-cane, onions, and peas. In general, these crops have been inserted into a cropping cycle which was previously dominated by the cultivation of sorghum and millet in two long seasons (monsoon and winter), with a low-activity hot season between them. In this situation, not only was there greater temporal slack during the year but each crop did not make intense, precise, and frequent demands on the time of farmers. While subsistence cropping in millet-growing areas does require certain key operations to be performed at certain times, both the length of the seasons and their internal activity structure leave considerable temporal flexibility. This flexibility ceases once major cash crops arrive on the scene, especially onions and peas, but also to some degree sugar-cane. The cultivation cycles for the commercial crops cross-cut the pre-existing calendric cycles which, for most farmers, require room for the basic subsistence crops, and also stretch considerably into the hot season, which was previously a

6. This important topic has not been paid much attention by students of agrarian life in South Asia; an important exception is Amin 1982.

slack period. Furthermore, the vegetable cash crops typically require more intense and carefully timed bursts of activity for weeding, watering, and fertilizer application. Finally, their own cycles of planting and harvesting frequently overlap with each other as well as with those of the main subsistence crops. As a result, especially for those farmers who are self-reliant in terms of family labour, much of the year is a scramble to juggle the cycles of these various crops, and most of them tend to have at least a small amount of their total acreage under some of these cash crops.

As crop seasonalities begin to jostle each other and crowd the time available to many farmers, other periodicities frequently become subordinated to them. Marriage celebrations are frequently timed not solely by reference to auspicious moments, as determined by the Hindu almanac, but must yield to the agricultural schedules of the wealthier families. Pilgrimages once undertaken with great liberality must now be handled more circumspectly, either by going shorter distances, or by staying away fewer days, or by leaving key members of the work force behind. Major village festivals and rituals seem no longer genuinely to set the pace and structure of the rural calendar, but rather to be islands of cosmological stability amidst an increasingly hurried flow of production-related activities. Even at the everyday level, women frequently find themselves performing important ritual tasks on the run: in the midst of rushing to work on someone's fields, while on the way to get water or firewood, or while tending the family goats or sheep.[7] In short, the traditional interactive rhythm of ritual and ecological periodicities is now increasingly penetrated and framed by the requirements of labour, energy, cash, and demand associated with the commercialization of agriculture. This does not seem to be a temporary shift in the way farmers in Vadi talk about their lives and experience the flow of time, in so far as we can tell by looking at what they say as well as what they do: it looks as if it is not likely to be reversed.

7 Conclusion

This essay has told a story whose plot has worked at two levels. The first level concerned the evolution of an agronomic discourse in Marathi, in the context of the region. The second level concerned the village of Vadi, and a rather more recent, and detailed, story of technical change in irrigation. It remains now to discuss the general implications of this story, by returning to the main moral issue raised in the introduction to the chapter: how are we to assess the benefits of technological change in such a case?

7. The phenomenological situation of poorer rural women is discussed in Appadurai forthcoming.

I suggested that my axiomatic criterion was the *value of reproduction* for any human community. I also suggested that the main requirement for the maintenance of this value was the *reproduction of core values*. By this I meant that our challenge was to establish, in a way that combines *our* perspectives with the insights of those we study, what core values need to be reproduced for the community itself to be reproduced, not necessarily in an unchanging fashion, but in a way that preserves its distinctive social life.

I believe that there is a set of deep links between agricultural and social life in Vadi, and in communities such as Vadi.[8] These links take many forms, but their critical expression is in a whole variety of what I call *centripetal* social forms. In ritual, in agricultural work, in men's work teams, in women's work teams, in ritualized service-exchange relationships, in relations between rich farmers, between them and poor farmers, and between poorer farmers themselves, there is a rich range of connections, not always determined by ties of caste or kinship, which are enduring, multi-functional, and built on amity. By external criteria, some of these relationships (such as those between landlords and tenants, money-lenders and creditors, richer and poorer farmers) might appear exploitative. But they are cross-cut by, and part and parcel of, other modes of interaction to which the language of exploitation would not appear to apply. Together, what these centripetal forms indicate is that the core value of this community is *sociality* itself. That is, though the forms of sociality have changed over time, there is still a widespread sense, instantiated in practice as well as in farmers' talk, that a form of social life built around centripetal pulls is the core value of this community.

It is this core value which is threatened by commercialization, as I have portrayed it in this chapter. At the level of discourse, I have tried to sketch a process which gradually divorces agronomy from agriculture, or, more loosely, divorces agriculture from agrarian relations. More specifically, at the normative heart of the new discourse is a conception of the farmer as a technologically sophisticated, credit-seeking, market-oriented person, whose goals are (in the current commercial sense), to maximize output, profit, and income. Although, particularly in the cultivation of sugar-cane, a powerful co-operative movement has emerged in Maharashtra, this does not controvert the general thrust of the new commercializing ideology, which aspires to create a farmer who is free of complex local ties. This is a farmer who responds to *centrifugal* pulls, largely commercial ones, which draw him away from the social demands of village life.

What is true at the macro-level of the formation of an agronomic discourse, is reflected in a complex way at the level of practice and talk

8. For a fine exploration of these links, see Schlesinger 1981: 233–74.

among the farmers of Vadi. As I have suggested in another context (Appadurai 1984), while the small farmers of Vadi are forced to participate in partnership and sharing arrangements if they wish to have any part in the opportunities of commercial agriculture, they do not regard these arrangements as desirable. They aspire to a situation where they might be 'big' farmers, who can enter this arena on their own, without recourse to complex sharing arrangements.

It is important here to distinguish co-operation as a *value* from co-operation as a *strategy*. In the traditional set-up, as I have construed it, the prime value of sociality is expressed in a variety of centripetal social forms, many of which involve co-operation. But as the commercialization process of the last century has made its ideological and institutional inroads, the *erosion* of such centripetal social forms has led to a situation where co-operation has been reduced to a *strategy* for subsistence. Particularly for poorer farmers, the aversion to partnership reflects a deep ambivalence about this reduction. They are willing to pursue it, for they see fewer and fewer alternative ways to assure subsistence in the world which they now confront. But they resist it because it is *only* a strategy, furthermore a risky one, and one that does not any more encode or imply broader or deeper social ties. The solution to this ambivalence is, therefore, not simply to create institutions which mediate the conflicts between micro-motives and aggregate outcomes (conflicts typified by the prisoner's dilemma). Rather it is to create institutional alternatives to the apparently inexorable march of commercialization. Only such alternatives will restore co-operation as a value, not merely a strategy.

This observation about the reduction of co-operation from a value to a strategy permits me to clarify the relationship between commercialization and individualism in the last century. This relationship has three features: (1) though the relationship between farmers and markets in Western India is far older than the last century, it is now a pervasive factor in more villages and in more transactions in such villages, and it affects more farmers in such villages. There is thus a great increase in the sort of individualism we associate with market-orientation. (2) For some farmers, this has meant the beginnings of a genuinely capitalist orientation to farming, which sees savings, investment, and profit as the goals of agricultural production. (3) For all *farmers*, rich or poor, social relations in production are increasingly seen as *strategic* interactions with other *individuals* (whether for survival or for profit), rather than as expressions of the values of sociality. This last shift is, in my judgement, the critical differentiating feature of the 'individualism' of the last century in rural Western India. Though it is so far visible largely in the domain of production, it will probably soon affect the ethos of consumption as well.

At this point, it may well be asked why the current situation is objectionable? Why can it not be seen as the dawn of a happy world of individualistic, market-oriented, profit-seeking farmers, reorganizing their social lives in keeping with their new-found economic opportunities? There are three answers to this question. The first, which I have already hinted at, is that for many of these farmers, the loss of knowledge (and the associated losses in social ties) that some of these changes bring is a bad risk, since they may well be pushed out of the commercial sphere and pushed back into the subsistence sphere in which such knowledge is not so irrelevant. The second reason is that these changes involve a steady reduction in the relative autonomy of the village as an economic arena, something which on the whole has not been shown to be of either absolute benefit to the nation or to more than a small number of villagers. But the third reason is the most important.

Most small farmers are obsessed with the desire to have a share (even a tiny one) in the market in agricultural commodities not because there is a natural entrepreneurial impulse in everyone, but because *cash* is the key to subsistence to an unprecedented degree in places like Vadi. That is, large-scale transformations in marketing, production, the division of labour, and monetization, have created a situation in which more and more transactions that are critical to subsistence require money. It is this desperate need for money which drives small farmers to push for a tiny piece of the commercial sector in agriculture, even in terribly involuted circumstances. For most of them, such participation in commercial agriculture is not the road to larger capital, growing income, and the status of 'big' farmer, but is, rather, the *sine qua non* of survival in a deeply monetized world.

In this context, there has been a profound transformation of the relationship between risk and sociality in rural life. Where, in the past, partnership arrangements (and sociality in general), of whatever sort, constituted values as well as hedges against risk, in the new circumstances of commercialized agriculture, partnerships (and sociality in general) are seen as strategies, as burdens, and indeed as *sources of risk* in agricultural enterprises. Thus, many poorer farmers are in a terrible predicament: they are pressed to participate in a commercial agriculture which pulls them away from a complex web of social ties; yet this pressure generally yields not new wealth but only precarious subsistence in a heavily monetized world. It is this double jeopardy of the centrifugality produced (both ideologically and practically) by the technical needs of commercialization which makes it a dubious proposition, from the point of view of the value of reproduction and the reproduction of values in Vadi.

REFERENCES

Amin, Shahid (1982) 'Small Peasant Commodity Production and Rural Indebtedness: The Culture of Sugarcane in Eastern U.P., *c.* 1880–1920', in Ranajit Guha (ed.), *Subaltern Studies*, i, New Delhi: Oxford University Press.

Amruttungal, Ramachandra (1852) *Jāgtījōt*, Poona: Board of Education.

Appadurai, Arjun (1984) 'Wells in Western India: Irrigation and Cooperation in an Agricultural Society', *Expedition* (University of Pennsylvania), 26/3: 3–14.

—— (1989) 'Transformations in the Culture of Agriculture', in Carla Borden (ed.), *Contemporary Indian Traditions*, Washington, DC: Smithsonian Institution Press.

—— (forthcoming) 'Dietary Improvisation in an Agricultural Situation', in Anne Sharman *et al.* (eds.) *Diet and Domestic Life in Society*, Philadelphia: Temple University Press.

Apte, Chintaman Moreshwar (1890) *Uttama Shētkari*, Akola: Vidharba Press.

Attwood, D. W. (1980) 'Irrigation and Imperialism: Water Distribution and the Origin of Enclave Capitalism in Rural Western India' (unpublished).

—— (1984) 'Capital and the Transformation of Agrarian Class Systems: Sugar Production in India', in Desai, Meghnad, Rudolph, S. H., and Rudra, A., (eds.) *Agrarian Power and Agricultural Productivity in South Asia*, Berkeley: University of California Press.

Banaji, J. (1977) 'Small Peasantry and Capitalist Domination: Deccan Districts in the Late Nineteenth Century', *Economic and Political Weekly*, 7/33–4: 1375–404.

Bayliss-Smith, T., and Wanmali, S., eds. (1984) *Understanding Green Revolutions: Agrarian Change and Development Planning in South Asia*, Cambridge: Cambridge University Press.

Catanach, I. J. (1970) *Rural Credit in Western India, 1875–1930*, Berkeley: University of California Press.

Charlesworth, N. (1985) *Peasants and Imperial Rule: Agriculture and Agrarian Society in the Bombay Presidency, 1850–1935*, Cambridge: Cambridge University Press.

Chaudhari, K. N., and Dewey, C., eds. (1979) *Economy and Society: Essays in Indian Economic and Social History*, New Delhi: Oxford University Press.

Durkheim, E. (1960) *The Division of Labor in Society*, trans. G. Simpson, Glencoe, Ill.: Free Press (French original 1893).

Fukazawa, H. (1983) 'Agrarian Relations: Western India', in Kumar (ed.) *The Cambridge Economic History of India*, ii, Cambridge: Cambridge University Press.

Hoy, David, ed. (1986) *Foucault: A Critical Reader*, Oxford: Basil Blackwell.

Keatinge, G. (1912) *Rural Economy in the Bombay Deccan*, London: Longmans Green.

—— (1921) *Agricultural Progress in Western India*, London: Longmans Green.

Khare, Kasinath Trimbak (1892) *Hindustānātīl Shētkaryānchī Sthithi va Shētkı ñchi Kāmēn*, Gyanprakash Press

Kumar, R. (1968) *Western India in the Nineteenth Century: A Study in the Social History of Maharashtra*, London: Routledge and Kegan Paul.

McAlpin, M. (1983) *Subject to Famine: Food Crises and Economic Change in Western India, 1860–1920*, Princeton: Princeton University Press.

Mann, H. H. (1917) *Economic Progress of the Land and Labour in a Deccan Village, No. 1*, London and Bombay: Humphrey Milford, Oxford University Press.

—— and Kanitkar, N. V. (1921) *Land and Labour in a Deccan Village, No. 2*, London and Bombay: Humphrey Milford, Oxford University Press.

Nipunge, H. L., ed. (1981) *Krishival Dāyiri 1981*, Poona: Pusphak Prakashan.
Perlin, F. (1978) 'Of White Whale and Countrymen in the Eighteenth Century Maratha Deccan: Extended Class Relations, Rights and the Problem of Rural Autonomy under the Old Regime', *Journal of Peasant Studies* (Jan.), 5/2: 172–237.
Saumerez Smith, Richard (1985) 'Rule-by-records and Rule-by-reports: Complementary Aspects of the British Imperial Rule of Law', *Contributions to Indian Sociology*, NS 19/1: 153–76.
Schlesinger, Lee (1981) 'Agriculture and Community in Maharashtra, India', in George Dalton (ed.), *Research in Economic Anthropology*, vol. iv, Greenwich, Conn.: JAI Press.
Wallace, Anthony (1970) *Culture and Personality*, 2nd edn., New York: Random House.

7

Losing Touch: The Cultural Conditions of Worker Accommodation and Resistance

STEPHEN A. MARGLIN

1 Introduction

This chapter continues a series of enquiries (Marglin 1974, 1979, 1984) which have focused on the role of profitability and capitalist class interest, as distinct from efficiency,[1] in shaping the organization of work. At issue here is the workers' side of the story, specifically the cultural underpinnings of resistance and accommodation to the capitalists' project of domination.

The argument is built up from several separate propositions. The first is that cultural variables are central to the outcome of conflict over the organization of work. What people value, how they know—both systems of values and systems of knowledge—affect whether, how, and with what degree of commitment people will defend themselves and their work against the capitalist (or the commissar, for that matter). Indeed, this chapter, although it assumes the importance of class struggle in determining the organization of work, asserts equally strongly that the parameters of class struggle are determined by cultural values. Even class

---

1. 'Efficiency' is the economists' preferred term for describing the virtue of the market. An efficient set of economic arrangements is one that precludes the provision of more of one good except at the sacrifice of some other good. 'Goods', it should be noted, has an elastic meaning: a good can be defined as narrowly as a specific commodity like bread or ice-cream or it can be stretched to mean the well-being of individuals. In its second meaning, an efficient set of arrangements is one which precludes increasing the well-being of one individual except at the expense of another.

The advantage of the more technical terminology of 'efficiency' over a more informal notion like 'the size of the economic pie' is that it permits comparison of situations where tastes differ: 'size of the pie' becomes ambiguous when some people like blackberry pie while others like apple pie. But taste differences are not matters of great moment for present purposes, and we lose correspondingly little if we take the informal route of identifying efficiency with pie size.

Observe that the economists' definition of efficiency is somewhat at odds with conventional usage. A businessman thinks he is increasing efficiency if he is successful in imposing a speed-up. But the economist will object that the higher output is at the expense of greater effort. It is not necessarily more efficient in the sense of providing more of one good without sacrificing something elsewhere.

itself is not born of economics alone, but of the union of economic interest and cultural justification. Classes act in history only when they are armed and legitimized by cultural values which are generally and widely held throughout the society. And culture not only empowers, it sets limits to class conflict. People struggle only to the extent that their common cultural heritage permits of different interpretations.

The first concrete application of this idea is that the tenacity with which workers defend their work arrangements depends on the meaning that they attach to their work. This meaning can take one of two forms, *holistic* or *individualistic*. *Holistic* meaning attaches significance to one's work because it is an integral part of a whole which commands the allegiance and assent of the community; *individualistic* meaning, by contrast, is a significance that one creates oneself through work.

The preconditions of holistic and individualistic meaning differ. Holistic meaning requires that work be embedded in the cultural fabric, that it be an expression of one's relationship to the cosmos rather than simply a matter of earning one's daily bread. Individualistic meaning requires that one be in control of process and product, without which the very project of *creating* meaning becomes unthinkable.

The problem for workers has been twofold, for Western culture fosters neither holistic nor individualistic meaning for most forms of work. First, the Judaeo-Christian and the Greek traditions disembed most work from a context that might make it meaningful. Second, starting with Plato and Aristotle, one system of knowledge has become hegemonic. The problem is that workers' knowledge is generally organized in terms of other, 'inferior', systems, with the result that it becomes the inferior knowledge of inferior people. The culture thus undermines workers' attempts to defend their control of work.

These arguments are developed in the sections that follow. After a sketch of the relevant background (Sections 2–4), we shall turn to the main ideas, the disembeddedness of work (Section 5) and the devaluation of workers' knowledge systems (Sections 6–10) in the West. Sections 11–13 highlight these ideas by contrasting the conception of work in Hindu culture as revealed by a case-study of a weaving community.

2 Meaning—Holistic and Individual

Work is, and undoubtedly will remain, a core element in establishing a sense of purpose and accomplishment, a sense of significance for one's entire life. Even to speak of the meaning of work is therefore necessarily to speak of the meaning of life, and to oppose the nihilism of Macbeth ('[Life] . . . is a tale/Told by an idiot, full of sound and fury,/Signifying nothing') or the utilitarianism of Freud ('What decides the purpose of life is the . . . pleasure principle' (1961: 23)).

Notwithstanding the scepticism, and indeed downright hostility, of the modern, secular, West to any attempt to invest life with meaning—'human presumptuousness' Freud called it (1961: 22)—human beings expend considerable energy to disprove Macbeth. Our loves, our friendships, our relations with parents and children, *our work*, are at least partially a function of a deep-seated drive to make our lives signify something. Certainly Freud's pleasure principle falls well short of explaining attitudes towards work and love, which Freud himself is supposed to have made the measure of successful psychological adjustment.

Social organization may facilitate or hinder the search for meaning. In non-individualistic, 'holistic', societies, the meaning of work is a cultural given, but this is the case only exceptionally in individualistic societies. When one is part of a 'cause'—the last one which commanded broad allegiance in the United States was the cause of defeating Germany and Japan during World War II—it is much like being part of the effort to build a cathedral in the non-individualistic Middle Ages: the particular job can be subordinated to the whole and derive its meaning from the meaning of the whole.

But the general situation of modern individualistic society is that there is no such transcendent cause. Instead, one must be both playwright and leading actor; we each must create our meaning both through the roles we write for ourselves and the way we act them. Doubtless it was much easier when parts in the theatre of life were socially given, and all one had to do was to interpret one's part.

There are thus two kinds of meaning that attach to work, or perhaps it is more accurate to speak of two separate paths through which work feeds into the meaning people attach to human existence. The first is a *holistic* meaning, with significance and purpose assigned to work by the common consent of the community. The glory of God or the defence of democracy, or for that matter the construction of socialism, all exemplify transcendent causes that have invested work with meaning at some places and times.

The second form of meaning is *individualistic*, a significance and purpose that the worker herself creates and asserts through her work. 'Symbolic immortality', to borrow a term from Robert Jay Lifton (1983: 21), 'something to point to' in the words of a steelworker whose story is the preface to Studs Terkel's *Working* (1972).[2] The achievements of work, more than the result of any other activity we undertake, give us grounds

2. 'Pyramids, Empire State Building—these things just don't happen. There's hard work behind it. I would like to see a building, say the Empire State, I would like to see on one side of it a foot-wide strip from top to bottom with the name of every bricklayer, the name of every electrician, with all the names. So when a guy walked by, he could take his son and say, "See, that's me on the forty-fifth floor. I put the steel beam in." Picasso can point to a painting. What can I point to? A writer can point to a book. Everybody should have something to point to' (p. xxxii).

believing that we might transcend our physical mortality, a belief already implicit in holistic meaning.

Control over process and product becomes central to any discussion of the meaning of work once we recognize the absence of a holistic meaning in contemporary Western society. For control is a necessary, if hardly sufficient, condition for investing one's work with individualistic meaning. But individual or even collective control by workers clashes with the capitalist project of domination. The central proposition of my first paper on work organization (Marglin 1974) was that two crucial steps in the history of work—the extension of the division of labour at the subproduct level and the concentration of production in factories—were instituted by capitalists in order to enhance their control. Subsequent papers (Marglin 1979, 1984) have been variations on the theme of control.[3]

3   The Division of Labour and the Rise of the Factory

Let me now briefly recapitulate the role of the division of labour in the perspective of control. My 'enemy' is evidently Adam Smith, for whom the efficiency of a highly developed division of labour was the starting-point of economic analysis. Indeed, Smith is commonly given credit for 'discovering' the division of labour. There is some justice in this, for certainly nobody before Smith (and, with the exception of Durkheim, nobody since) has made the division of labour so central to his argument. But the credit should be for emphasis, not discovery. The Greeks anticipated Smith in all important respects, down to the size of the market as the main factor limiting the division of labour (Xenophon). Plato went one better than Smith. In the *Republic*, the putative efficiency of the *economic* division of labour is the basis of the argument for a *political* division of labour. The chief drawback of democracy is precisely that everybody does everything, a defect which Plato's own blueprint of a specialized political caste was supposed to remedy.

3. Observe that control is not being opposed to profit. Contrary to 'invisible hand' arguments, in which profitability is a function of efficiency alone, profitability is here held to depend jointly on control and efficiency. Efficiency at best creates a *potential* profit; without control the capitalist cannot realize that profit. Thus organizational forms which enhance capitalist control may increase profits and find favour with capitalists even if they affect productivity and efficiency adversely. Conversely, more efficient ways of organizing production which reduce capitalist control may end up reducing profits and being rejected by capitalists.

This is not to say that businessmen actually do maximize profits. This is a controversial point on which it is unnecessary for present purposes to take a view one way or another. To assume that capitalists are motivated solely by profits may be an overly narrow, economistic perspective, but there is no need for present purposes to assume that control is an end in itself which is sought independently of its contribution to profits. In the present circumstances Occam's Razor suggests that control be regarded simply as a means to profit. *Entia non sunt multiplicanda praeter necessitatem.* (But see Albert Hirschman 1984.)

Neither Smith nor the Greeks distinguished between the division of labour at the product level and the division of labour at the subproduct level, the division of labour *between* workshops and the division of labour *within* the workshop. Both were seen as reflecting only efficiency considerations, the second being simply an extension of the first as the size of the market becomes large enough to warrant further specialization.

Karl Marx perceived an important difference once the division of labour ruled within the workshop as well as without: the division of labour at the subproduct level, the technical or detailed division of labour in Marx's terminology, makes the worker dependent on the capitalist. By contrast, the division of labour at the product level, the social division of labour, in no way presupposes the capitalist as integrator of the production process.

In the main, however, Marx followed Smith in invoking efficiency to explain the extension of the division of labour from the social to the technical level. The increased dependence of the workman on the boss was simply the unfortunate by-product. In this respect I differ from Marx; I argue that what Marx understood to be a by-product was in fact intentional.

The problem of the capitalist, as seen in my perspective, is to maintain a position for himself in the production process. Sometimes an adequate position is made possible by high capital requirements and indivisibilities, which put the activity beyond the reach of the individual workman or even of an association of workmen. Coal-mines and shipyards and even Arkwright's spinning mill come to mind as examples. But these are, I believe, the exceptions rather than the rule.

In the general case indivisibilities and associated capital requirements are not sufficient to maintain a position for the capitalist in the production process. Here, I have argued (Marglin 1974), the capitalist maintains his role by specializing workers to particular tasks, reserving to himself a critical task, frequently the task of integrating the separate operations into a marketable product. This allows him to stand between the workers and the product market, obliging the workers to sell their labour power rather than the product of their labour. Robert Cookson, a British woollen manufacturer in the period of the industrial revolution, succinctly put the essential point to a parliamentary committee: 'Suppose a man goes into a room and is confined in a room where there are twelve, thirteen, or fourteen looms, how is that man to be proficient in any part of the business than that?' (*Report from the Select Committee to Consider the State of Woollen Manufacture in England*, British Parliamentary Papers (1806), 1, p. 74. Quoted in Morris 1972.) Lest the committee harbour any doubts about his meaning, Cookson answered his own question: 'People trained up in a manufactory are never likely to set up for themselves.'

Thus, division of labour at the subproduct level, or more accurately, specialization at the subproduct level, became an instrument of capitalist control. Even if less efficient than alternative forms of work organization in which the worker exercised more control, a highly developed division of labour would enhance the capitalist's control over the production process and increase his profits.

Specialization ensured the dependence of the worker on the capitalist, but it did not get him to work. The problem of discipline was of course not a new one. Xenophon in the fourth century BC, Columella in the first century AD, Walter of Henley and other medieval writers, addressed the problem of worker discipline, anticipating such thoroughly modern ideas as incentive systems (Columella) and even time and motion studies (Walter). But at the time of the industrial revolution the legal freedom of the workers compounded the problem of discipline. The worker laboured primarily under economic rather than political compulsion, and the market was not much help.

Capitalists consistently complained about the perversity of the labour market. Higher wages, instead of coaxing out more effort, served only to reduce the worker's dependence, to the point that one eighteenth-century observer noted 'the sentiment universal' among cotton manufacturers 'that their best friend is high provisions' (Arthur Young 1770). A little later, the same observer put the point in somewhat stronger terms: 'every one but an idiot knows that the lower classes must be kept poor, or they will never be industrious' (quoted in Thompson 1963: 358).

The putting-out system made matters worse: in his own cottage the worker had control of raw materials and set the pace of his work. His control over raw materials led to endless squabbles over product quality as well as over embezzlement and fraud. (The worker was in a position to substitute inferior goods; give short weight; put 'wastes' to his own, rather than the boss's profit.) Control over the pace of work increased the possibilities for perverse—from the boss's point of view—responses to the incentive of higher wages.

No wonder that capitalists sought ways of limiting workers' control: organizational forms in which the boss, not the worker, fixed the hours and intensity of work, and where the worker would labour under the eye of a boss so that the fringe benefits (the worker's view of fraud and embezzlement) that accrued from control of raw materials would be harder to come by. The end result of this search was the factory.

This is not to suggest that efficiency considerations (in the sense of note 1) played no role in the rise of the factory. Indeed, in some industries, such as cotton textiles, efficiency considerations may have been very important. The transition from cottage to factory in cotton appears to have been predicated on the greater efficiency of the water-mill and steam-engine and the associated technical compulsion to centralization.

Boilers could not be practically adapted to the dispersed production of the putting-out system.

But two aspects of the transition from cottage to factory make it difficult to accept the proposition that efficiency considerations were generally decisive. On the one hand, the transition from cottage to factory also took place without the appreciable change in technology that accompanied the shift in cotton spinning and weaving. Woollen textiles are a case in point: the first woollen mills did not make use of water- or steam-based technologies, but utilized the same hand-powered technologies that workers had in their own homes. On the other hand, where workers were sufficiently powerful and motivated to resist factory organization, as in the case of the Coventry silk ribbon weavers, they were able to adapt steam-powered technologies to their own purposes. In Coventry, weavers 'rented' capital from capitalists: the capitalist's steam-engine powered a shaft that ran through the lofts of a row of attached houses, the lofts being the workshops in which the weavers' looms were located (Prest 1960).

The existence of industries like woollens in which factories arose without any technological innovation argues against the *necessity* of a technological basis for the factory. The existence of non-factory forms of organization around a new technology like steam, as deployed by the Coventry ribbon weavers, argues against the *sufficiency* of a technological explanation.

4 *The Evolution of Production Relations*

The subproduct division of labour and the factory were of course neither the beginning nor the end of capitalist innovation in the organization of work. Capitalists established their dominance over production only gradually; even in the late nineteenth century, workers—at least some of them—exercised substantial control over important aspects of work which would today, in the United States at least, be regarded as 'management prerogatives': for example, hiring and firing of assistants, setting work rules, and distributing the workers' share of the pie (Montgomery 1979, Buttrick 1952).

The basis of this control was twofold. First, the working class maintained a cohesion reflected in strikes and other forms of mutual support. Second, knowledge and skills were carefully cultivated and protected from outsiders—particularly from the boss and his agents. 'The boss's brains', according to a popular aphorism of a hundred years ago, 'are under the worker's cap.' In the words of Frederick Winslow Taylor, the father of scientific management,

foremen and superintendents know better than anyone else, that their own knowledge and personal skill falls far short of the combined knowledge and dexterity of all the workmen under them. The most experienced managers therefore frankly place before their workmen the problem of doing the work in the best and most economical way (1967: 32).

To consolidate and extend their dominance over production, capitalists had a double task, first to break the solidarity of the workers and, second, to restructure production so as to reduce to a minimum the role of workers' knowledge and skills. The destruction of solidarity focused on transforming the orientation of the trade-union movement to 'business unionism', with a narrow focus on the dollar and an almost total abdication from issues of control. The role of confrontations, of which the Pullman and Homestead strikes are representative US examples, was central to this process. These were setbacks from which the labour movement took decades to recover.

In the restructuring of work key steps were the development of what Richard Edwards (1979) has labelled *technical* and *bureaucratic* control, symbolized by the assembly line and the rule book. Both were attempts to depersonalize authority relations, to legitimize capitalist control by appealing to the shared cultural value of the superiority of impersonal to personal relations (Banuri, Chapter 3 above). The intention of both technical and bureaucratic control was to create and foster the impression of a transcendent authority—the assembly line or the rule book—to which all, boss and worker alike, are subject. What the capitalist forgets to mention is that somebody makes the rules, just as somebody sets the speed of the line.

The capitalist project of reorganizing work was epitomized by scientific management, or 'Taylorism' as it is sometimes called in honour of its principal founding father, whose description of the traditional, 'pre-scientific', state of affairs was earlier quoted at length. Contrasting his proposal with traditional systems of organizing production, Taylor (1967) had this to say:

Under scientific management . . . the managers assume . . . the burden of gathering together all of the traditional knowledge which in the past has been possessed by the workmen and then of classifying, tabulating, and reducing this knowledge to rules, laws, and formulae (p. 36). These replace the judgment of the individual workman (p. 37). Thus all of the planning which under the old system was done by the workman, as a result of his personal experience, must of necessity under the new system be done by management in accordance with the law of the science (p. 38).

Scientific management has been the subject of considerable controversy. Even the degree to which it has succeeded in eliminating the worker as a thinking participant in the production process is controversial. My own view is that friend and foe alike have misread Taylor's project as accomplished fact.[4] There is however no gainsaying the considerable success achieved by capital in carrying through the larger project of which scientific management was a part, that of both reorganizing the workplace and channelling the expression of worker opposition into 'bread and butter' issues of pay and employment security.

It has been emphasized that these changes could not be brought about by unilateral fiat on the part of capital. They were rather the outcome of struggle, in which both resistance and accommodation played important parts. But notwithstanding protracted and sometimes heroic resistance, the fact is that accommodation predominated.

There are many reasons for this. Capitalists wielded disproportionate power, politically as well as economically. Capitalism also delivered the goods, to use Herbert Marcuse's (1966) apt phrase; the restructuring both of work and of the field of resistance took place during a period of rapid growth of real wages. This is well known and needs no elaboration.

What is less well understood is the cultural dimension of class struggle. Indeed, a premiss of this chapter is that classes do not act in history until they are armed by culture, as culture normally finds expression in setting the terms of class conflict. Resistance to oppression, like oppression itself, is invariably the union of class interest with cultural justification. The accommodation of the working class to capitalist domination can only be comprehended when we understand the limits of the cultural basis for working-class resistance.

My thesis is that the capitalist class held the high ground not only economically and politically, but culturally as well. For, on the one hand, work was never embedded in the life of the Western community and the Western cosmic order, as it is in holistic societies. (Lutheran Protestantism and the communities coming under its sway present an exception that tests this rule.) Neither was the worker empowered by culture to defend the union of conceptualization and execution which underpins control by the individual worker. So the worker was unable to find the holistic meaning immanent in embedded work and he was discouraged by cultural values which he shared with the capitalist from defending the conditions of individualistic meaning.

5   The Cultural Roots of Disembeddedness

In the West work stands outside, if not actually opposed to, life. As part of the economic sphere, work is ordinarily reduced to an instrumental

4. Taylor himself was far from the lackey of capital he is portrayed by critics on the left (for instance, Braverman 1974). Over time he became as suspicious of capital as he was of labour. Of course, capitalists made use of Taylor. But then so did Lenin, whose encomiums for scientific management were already prefigured in Marx's characterization of 'socialized man, the associated producers, rationally regulating their interchange with Nature, bringing it under their collective control . . . and achieving this with the least

status within a pleasure/pain calculus, questions of meaning reduced to quality of work-life or on-the-job satisfaction. The disembeddedness of work is doubtless related to a larger separation of the economic from its social, political, and moral context, the central focus of Karl Polanyi's (1944) analysis of the development of capitalism. One can fault Polanyi for telescoping into the eighteenth and nineteenth centuries a process which had gained considerable momentum by the thirteenth. But if we recognize the origins of the 'economy' in medieval society, particularly the transformation of land and labour into 'commodities', we must reckon with the even greater remoteness of the disembeddedness of work.

This disembeddedness has roots in both Greek and Judaeo-Christian conceptions of work, particularly manual work, and its relationship to the purposes of human existence. Plato and Aristotle held the workman in equal contempt, though each had a different theory of how and why manual labour disqualified one from the higher pursuits of philosophy and politics. Plato, as has been observed, modelled the ideal polity of the Republic on the putative efficiency of the division of labour and specialization, buttressing this argument with an elaborate theory of knowledge (to which we shall return in another context). Aristotle, disputing both Plato's views on the polity and his theory of knowledge, nevertheless shared his views on the division of labour.[5] Aristotle held even the labour of directing other people's work in low regard. 'This science [of direction] is of no particular importance or dignity . . . Therefore all people rich enough to be able to avoid personal trouble have a steward who takes this office while they themselves engage in politics or philosophy' (*Politics*, 1255^b 32–7).

Xenophon was even more condemning:

The mechanical arts utterly ruin the bodies of those who work at them, compelling them to sit still and remain indoors, or in some cases even to spend the whole day by a fire. And when the bodies are made effeminate, the souls too become more diseased. Lack of leisure to join in the concerns of friends and of the city is another condition of those that are called mechanical; those who practice them are reported to be bad friends as well as bad defenders of their fatherlands. Indeed, in some of the cities, especially those reputed to be good at war, no

expenditure of energy . . .' (Marx 1894: 800). Sudhir Kakar 1970 has written a rewarding psychobiography of Taylor, including an account of the experiences which soured Taylor on captains of industry.

5. Plato, *Republic*, 368–70; Aristotle, *Politics*, 1252–4. The agreement holds even as to the basis of specialization. We can distinguish between Smithian and Ricardian theories of the division of labour, the first arguing the efficiency of specialization in terms of *environment* (that is, learned behaviour) and the second in terms of *heredity* (endowment). Smith's arguments for such specialization are couched in terms of learned behaviour and in no way presuppose a genetic disposition or proclivity to one kind of work or another (1937). Ricardo's theory of specialization presupposes an innate 'comparative advantage' based on differences in endowments (1951). In this typology both Plato and Aristotle are at the Ricardian end of the spectrum.

citizen is allowed to work at the mechanical arts (*Oeconomicus*, iv. 2–3, Strauss 1970: 17).

Xenophon makes an exception for agriculture. Agriculture was argued to be physically superior, complementary to rather than subversive of military preparedness (*Oeconomicus*, v) and thus at the service of and embedded in the highest aims of the political community. But for Xenophon agricultural labour was exceptional in its moral superiority too, for it was embedded in the cosmos in ways in which the craftsman's work was not and could not be. '[T]he earth, *being a goddess* [*emphasis added*], teaches justice to those who are able to learn, for she gives the most goods to those who serve her best' (ibid. v. 12).

In contrast with the Judaeo-Christian origin myth, labour on the land is not punishment for sin but the fall-out from internecine struggle among the gods; according to Hesiod, it all starts with Prometheus, or rather with Zeus' retaliation for Prometheus' transgressions:

[T]he gods keep hidden from men the means of life. Else you would easily do work enough in a day to supply you for a full year even without working . . . But Zeus in the anger of his heart hid it, because Prometheus the crafty deceived him; therefore he planned sorrow and mischief against men (Hesiod, *Works and Days*, l. 42–50).

Hesiod goes on to sing the praises of agriculture and the agriculturalist, praises that are echoed in Western conceptions of the good life and the good society from Virgil to Thomas Jefferson. The French classicist Jean-Pierre Vernant summarizes the distinctive embeddedness of agriculture in Greek thought this way:

Agriculture remains . . . integrated into a system of religious representation . . . Working the land. . . is participation in an order superior to man, at once natural and divine. It is in this religious context that the aspect of effort, in agricultural labour, takes on a particular significance: the confrontation with the task imposed, the difficult and strained occupation, acquire value and prestige in the measure in which a relationship with the divine is established, a kind of reciprocal tie. Labour can then appear meritorious as the counterpart of exigencies and of divine justice, in the most general sense, *arete* [virtue]. There is in this a theme which comes to equilibrate in the moral reflexion of Greece the affirmation of the superiority of pure thought over action (Vernant 1982 ii. 23–4).

The Judaeo-Christian tradition does not afford even this exception. At least until the Reformation, work appears to have largely negative attributes. Indeed, it lies outside the fundamental concerns of the Judaeo-Christian world-view. True, agriculture starts off promisingly enough: 'The Lord God took the man and put him in the garden of Eden to till it and keep it' (Genesis 2: 15). But after Adam and Eve eat of the forbidden fruit, God condemns the one to labour in the fields and the other to labour in childbirth.[6] As punishment for original sin, work clearly has religious connotations, but these are largely negative.

The specifically Christian innovations hardly help. The Sermon on the Mount directs us to imitate the fauna and flora: '. . . the birds of the air . . . neither sow nor reap nor gather into barns, and yet your heavenly Father feeds them . . . the lilies of the field . . . they neither toil nor spin; yet I tell you, even Solomon in all his glory was not arrayed like one of these' (Matthew 6: 26–9).

St Paul is generally represented as having a more positive attitude towards work. To be sure, Paul said 'If any one will not work, let him not eat' (2 Thessalonians 3: 10). But Paul found no positive value in labour. Rather, work was preferable to idleness, breeding ground for 'busybodies'. No more is said for honest toil than that it avoids the temptations of idleness and sloth.

By the Middle Ages, the intransigence of the Sermon on the Mount had been further mellowed by the exigencies of living in and governing this world. But Christianity remains ambivalent towards work. The ideal remains trust in God to fulfil all of one's needs, but the reality is a social, political, and economic order which requires a diversity of labours for its maintenance and reproduction.

Piers Plowman, the dream allegory written by William Langland, an otherwise obscure fourteenth-century English cleric, illustrates the ambivalence.[7] The first version extant has 'Truth' pardoning the sins not only of Piers, but along with him the sins of 'every labourer on earth who lives by his hands, who earns his own wages and gets them honestly, living in charity and obeying the Law' (Book vii). This version of the text ends with Piers recognizing the 'pardon' as nothing but an excerpt from the Athanasian Creed. In a rage, he destroys the bogus pardon, invoking the Sermon on the Mount to justify his decision to 'give up my sowing, and cease from all this hard labour'.

A later version of *Piers* carries the ambivalence further. Additional text transforms Piers into St Peter, who, as Christ's vicar, presents the division of labour as 'diversities of gifts, but the same Spirit'. For the sake of social harmony 'each craft must love the other' (Book xix).[8] A key difference from the first portion of the text is the injunction that 'you must clothe and feed yourselves', a departure from the birds-of-the-air, lilies-of-the-field view with which the earlier text concludes.

6. Is it to Genesis we owe the double meaning of 'labour'?
7. Why Langland rather than Aquinas or Dante as the representative medieval Christian? A thorough study of the issues raised here would doubtless include all three, but, as a low-ranking cleric, Langland is probably closer to popular belief than others.
8. Tolerance and mutual respect are enjoined in a remarkable passage which prefigures the Rawlsian emphasis on suppressing individual circumstances in arriving at a just social contract: 'Some occupations are cleaner than others' said Grace, 'but you can be sure that the man who works at the pleasantest job could have been put to the foulest. So

Three points are worth making here. First we should take note of a problem with which medieval Christians—from more or less orthodox philosophers and theologians to heretics and rebels—wrestled: the problem of coming to terms with the transformation of Christianity from a religion of oppressed and marginalized minorities in the Roman world to Christianity as the official religion of the oppressors as well as the oppressed. In this respect, the transformation of Piers into St Peter is significant, reflecting the change of Christ as the Humble and Humiliated Redeemer into the Powerful and Glorious Ruler, and his Church from a federation of local bands of the faithful into the most powerful institution of Christendom (!), an institution which could hardly afford to take seriously the birds of the air or the lilies of the field as models for human attitudes towards work.

But even then, and this is the second of the three observations suggested by the later Piers, work is not embedded in the Christian scheme of salvation. It reflects rather the Pauline disposition towards the lesser of evils. Each may be endowed by the Holy Ghost (Grace in the allegory) with a 'gift' to permit him to gain an honest living, but this is to fulfil no cosmic plan, no divine order. No one comes into touch with the Godhead through his gift. Rather, the point is, as for Paul, 'that Idleness, Envy and Pride should never get the better of him' (Book xix).

At the end of Piers's story, however, and this is the final point to be made here, the institutional needs of the Church are again subordinated to the Sermon on the Mount. 'Nature' invokes the power of love:

'Learn to Love, said Nature, and give up everything else.'
'But how shall I clothe and feed myself and make a living?'
'If you love sincerely,' he said, 'you will never lack food and clothing as long as you live' (Book xx).

How do we account for Langland's pervasive ambivalence? It undoubtedly owes something to the ambivalence of his own position as a lowly cleric. Closer to the mass of peasants than to any seat of temporal power (he has harsh words for priests who prefer the high life of London to their country parishes), Langland could pay closer attention to the spiritual message of Christianity than to the administrative exigencies of the Church.

In short, in so far as Piers Plowman speaks for medieval Christians, work is part of the social order, but this social order remains, even after a millennium, a makeshift and transitory order. It is a holding pattern of social existence still awaiting the Antichrist and the Last Judgement. Like marriage, work continues to be represented in the Pauline manner, as a lesser of evils. Do-Well, Langland's Everyman, may require work to avoid

you must all remember that your talents are gifts from me. Let no profession despise another, but love one another as brothers' (Book xix).

idleness, but the seeker after salvation who breaks out of the holding pattern can trust to God for all his needs—like birds and lilies.

Thus, at the end of the Middle Ages, as at the dawn of Christianity, work remains outside the central purpose of human existence. But the Reformation brings a dramatic change in attitudes towards work. Specifically, in the Lutheran dispensation, the 'calling' becomes central to the religious life; work is firmly embedded in the Lutheran conception of divine and human purpose.

It is, however, important to separate the embeddedness of work in Lutheran communities from the more general question of the link between Protestant religion and capitalist economy. Max Weber (1930) and R. H. Tawney (1938), though arguing opposite sides of the case, both affirm a strong link between the Puritan doctrine derived from John Calvin and the rise of English capitalism. From our perspective, even if we accept Weber's position, the effects of Calvinism are ambiguous. For one thing, Calvinism fundamentally alters the notion of calling so as once again to disembed work. Instead of a calling to a particular line of work, Calvinism emphasizes *election* or predestination. One's worldly activity is now important only as a sign of God's favour or disfavour: economic success is a superficial characteristic of (if, to be sure, hardly a sufficient condition for) salvation. As a sign of divine grace, the work one does becomes less important than the rewards one receives for the work. Calvinism embeds money, not work. Richard Baxter's memoirs, written in the waning years of the seventeenth century, make this clear (quoted in Tawney 1938: 241):

If God show you a way in which you can lawfully get more than in another way (without wrong to your soul or to any other), if you refuse this, and choose the less gainful way, you cross one of the ends of your Calling, and you refuse to be God's steward.

Within Germany and the Nordic countries, Lutheran ideas about work may still be a motive force behind a continuing (craft) dedication to quality. But elsewhere, modern Protestantism would appear to owe more to Calvin than to Luther. In the United States, for example, virtually all that survives of the Lutheran idea of a 'calling' is that the non-academic, blue-collar wing of the American secondary school often goes under the name of 'vocational education'.

The Marxian vision of a post-capitalist, even a post-socialist, Utopia no more embeds work than does the Greek or Judaeo-Christian world-view. Marx had no conception of an organic or holistic society, with a unified world-view in which work would be embedded. Louis Dumont (1977) has rightly emphasized the extent to which Marx shared the individualism of his culture: of course he differed fundamentally from the dominant ideology in his insistence that capitalism stifled the individual, but this is not the same as taking issue with individualism in and of itself. His paean to work in the *German Ideology*—

In communist society, where nobody has one exclusive sphere of activity but each can become accomplished in any branch he works, society regulates the general production and thus makes it possible for me to do one thing today and another tomorrow, to hunt in the morning, fish in the afternoon, rear cattle in the evening, criticize after dinner, just as I have a mind, without ever becoming hunter, fisherman, shepherd, or critic (Marx and Engels 1846: 22).

—has to be understood in terms of the possibilities of individualistic rather than holistic meaning.

Indeed, it is questionable whether Marx would consider hunting, fishing, cattle-rearing, and criticism as work at all. Heir to both Greek and Judaeo-Christian attitudes, he would, arguably, assign all this to the realm of leisure. In the realm of work, however society might be organized, the best Marx hoped for (as we have observed in note 4) is 'rationally regulating the interchange with Nature . . . and achieving this with the least expenditure of energy'. To quote the relevant passage at length:

In fact, the realm of freedom actually begins only where labour which is determined by necessity and mundane considerations ceases; thus in the very nature of things it lies beyond the sphere of actual material production. Just as the savage must wrestle with Nature to satisfy his wants, to maintain and reproduce life, so must civilized man, and he must do so in all social formations and under all possible modes of production. With his development this realm of physical necessity expands as a result of his wants; but at the same time, the forces of production which satisfy these wants also increase. Freedom in this field can only consist in socialized man, the associated producers, rationally regulating their interchange with Nature, bringing it under their common control, instead of being ruled by it as by the blind forces of Nature; and achieving this with the least expenditure of energy and under conditions most favourable to, and worthy of, their human nature. But it nonetheless still remains a realm of necessity. Beyond it begins that development of human energy which is an end in itself, the true realm of freedom, which, however, can blossom forth only with this realm of necessity as its basis. The shortening of the working-day is its basic prerequisite (Marx 1894: 799–800).

We have considerably shortened the working day since Marx's time, but we are no closer to a society in which either work or leisure is meaningful. Probably we cannot approach either goal so long as the two are separate and distinct, with work—like chicken-pox—conceived of as something to be got over as quickly as possible.

6 Knowledge Systems: Techne and Episteme

The disembeddedness of work means that a defence against the capitalist project of assuming control of process and product could not be based on the cultural significance of the worker's activity, on its *holistic* meaning.

But what if cloth-making or gun-making or wheel-making had the personal significance for the weaver or the gunsmith or the wheelwright that teaching and research have for the university professor? What if the same possibilities for investing work with *individualistic* meaning were perceived in the first set of occupations as in the second? Is it not plausible that the prerequisites of meaningful work would have been defended more passionately? The premiss of the argument that will be made in this section is that workers' accommodation to the capitalist project of controlling work was facilitated by the shared cultural assumptions of workers and capitalists which devalued the worker's efforts. Specifically, it will be argued, first, that a basis of workers' control of the production process was a system of knowledge that intimately linked conception and execution; and, second, that this system of knowledge was implicitly regarded—by workers and capitalists alike—as inferior to the knowledge system which capitalists used to restructure production so as to separate conception from execution, the better to bring execution under their control.

Scientific management provides a useful and important text for examining this argument, and the cultural values at issue are once again deeply rooted in Western culture. But before we attempt to read the text or explore its roots, we require much more clarity concerning what is meant by the notion of a *system* of knowledge. 'Knowledge system' has by now come to have a fairly wide currency, frequently being associated with French structuralists and post-structuralists of the ilk of Claude Lévi-Strauss and Michel Foucault. But the concept is used too idiosyncratically to have a standard meaning to which one can refer.

Knowledge system here is used to characterize different ways of knowing in terms of four characteristics: epistemology, transmission, innovation, and power. *Epistemology* is the first issue: how do we know what we know? Every system of knowledge has its own theory of knowledge, that is, its own theory of what counts as knowledge. *Transmission* is closely related to epistemology. How do we go about distributing and receiving knowledge? *Innovation* refers to the process of change: how does the content of what we (collectively) know get modified over time? Finally, *power*: what are the political relationships between members of a community who make use, in greater or lesser measure, of the same system of knowledge? And how does a particular knowledge community relate to other knowledge communities?

The point of the term *system* is twofold. Its first purpose is to suggest that epistemology, transmission, innovation, and power are not attributes of knowledge in general but characteristics of particular ways of knowing. There is no single epistemology, but specific epistemologies which belong to distinct ways of knowing. Equally there are distinctive ways of transmitting and modifying knowledge over time. And different ways of knowing imply different power relationships among the people who share knowledge and between 'insiders' and 'outsiders'.

The *links* among these several characteristics are a second systematic aspect of knowledge. How we know and how we learn and teach, how we innovate and how we relate to power—these characteristics of knowledge mutually interact, as well as interacting with the basic constructions that underlie each particular way of knowing.

All this may become clearer if we concretize the discussion in terms of distinct knowledge systems which I shall call *techne* and *episteme*. It should be explained that the Greek terms are intended to evoke rather than to define; *techne* and *episteme* will be defined, not by (approximate) English equivalents of the Greek, but by a series of oppositions.

On the one hand, *episteme* is knowledge based on *logical deduction from self-evident first principles.* The best model is perhaps Euclidean geometry, though Euclid's axioms have turned out with the passage of time to be less self-evident than had once been supposed—we now have a variety of geometries each with its own axiomatic basis. 'Logical deduction' implies proceeding by small steps with nothing left out, nothing left to chance or to the imagination. Besides the mathematical theorem, the computer program comes to mind as a model of epistemic knowledge.

Epistemic knowledge is *analytic.* It decomposes, breaks down, a body of knowledge into its components. It is thus directly and immediately reproducible. It is fully *articulate*, and within *episteme* it may be said that what cannot be articulated does not even count as knowledge.

Episteme lays claims to *universality*, to being applicable at all times and places to all questions. Indeed adherents of *episteme* do not in general see it as one system of knowledge among many, but as knowledge pure and simple.

Epistemic knowledge is purely *cerebral.* Mind is separate from body, and *episteme* pertains to the mind alone. The statement 'I feel there is something wrong with what you are saying', which is to say 'I sense something is wrong, but I cannot articulate what or why', has no place within *episteme.*

Even when pressed into action, *episteme* is *theoretical.* Once the tentative and provisional nature of any axiomatic scheme is recognized, epistemic statements are necessarily hypotheses. Indeed, without entering into the nuances of the debate between Karl Popper (1968) and his critics (Kuhn 1970; Lakatos 1970; Putnam 1974) it can be said that *episteme* is geared one way or another to *verification.* Its very procedure, the insistence on small steps that follow immediately and directly upon one another, precludes discovery and creativity. To discover or to create through *episteme* would be like the proverbial monkey typing Shakespeare: he

Table 3.   Corresponding Attributes of *Episteme* and *Techne*

Episteme	*Techne*
Logical deduction/Self-evident axioms	Intuition/Authority
Analytic	Indecomposable
Articulate	Implicit
Universal	Contextual
Cerebral	Tactile/Emotional
Theoretical	Practical
Verification	Discovery/Creativity
Impersonal	Personal
Egalitarian internally/	Hierarchical internally/
Hierarchical externally	Pluralistic externally

might some day do it, but we would be hard pressed to find the wheat among the chaff.

Finally, *episteme* is *impersonal* knowledge. Like the Christian God (Romans 2: 11), *episteme* is impartial; it is in principle accessible to all on equal terms. It is thus not only theoretical knowledge, it is theoretical knowledge of theoretical equals. By contrast, like the Christian faith, *episteme* not only distinguishes those within from those outside the knowledge community; as Christianity denies the possibility of salvation to unbelievers, *episteme disenfranchises* those outside. From the universalistic claim of *episteme* it is an easy and direct step to the view that those lacking in *episteme* are lacking in knowledge itself. Table 3 opposes these attributes of *episteme* to corresponding attributes of *techne*.

In contrast with the basis of *episteme* in logical deduction from self-evident axioms, the bases of *techne* are as varied as the *authority* of recognized masters to one's own *intuition*. Opposed to the small steps of *episteme* are both received doctrine and the imaginative leaps which all at once enable one to fit the jigsaw puzzle together. It is in either case a knowledge of the whole, difficult to break down into parts. In contrast with the analytic nature of *episteme*, *techne* is *indecomposable*.

Possessors of *techne* often find it impossible to articulate their knowledge. They are generally aware that they possess special knowledge, but their knowledge is *implicit* rather than explicit. It is revealed in production of cloth or creation of a painting or performance of a ritual, not in manuals for weavers, artists, or priests.

Technic knowledge makes no claims to universality. It is specialized in nature and closely allied to time and place. It always exists for a particular purpose at hand; *techne* is *contextual*.

Techne belies the mind/body dualism which is basic to *episteme*. Under *techne* one knows with and through one's hands and eyes and heart as well as with one's head. *Techne* is knowledge which gives due weight to what Martha Nussbaum and Amartya Sen (1989: 316) have called the 'cognitive role of the emotions' as well as to the knowledge of touch. Feeling, in both senses of the term, is central to *techne*; *techne* is at once both *tactile* and *emotional*.

Techne is intensely *practical*, to the point that, as has been suggested, it reveals itself only through practice. This is not to deny the existence of an underlying theory, but the theory is implicit rather than explicit, not necessarily available, perhaps not even usually available, to practitioners.

Technic knowledge is geared to *creation* and *discovery* rather than to verification. Even a mathematical theorem is largely the product of *techne*, although the proof must, by the very requirements of the knowledge system on which mathematics is based, be cast in terms of *episteme*.

Finally, where *episteme* is impersonal, *techne* is not and cannot be. It normally exists in networks of relationships and cannot be transmitted or even maintained apart from these relationships. The normal avenues of transmission—parent–child, master–apprentice, *guru–shisha*—are intensely *personal* (cf. Chapter 3).

These are not normally relationships among equals. There is a hierarchy blending age, power, and knowledge. But it should be observed that the hierarchy is typically linear rather than pyramidal, as wide at the top as at the base. Thus those at the bottom have a reasonable expectation (though no guarantee) of moving up to the top with the passage of time. It is the hierarchy of the guild, where every apprentice can expect to be a master, not that of the factory, where few workers can become foremen, let alone executives.[9]

If *techne* is internally hierarchical, it is more open externally. Laying no claim to universality, recognizing limits of time, place, and purpose, *techne* does not inherently subordinate those outside a particular community of knowledge to those inside the community. *Techne* may not be inherently egalitarian in terms of its external relations, but it is at least *pluralistic*.

In terms of the four characteristics that have been proposed to distinguish knowledge systems, the differences between *episteme* and *techne* are striking. *Episteme* recognizes as knowledge only that which is derived by the rules of logic from axioms acceptable as self-evident first principles. *Techne* by contrast recognizes a variety of avenues to knowledge, from authority to immediate experience: the test of knowledge is practical efficacy.

The transmission mechanisms are as different as the epistemologies.

---

9. It can also be a hierarchy of sex, in which case the linearity notion obviously does not apply. But traditional societies typically allocate separate *technai* to men and women, so that in so far as power relationships between sexes are related to knowledge they reflect rules of power *between* rather than *within* knowledge systems. Carol Gilligan's well-known work, *In A Different Voice* (1982), can be interpreted as a defence of (feminine) *techne* against (masculine) *episteme*.

Epistemic knowledge in principle is accessible through pure ratiocination, but in practice, *episteme* is generally acquired through formal schooling. Indeed knowledge in the West has more and more come to be equated with what is taught in the schools, and the schools in general are dedicated to *episteme*,[10] so much so that a young friend suggested opposing book knowledge and street knowledge in place of the opposition between *episteme* and *techne*. The canonical way of transmitting *techne* is, as has been indicated, through a personal nexus epitomized by the master–apprentice relationship. The master's example more than any precept instructs the apprentice, who absorbs almost unconsciously what he is taught. Almost anybody can acquire the rudiments of a craft in this way, but quality is a matter of intuition, of a heightened sense of touch and feel developed through years of practice.

Epistemic innovation leads a double life. The formal model allows one only to replace an erroneous logical derivation with a correct one or to change the assumptions. One can supplement existing axioms, or, more rarely, replace existing axioms by new ones, as Newton did for his predecessors and Einstein did for Newton. With new axioms one can proceed to new theorems by old methods: the new theorems are simply logical entailments of the new assumptions. In practice, as has been noted, a considerable admixture of *techne* is involved even in epistemic innovation: the innovator has to know where he is going and the map is provided by his intuition rather than his logic. Technic innovation is largely a matter of trial and error. This is not to say it is haphazard, but the underlying structure of technic innovation, like the *techne* it modifies, is often hidden from the innovator himself.

If knowledge is a text, the canonical form of epistemic innovation is *criticism*. Innovation takes the form of a direct assault, a challenge to logic or to first principles themselves. The canonical form of technic innovation, by contrast, is *commentary*, emendation and explanation of the text. The authority of the fathers is not challenged but reinterpreted. For this reason, epistemic innovation can flourish only in a community of equals, where respect for personal authority is relatively attenuated. The attacks of Peter Abelard on the doctrinal authority of popes and saints presupposed that in the West even religious knowledge had, by the year AD 1100, come to be regarded as epistemic in nature.

Episteme and *techne* reverse internal and external power relations. As has been noted, *episteme* assumes a community of equals, whose superior

10. There are exceptions; the law and business faculties of my own university have since their inception given pride of place to the 'case method' of instruction, which attempts to condense the *techne* of the law office and the executive suite into a form accessible to students, and to allow learning to take place in a simulated environment in which mistakes are not too costly. But even these exceptions are coming increasingly under fire from the epistemic academic establishment.

knowledge makes them collectively and individually superior to those
outside. *Techne*, by contrast, presupposes a hierarchy of knowledge and
a corresponding hierarchy of power within the knowledge community.
But the community as a whole can relate in different ways to other
communities. According to context, it can be more knowledgeable, and
hence wield greater power, or less knowledgeable and correspondingly
weaker.

It will be recognized that *episteme* and *techne* are ideal types. *Episteme*
comes close to what many mean by science, and 'science' is indeed one
of the words used to translate the Greek. ('Knowledge' is another
translation, which suggests that the claims of *episteme* to universality are
long-standing.) *Techne* is more difficult to pin down. As the root indicates,
it contains elements of 'technique'; 'art', one translation of *techne*, conveys
some of its flavour. But contemporary scholarship glosses both *episteme*
and *techne* as 'science', a translation perhaps more congenial to my
purposes in its emphasis on the common field of these terms (see
Nussbaum 1986: 444). In any case an opposition between 'science' and
'art' would unduly and prematurely constrain the meaning of these terms,
and the very openness of the Greek terms (to those of us who would
claim to be largely innocent of classical Greek) has much to commend it
at this stage of our proceedings.

Oliver Sacks has written of a condition called Tourette's syndrome, a
nervous disorder 'characterized by an excess of nervous energy, and a
great production and extravagance of strange motions and notions' (1985:
87). An element of Sacks's story is that Tourette's syndrome simply
dropped out of sight soon after its identification in the late nineteenth
century. 'Dropped out of sight' may appear a peculiar locution, but as
Sacks tells the story it is quite accurate: there is no indication that
Tourette's syndrome occurred with any less frequency, but it went
unnoticed by the medical profession for the better part of a century, until
it was restored to respectability, in part through Sacks's own efforts, in
the 1970s. It is now a flourishing disease—in the sense of having not
only medical legitimacy but also an association of victims and their
sympathizers. The interesting question for our purposes is how an obvious
and dramatic disorder like Tourette's syndrome could go from visibility
to invisibility and back.

In our terminology, Sacks's answer is that as Western medicine became
increasingly epistemic in the twentieth century, there was less and less
place for disorders for which no organic basis had been found. The
medical knowledge system defined medical knowledge, and what didn't
fit simply dropped from view. As far as the medical profession was
concerned, Tourette's syndrome ceased to exist. The rediscovery of
Tourette's syndrome is a tribute to the efforts of Sacks and those affected

by Tourette's to resist the monopoly of medical *episteme*. Although friends and disciples of medical *episteme* might take comfort in the subsequent identification of an organic basis for Tourette's syndrome, Sacks emphasizes that neither the disorder nor its management can be conceptualized in purely epistemic terms.

Sacks remarks in passing that he was alerted to the importance of Tourette's syndrome by an experience that occurred the day after he clinically observed a patient with Tourette's: within the space of a single hour, he noticed three more examples of a disorder that the more charitable of his colleagues had labelled extremely rare and the less charitable had termed mythical.

I have much the same feeling about *techne* and *episteme*. Having once been sensitized, I now see them everywhere. This is of course simply a way of recognizing that the distinction between *episteme* and *techne* has considerable overlap with a variety of dichotomies that others have proposed to distinguish ways of knowing. The best known, perhaps, is Robert Pirsig's distinction between classical and romantic knowledge in *Zen and the Art of Motorcycle Maintenance* (1976). 'A classical understanding', according to Pirsig, 'sees the world primarily as underlying from itself. A romantic understanding sees it primarily in terms of immediate experience' (p. 66). The emphasis is different but 'classical' clearly resonates with epistemic, and 'romantic' with technic. Even closer, perhaps, is Michael Polanyi's (1958) characterization of 'tacit' knowledge as a distinctive way of knowing, in which touch and feel play an essential role—as they do in my characterization of *techne*. In a different context, Ian Hacking (1975) has argued that the persistence until the Renaissance of a conception of knowledge as logical deduction from self-evident first principles was the major obstacle to the development of a theory of probability. Probability, for Hacking, can emerge only when the warp of a stochastic conception of events becomes enmeshed with the weft of less than certain knowledge, knowledge which varies with empirical evidence, a conception completely at odds with the certainty of logical deduction from a sound axiomatic base.[11] Finally, in yet another context, Jerome Bruner (1962) has distinguished between 'right-handed' and 'left-handed' knowledge, the first stressing logic and the second intuition, a distinction easily assimilable to the opposition between *episteme* and *techne*.

Free association (a *techne* in itself) leads from Jerome Bruner back to Oliver Sacks. His best-seller of 1985, *The Man Who Mistook His Wife for a Hat*, has already been mined for Tourette's syndrome. But there is much more to this book. The *Clinical Tales* of its subtitle are the vehicle

---

11. In Hacking's formulation, 'knowledge' (*episteme* in present terminology) is opposed not to *techne*, but to 'opinion', roughly speaking, received doctrine. Of course, the role of received doctrine is sufficiently important in the present conception of *techne* as to suggest at least a family resemblance between the two concepts.

for a plea for a new system of medical knowledge (my terminology, not Sacks's), one that integrates *techne* and *episteme* and is thus worthy of the complexity of human order and disorder, in which mind, body, and soul are inextricably intertwined.

The disorders Sacks recounts can be seen in my terms as imbalances of *techne* and *episteme*. The patient from whom the book takes its name, for instance, suffering from visual agnosia, had totally lost the *techne* required to distinguish a hat from a head. He lacked *judgement*, quintessentially a matter of *techne* rather than *episteme*. Looking at pictures, 'He failed to see the whole, seeing only details, which he spotted like blips on a radar screen' (p. 9). A rose which Sacks offers the patient for examination becomes ' "a convoluted red form with a green linear attachment" ' (p. 12).

With much assistance from his wife, Sacks's patient managed to maintain a semblance of carrying out the daily functions of life by reorganizing them into an epistemic system. As long as he could break down an activity like dressing or eating into a series of detailed operations, he could cope, but, just as he was totally at a loss in seeing a whole picture, he was totally unable to carry through an operation which could not be decomposed into details. *Episteme* is clearly insufficient to organize experience.[12]

Now to the Bruner connection. Imbalances of *techne* and *episteme* can frequently be related to right- and left-hemisphere lesions, and one is therefore tempted to reduce *techne* and *episteme* to an organic phenomenon, locating *techne* in the right side of the brain and *episteme* in the left. In fact, when I met Dr Sacks in the autumn of 1986, I put this possibility to him, but he was quite hostile to the idea. It would be a great mistake, he warned, to attempt to assign normal mental functions to one hemisphere or the other on the basis of pathologies. The mind, one may infer, is indecomposable, like *techne* itself.

It has been remarked that *techne* and *episteme* are ideal types. It is not surprising therefore that in pure form, by itself, *techne* or *episteme* will function with comic, bizarre, or grotesque results, as in Sacks's clinical histories. But the practical requirement that *episteme* and *techne* co-operate

12. Adam Smith attached great importance to the division of labour as a stimulus to invention. 'Men', he observed in the *Wealth of Nations*, 'are much more likely to discover easier and readier methods of attaining any object, when the whole attention of their minds is directed towards that singular object, than when it is dissipated among a great variety of things' (1937: 9). An extraordinary claim, when we consider that invention requires an appreciation of the connections between various parts of the process, such as is achieved by integrating rather than dividing labour. Smith's claim makes more sense when it is recognized that he had in mind as potential inventors 'philosophers or men of speculation, whose trade it is not to do any thing but to observe every thing; and who, upon that account, are often capable of combining together the powers of the most distant and dissimilar objects' (p. 10). For Smith's 'philosophers', knowledge of production is in our terms necessarily epistemic. They stand outside the production process and comprehend it only if it is broken down into its components.

does not prevent a universalizing *episteme* from pushing its claim to a monopoly of knowledge.

Having illustrated this tendency by the ups and downs of Tourette's syndrome, let me turn to an example closer to home, one drawn from economics. Milton Friedman is well known outside the economics profession for his extreme opposition to government intervention in the economy; Victorian England looks positively *dirigiste* in comparison with Friedman's ideal. Friedman is equally well known inside the profession for his contributions to economic theory, most of which are regarded as quite within the mainstream, if somewhat towards one end of the spectrum. Among the less controversial contributions is an article on methodology which has become a classic in the field, 'The Methodology of Positive Economics' (1953). One strand of Friedman's argument is particularly important for our present purposes.

The point of the article is that we should judge a theory by its conclusions, by how well it squares with observation, not by its premisses—a position on its face perhaps not uncongenial to those who operate primarily in terms of *techne*. But Friedman's purpose is not to defend *techne*; rather it is to defend an *episteme* shorn even of the minimal grounding in experience implied by the requirement that its premisses be self-evident.

One of Friedman's arguments is particularly salient for our purposes. His text is the postulate that individual behaviour is governed by utility maximization, economists' jargon for Jeremy Bentham's pleasure/pain calculus. It really doesn't matter whether or not individuals actually perform such calculations, Friedman assures us. What matters is whether they act *as if* they maximize utility. Friedman offers a striking analogy to illustrate and defend the 'as if' argument. He invites us to consider a superb billiard player lining up a delicate shot. This billiard player does not write down, much less attempt to explicitly solve, the complicated differential equations of the interactions of the billiard balls. It is enough, according to Friedman, that the successful billiard player acts *as if* she were an expert in differential equations.

Economists have generally found the billiard analogy compelling, and indeed it is compelling—if we are prepared to grant that all knowledge is epistemic. For in that case the billiard player must willy-nilly be a closet mathematician (and a superior one at that, since no closed-form solution exists for the three-body problem which is the epistemic essence of billiards). But this identification of knowledge with *episteme* is precisely the point at issue. Friedman has no warrant—apart from the weight of Western intellectual tradition—to reduce the billiard player's *techne* to the mathematician's *episteme*. In the present perspective, her knowledge is of an entirely different kind, belonging to a different system, and it is no more instructive to suggest that the billiard player lines up her shots 'as if' she were a mathematician than to suggest that the mathematician solves her equations 'as if' she were trying to make a score at the billiard table. *Techne* cannot be reduced to *episteme* any more than *episteme* can be reduced to *techne*.

Let me take another example from economics. In 1921 another great economist of the so-called Chicago School, Frank Knight, proposed to distinguish two kinds of chance, 'risk' and 'uncertainty'. In Knight's language, risk applies to the class of chancy events for which an underlying probability distribution is known. Customary examples are the chances of an American woman aged fifty-three surviving for ten years, or the temperature in Helsinki exceeding 30°C on a July day between now and the year 2000. Uncertainty applies to the class of events which are not only chancy, but for which not even an underlying probability distribution is known. Examples are the extent of the market for videophones by the end of the century, or Israeli acceptance of a Palestinian state before this book is published. In Knight's view, there is an essential difference between the two classes of events: a fifty-three-year-old woman can buy ten-year term insurance, the cost of which will reflect the actuary's mortality tables, but, when all is said and done, the videophone manufacturer must rely on his hunches about the future of communications technologies: he cannot insure an investment in videophone-making machinery against the failure of a market to materialize.

For Knight, the point of the distinction is that whereas risk can be made routine ('epistemized', I should say) through such devices as insurance, uncertainty requires a special class of economic agents. Profit is the reward of those whose superior *techne* (once again my word, not Knight's) guides them to business strategies which are eventually validated by the market. Loss is the penalty for inferior *techne*.

This is not the place to examine or criticize Knight's theory. Indeed, my interest lies elsewhere, with the subsequent history of the economics of chance. In a word, like Tourette's syndrome, and for much the same reason, uncertainty has more or less disappeared from sight. Mainstream economic theory assimilates uncertainty to risk by the device of subjective probabilities. The first step in the argument is to blur the Knightian distinction by observing that, at the risk end of the spectrum, we can never 'really' know a probability distribution; we only have more or less relevant information on particular samples. By the same token, at the uncertainty end, we are never totally without information about the likelihood of alternative outcomes. Moreover, the institutional lines are blurred too: markets exist in a wide range of situations that are closer to uncertainty than to risk, for instance, futures markets in commodities and the *ad hoc* insurance contracts that have long been the speciality of Lloyd's of London.

The blurring of the distinction between risk and uncertainty in practice ignores the obvious in Knight's theory—that these categories are ideal types. (Knight was after all a student of Max Weber.) The existence of mixed cases and fuzzy lines becomes the pretext for abolishing the distinction altogether. If one is disposed in that direction, it is an easy intellectual step from the fuzziness at the edges of the distinction to the idea that *all* probabilities are personal or subjective in nature. And this indeed is the dominant view in mainstream economic theory today. As with utility maximization, it does not matter for the theory whether individuals consciously calculate the subjective probability distributions required by the theory. 'As if' behaviour will do just fine.

What accounts for the success of subjective probability theory? Certainly not its predictive power. Ever since the theory was elaborated, critics have observed that untutored individuals violate the precept of uniform treatment of risk and uncertainty (see, for example, Ellsberg 1961). Indeed many persist in going their own way even in the face of instruction. But neither the criticism nor the supporting evidence has had perceptible influence on the status of the theory.[13]

It is not predictive power but theoretical unity which commends subjective probability to the mainstream. The hidden agenda is to eliminate *techne* and any action based on *techne* from economic theory so as to maintain the epistemic purity of the economic conception of knowledge and behaviour. The *techne* of coping with uncertainty, like all *technai*, is subsumed as an inferior form of *episteme*, rather than being regarded as a distinct, complementary system of knowledge and basis for action.[14]

These examples are meant to illustrate two basic points about *episteme* and *techne*, first, the complementarity of the two systems of knowledge

13. Subjective probability theory does have one great virtue. It emphasizes that reality is constructed rather than objectively given, an idea immanent in neo-Keynesian views of the dynamics of the capitalist economy (see Chapter 1 above, Marglin 1987, Marglin and Bhaduri 1989). But this is hardly the basis for its appeal to mainstream economists, for whom this aspect of Keynes is totally alien.

14. Economists will recognize that subjective probability theory does not necessarily do away with the need for a *techne* of coping with an uncertain future. As the standard theory is customarily stated, *episteme* suffices because subjective probability is teamed up with the somewhat fanciful notion of complete contingent commodity markets. In this theory, subjective probability is limited to expressing the likelihood of alternative 'states of the world', a notion that includes whatever information is relevant to the contracting parties, whether it be a temperature in Helsinki in excess of 30°C, which might be relevant to manufacturers of soft drinks, ice-cream, and sun-tan lotion, or the end of hostilities in the Middle East, which might be relevant to arms manufacturers. In the standard theory, the prices that would obtain in each state are assumed to be known with certainty, as the outcome of trading in contingent commodity markets. Contingent markets are markets in which delivery is contingent on a particular state of the world actually occurring. Conjured out of a warp of future markets (such as the market for no. 2 corn to be delivered in Kansas City next December) and a weft of *ad-hoc* insurance (*à la* Lloyd's of London), contingent commodity markets are not quite

STEPHEN A. MARGLIN 243

in everyday life, and, second, the attempt of *episteme* to crowd out *techne* in fields as diverse as economics and medicine. But all this is by way of introduction to the main theme: the interaction between *techne* and *episteme* in production and in the struggle over control of the production process.

7 Techne and Episteme in Production: The Wheelwright's Shop

Though practical knowledge invariably combines the two systems, workers' knowledge has traditionally been organized much more in terms of *techne* than in terms of *episteme*. The extent to which *techne* predominates is well illustrated by George Sturt's account of wheelwrights and their work in a small town in Victorian England. Sturt's account was first published in 1923 and has been reprinted ten times since, its enduring

far away.

whose influence 'I felt that man's
' (Sturt 1923: 12). Unfortunately,
ter wheelwrights, Sturt had not
ing man, a lack he was to regret
d him in 1884 to abandon the
a teacher, for the wheelwright's
ry he was to be the proprietor.

predilections, his description of

eye and hand were left to their own
y by art but not by reasoning the
loes; and so too a good smith knew
d be made for a five foot wheel and
t it in his bones. It was a perception
no reasoning. Every detail stood by
: or by tradition.

why a cart wheel needed a certain

-economist. The difficulty comes not in
market, but in positing ubiquity. To reduce
s, subjective probability is coupled to the
: is provision for every possible commodity
contingency that is economically relevant.
probability distribution over states of the
:tion on the basis of utility maximization.
ribution over contingent market prices as
is to show the logical possibility of an
in world, the peculiarity of the assumptions
pposite direction, namely the impossibility

convexity . . . none of [the men], any more than myself could have explained why it had to be so (pp. 19–20).

Equally arresting is the power that knowledge gave the worker:

. . . I have known old-fashioned workmen refuse to use likely-looking timber because they held it to be unfit for the job.

And they knew. The skilled workman was the final judge. Under the plane (it is little used now) or under the axe (it is all but obsolete) timber disclosed qualities hardly to be found otherwise. My own eyes know because my own hands have felt, but I cannot teach an outsider, the difference between ash that is 'tough as whipcord,' and ash that is 'frow as a carrot,' or 'doaty,' or 'biscuity.' In oak, in beech, these differences are equally plain, yet only to those who have been initiated by practical work (p. 24).

All the elements of *techne* are present. The emphasis on touch and feel, trial and error, and tradition: 'My own eyes know because my own hands have felt . . .'. The knowledge that cannot be articulated: 'but I cannot teach an outsider . . .'.

Tradition and rule of thumb come before understanding. Sturt indeed spends an entire chapter (ch. 18) explaining 'dish', the convexity necessary for a proper wheel to which the extensive quotation above alludes. Sturt emphasizes that wheelwrights—that he himself—was putting dish into wheels long before he understood why. For the men, that their fathers had built wheels this way was reason enough. Only 'intellectuals' like himself felt it necessary to epistemize the lore of wheel and wagon construction. As Sturt wrote in another context, 'No rule of or scale of foreway was known in my shop, but wheelwrights of great experience could get the right effect by exercising their judgment on it' (p. 137).

Sturt's summary deserves to be quoted at length:

The nature of this knowledge should be noted. It was set out in no book. It was not scientific. I never met a man who professed other than an empirical acquaintance with the waggon builder's lore . . .

In a farm yard, in tap room, at market, the details were discussed over and over again; they were gathered together for remembrance in village workshop . . . the whole body of knowledge was a mystery, a piece of folk knowledge, residing in the folk collectively, but never wholly in any individual (pp. 73–4).

Sturt must have been aware of the irony. Having lived far enough into the twentieth century to see a world which had no further use for the wheelwright's *techne*, Sturt sought to preserve this *techne* by recasting it as *episteme*: one almost feels capable of crafting an entire wagon after reading *The Wheelwright's Shop*, but undoubtedly this is the spell of Sturt's *techne*—as author rather than wheelwright.

The automobile must bear final responsibility for the demise of the wheelwright's craft, but even before the automobile, innovations in the technology of wheel manufacture had combined with the extension of the market wrought by the railway to change the business environment in which Sturt and others like him operated. Moreover, the production relations of Sturt's shop had a dynamic of their own, which nicely illustrates the power relations that inhere in *techne*.

Long before the advent of the automobile, Sturt began a saga of innovation, one that started from disillusionment. Within a few years of taking over from his father, Sturt abandoned Ruskin:

I realized how impossible it would be to carry out any of the Ruskinian notions, any of the fantastic dreams of profit sharing, with which I started. The men in the shop, eaten up with petty jealousies, would not have made any ideals work at all (p. 200).

Sturt did not spare himself. He, as well as the men, was to blame: 'under my ignorant management, the men had grown not so much lazy as leisurely' (p. 200).

Sturt evidently felt himself caught between the proverbial rock and the equally proverbial hard place:

To discharge the men was not to be thought of. How could I ever find fault with those who had taught me what little I knew of the trade and who could but be only too well aware of how little that was? Moreover they were my friends. Business was troublesome even on the best of terms, but I could not have found the heart to go on with it at all at the cost of the friction which must have come if I had begun trying to 'speed up' my friends and instructors. Meanwhile, none the less, the trade these friends of mine depended on for a living was slipping away, partly by their own fault (p. 200).

'What', Sturt asks rhetorically, 'was to be done?' His solution was less original than the anguish it caused him:

Eventually—probably in 1889—I set up machinery: a gas engine, with saws, lathe, drill, and grindstone. And this device, if it saved the situation, was (as was long afterwards plain) the beginning of the end of the old style of business . . .
. . . there in my old-fashioned shop the new machinery had almost forced its way in—the thin end of the wedge of scientific engineering . . . 'The men', though still my friends, as I fancied, became machine 'hands'. Unintentionally, I had made them servants waiting on gas combustion . . . they were under the power of molecular forces. But to this day the few survivors of them do not know it. They think 'Unrest' most wicked (pp. 200–1).

Some will read the conclusion to Sturt's tale as simple sentimentality. One cannot have gas-driven machinery without the new production relations it entails. But a close reading suggests a different interpretation.

Consider the nature of authority in a shop like Sturt's. Formally the boss's power rests in ownership. But substantively ownership is an insufficient basis. To command effectively requires legitimacy, and to achieve legitimacy requires that the boss be a superior wheelwright. A legitimate ruler commands by example as well as by fiat. He sets the pace because he knows by experience what constitutes a fair day's work and he can, if need be, do that much and more.

George Sturt's father commanded by example. So did his grandfather. As superiors in *techne*, both held the respect as well as the affection of the men. But lacking the apprenticeship necessary for the development of superior skill, Sturt could only, as he says, lay claim to their friendship—not to their respect. Unable to exercise power in the traditional 'mechanical' mode based on a superior command of *techne*, Sturt, in this reading, turns to a new 'organic' mode; a new technology makes the men dependent on him in a new way in which their traditional knowledge plays a much diminished role. With gas-driven machinery comes a new system of knowledge, 'scientific engineering', in which Sturt is on a more than even footing.

It is not machinery which gave rise to a new system of production relations, but the need for a new system of production relations which led to the introduction of particular kinds of machinery. Had Sturt been able to command in the way of his forefathers, gas-driven machinery need not have transformed production relations any more than the steam-powered looms transformed the production relations of Coventry ribbon weavers (Prest 1960, summarized above in Section 3).

8   *Scientific Management*

Sturt's problem was fundamentally the same as Frederick Taylor's. In the words of the father of scientific management, 'The shop was really run by the workmen, and not by the bosses. The workmen together had carefully planned just how fast each job should be done, and they had set a pace for each machine throughout the shop' (Taylor 1967: 48–9).

Appointed a gang boss in the Midvale Steel Company, Taylor set about challenging worker control. Lacking Sturt's fastidiousness—his father and grandfather had not run the shop before him—Taylor was initially determined not to let any bonds of affection (which in Taylor's case were unlikely in any case to have been reciprocal—see Kakar 1970) stand in his way.

The story of scientific management begins with his essentially pyrrhic victory in those early Midvale efforts. Despite considerable success, he regarded these efforts as a failure—for the same reason that made George Sturt hesitate to intervene at all. As Taylor later told the story (Taylor 1967: 52–3), it was anguish at the 'bitter relations' caused by these first attempts to take control of production which spurred him on to more fundamental efforts at reorganizing work. It is these later efforts that he labelled 'scientific management' and which others have called simply 'Taylorism'.

Evidently there was not only a residue of bitter relations, but continuing resistance to Taylor's efforts to speed up work. The immediate problem was 'the ignorance of the management as to what really constitutes a proper day's work for a workman' (p. 53).[15] But underlying the problem of a fair day's work was a more basic problem of knowledge. The narrative continues: 'He [Taylor] fully realized that, although he was foreman of the shop, the combined knowledge and skill of the workmen who were under him was certainly ten times as great as his own' (p. 53).

In our terminology, the underlying problem, as perceived by Taylor, was a knowledge system based on *techne*. Within it, he could never hope for a decisive victory; as long as his project took the form of a simple appropriation of the worker's *techne*, success would be at best partial. His vision of total dominance required a thoroughgoing reorganization of the knowledge of production, as the basis for a thoroughgoing reorganization of production itself. Only a recapitulation of workers' knowledge in the form of an *episteme* to which management alone had access would provide a firm basis for managerial control. Only such a recapitulation would allow management to escape the constraints of subordinating production to the worker's *techne*, within which the best the manager can do is

frankly to place before the workmen the problem of doing the work in the best and most economical way . . . inducing each workman to use his best endeavour, his hardest work, all his traditional knowledge, his skill, his ingenuity, and his good will—in a word, his 'initiative', so as to yield the largest possible return to his employers (p. 32).

Taylor knew *techne* all right—he has articulated it in this passage as nearly as one can—and he knew it for the obstacle it was to managerial control. To remove this obstacle, not only must managers get hold of the knowledge of workers, they must change its form. Thus scientific management is not simply appropriation, it is also transformation. Reread the passage from *The Principles of Scientific Management* which was used in Section 4 to describe the basic idea of Taylorism:

Under scientific management, the managers assume . . . the burden of gathering

---

15. Taylor had amplified this observation in testifying before a governmental commission, 'When I got to be a foreman of the shop and had finally won out and we had an agreement among the men that there would be so much work done—not a full day's work, but a pretty good day's work—we all came to an understanding, and had no further fighting. Then I tried to analyze it, and said: The main trouble with this thing is that you have been quarrelling because there have been no proper standards for a day's work. You do not know what a proper day's work is. Those fellows know the times more than you do, but personally, we do not know anything about what a day's work is. We make a bluff at it and the other side makes a guess at it and then we fight. The great thing is that we do not know what is a proper day's work.' (Testimony before the Industrial Relations Commission, cited in Copley 1923.)

together all of the traditional knowledge which in the past has been possessed by the workmen and then of classifying, tabulating, and reducing this knowledge to rules, laws, and formulae (p. 36). These replace the judgment of the individual workman (p. 37). Thus all of the planning which under the old system was done by the workman, as a result of his personal experience, must of necessity under the new system be done by management in accordance with the laws of the science (p. 38).

Taylor was sanguine about the consequences of separating execution from control. As was indicated in note 4, he was never the lackey of capital which critics on the left have consistently portrayed him: his suspicions and resentments of capitalists ran as deep as his reservations about workers (Kakar 1970). Rather, he saw scientific management as a third way, a way of making 'the interests of the workmen and the management . . . the same, instead of antagonistic' (pp. 52–3). According to Taylor, and there is every reason to believe he was being sincere,

Scientific management . . . has for its very foundation the firm conviction that the true interests of employés and employers are one and the same; that prosperity for the employer cannot exist through a long term of years unless it is accompanied by prosperity for the employé, and *vice versa*; and that it is possible to give the worker what he wants—high wages—and the employer what he wants—a low labour cost—for his manufactures (p. 10).

Taylor paid less attention to the non-material interests of the worker and dealt with these interests in a contradictory fashion. He first suggested that scientific management would actually increase workers' on-the-job satisfaction; but he immediately fell back on the argument that the omelette of progress required a few broken eggs. On the one hand (pp. 120–1),

All of us are grown-up children and it is equally true that the average workman will work with the greatest satisfaction, both to himself and to his employer, when he is given each day a definite task which he is to perform in a given time, and which constitutes a proper day's work for a good workman. This furnishes the workman with a clear-cut standard, by which he can throughout the day measure his own progress, and the accomplishment of which affords him the greatest satisfaction.

On the other hand (p. 125),

Now when through all of this teaching and this minute instruction the work is apparently made so smooth and easy for the workman, the first impression is that this all makes him a mere automaton, a wooden man. As the workmen frequently say when they first come under the system, 'Why, I am not allowed to think or move without someone interfering or doing it for me!' The same criticism and objection, however, can be raised against all other modern subdivision of labour.

Taylor's guinea-pigs were less enthusiastic about separating conception and execution. Charles Shartle, a subordinate, later reminisced

... he [Taylor] would always say that he had others to think, and we are supposed to do the work. I remember he said to me, many times, I have you for your strength and mechanical ability, and we have other men paid for thinking, and I think he used to try to carry this out pretty well. But I would never admit to him that I was not allowed to think. We used to have some pretty hot arguments just over this point. (Charles Shartle, *Recollections*, Taylor Collection, Stevens Institute of Technology, Hoboken, New Jersey. Quoted in Kakar 1970: 98–9.)

In the end, Taylor never achieved more than the partial success he enjoyed when working within the framework of *techne*. Running a factory on *episteme* alone was a fantasy. Like one of Oliver Sacks's more extremely afflicted patients, a factory run on pure *episteme* might be grotesque or comical, but it could never function with any semblance of normality.[16]

9   Numerical Control

But such is the power of ideas that the project of epistemizing production has never been abandoned. David Noble's book, *Forces of Production* (1984), is a superbly instructive chronicle of scientific management reincarnated in the automation of machine-tool manufacture. Noble's story describes how a particular strategy of automation, numerical control (or N/C) came to dominate in the United States. The other side of Noble's tale is why the alternative, record playback (or R/P) was put aside.

Recast in our terminology, the choice was between a technology based on *episteme* and one based on *techne*. Whereas N/C, the epistemic technology, attempted to bypass the skilled machinist altogether, R/P built directly on the skilled machinist's *techne*. N/C envisioned a direct transition from the blueprint of a part into a series of instructions expressed in mathematical form with the help of a computer, which, once encoded on a magnetic tape or punched paper, were supposed to activate the machine tool to perform an appropriate series of operations. By contrast, R/P prepared the tape by recording the motions of a skilled machinist. Noble describes the difference between the two technologies thus:

Whereas with the motional approach, the skills and tacit knowledge of the machinist were automatically recorded as he interpreted the blueprint and put the machine through its paces manually, without ever having to be formally or explicitly articulated, with N/C, all interpretation was performed by a 'part programmer,' at his office desk, who was required to spell out precisely in

16. Whyte 1961, ch. 10, and Burawoy 1979 provide excellent accounts of scientific management in operation in the same plant at an interval of 30 years. (The account in Whyte was contributed by Donald Roy. See Roy 1952a, 1952b for a more detailed discussion of the dynamics of boss–worker relations in the plant during the 1940s.)

mathematical and algorithmic terms what had heretofore been largely sight, sound, and feel (p. 84).

The merits of N/C in terms of efficiency were in Noble's view dubious, to say the least, though their economic defects were hidden for a long time by the generosity of the United States Air Force in supporting the research and development of N/C technologies. Rather, the appeal of N/C was the fantasy of a production process so thoroughly epistemized that workers, at least skilled workers, would no longer be necessary. His imagination stirred by a demonstration at the Massachusetts Institute of Technology (a prime contractor in the early development of N/C), one early enthusiast wrote to the MIT project leader in early 1952 that N/C 'signals "our emancipation from human workers"' (Noble 1984: 235).

Shortly thereafter, in 1954, the trade magazine *American Machinist* observed more soberly: 'Numerical control is not a strictly metalworking technique, it is a philosophy of control' (quoted in Noble 1984: 237–8). In 1976, with two decades of hindsight, *Iron Age* reached a similar conclusion: 'The fundamental advantages of numerical control [is that] it brings production control to the Engineering Department' (p. 238).

This was still part fantasy. The reality, in Noble's view, was that N/C was a costly and cumbersome technology which had little built-in flexibility to cope with the variety of conditions under which production actually takes place. 'Different materials, temperatures, irregularities in the workpiece, tool-wear, machine malfunction—all of them would affect reproduction accuracy and their final quality' (Noble 1984: 151). And require, willy-nilly, the intervention of the machinist's *techne*. Indeed, although, in the words of a production supervisor, 'The whole purpose of N/C is to remove the operator from the process' (p. 242), operators had to learn to read the tapes in order to make adjustments for changes in operating conditions. 'N/Cs are supposed to be like magic,' observed one operator, 'but all you can do automatically is produce scrap.'[17]

Of course R/P technologies were not immune to these problems. The difference between R/P and N/C lay in how the control tapes were prepared rather than in how these tapes were operated.[18] For the most part the architects of R/P as well as of N/C technologies had imagined that the system would function with minimal operator intervention, and what little was required could be handled by unskilled workers (Noble

17. And worse. One machine operator reported on the potentially fatal consequences of a programming error: 'He tabbed it wrong one time and we were in a hole; I had a two-inch drill and I was seven inches in the hole. The machine took off and it threw that drill fifty feet down the shop. It weighed two pounds and it just missed me; it went over the helper's head and took his hat off. So after that I said, "I'm going to know this thing, because this might kill me"' (p. 246).

18. But see Noble (1984: 164) for the view that R/P systems inherently gave the operator control over production speeds.

1984: 151). In short, the designers of R/P also saw little need to incorporate provision for the operator to 'override' the program when conditions warranted.

There was however an essential philosophical difference between these two approaches: the N/C system, based on pure *episteme*, presupposed the redundancy of the machinist and his *techne*; the R/P system by contrast built on that *techne*. Practically, under an R/P technology the skilled machinist would still be available on the shop-floor when his *techne* was required. The goal of N/C technology was to eliminate the skilled machinist altogether.

It is unfortunate that Nobel could not include more comparative material in his study; the experience of other countries, to judge from the tantalizing hints Noble drops along the way, has been different in ways of direct relevance to our primary concern. In particular, Japan provides a revealing contrast with the American predilection towards complex N/C systems, and the corresponding rejection of simpler R/P systems (see Noble 1984: 169 n. and 182 n.). In a comparative study of the Japanese and American firm, Masahiko Aoki (1988) remarks specifically on this difference; for Aoki it reflects a Japanese attitude towards workers' knowledge fundamentally different from the attitudes that characterize the West.

This brings us to one of the basic questions of this essay: how does the nature and role of knowledge in the production process figure in the odd mixture of resistance and accommodation with which workers have received technical changes that have undermined their autonomy? Resistance is perhaps the easier part of the story. Workers are able to resist successfully because their *techne* is essential to the production process. Noble's operator spoke volumes when he observed that 'all you can do automatically [*read "epistemically"*] is produce scrap'. The point is that *episteme* can never be a self- sufficient system for organizing thought, much less action.[19] As Pirsig remarked of 'classical' knowledge in *Zen and the Art of Motorcycle Maintenance*, 'the motorcycle, so described, is almost impossible to understand unless you already know how one works. The immediate surface expressions that are essential for primary understanding are gone. Only the underlying form is left' (1976: 71). Practical managers, however disposed they might be to *episteme* and the control it promises, come eventually to learn its limits. One executive had this to say in 1957 to a meeting of the Electronics Industry Association:

19. Even at the level of pure thought. Gödel, at least as he is translated for the non-specialist (see, for example, Kline 1980: 260–4), is supposed to have demonstrated the impossibility of a consistent and complete theory on *any* set of axioms: either there will be inconsistencies (theorems which will be at once 'true' and 'false') or there will be incompleteness (theorems whose truth status cannot be determined). With this unpromising beginning, it is hard to see how one would even be tempted to rely on pure *episteme*.

In my opinion there is too much talk about giant brains, computer-controlled factories, and the abolition of the factory worker . . . N/C will never be able to do away with factory workers . . . experience leads me to believe that the engineer is incapable of doing an efficient job without the know-how of the factory worker (quoted in Noble 1984: 236).

An article in *Fortune* put it this way: 'Factory operations may seem orderly enough until you try to describe them in computer programs, then they begin to look quite irregular' (quoted in Noble 1984: 344).

The limitations of *episteme* are a running theme of Noble's account of the introduction of N/C technologies. On the shop-floor, the focal point was control over machine speeds. On the one hand, machine speed was, as it were, the cutting edge of managerial control. On the other hand, the variations of conditions made it necessary for managers to permit workers to use their judgement in deciding when to override the computer program. But the capacity to override was at the same time the capacity to 'pace' and maintain 'stints'—the very heart of the traditional system that management had been struggling against since well before Taylor's time. As Noble put it, 'Management attempts to control the freedom of the work force invariably run up against the contradiction that the freedom is necessary for quality production' (p. 277).

Accommodation is more difficult to explain. Since time out of mind workers have been concerned with the effects of technical change, beginning with the most obvious question of the effects on employment. But in the end, resistance on the shop-floor is limited to the kind of guerilla struggle that uses overrides to pace production or in the kind of rearguard action that defends job classifications against 'deskilling'.

It is easy to understand why individual workers have not played an active role in influencing the course of innovation. Isolated from the design process by the very organization of work under capitalism and by their own limitations in the *episteme* of production, workers are necessarily on the receiving end.

But the same arguments cannot apply to the trade unions. All the same, trade union intervention in the process of technical change has, in the United States at least, long been marked by reticence, hesitation, and timidity—when it occurs at all.

The trade union imagination is limited to protecting the jobs and incomes of the existing labour force, a strategy successfully pursued for many years by John L. Lewis of the United Mine Workers. Unions no more than individual workers have sought a role in shaping the content of technical change.

Noble's account of the unions' role in the automation of machine-tool production fits this general picture. Even when their assistance was actively sought by the developers of 'Specialmatic', a rarity as a technology more conducive to worker control, the labour unions showed little interest and less enthusiasm. According to Noble, 'labour unions in the metalworking industries never championed the Specialmatic, or any other potentially labour-oriented technological advance for that matter, leaving such decisions to management alone' (1984: 95–6). In short, the trade union attitude was that of Harry Bridges, the militant leader of the International Longshoremen, who 'concluded that the fate of technology was irresistible and that [labour] would have to "adjust" to survive' (quoted in Noble 1984: 259).

This fatalism, of course, has many roots. It has already been observed that the emergence of 'business unionism' in America was itself the outcome of a protracted struggle. But the abdication of trade unions with respect to questions of technology, more precisely the *content* of technology, cannot in my judgement be understood without reference to the cultural values attached to *episteme*. In the West *episteme* is held at the very least to be a superior form of knowledge, if not the *only* form of knowledge. Moreover this value is widely held. It may serve the interests of capital in legitimizing scientific management (or indeed any enterprise that can lay claim to being 'scientific'), but it derives its legitimacy from the circumstance that workers as well as capitalists, craftsmen as well as schoolmen, believe in the superiority of *episteme* over *techne*. This shared belief, in my view, is a key ingredient in the accommodation of workers and their leaders to the project of capitalist domination of production. If you believe that *episteme* subsumes *techne*, it is hard to make a determined defence of your *techne*.

10   The Marginalization of Techne

The glorification of *episteme* in Western culture has a long history. The term, along with *techne*, is of course Greek, but there is much dispute among students of classical Greek civilization over how these terms were used and understood by different Greeks at different times. A formal distinction between the two terms somewhat along present lines is made by Aristotle in the *Nichomachean Ethics* ($1139^b 14$–$40^a 24$), but the salient issue is less the precise nature of the distinction between the two than the subordination of the one to the other.[20] There is first of course class politics: in so far as *techne* referred to the craftsman's knowledge of production, it is to be expected that it would be subordinated along with

---

20. Aristotle, it should be observed, is inconsistent in his usage of *techne* and *episteme* (see Nussbaum 1986: 444), and earlier writers, including Plato, appear to have used the terms almost interchangeably, at least in those areas that are of concern to the present enquiry (Lyons 1969, Nussbaum 1986: 444). In particular, Nussbaum ascribes to *techne* (pp. 94–6) many of the characteristics that I have not only ascribed to *episteme*, but have made pivotal in distinguishing between the two.

the craftsman himself. But if Plato is any guide, the upper-class Greek conception of the craftsman must have been ambivalent: the craftsman figures prominently in the Platonic origin myth, creation itself being the work of a *demiurgos*, a craftsman; and the craftsman's *techne* appears and reappears in the Platonic dialogues as the model of purposive knowledge (Klosko 1986: 28, 41; Vidal-Naquet 1983: 293). The ambivalence may stem from a very real tension between the essential role of the craftsman and his knowledge to the well-being of the *polis* on the one hand and the inferior position of the craftsman on the other (Vidal-Naquet 1983: 289–316).

But more than power politics is at issue: Greek theories of knowledge, Jean-Pierre Vernant has suggested, led to the devaluation of technical knowledge, the artisan's *techne*, because production involved contamination of pure knowledge, which deals with the unchanging and the certain, by the unpredictable. Unlike *episteme*, technical knowledge deals with approximation, 'to which neither exact measure nor precise calculation applies' (Vernant 1982, ii: 51). Thus

Artisanal *techne* is not real knowledge. The artisan's . . . *techne* rests upon fidelity to a tradition which is not of a scientific order but outside of which would hand him over, disarmed, to chance. Experience can teach him nothing because in the situation in which he finds himself placed—between rational knowledge on the one hand and *tuche*, chance, on the other—there is for him neither theory nor facts capable of verifying theory; there is no experience in the proper sense. By the strict rules which his art necessitates, he imitates blindly the rigour and sureness of rational procedure; but he has also to adapt himself, thanks to a sort of flair acquired in the practice of his profession, to the unpredictable and the chancy, which the material on which he acts always has in greater or lesser degree (Vernant 1982, ii: 59).

Citing the poet Agathon, Aristotle summarizes the problem succinctly (*Nichomachean Ethics*, 1140^{a}20): 'Art [*techne*] loves chance, and chance art', and this, if we follow Vernant's interpretation, must lower the status of *techne*.

The association of *techne* with chance recalls Pierre Vidal-Naquet's eloquent evocation of the opposition between order and disorder in the evolution of Greek thought and social institutions. Lacking a theory of probability, the Greeks identified chance with disorder, and knowledge of random variability was not knowledge at all (Hacking 1975). One might suggest that for the Greeks *episteme* was not only the knowledge system of science but the knowledge system as well of social order, and its attractions the attractions of stability. The craftsman and his *techne* represent—to borrow a phrase Vidal-Naquet employs in a different context—'disorder and the individual exploit' (1983: 174).[21]

Worse, *techne*, certainly the artisan's *techne*, was bound up with *empeiria*, experience, and therefore further contaminated by its contact with the concrete and the practical. '*Empeiria*, experience, . . . is neither experimentation nor experimental thought but practical knowledge obtained by groping (*tâtonnements*). To the extent it comes more closely into contact with the physically concrete, theory [i.e. *episteme*] loses its rigour and ceases to be itself. It is not applied to, but degraded in, facts (Vernant 1982: 52). Indeed, Plato appears to use the term *empeiria* to describe characteristics of craft production that I have described in terms of *techne*.[22] But whatever the names, the distinction between types of knowledge is central to Plato's philosophy. The *Republic* is categorical about the inferiority of the craftsman's knowledge. Socrates expresses the Platonic view in terms of the relation between the knowledge of the horseman who uses the bit and bridle and the craftsman who makes them. 'Is it not true,' Socrates asks, 'that not even the craftsmen who make them know [how they should be made] but only the horseman who understands their use?' (601 C). At issue is a difference not between *episteme* and *techne* (see footnote 20) but one between *episteme* and *techne* on the other hand and *ortha doxa* (right opinion) on the other. Socrates continues:

It follows, then, that the user must know most about the performance of the thing he uses and must report on its good or bad points to the maker. The flute-player, for example, will tell the instrument-maker how well his flutes serve the player's purpose, and the other will submit to be instructed about how they should be made. So the man who uses any implement will speak of its merits and defects with knowledge, whereas the maker will take his work and possess no more than a correct belief, which he is obliged to obtain by listening to the man who knows (601 D–E).

The terminology may be different, but there is no question that the knowledge of the craftsman is of a different, and inferior, sort.

21. Vidal-Naquet, along with Marcel Detienne and Vernant 1974 have emphasized *mètis* (after Metis, first wife of Zeus and mother of Athena) as a separate system of knowledge within classical Greek culture. *Mètis* connotes cunning, trickiness, deception—all relevant to the struggle over control of production as well as to the mythic struggles of gods and heroes. A separate study would be required to analyse the relationship between *mètis*, *episteme*, and *techne* in the production process. Suffice it to say that from my perspective it is not an accident that 'crafty' captures an important aspect of *mètis*.

22. In *Gorgias* (465 A) Plato has Socrates say with respect to the art of cooking: 'I say it is not an art, but a habitude [*empeiria*], since it has no account to give of the real nature of the things it applies, and so cannot tell the cause of any of them. I refuse to give the name of art [*techne*] to anything that is irrational.' In *Philebus* (55 D–E) Socrates asks his interlocutor to 'consider whether in the manual arts [*cheirotechnikai*] one part is more allied to knowledge [*episteme*], and the other less, and the one should be regarded as purest, the other as less pure.' He goes on to assert, '[I]f arithmetic and the sciences of measurement and weighing were taken away from all arts [*technai*], what was left of any of them would be, so to speak, pretty worthless.'

For Aristotle too the craftsman left to his own devices could lay claim
only to an inferior grade of knowledge. Indeed Aristotle even takes over
the parable of the flute-maker and the flute-player and with Plato
stigmatizes the craftsman's knowledge as simply 'right opinion' (*Politics*,
1277^{b}27–30). (But it is for 'experts in the science of mensuration to elect
a land surveyor and for experts in navigation to choose a pilot' (*Politics*,
1282^{a}9–10). Foolish consistency is the hobgoblin of little minds.) Aristotle
believed that there could be an *episteme*—albeit an inferior one—of even
the slave's work, an episteme for instance of cooking (ibid. 1255^{b}26–32).
In this respect, Aristotle is the true precursor of Taylor.

It is evidently too much to assert that the conception of knowledge,
and particularly of craft knowledge, held by certain Greek philosophers
determined the Western conception for all time to come. In the first place,
alternative readings of the Greeks are possible, as modern scholarship has
amply demonstrated. For instance, in contrast to the dominant reading
of 'the Greek' (that is, Plato's and Aristotle's) conception of knowledge
as limited to that which is logically derivable from self-evident first
principles, which is my notion of *episteme*, Martha Nussbaum (1986:
290 ff.) has suggested that Aristotle in particular had a much more elastic
view. In Nussbaum's interpretation, Aristotle's conception of practical
wisdom, the knowledge of life, differs from the *episteme* of mathematics
and natural science precisely in its reliance upon the emotions, experience,
and other aspects of what I have assigned to the realm of *techne*. In
Nussbaum's reading, Aristotle assigns practical wisdom to a distinct place
from *episteme*, but it is not an inferior one.

It is significant however that such an interpretation has a relatively
recent pedigree, whereas the dominant reading goes back at least to Thomas
Aquinas. And the dominant reading, while a matter of interpretation, is
not an invention out of whole cloth. The power of *episteme* in the modern
West is hardly conceivable without deep roots in the past.

11   *The Handloom Weavers of Nuapatna*

Much of the foregoing is necessarily speculative. It deals with a side of
history that mainstream historians and social theorists have largely ignored.
Those of a Marxist bent, seeing culture as derivative of economic and
technological conditions, have, for their part, preferred to see the
accommodation of workers to the capitalist project of controlling production in terms of the political and economic power of a dominant class,
rather than in terms of a shared cultural heritage that devalues work along
with the knowledge of the worker.

Even if there were more solid scholarly foundations to build on, it
would be difficult, as long as we stay within the history of work in the

West, to gain any perspective on what might have been or, for that matter, what still might be. It is for this reason that we now shift gears abruptly, to examine the political economy and cultural basis of work in a traditional, non-Western, setting.

I first visited Nuapatna, in the Indian state of Orissa, during the winter of 1985-6, in search of cross-cultural counterpoint to my historical and theoretical studies of work organization in the West. I was attracted by the possibility of observing on the ground the social organization of an industry—handloom weaving—that in Europe had been consigned to the history books a century and a half ago.

I had little idea of what to expect. My information was limited to the bare fact that Nuapatna had for hundreds of years been a centre of a particular kind of handloom weaving, *ikat*.

Ikat is a form of tie and dye in which dye is applied to the yarn prior to the actual weaving process, rather than to the finished cloth.[23] The origins of this art are lost in the mists of time, and centres of *ikat* production have been found from South-East Asia[24] and Japan to West Africa and South America. *Ikat* was once produced in many places in India, but apart from a remnant of a few families who still produce *ikat* fabrics in Gujarat in Western India, only three centres of *ikat* survive in the subcontinent, two of which are in Orissa, the third in neighbouring Andhra Pradesh.

This is not the place to tell the story of Nuapatna *ikat*. I have here the more limited aim of examining the basis of its survival and growth, with particular attention to the issues of embeddedness and knowledge systems that have loomed so large in my analysis of the cultural constraints that operate in the West. Accordingly my description of the political economy of Nuapatna will be kept to a minimum consistent with providing the necessary context.

Nuapatna, located at 86° E, 20° N, had a population of 3,500 according to the census of 1971, the latest from which detailed data are available. Of this number, 650, two-thirds of the paid labour force, are listed in the census as engaged in household industry, and most of these people would be weavers. A round number of 500 would probably not be far off for the population of active weavers, but that would exclude a large number of ancillary workers, women and children, and is better interpreted as the number of looms rather than the number of those involved in weaving. Moreover, these numbers refer to Nuapatna proper. The adjoining villages

23. Dyeing is by the so-called 'resist' method, in which bundles of yarn are divided into several segments according to the design, and segments to which dye is not to be applied are wrapped in cylinders, originally of leaf, now generally of plastic, before immersion into the dye. Colours are applied sequentially with different portions of the yarn sealed off from the dyes in turn.

24. The name *ikat* is Malayan in origin (Mohanty and Krishna 1974). The Oriya word is *bandha*. Both *ikat* and *bandha* come from words that mean to tie or to bind.

also have their share of weavers, and all in all 1,000 looms would be at least the right order of magnitude.

Nuapatna's population, though probably not the number of looms, has increased substantially since 1971, but that gets us ahead of the story. It is the largest village in Tigria *tahsil* (the *tahsil* is the smallest unit in the administrative hierarchy) but it is not the *tahsil* headquarters. That honour belongs to the village of Tigria, seat of the tiny princely state which bore this name in the pre-Independence period. Nuapatna is situated two miles from the Mahanadi, the great river that divides the state of Orissa in two, still not spanned by a bridge for hundreds of miles upstream of Cuttack, the large commercial centre near its mouth in the Bay of Bengal.[25]

The first reference to weaving in Nuapatna dates from the reign of Ranchandradev II, ruler of the kingdom of Puri in the early eighteenth century and suzerain of the Raja of Tigria and many other such minor rulers. A document in the temple archives—Puri is a pilgrimage centre and site of the great temple of Jagannātha—records an order of the Puri king concerning the production of *Gītagovindakhanduā*. By order of the king, the production of *Gītagovindakhanduā* is to be transferred from the village of Kenduli, the birthplace of the author of the *Gīta Govinda*, to *Nuapatna, specifically to 'eight brother weavers . . . who were to be remunerated for their labour . . . by way of Bhoga-praśād* [food offered to the temple deities and then distributed to the people] *and other gifts'* (Mohanty and Krishna 1974: 20).[26]

A mid-eighteenth-century British visitor, one Thomas Motte, also makes reference to weaving in Nuapatna. Motte recounts that the Raja of Tigria invited weavers who were victims of the depredations of a neighbouring raja to settle in Nuapatna (Mohanty and Krishna 1974: 20).

Interestingly, a gazetteer of the princely states of Orissa, written at the turn of the present century by a member of the Indian Civil Service, L. E. B. Cobden-Ramsay, makes no reference whatsoever to Nuapatna or to *ikat*. This absence is all the more striking since under the heading 'occupations, manufactures, and trade' other places, including a nearby village in the adjoining princely state of Baramba, are mentioned as centres of weaving of high-quality cloth and design (Cobden-Ramsay 1982: 81, 322–3).

25. In pre-Independence days the Mahanadi was a principal avenue of transport and trade, but not apparently for the Nuapatna cloth trade. Before the bus and truck arrived on the scene, however, at about the time of Independence, forty years ago, the chief means of transporting textiles to the Cuttack market was to carry a load of cloth atop one's head, a journey that took the better part of two days.
26. A *khanduā* is a shawl used to cover the upper body, and a *Gītagovindakhanduā* is the shawl used to cover the images of the gods in the Puri temple. The special *khanduā* in question gets its name from the 12th-century devotional poem, the *Gīta Govinda*, the song of Govinda (Lord Jagannātha), a verse of which is woven into the fabric by the *ikat* method.

This may well indicate the low state into which Nuapatna weaving had fallen in the latter days of the Raj.[27] The general view among the older weavers of Nuapatna, certainly, is that their craft had fallen on hard times during their youth. To be sure, the tradition of weaving for the Jagannātha temple never died. Moreover, elaborate *ikat* saris survive from the early part of the century, and there was apparently a limited market for *silamajoḍa*, a garment of raw silk traditionally worn by the groom at Hindu weddings. But most of the weavers were reduced to producing for the wage-goods market, in which demand was limited to coarse (20-count[28] and lower) fabrics with little ornamentation.

Local people credit the late Arjun Subuddhi for the revival of Nuapatna *ikat*. Arjun Subuddhi, whose surname is an honorific granted by the Raja of Tigria for his service to the state as a tax-collector and for his proficiency as a musician, certainly lived up to his name (*su* = good and *buddhi* = intellect). Born in 1905 to a weaving caste family who had established themselves as putters-out, Subuddhi was trained in the traditional art of his caste, and according to his son (who provided most of the details of his father's life to my collaborator, Purna Chandra Mishra), he was himself a proficient weaver. But his life's work lay elsewhere. In addition to his duties as tax-collector, he took part in the family putting-out business, and in travelling to Cuttack to sell Nuapatna cloth—today an hour and a half by car on a hard-surfaced road, but before Independence a day and a half away—he acquired a knowledge of the market that he later put to use not only for his own benefit but for the benefit of the entire village.

One anecdote recounted by his son will convey something of Arjun Subuddhi's business talent. Seeing that middlemen and brokers, referred to by Subuddhi's son as 'rich businessmen of Cuttack', were taking an inordinate share of the profit, he contrived to learn the names and addresses of the people in Calcutta and Bombay with whom they dealt. He was thereby able to establish direct connections with Bombay and Calcutta businessmen and began to send cloth directly to these distant merchants by post. He also had sample books made up and distributed.

Through his business travels, Arjun Subuddhi became aware of the

27. An alternative explanation, favoured by Alfred Buehler and his collaborators, is that elaborate *ikat* motifs are a late 19th-century or early 20th-century innovation in Orissa, and that *Gītagovindakhanduā* were in earlier times embroidered rather than woven with tie-dyed yarns (Buehler *et al.* 1980: 70).

28. Count is a measure of the fineness of cotton yarn, defined as the ratio of the number of yards of a single thread required for a pound of yarn to 840. Thus if 8,400 yards of a single thread weighed one pound, the count would be 10. Coarse yarns are those below 40 count. Medium yarns are 40–60 count. Fine counts are 80 and above. Nuapatna yarns rarely go above 80 count, although I have encountered 100 count yarn and 2 × 120 count mercerized yarn. (Mercerizing is a finishing process for adding resilience to the yarn, and 2 × 120 means that 2 strands of 120 count yarn are twisted together for additional strength.)

popularity of Sambalpuri fabrics, Sambalpur being the other (and more renowned) centre of *ikat* in Orissa. Around the time of Independence he sojourned in the Sambalpur area and, a weaver himself, was able to assess the problems of learning the Sambalpuri technique and design.

He took three weavers with him on one of these trips, that they might learn at least the rudiments of the Sambalpuri art. Returning to Nuapatna, Subuddhi set the three (one of whom was still alive during my time in Nuapatna but too feeble to be interviewed) to work on Sambalpuri designs, advancing materials and guaranteeing to purchase the products even if there were mistakes in them that rendered them unfit for market. He would bear the risks.

The three gradually mastered the Sambalpuri art and the process of diffusion began. Once again Arjun Subuddhi provided encouragement, both economic and psychological, but according to many accounts the weavers were reluctant to experiment. Reportedly, the weavers feared that they would not become proficient enough to turn out quality goods and that even if they did, the goods would not find markets.

The difficulty with this explanation of the weavers' reluctance to adopt the new designs and techniques is that it was not their own resources but Arjun Subuddhi's that were on the table. For the weavers, the problem might have been some combination of identification with Arjun Subuddhi, concern for their own reputations and sense of self, and, finally, a fear of the unknown. These are not variables with which economists are comfortable, but having myself attempted a relatively minor marketing innovation in Nuapatna, I am disposed to believe the accounts of an unfocused reluctance.

In any event, the obstacles were overcome and the economy of Nuapatna was transformed. *Ikat* weaving became quite general, to the point that **Nuapatna has come to rival Sambalpur as a centre of this art.**

How much of the credit is due Arjun Subuddhi? A fair answer must allow for two factors which might diminish Arjun Subuddhi's role. The first is a cultural tendency towards cults of personality, the tendency to personify what might in the West be described in terms of an impersonal process of technological innovation and diffusion (cf. Chapter 3). The second is that at about the same time, other actors, chiefly governmental, were getting into the picture, and it is hard to sort out the contributions of all these agents of change. None the less, when all is said and done, I am persuaded of the general accuracy of the account I have rendered and its stress on Arjun Subuddhi's role.

A more difficult problem is to identify with any precision the nature of Arjun Subuddhi's innovation. The problem is not to identify Subuddhi's legacy, but to discover the situation before he transformed it. There is general agreement that Nuapatna weavers had fallen on hard times and that the majority of weavers produced coarse cotton cloth for a mass

market. What is in doubt is the extent to which the minority practised
the craft of *ikat*. It is probable that fine weaving included a great deal of
embroidery, especially on *silamajoḍa*. It still does, particularly on the
borders of saris, but the effect is now achieved mechanically by means of
dobbies on the loom whereas earlier it was a much more time-consuming,
hand process.

But many people, including Arjun Subuddhi's son, assert much more,
to wit, that Arjun Subuddhi *introduced ikat* to Nuapatna. On the face of
it this assertion is implausible. Whatever their origin, *ikat Gīta-govindakhanduā* survive from the late nineteenth century, as do *ikat* saris
(Mohanty and Krishna 1974). If not a total novelty, however, it is likely
that before Subuddhi, *ikat* was limited to a small number of weavers
who worked in silk and produced either for the Puri temple or for the
luxury market; and that apart from the expense of the fabric, the nature
of the production process made it too labour-intensive and therefore too
costly for ordinary consumers (even with weavers receiving the low wages
which prevailed, and still prevail, in the handloom industry).

The technical difficulty was that the tie and dye process was applied to
the weft, and therefore each pic had to be adjusted individually, a
time-consuming and laborious process. The secret of the success of
Sambalpur was that the tie and dye was concentrated on the warp,
particularly on the border of the sari. According to the elaborateness of
the design, some weft tie and dye might still be incorporated into the
design, particularly at one end of the sari, called the *pallav* or *anchal*; the
Sambalpuri method allowed considerable latitude in this matter. The *ikat*
border provided a pleasing effect—and at a sufficiently low cost that the
technique could be employed on cotton cloth destined for the mass market.

Thus the frequently heard claim that Arjun Subuddhi brought *ikat* to
Nuapatna is probably correct up to a point. It is likely that he introduced
warp ikat and made it possible for cotton weavers to utilize tie and dye
yarns in their work. This was an enormous achievement, and it is
no wonder that Arjun Subuddhi is revered throughout the weaving
community.

Arjun Subuddhi died in 1961, but even before his death a second
innovation was introduced that was to have a profound impact on the
political economy of weaving. In 1955, the first co-operative society began
operation, with Arjun Subuddhi as its president. Co-operatives in name
only, the societies (the English word has been taken over into Oriya) are
in fact modern-day putters-out, advancing materials to the weavers and
frequently stipulating the design as well. Even the terminology is more
capitalist than co-operative: the weaver gets *majuri* (labour charge) and
the society gets the profit. Four societies now dominate the scene in
Nuapatna, but they have not completely displaced the private-sector

putters-out. Traditional putters-out, locally called *mahājans*[29] still flourish, and there are even a few small, private handloom factories in operation.[30]

The Nuapatna co-operatives compete with the *mahājans*, but it is a symbiotic rather than a rivalrous competition. Arjun Subuddhi carried on his private business while he was president of the No. 1 Handloom Weavers' Cooperative Society, and the tradition of *mahājans* holding office in the societies continues.

Although the overwhelming majority are independent in the sense that they own their own looms and weave in their own houses, I have never encountered nor even heard of a completely self-sufficient, independent weaver who provides all his own working capital. However, all other conceivable combinations seem to exist. It is not unusual for a father and son living in the same household to be members of different co-operative societies, or for a weaver of a batch of saris for the co-operative society to sell a few of the batch on his own account, refunding the cost of materials to the society. He might also piggy-back a few additional saris, for which he supplies the working capital, on to a batch produced for the co-operative society. One weaver of my acquaintance sold a sari to a local *mahājan* when the co-operative society, strapped for funds, could not pay him the labour charge.

The scales would appear to be loaded against the *mahājan*. The co-operative societies have access to subsidized credit and are the beneficiaries of other subsidies as well. But the *mahājan* has one great advantage. The co-operative societies are generally barred from providing credit to their members except for productive purposes and this takes the form of advances of materials only. The *mahājan* operates under no such restriction, and loans extended for anything from marriages and funeral expenses to house construction are an important aspect of the complex connections between *mahājans* and weavers.

It is not easy to explain the dependence of the weavers on the co-operative societies and the *mahājans*. A purely economic explanation has some power: the putter-out not only supplies credit, but keeps abreast of the market, a function that is particularly important in the market for saris, where, as in other clothing markets, fashion predominates. As early as 1613, Peter Floris, the principal merchant on the *Globe*, which undertook the seventh voyage of the English East India Company, learned the hard way the importance of judging the market correctly.[31] This excerpt from Floris's journal describes a costly error of judgement:

29. According to *Hobson-Jobson* (Yule and Burnell 1903: 536), the word comes from the Sanskrit for great (*mahā*) people (*jan*). Its closest English equivalent is businessmen, but *mahājan* carries a greater connotation of power and importance.

30. The largest and most successful weavers' co-operative society in Orissa, the Sambalpuri Bastralya, itself maintains three handloom factories. But that is another story.

31. This voyage was innovative and portentous, in that its mission was not simply trade between Europe and the Indies. Most of the voyage, lasting from 1611 to 1615, was

Butt a greate oversight hath bene committed in the bespeaking of the foresayd Maleys cloth, to witte, the *pattas*, *dragans*, *salalus* and theyr sortes, for they have all of theym, to witte, the Petapaolishe cl[o]ath, a little narrowe white edge, and the upright [proper] Maleys cl[o]ath muste bee withoute it, as the cl[o]ath of Paleacatte was; wherein those of Maleys are so curious [i.e. particular] that they will not once putte foorth theyr handes to looke uppon theym; and, yf I had not nowe founde it by experience, I had never believed it, that so small a faulte should cause so great an abatement in the pryce . . . (Floris 1934: 71).

However, the role of the putter-out in interpreting the state of fashion does not fall from heaven but from the organization of marketing. There is virtually no local wholesale market for Nuapatna fabrics despite the possibilities that exist. In the first place there is a twice-weekly market to which local traders come to sell their wares. This market is heavily patronized by local people; it is the main source of fresh vegetables and a source as well of staple foods, rice and pulses. There is even a small section of the market devoted to cloth. There are also two or three permanent shops on the main road, as well as the co-operative societies, which deal exclusively in cloth goods.

But all this operates on the retail level. In the absence of a wholesale market regularly visited by outside traders, the individual weaver has no way, even if he were so disposed, of informing himself about the course of fashion and dealing with a thick (as opposed to thin) market, of selling on a regular basis the fruit of his labour rather than his labour power.

Not that the weaver is typically so disposed. There are, or can be, significant personal ties that bind the *mahājan* and the weaver to each other, as I have seen not only in Nuapatna, but in other weaving centres as well. It would be a mistake to reduce this relationship to an economic one.[32]

Even when the personal tie is much diminished, as is the case when the *mahājan* becomes the co-operative society, the putter-out plays a role that goes beyond the narrowly economic. Over several months in early 1987 I attempted to establish a direct connection between several weaving families and Central Cottage Industries, a Government of India

spent *producing* goods in India for trade in South-East Asia. Textiles were the chief product.

32. The most striking example was provided by a brief encounter with a prosperous and prominent family of weavers in Barpali, a centre of *ikat* in Sambalpur district. On a previous trip several years back, Purna Chandra Mishra had taken photographs of the family and particularly the head of the family, a distinguished weaver. As the photographs had been returned with the notation 'addressee unknown', Mishra was taking advantage of our visit to deliver the photographs in person. It turned out that the patriarch had died some months before, and our visit was a great consolation and even an occasion of joy: the family had no photographs of the old man. Amid the rejoicing, the three brothers, themselves proficient and even prize-winning weavers, sent immediately for the *mahājan* so that he could join in the joy of the occasion. The young men's warm feeling for the *mahājan* could not have been fabricated; clearly much more than an economic nexus was at work here.

undertaking that has had considerable success in marketing handicrafts to affluent tourists and Indians alike in the chief cities. Once again, this is not the place for that story. Suffice it to say that for the most part my efforts failed. Nominally the inability of CCI representatives to provide an advance for materials was the sticking point; the weavers frequently complained of their poverty and attributed their reluctance to execute orders from the CCI to their shortage of working capital. But in my view the obstacle was not so much poverty, illiquidity, or the extra risks involved in working without an advance. It was the unfamiliarity of an unconventional mode, the same reluctance that made their fathers hesitate to adopt Arjun Subuddhi's innovations. The advance provided by the *mahājan* or the co-operative society plays an economic role of course; but it is also a symbolic guarantee of continuity and reciprocity.

Whatever its sources and reasons, the dominance of putters-out is significant. Whether it be the East India Company or Arjun Subuddhi or the co-operative societies providing the designs, for the producer the union of conception and execution is ruptured. A senior official of the state government with many years experience of the handloom industry, whom I interviewed in January 1986, was totally pessimistic: 'In Nuapatna [he said] the weavers used to weave for pleasure as well as for bread, but now it is just for bread. The aesthetic touch is lost . . . Now his creative talent is lost, and his work has become like a carbon paper in a typewriter.'

This is very likely an overstatement. In the first place the halcyon days were never so halcyon. Those who produced 20-count plain saris were hardly in a position to exercise their creative talents. More important, a measure of artistic independence and creativity is present even today. The relationship of the putter-out to the weaver is certainly hierarchial, but it is at the same time a personal rather than an impersonal one (see Chapter 3 above). There is considerable room for give and take between the weaver and the putter-out, especially for experienced, accomplished, and senior weavers. There is also room for improvisation. The most skilled among the Nuapatna weavers are clearly artists—and regard themselves as such. Listen to one of them, Narasingha Paramanik, in a conversation with Purna Chandra Mishra in the spring of 1986:

Let my Suresh [*Paramanik's son, then a young man of seventeen and already an accomplished weaver*] learn everything that I know and then at least my soul will be happy to take rest. This is what I want—let him learn everything and then let him do what he feels like doing. [*Suresh had, earlier on in the interview, been reported by his father as being more interested in money than in art.*] I mean to say let this art live, let it not be sold.

The co-operative society says that I should give them these beautiful designs. 'We will decorate the society.' But I do not; they are my creations and I do not like to sell these designs and to earn money in this way. I do not like it.

If you weave a design and that goes to market [*Mishra asks*], other weavers will be able to learn it, isn't that so?

Let them learn; this way I will give more exercise and additional tasks to the weavers. Only the weavers who have a good brain can copy the design, but when I see the designs being copied, as the primary man I will change and modify them. This is a *khela* [*play or game*]—this is what good weavers feel and need. I would like to stay in this art—playing, playing, thus finishing life, coming to the end to die. But before my death I want to see how my son plays.

Besides a measure of artistic independence, the Nuapatna weaver enjoys the considerable flexibility that attaches to cottage industry. He is free to begin and end work as he pleases, to determine the intensity and pace of work, in short, to set his own rhythm. I have seen at first hand varied uses to which this flexibility is put: on one visit to Nuapatna I was frustrated by my inability to interview Narasingha Paramanik because he was attending a week-long reading of a religious text in a local Hindu temple. On another visit, Dharmananda Sahu was away from the village altogether at his son-in-law's house in another part of the state. Another time, Arjuna Patra was unavailable, attending to preparations for the marriage of one of his sons.

The scope for creativity and the scope for flexibility play a role in the vitality of Nuapatna weaving. This is certainly part of the 'compensating differential' that economists invoke, *deus ex machina*, when individuals fail to respond to pecuniary incentives. For it is clear that the attractions of weaving are not financial. Nobody can say with certainty how much the weaver earns per hour or day of work—not even the weaver himself. For one thing the irregularity of his work—the flip side of the flexibility that makes weaving attractive—makes it difficult to measure productivity, and productivity measures are essential to estimate earnings since earnings are by the piece. For another, the preparatory work (*talikāma*) is carried out a bit at a time rather than at a single stretch, frequently by women, who do this work when they have free time between other household chores; or else it is done by children and old folks, whose rhythms make comparison with the labour time of adult males exceedingly difficult. But when all is said and done, I judge the range of earnings for 'full-time' adult males in 1986–7 to have been from Rs 10 to Rs 20 per day of eight hours, with most of the weavers crowded down towards the bottom end of the scale. At Rs 1.00 = $0.08, Rs 10 is not a high daily wage, not even by Nuapatna standards. Even if differences in the cost of living are taken into account—rice, the staple food, at that time cost from Rs 3 to Rs 3.50 ($0.25 to $0.30) per kilogram—this remains a low wage. By comparison, agricultural labourers reportedly earn Rs 10 for a five-hour day and Rs 15 for eight hours, although the relevance of this comparison is diminished by the seasonal nature of agriculture in Nuapatna.

More relevant is the possibility of factory work. On 30 October 1984,

Indira Gandhi inaugurated the J-Spin mill at Nuapatna, her last public act before being assassinated by her own security guards. J-Spin, short for Shri Jagannath Weavers' Co-operative Spinning Mill, is once again a story unto itself, and here I shall skip over most of what does not impinge directly on present concerns. J-Spin, like many public sector enterprises, was created for a number of purposes: rural employment and an assured supply of high-count cotton yarns to the co-operative sector at 'reasonable' prices are the official reasons, but it is hardly coincidental that the mill is situated in the constituency of the Chief Minister of Orissa, J. B. Patnaik.

The main point for present purposes is that J-Spin, carrying 750 people on its rolls in order to assure the presence of 550 in its three-shift operation, paid a minimum of Rs 12.50 per day (as of spring 1987—a rise to Rs 13.25 retroactive to the first of the year was in the works as I was leaving in April), plus fringe benefits (bonus, vacation pay, pension fund, medical insurance) that on my calculations are worth approximately 25 per cent of one's base pay. Many operatives earn substantially more. Piecers, for example, earned Rs 17.50 per day, and reelers (mostly women who are paid piece rates) reportedly averaged Rs 15–16 per day, with some earning as much as Rs 25. None of this work requires more than a few months' on-the-job training.

It is not particularly desirable work—income and security apart. The noise and the dust are oppressive, as was the heat on the day of my first visit in January 1986. (The heat becomes less of a problem, at least relatively, in March and April, when outside temperatures climb to 40°C.) The work is itself boring and the routine stultifying.

Blake's 'satanic mills' spring easily to mind; apart from neon lights, J-Spin hardly seems an improvement over nineteenth-century English spinning mills. And even here, the gain is not without its corresponding cost: artificial lighting obviates any necessity of windows, and one cannot in fact see the open sky from inside the mill. One mill executive, a particularly perceptive as well as open individual, told me, 'people feel it to be like a big prison'.[33]

But there is nevertheless no problem recruiting workers: mill wages and employment security are not easily come by in India, particularly in rural Orissa. Recruitment is through a cumbersome process in which the local employment exchange supplies names to the mill; new engagements are then vetted by a committee of local notables whose function, it was explained to me, is to ensure an equitable distribution of the available jobs within the Nuapatna area, a special concern to the Chief Minister, in whose parliamentary constituency the mill lies.

33. My four-year-old was to have accompanied her mother on a tour of the plant during one of my visits. Jessica, who had with great equanimity dealt with all the novelties of India, began to scream upon entering the mill and could not be soothed within its walls. The tour was aborted.

Local people are more sceptical of the committee's purpose. The going price of a job at the mill, I heard on more than one occasion, is upwards of Rs 1,000. In any case, the intricacies of hiring procedures were more important when the mill first went into operation than now. Precious few openings come up at the mill, and, shortly before my departure from India in the spring of 1987, I was told by a member of the committee of notables that no new workers had been hired in the last year, despite the 'voluntary' departure of 41 leaders of an unsuccessful strike over the position of temporary workers in the summer of 1986.

But one fact stands out. Practically no weavers work at the mill, and the few that do appear to be there for very special reasons, as in the case of one young woman in her twenties I interviewed who still lived at home in a society where for women of her class marriage was the well-nigh universal rule. Had her husband sent her home? Was she unable to bear children and therefore unmarriageable? The questions were too delicate to put.

As has been observed, economists will have no trouble digesting the reluctance of weavers to enter the mill: the standard explanation is that the income differential simply does not compensate for the added onerousness of factory work. I have no desire to pick a quarrel, especially since this explanation undoubtedly does capture some of what is at issue; the independence and flexibility on the one hand and the regimentation and physical discomfort on the other undoubtedly contribute to the weavers' willingness to forego the economic gains available in the factory.

But I think there is much more to the story. The weaver's work is embedded in the very fabric of his being in ways that are scarcely comprehensible to Westerners of this day and age. And his *techne* is on a more secure footing culturally than is the Western craftsman's. These considerations at the very least reinforce the pecuniary and non-pecuniary utility the weaver derives from his work. Arguably, these considerations dominate and make a utility calculus superfluous.

12   The Embeddedness of the Weaver's Craft

Let me take up the issue of embeddedness first. It has been noted that the earliest reference to Nuapatna weaving is from a temple document going back to the early eighteenth century. The connection continues to this day, and the weaving of *Gītagovindakhanduā* is as much a religious as an economic act, one moreover that is ritually loaded.

The weaver of these temple garments must take special care that the work is perfectly executed, and even more care not to pollute cloth destined for Lord Jagannātha or his brother or sister. His diet is restricted to pure foods, to one meal of rice, boiled vegetables, and *ghee* (clarified butter); meat, fish, and vegetable oil are specifically forbidden. He may not chew betel nut or talk while weaving for fear of polluting the cloth with his saliva. The weaver cannot have his hair cut or his face shaven, again for fear of pollution. He must abstain from sexual intercourse. He cannot weave the *Gītagovindakhanduā* if a birth or death occurs in the house—even a birth, although auspicious, involves the household in ritual impurities (Apffel Marglin 1985). Special clothes are worn during the weaving, clothes that are kept clean and therefore free from pollution.

Nobody else touches the cloth or the loom, and even the weaver himself avoids touching the frame of the loom with his feet (the pedal excepted). Small children may be ritually contaminated by bodily excretions as well as contaminating their mothers and other caretakers, so both must be kept away from the loom. Menstruating women are particularly polluted, and to be on the safe side *all* women are kept away from the loom and the *tantaghara* (the room in which the loom sits, generally the room facing the street). Even the shadow of a child or woman should not fall on the loom.[34]

I cannot judge how far these traditional procedures and restrictions are actually followed. One informant, an old man who earlier had been a traditional supplier, suggested that the decline of the Puri temple had affected the weaving of *Gītagovindakhanduā*.[35] According to this man, the weaving of these sacred garments has become a business like any other: 'some big businessmen get [an] order from the temple administrator and come here and place the order with the cooperative society. The society gives this order not to us, [but] to some people of their own and they do not take care.'

On the other hand, my own attempts to place an order for *Gīta-govindakhanduā*, as well as similar attempts of Central Cottage Industries, were repeatedly frustrated. There was great reluctance to take on the responsibility for providing *Gītagovindakhanduā* for any other purposes than the traditional temple ones. The tradition may be at risk, but it is hardly a thing of the past.

Everyday weaving is less ritually loaded, but it is still deeply embedded in the weaver's definition of himself and the meaning of his life. A religious attitude is pervasive. Most weavers stressed the importance of beginning the work day with a purificatory bath. A brief ceremony of

34. Interestingly none of these restrictions apply to the *talikāma* (the preparatory arrangements), only to the actual weaving itself. I am unable to provide a reason for this distinction.

35. Prior to 1955, Puri temple was administered by the Raja of Puri, the only public role remaining to him after the British deprived him of his temporal authority in the 19th century. Since 1955, when the lands that supported the temple were confiscated, the temple has been subsidized and administered by the Government of Orissa (Apffel Marglin 1985).

worship precedes the actual commencement of work. The post (or *khuṇṭa*) on the right side of the loom, which bears the weight of the loom, is worshipped as the seat of the god Visvakarma (who is worshipped in many crafts as the god of the tools of the trade). The *Visvakarmakhuṇṭa* is invariably made of wood of the neem tree, the same wood that is used for the images of Jagannātha and his brother and sister in the Puri temple. By contrast, the rest of the loom can be made of any wood, and the choice is dictated by price and quality. The *Visvakarmakhuṇṭa* is normally decorated with a *bānā* (a narrow strip of cloth) which represents the first offering of a new year or a new project. As new offerings are put in place, old ones are taken by an older member of the household to a pond, river, or tank (artificial pond) and put into the water.

Rules of purity and pollution are in force, but in an attenuated form relative to the weaving of *Gītagovindakhanduā*. For instance, menstruating women are forbidden to enter the *tantaghara* or to touch the loom and its ancillary equipment for a week. And though even untouchables can enter the *tantaghara*, visitors must take care not to touch the loom, especially with their feet.

Weaving is nominally a seven-day per week operation, but we have seen that work is frequently interrupted for other pursuits. It is also punctuated by holidays on which work stops altogether. Of special interest is the festival of *aṇukūla* (good beginning). At the time of the *aṇukūla*, unlike other holidays, it is imperative that some cloth be woven, for this is essential to the ritual of 'good beginning'. The timing of the ritual differs according to caste (there are four weaving castes in Nuapatna), but the ritual itself appears to follow the same general form. The first step is a thorough cleaning of the *tantaghara* and of the loom itself. The *Visvakarmakhuṇṭa* is disengaged, so that the loom is at rest. During the day no work is done, and in the evening there is a ceremony of worship of the loom (*tantapūjā*) conducted by the head of the family (rather than by a Brahmin priest). On the next day, some cloth is woven. The newly woven cloth is immediately sold, traditionally to a *mahājan*, but the *mahājan* has in recent times been displaced by the co-operative society.

In December 1987 Purna Chandra Mishra attended the *pūjā* in the house of a leading weaver of Nuapatna, a collateral descendent of Arjun Subuddhi. His description of the *pūjā* includes offerings of food, water, flowers, and incense to the loom, particularly to the *Visvakarmakhuṇṭa*. The *pūjā* also included a reading from the caste *purāṇa*,[36] which recounts the origin of weaving and weavers and, seemingly unrelated, the difficulties of the original weaver with the original *mahājan*. A part of the ritual symbolically re-enacts these difficulties: a new *bānā* is reduced to ashes

---

36. *Purāṇa* means old, but refers in context to the document that mythically describes caste origins.

over the flame of an oil lamp. A little oil is added to the ashes to make a paste, and the paste is applied to the face of a straw *mahājan*, sitting on a straw horse. The straw *mahājan*, his face blackened by the paste, is a silent witness to the *pūjā*. At the end of the *pūjā*, there is general rejoicing. The flame from the *bānā* burns big and bright, a portent of prosperity for the house of Viswanath and Bansidhar Das. *Praśād*, the food first offered to the gods, is distributed to family and friends.

It is inauspicious to see the blackened face of the bad *mahājan* after the ceremony. Accordingly, the next day, the head of the family will dispose of the figure of the *mahājan* on horseback in the village tank (the artificial pond that serves as a place for people and animals to bathe, and for the washing of clothes).

A weaver whom Mishra had interviewed the previous year interpreted the ritual blackening of the *mahājan*'s face as a representation of the result of a bargain in which the weaver is unsatisfied with the price. 'The weaver . . . becomes angry and . . . sets fire to a piece of cloth, and by its ashes the face of the *mahājan* is disfigured.' This view is consistent with the sequel. The cloth woven the next day as part of the *anukūla* is sold to the *mahājan* or co-operative society for whom the weaver customarily works. The putter-out buys the cloth and adds gifts of food and clothing to the purchase price (a *dhoti*, the *anukūla dhoti*, was specifically mentioned by one weaver, but I do not know how common it is). All accounts stressed the importance of the money being paid over 'quickly', that is, without hesitation or quibble.

The *purāṇa* of one of the weaver castes, the Asini Pataras, tells the following story. The first weaver, Siva Das, is in debt to a *mahājan* and cannot repay the loan. Significantly, he has borrowed money to perform a proper *pūjā* at the festival of *pauṣa māsa sukla pakṣa nabamī*, the ninth day of the waxing moon in the lunar month of Pausa (December/January), on which the *anukūla* falls. The *mahājan* is repeatedly put off by Siva Das when he comes for his money. A year passes, and another *nabamī* festival claims the money Siva Das might have used to pay off the loan. Finally the *mahājan* proposes to foreclose on the bundle of cloth which has been left as security for the loan. Opening the bundle, the *mahājan* exclaims, 'Oh, how beautiful—what is the price?' Siva Das, encouraged by Visvakarma, replies, 'I will not sell it for less than Rs 500. I would sooner throw it into the fire.' The *mahājan* responds, 'Then keep your cloth and pay back my money.' Siva Das repays the loan in kind, saying, 'Take as much of this *cidr bastra* [old and torn cloth] as is required to pay off the loan.' This done, he throws the first bundle into the fire, and does *pūjā* to the family god (*Iṣṭadeva*).

It requires neither deep analysis nor arcane methodology to see how the religious and the economic meet in ritual and myth. Relations with the *mahājans* (old or new) are a constant concern of the weaver. Ragha

Rana, the weaver who had diverted saris from the co-operative society to a *mahājan* because the society was illiquid and could not pay the labour charge, remarked pointedly that the *mahājan* had paid at once. The conflictual part of the ritual is more ambiguous. Ostensibly an assertion of the weaver's power *vis-à-vis* the *mahājan*, it is more likely to be the assertion of an ideal little realized in practice than a statement of fact, present or past.

The myth is curious. The *purāṇa* depicts the weaver as improvident, the *mahājan* as patient and even accommodating. No Shylock he! The virtue of the weaver lies in his devotion to the gods and to his craft. Shame before the *mahājan* does not deter him from devoting his limited funds to the *nabamī* festival, funds which he might have used to repay his debt. The claims of men cannot be put ahead of the claims of the gods. Nor will he bargain about the worth of his art. Sooner let his creation be consumed by the fire than let it be the object of haggling.

The first part of this *purāṇa* reinforces an image of the weaver which in Western terms could at best be regarded as ambivalent, but which for the weavers themselves, whom I questioned extensively on this subject, is clearly positive. This part of the *purāṇa* recounts the invention of cloth. The gods, finding their nakedness ugly (not shameful, as did Adam and Eve but simply ugly) first contrive to steal the original cotton seed from a demon who has it firmly implanted in his forehead. But Kapisura, the demon, has been given the boon that 'he will not be killed in the house or outside, nor in daylight or at night, nor by any weapon. Nor will he burn or drown.' He must be tricked, and tricked he is.[37] Krishna takes the form of lice and infests the demon's hair. Chakradhara (Vishnu with the discus) appears in the form of a *kāminī* (lustful woman) and offers to remove the lice that infest Kapisura's hair. On the pretext that the light is too faint in the house, it being twilight (and thus neither daylight nor night), the *kāminī* coaxes the demon out under the eaves of the house (neither outside nor inside) and Krishna, taking his own form, breaks the demon's head in two with his bare hands (no weapon is involved, and the demon neither burns nor drowns).[38]

After the cotton seed has been liberated from the demon, it is planted. The gods, attracted by the beauty of the cotton plants in bloom, pluck all the flowers. Once again a trick is employed to make them desist so that the flower might develop into fruit. Brahma tells the cultivators to smear a little blood on the flowers: the gods will not pluck flowers so

37. The *mètis* (craftiness) of the gods recalls the original *Mètis*. See n. 20 above, and Detienne and Vernant 1974.
38. The demon's boon is related explicitly, but the circumvention of the boon is not. The story simply recounts that the *kāminī* lures the demon outside under the eaves, on the pretext that there is insufficient light in the house to see the lice. There is no need for more explanation. The boon and its remedy, a standard device in Hindu mythology, would be familiar to the listener.

polluted. This done, the plants bear fruit. When the cotton is harvested and men are set to work spinning yarn, the weaver enters the picture.

Brahma, who has masterminded the operation from seed to yarn, turns over further responsibility to Vishnu. From a lump of earth Vishnu creates an image and gives life to the image; thus are created Siva Das, the first weaver, and Swati Devi, his wife. Siva Das is willing but ignorant. 'What is our work?' he asks. 'What are we to do?' Vishnu tells him and then leads him step by step through the preparatory processes of weaving. Siva Das is particularly troubled by the step at which the yarn is starched, since the customary starch is water in which rice has been cooked. 'How will we avoid the pollution of the rice water?' Siva Das asks Vishnu. 'Wind the starched yarn on the spindle in the sun,' Vishnu counsels the weaver, 'and the pollution will go away.'

Then the gods, in heavenly convocation, ask Vishnu how the cloth will actually be woven. Vishnu names all the parts of the loom, and the gods volunteer to become these parts. 'I will become the *khila* [the peg which holds the loom together],' says Angira. 'And I', says Narada, 'the *dungi* [needle].' Brahma offers himself as the *bharā* [treadle]. And so on down the list.

But, Vishnu observes, as matters stand the loom is useless. Someone must bear the load and support the loom. 'You know best,' responds Brahma. But, says Vishnu, no one will bear the load and support the entire loom unless he is given the first cloth. The other gods reply, so be it. Then Vishnu says, 'I will come as Visvakarma Vasudev and will bear the load. I will give the necessary support.' Hearing this, the other gods bow down to Vishnu, and Vishnu orders Siva Das to begin weaving.

Siva Das inquires as to the exact day he is to make the loom ready and do the *pūjā*. Vishnu tells him that he should do the *pūjā* on the ninth day (*nabamī*) of the bright fortnight (*sukla pakṣa*) of the month of Pausa and on the tenth day he should begin to weave (*tantabuna aṇukūla*).

So it was done; the first fruits of the loom were duly offered to Visvakarma Vasudev, and subsequent products to the other gods. The gods were overjoyed and, wishing to reward the weaver, offered him a boon of his choice. 'Let me be given the boon that I earn enough in one day's weaving to eat throughout the year,' Siva Das said. And this was done too.

When Siva Das returns home, his wife asks him what had happened. He tells Swati Devi about the boon. Far from being pleased, she says, 'What have you done? It is not good. Our children will be undisciplined (*ayogya*). Go back and tell the gods you have made a mistake. Ask for another boon. Say

> Niti araji, niti khāibi
> Jalāguḍi bāṭe, bela cāhinbi
> (I will earn everyday, I will eat everyday
> I will see the passage of time through the window).'

Siva Das does as his wife bids him, and the gods grant him the new boon. 'Both Siva and his wife are glad. The couple spend their time pleasantly.'

This ends the story of the creation. But at the same time it sets the stage for the tale of the weaver and the *mahājan*. The month of Pausa is about to come and Siva Das realizes that he has no money to prepare a proper *pūjā* for *nabamī*. He remembers the bundle of cloth and sets off for the house of the *mahājan*. The second part of the *purāna*, which has already been summarized, unfolds.

What must be remembered in interpreting this story is that the Nuapatna weaver, like most Indians, is much closer to his or her origin myth than Westerners are to theirs. Even 'believing' Christians and Jews, fundamentalists apart, are taught from an early age to take their biblical myths with a grain of salt. I can remember one of my children explaining to me at the age of six or seven that the parting of the Red Sea was 'just a story' and that it was 'really' tidal action rather than the hand of the Lord at work. Traditional Indians make no such distinction. The mythic and the real are not separate domains (cf. Chapter 4). The parts of the loom are not metaphorical gods or representations of gods, they *are* gods. And Visvakarma supports the loom today as he did for Siva Das. The concerns of Siva Das—why am I here? how do I avoid pollution? who takes precedence, the *mahājan* or the *Iṣṭadeva?*—are equally the concerns of today's weaver.

And the answers are to be found in the *purāna*. The weaver works for his daily bread, to be sure, but he was put on this earth to add to the glory of the gods, not simply to make a living. And pollution? Pollution is to be surmounted, but it cannot be avoided entirely. Why, without pollution, the cotton bloom would never mature into fruit and the yarn could not be starched.

In this light, the 'boon' of working every day to eat that day is of particular interest. In one sense it is highly negative, very much like the Pauline injunction 'if anyone will not work, let him not eat': its chief virtue is to avoid the sloth and dissolution to which idleness must lead, the *ayogya* or indiscipline that Swati Devi fears for her children if they need work only one day per year. But in another sense, the contrast with both the Greek and Judaeo-Christian origin myths is striking: the by-product of conflict among the gods in the one case, a just punishment for man's transgressions against the divine in the second. For the Hindu weaver labour is a boon. The contrast with the Sermon on the Mount is also striking: the Hindu weaver is not to expect to be fed like the birds or clothed like the lilies, for God helps him who helps himself. However, the attitude towards time, calculation, and accumulation of worldly goods does recall the Sermon on the Mount: one is not to lay up stores of treasure, but to take each day as it comes with little heed for the morrow.

With this attitude his dependence on the *mahājan* is less cause for wonder. It is as much a psychological as an economic dependence, and it serves no useful purpose to try to reduce the one to the other, whether the reduction be a Marxian one in which psychology is a reflection of economics ('the weaver is psychologically dependent because he is poor') or a neo-conservative one in which economics grows out of psychology ('the weaver is poor because he lacks psychological independence').

The bottom line is that the Nuapatna weavers' relationship to their craft cannot be reduced to the bottom line. Their work is deeply embedded in their life—who they are, why they are here. In the West, only the original Lutheran notion of a 'calling' would seem to approach the religious quality that work has for the weaving castes of Nuapatna. Narasingha Paramanik was no doubt posing a bit when he said to me, 'More money is not good. I am satisfied with Rs 5; I don't want to run for Rs 10. If one gets too much, it is not good. Let Suresh [his son] earn name and fame as a weaver.' But there is more than a grain of truth in this pose. If Suresh's future is in doubt—he talks of opening a shop to sell cloth—it is not for lack of parental guidance, but because the modern world is fast closing in on Nuapatna.

13 Ikat as Techne

Ikat is the embodiment of *techne*. No manuals, no texts, everything passed down from father to son (and increasingly, but that again is another story, to daughters and wives as well).[39] On my second visit to Nuapatna, I enquired of a weaver how his teenaged son learned the craft. Easy, he replied. He simply watched how we adults did it. Much later, I asked a little girl of seven or eight how she had learned to draw raw silk from the cocoon and twist it into thread. She made no reply, but a little boy of five who was sitting at her side, presumably her brother, chimed in with a smile, 'Spinning, spinning, spun' (*kāṭu, kāṭu, kāṭilā*), which pithily sums up the process for learning any *techne*.

It is not to be doubted that *ikat* is a *techne*, closely adhering to the theories of knowledge, communication, innovation, and power outlined in Section 6 of this chapter. What remains at issue is the significance of this fact. Some will find it irrelevant to the survival of *ikat*, and the likelihood of epistemization, mechanization, and technological unemployment. It certainly can be argued that *ikat* remains a *techne* only because it is in nobody's interest to epistemize it. The economic motivation

39. I err. Bijoy Chandra Mohanty and Kalyan Krishna 1974 have described the *ikat* process. But I defy anybody who is not already initiated into the art to make head or tail of their description, and those who are initiated have neither need nor facility for epistemic explanation.

to epistemize would be to lay the basis for mechanization, but with the best weavers commanding a wage of less than $2.00 per day and the majority hardly $1.00, there would seem to be little room for profit in mechanizing the weavers' art. *Ikat*, in this view, survives as a *techne* only because of the poverty of the craftsman.

At the other extreme, the technostructure of officialdom, both public and private, generally views the obstacles to mechanization as insurmountable. The tie and dye process is seen as inherently imperfect, and nothing but the judgement, skill, and dexterity of the weaver can compensate for these imperfections.

The weavers, for their part, live in continual fear of technological displacement. My collaborator and I were for a long time suspected of ulterior motives: that we would use the information we were gathering to take the very rice from their mouths. However benign our intentions, they had good reason for their suspicions. A Japanese delegation had reportedly visited Nuapatna a few years back and cleared out the stocks of the co-operative societies in an unsuccessful attempt to adapt Nuapatna *ikat* design and method to mechanization.

Though this report was never confirmed, it was a fact that cheap imitation tie and dye, so-called *bapta* print saris (which bear the same relation to real tie and dye that the classics comics of my youth bore to the classics themselves) had flooded the market between my first visit in the winter of 1985–6 and my return a year later. The one appeal of these mill-made fabrics from Bombay was price, but this was sufficient—for the time being at least—for Nuapatna products to accumulate on the shelves of the co-operative societies and the *mahājans'* shops.

One might be optimistic for the longer run. A similar thing had happened in Sambalpur a couple of years earlier, and the pendulum of fashion had turned back to the local product when the mill-made saris demonstrated over the course of a few months the inferior durability of both fabric and colour. But for the moment, the invasion was playing havoc. Large numbers of weavers were shifting from cotton to silk; as a luxury-market product, silk was, for the moment anyway, immune to competition from low-quality imitations. And everybody was nervous about the future of the trade.

My own judgement is that although the Nuapatna weavers are reasonably secure for the moment, there is in the long run no technical obstacle to a partial epistemization and mechanization of *ikat*. On the other hand, a completely automatic process seems no more possible than a completely automatic process of machine-tool manufacture.

The real issue, unless the continued poverty of the weavers decides the issue in favour of the status quo, is what the mix of *episteme* and *techne* will be: whether automation will be used to make the weaver increasingly an appendage of the machine and the weaver's *techne* subservient to the *episteme* of the *mahājans* of the twenty-first century (whoever they might be), or whether automation will be used to enhance the power of the weavers by making *episteme* serve their *techne*.

The die is hardly cast. The predilections of India's political, business, and academic leadership are clear. Sharing the largely unconscious presuppositions of their Western counterparts with respect to the superiority of *episteme* over *techne*, they will see little to be gained from the second scenario. Indeed, in these quarters it will probably be dismissed as Utopian idealism, however much lip-service may be paid to that arch-idealist, Mohandas Gandhi.

But the possibilities on the other side should not be underestimated. The resilience of Orissan *ikat* weavers, I have suggested, is not finally reducible to an economic analysis, because the resilience is fortified by the embeddedness of the weavers' work in their life. I would add, somewhat more tentatively, the hypothesis that traditional Indian attitudes toward *episteme* and *techne* leave the weaver more cultural room to defend his *techne*.

Tradition of course grants the Brahmin superiority over other castes and accordingly grants his knowledge a superiority over the *technai* of other castes. But this hierarchy differs in a fundamental way from the hierarchical dominance of *episteme* over *techne* in the West; no attempt is made in India to reduce *techne* to an inferior form of *episteme* or to deny its very existence. On the contrary: just as each caste is accorded its distinct and necessary role in a well-ordered cosmos (see Chapter 4), so must the *techne* of each caste be recognized as distinct and necessary.

Indeed, the *Bhagavad Gītā* can be read as (at the very least) denying superiority to the Indian equivalent of *episteme* over *techne*.[40] Such a reading, to be sure, is hardly necessary or even obvious, for it requires us to interpret passages (such as chs. iii and v) where disciplined action is compared with contemplative reasoning as implicating alternative knowledge systems. The terms *sāṃkhya* and (*karma*) *yoga*, which are used in the *Gītā* to distinguish 'reason-method' from 'discipline' as paths to Truth, certainly do not map directly on to *episteme* and *techne*. But the indirect links, via *jñāna* and *vijñāna*, are at least suggestive. Franklin Edgerton, eminent Sanskritist of the inter-war period and translator/commentator of the *Gītā*, identifies *sāṃkhya* with *jñāna* (1944: 166) and he elsewhere glosses *jñāna* as 'theoretical knowledge' and 'abstract, unapplied knowledge' (1933: 218, 220). Although *karma yoga* is never

---

40. It would take a much better understanding of Indian knowledge systems than I could ever claim even to outline the contours of the field. But a priori it is highly unlikely that Western *episteme* in particular will map isomorphically on to an Indian equivalent: J. F. Staal 1965 argues that Euclidean geometry is not the canonical form of rationality (read *episteme*) in India. In Staal's view, grammar rather than axiomatic mathematics is the canonical Indian *episteme*, and Panini rather than Euclid is the model.

equated with *vijñāna*, the emphasis in *yoga* on the 'practical' as against the 'intellectual' (Edgerton 1944: 165–6) arguably implicates *vijñāna*, which Edgerton glosses as 'practical or applied knowledge' (1933: 218–20). If we are on track in identifying *yoga* with *vijñāna*, it becomes easy to see a distinction like that between *episteme* and *techne* implicit in the distinction between *sāṁkhya* and *yoga*. But any insistence on a hierarchical ordering—on superiority and inferiority—perhaps misses the point. The main emphasis of the *Gītā* is on the unity of *sāṁkhya* and *yoga* (v. 4–5), and on the idea that context—in particular the individual's birth—determines the suitability of one path or the other, an idea which fits very well with the notion of complementarity between *techne* and *episteme*.

This is of course highly speculative. What is not speculative is that if the *ikat* weavers of Nuapatna are to defend their art, the best defence will be found in a critical assessment of their own cultural traditions, not in an uncritical acceptance of the West.

For all their conservative resistance to change, Nuapatna weavers have proved themselves remarkably adaptable. The innovation wrought by Arjun Subuddhi has already been recounted. But alongside these changes there have been numerous others. The substitutions of chemical dyes for vegetable dyes, modification of the length and breadth of the fabrics, technical improvements to the loom itself—individually these are much less dramatic than the new life given to *ikat* by adopting the Sambalpuri style of tie and dye; but together they indicate the possibilities for evolution and adaptation within the traditional system. Only time will tell if these possibilities extend to the computer age.

14   Conclusion

This essay has put forward the argument that in the West workers have largely accommodated themselves to the capitalist project of dominating the workplace because Western culture provides neither compelling reasons nor compelling means for workers to resist this project. In contrast to Hindu culture, workers who are heirs to the Greek and Judaeo-Christian traditions find both that their work stands outside the cosmic order and that the system of knowledge in which their work is organized is held to be an inferior system, if indeed it counts as knowledge at all. Lacking both cultural reason and cultural means to defend himself, the worker has been, to paraphrase Thomas Jefferson, easy prey for the designs of capitalist ambition.

It seems to me this argument has profound implications for the project of building a decent society. Socialists in particular have consistently stressed the importance of work organization in their project, and it is, in my opinion, right to do so. With less consistency, socialists have neglected the role of culture in shaping both the possibilities for, and the constraints on, work organization.

We in the West probably do not have the option of embedding work in our cosmology. We perhaps have more control over our theory of knowledge. We must at least hope so, for, if not, the socialist project is probably doomed. As Robert Pirsig put it (1974: 94),

[T]o tear down a factory or to revolt against a government or to avoid repair of a motorcycle because it is a system is to attack effects rather than causes; and as long as the attack is upon effects only, no change is possible. The true system, the real system, is our present construction of systematic thought itself, rationality itself, and if a factory is torn down but the rationality which produced it is left standing, then that rationality will simply produce another factory. If a revolution destroys a systematic government, but the systematic patterns of thought that produced that government are left intact, then those patterns will repeat themselves in the succeeding government.

The same socialist project which has exalted workplace democracy as the foundation of a decent society denies this foundation by making participation conditional on accepting the dominant knowledge system: workers are free to participate on condition that they accept the knowledge system of the party cadres and the engineers. But that is an option open only to a minority. As there is room for only so many cadres and engineers, most must remain workers, consigned to inferior status by virtue of the inferiority of their knowledge.

The point of my argument is not to glorify but to rediscover and to legitimize *techne*; to argue for a balance and even for a tension between *techne* and *episteme*. I have neither the intention nor the need to denigrate *episteme* in order to attack the hierarchical ordering in which *episteme* is placed above *techne*; my purpose is to argue against an imbalance that puts the very project of erecting a decent society at risk.

Outside the West, conditions are at once more problematic and more promising. To take India as a concrete example, the problems of poverty and internal conflict are intertwined with the problems posed by the encounter, cultural as well as economic, with the West. The economic consequences of that encounter are ambiguous. Whether the British deindustrialized India or laid the basis for its industrialization (or perhaps did some of each) is still debated by scholars and the issue will perhaps never be settled.

But the cultural consequences seem to me to be much more clear-cut. If India is to build a society on the foundations of democratic and participatory work organization, it will do better to follow the impulse of Mohandas Gandhi and his kind to look to India's own tradition than to follow the impulse of the ilk of Rajiv Gandhi to look to the West.

REFERENCES

Aoki, Masahiko (1988) *Information, Incentives and Bargaining in the Japanese Economy*, Cambridge: Cambridge University Press.

Apffel Marglin, Frédérique (1985) [catalogued under Marglin, Frédérique Apffel] *Wives of the God King: The Rituals of the Devadasis of Puri*, New Delhi and Oxford: Oxford University Press.

Aristotle (1934) *Nichomachean Ethics*, trans H. Rackham, Cambridge, Mass.: Harvard University Press.

—— (1944) *Politics*, trans. H. Rackham, Cambridge, Mass.: Harvard University Press.

Braverman, Harry (1974) *Labor and Monopoly Capital: The Degradation of Work in the Twentieth Century*, New York: Monthly Review Press.

Bruner, Jerome (1962) *On Knowing: Essays for the Left Hand*, Cambridge, Mass.: Harvard University Press, 1979.

Buehler, Alfred, Fischer, Eberhard, and Nabholz, Marie-Louise (1980) *Indian Tie-Dyed Fabrics*, Ahmedabad: Calico Museum of Textiles.

Burawoy, Michael (1979) *Manufacturing Consent*, Chicago: the University of Chicago Press.

Buttrick, John (1952) 'The Inside Contract System', *Journal of Economic History*, 12: 205–21.

Cobden-Ramsay, L. E. B. (1982) *Feudatory States of Orissa*, Calcutta: Firma KLM (first published 1910).

Copley, Frank B. (1923) *Frederick W. Taylor, Father of Scientific Management*, vol. i, New York: Harper & Row.

Detienne, Marcel, and Vernant, Jean-Pierre (1974) *Les Ruses de l'Intelligence: la Mètis des Grecs*, Paris: Flammarion.

Dumont, Louis (1977) *From Mandeville to Marx: The Genesis and Triumph of Economic Ideology*, Chicago: Chicago University Press.

Edgerton, Franklin (1933) 'Jñāna and Vijñāna', Otto Stein and Wilhelm Gampert (eds.), *Festschrift Moriz Winternitz*, Leipzig: Harrassowitz.

—— (1944) *The Bhagavad Gita*, Cambridge, Mass.: Harvard University Press.

Edwards, Richard (1979) *Contested Terrain: The Transformation of the Workplace in the Twentieth Century*, New York: Basic Books.

Ellsberg, Daniel (1961) 'Risk, Ambiguity, and the Savage Axioms', *Quarterly Journal of Economics*, 75: 643–69.

Floris, Peter (1934) *Voyage of Floris to the East Indies*, ed. W. H. Moreland, London: The Hakluyt Society.

Freud, Sigmund (1961) *Civilization and its Discontents*, ed. J. Strachey, New York: W. W. Norton (first published 1930).

Friedman, Milton (1953) 'The Methodology of Positive Economics', in *Essays in Positive Economics*, Chicago: University of Chicago Press.

Gilligan, Carol (1982) *In a Different Voice: Psychological Theory and Women's Development*, Cambridge, Mass.: Harvard University Press.

Hacking, Ian (1975) *The Emergence of Probability: A Philosophical Study of Early Ideas About Probability, Induction and Statistical Inference*, Cambridge: Cambridge University Press.

Hesiod (1914) 'Works and Days', in *The Homeric Hymns and Homerica*, trans. Hugh Evelyn-White, Cambridge, Mass.: Harvard University Press.

Hirschman, Albert (1984) 'Against Parsimony', *Economics and Philosophy*, 7: 7–21.

Kakar, Sudhir (1970) *Frederick Taylor: A Study in Personality and Innovation*, Cambridge, Mass.: MIT Press.

Kline, Morris (1980) *Mathematics: The Loss of Certainty*, New York: Oxford University Press.

Klosko, George (1986) *The Development of Plato's Political Theory*, New York and London: Methuen.

Knight, Frank (1921) *Risk, Uncertainty and Profit*, Boston and New York: Houghton Mifflin Company.

Kuhn, Thomas (1970) *The Structure of Scientific Revolutions*, International Encyclopedia of Unified Science, vol. ii, no. 2, Chicago: University of Chicago Press, 2nd edn. (first published 1962).

Lakatos, Imre (1970) 'Falsification and the Methodology of Scientific Research Programmes', in Imre Lakatos and Alan Musgrave (eds.), *Criticism and the Growth of Knowledge*, Cambridge: Cambridge University Press.

Langland, William (1959) *Piers the Ploughman*, ed. J. F. Goodridge, Hammondsworth: Penguin.

Lifton, Robert Jay (1983) *The Broken Connection: On Death and the Continuity of Life*, New York: Basic Books.

Lyons, John (1969) *Structural Semantics: An Analysis of Part of the Vocabulary of Plato*, Oxford: Basil Blackwell.

Marcuse, Herbert (1966) *One Dimensional Man: Studies in the Ideology of Advanced Industrial Society*, Boston: Beacon Press.

Marglin, Stephen (1974) 'What Do Bosses Do? The Origins and Functions of Hierarchy in Capitalist Production', Part I, *Review of Radical Political Economics*, 60: 60–112, repr. in A. Gorz (ed.) *The Division of Labour*, Sussex: Harvester, 1976.

—— (1979) 'Catching Flies with Honey: An Inquiry into Management Initiatives to Humanize Work', *Economic Analysis and Workers' Management*, 12: 473–87.

—— (1984) 'Knowledge and Power', in Frank Stephen (ed.), *Firms, Organization and Labour*, London: Macmillan.

—— (1987) 'Investment and Accumulation', in John Eatwell, Murray Milgate, and Peter Newman (eds.), *The New Palgrave*, London: Macmillan.

—— and Bhaduri, Amit (1990) 'Profit Squeeze and Keynesian Theory', in Stephen Marglin and Juliet Schor (eds.), *The Golden Age of Capitalism*, Oxford: Clarendon Press.

Marx, Karl (1959) *Capital*, vol. iii, Moscow: Foreign Languages Publishing House (first published 1894).

—— and Engels, F. (1947) *German Ideology*, ed. R. Pascal, New York: International (first published 1846).

Mohanty, Bijoy Chandra, and Krishna, Kalyan (1974) *Ikat Fabrics of Orissa and Andhra Pradesh*, Ahmedabad: Calico Museum of Textiles.

Montgomery, David (1979) *Workers' Control in America*, Cambridge: Cambridge University Press.

Morris, Frederic (1972) 'From Cottage to Factory', (unpublished senior honours thesis) Harvard College.

Noble, David F. (1984) *Forces of Production: A Social History of Automation*, New York: Oxford University Press.

Nussbaum, Martha (1986) *The Fragility of Goodness: Luck and Ethics in Greek Tragedy and Philosophy*, Cambridge: Cambridge University Press.

—— and Sen, Amartya (1989) 'Internal Criticism and Indian Rationalist Traditions', in Michael Krausz (ed.), *Relativism: Interpretation and Confrontation*, Notre Dame: Notre Dame University Press.

Pirsig, Robert (1976) *Zen and the Art of Motorcycle Maintenance: An Inquiry into Values*, London: Transworld.

Plato (1925) 'Gorgias' in *Lysis, Symposium, and Gorgias*, trans. W. R. M. Lamb, Cambridge, Mass.: Harvard University Press.

—— (1925) 'Philebus' in *Statesman, Philebus, and Ion*, trans. Harold N. Fowler and W. R. M. Lamb, Cambridge, Mass.: Harvard University Press.

—— (1941) *The Republic of Plato*, trans. F. Cornford, New York and London: Oxford University Press.

Polanyi, Karl (1944) *The Great Transformation*, New York: Rinehart.

Polanyi, Michael (1958) *Personal Knowledge: Towards a Post-Critical Philosophy*, Chicago: University of Chicago Press.

Popper, Karl (1968) *The Logic of Scientific Discovery*, New York: Harper & Row.

Prest, John (1960) *The Industrial Revolution in Coventry*, Oxford: Oxford University Press.

Putnam, Hilary (1974) 'The Corroboration of Scientific Theories', *The Philosophy of Karl Popper*, ed. K. Schilpp, La Salle, Ill.: Open Court.

Ricardo, David (1951) *On the Principles of Political Economy and Taxation*, ed. P. Sraffa with the collaboration of M. H. Dobb, Cambridge: Cambridge University Press (first published 1817, 3rd edn. 1821).

Roy, Donald (1952a) 'Quota Restriction and Goldbricking in a Machine Shop', *American Journal of Sociology*, 57: 427–42.

—— (1952b) 'Restrictions of Output in a Piecework Machine Shop', (Ph.D. dissertation) University of Chicago.

Sacks, Oliver (1985) *The Man Who Mistook His Wife for a Hat: And Other Clinical Tales*, New York: Summit Books.

Smith, Adam (1937) *The Wealth of Nations*, ed. E. Canaan, New York: Random House (first published 1776).

Staal, J. F. (1965) 'Euclid and Panini', *Philosophy East and West*, 15: 99–115.

Strauss, Leo (1970) *Xenophon's Socratic Discourse: An Interpretation of the Oeconomicus* (trans. of the *Oeconomicus* by Carnes Lord), Ithaca: Cornell University Press.

Sturt, George (1923) *The Wheelwright's Shop*, Cambridge: Cambridge University Press.

Tawney, R. H. (1938) *Religion and the Rise of Capitalism: A Historical Study*, Harmondsworth: Penguin (first published 1926).

Taylor, Frederick (1967) *The Principles of Scientific Management*, New York: Norton (first published 1911).

Terkel, Studs (1972) *Working*, New York: Random House.

Thompson, E. P. (1963) *The Making of the English Working Class*, New York: Vintage Books.

Vernant, Jean-Pierre (1982) *Mythe et Pensée chez les Grecs: Études de Psychologie Historique*, vol. ii, Paris: François Maspero (first published 1965).

Vidal-Naquet, Pierre (1983) *Le Chasseur Noir: Formes de Pensée et Formes de Societé dans le Monde Grec*, Paris: La Découverte/Maspero.

Weber, Max (1930) *The Protestant Ethic and the Spirit of Capitalism*, trans. Talcott Parsons, New York: Scribner's and London: George Allen and Unwin (first published 1904–5).

Whyte, William F. (1955) *Money and Motivation: An Analysis of Incentives in Industry*, New York: Harper & Row.

Young, Arthur (1770) *A Six Months' Tour Through the North of England*, London: W. Strahan.

Yule, Henry and A. C. Burnell (1903) *Hobson-Jobson: A Glossary of Colloquial Anglo-Indian Words and Phrases, and of Kindred Terms, Etymological, Historical, Geographical and Discursive*, 2nd edn., ed. William Crooke, London: John Murray (first published 1886).

INDEX

Printed in the United States
2592